David Foster Wallace is the author of the novels *Infinite Jest* and *The Broom of the System*, the story collections *Girl with Curious Hair* and *Brief Interviews with Hideous Men*, and the essay collections *A Supposedly Fun Thing I'll Never Do Again* and *Consider the Lobster*. His writings have appeared in *Esquire*, *Harper's*, *The New Republic*, *The New Yorker*, *The Paris Review* and other magazines. He is the recipient of a MacArthur Fellowship, the Lannan Award for Fiction, the *Paris Review*'s Aga Khan Prize and John Train Prize for Humour, and the O. Henry Award. David Foster Wallace died in 2008.

Infinite Jest

'Extraordinary . . . an astonishing and vast epic of contemporary American culture . . . Wallace's exuberance and intellectual impishness are a delight . . . Wallace is a superb comedian of culture'   James Wood, *Guardian*

'Enormously readable and quite ridiculously entertaining . . . a book of our times'

Anthony Quinn, *Daily Telegraph*

'Ambitious, accomplished, deeply humorous, brilliant and witty and moving. A literary sensation'

Independent

The Broom of the System

'Daring . . . hilarious . . . enigmatic . . . wonderfully odd . . . a zany picaresque adventure of contemporary America run amok'   *New York Times*

'Dazzling . . . exhilarating . . . bizarre . . . sweepingly successful . . . engaging and haunting . . . a remarkable book with a lot of prestidigitation in it . . . Wallace's talent is consistently impressive'   *San Francisco Chronicle*

'Brilliant . . . metafiction of the kind not seen since the heyday of John Barth and Donald Barthelme, and William Gass and William Gaddis and, oh yes, Thomas Pynchon'   *Los Angeles Times*

Also by David Foster Wallace

David
Foster
Wallace

A supposedly
fun thing
I'll never do again

Essays and Arguments

ABACUS

First published in the United States of America
by Little, Brown and Company 1997
First published in Great Britain by Abacus in 1998

*The following essays have appeared previously (in somewhat different
[and sometimes way shorter] forms):*

"Derivative Sport in Tornado Alley," "Getting Away from Pretty Much Being Away from It All,"
and "A Supposedly Fun Thing I'll Never Do Again" in *Harper's* in 1992, 1994, and 1996 under the
respective titles "Tennis, Trigonometry, Tornadoes," "Ticket to the Fair," and "Shipping Out."
"Derivative Sport in Tornado Alley" in Michael Martone, ed., *Townships*
(University of Iowa Press, 1993).
"E Unibus Pluram: Television and U.S. Fiction" in *The Review of Contemporary Fiction* in 1993.
"Greatly Exaggerated" in the *Harvard Book Review* in 1992.
"David Lynch Keeps His Head" in *Premiere* in 1996.
"Tennis Player Michael Joyce's Professional Artistry as a Paradigm of Certain Stuff About Choice,
Freedom, Limitation, Joy, Grotesquerie, and Human Completeness" in *Esquire* in 1996
under the title "The String Theory."

A CIP catalogue record for this book
is available from the British Library.

ISBN 978-0-349-11001-1

Printed and bound in Great Britain by
Clays Ltd, Elcograf S.p.A.

Papers used by Abacus are from well-managed forests
and other responsible sources.

Abacus
An imprint of
Little, Brown Book Group
Carmelite House
50 Victoria Embankment
London EC4Y 0DZ

An Hachette UK Company
www.hachette.co.uk

www.littlebrown.co.uk

To Colin Harrison and Michael Pietsch

a supposedly fun thing i'll never do again

table of contents

derivative sport in tornado alley

When I left my boxed township of Illinois farmland to attend my dad's alma mater in the lurid jutting Berkshires of western Massachusetts, I all of a sudden developed a jones for mathematics. I'm starting to see why this was so. College math evokes and catharts a Midwesterner's sickness for home. I'd grown up inside vectors, lines and lines athwart lines, grids — and, on the scale of horizons, broad curving lines of geographic force, the weird topographical drain-swirl of a whole lot of ice-ironed land that sits and spins atop plates. The area behind and below these broad curves at the seam of land and sky I could plot by eye way before I came to know infinitesimals as easements, an integral as schema. Math at a hilly Eastern school was like waking up; it dismantled memory and put it in light. Calculus was, quite literally, child's play.

In late childhood I learned how to play tennis on the blacktop courts of a small public park carved from farmland that had been nitrogenized too often to farm anymore. This was in my home of Philo, Illinois, a tiny collection of corn silos and war-era Levittown homes whose native residents did little but sell crop insurance and nitrogen fertilizer and herbicide and collect property taxes from the young academics at nearby Champaign-Urbana's university, whose ranks swelled enough in the flush 1960s to make outlying non sequiturs like "farm and bedroom community" lucid.

Between the ages of twelve and fifteen I was a near-great junior tennis player. I made my competitive bones beating up on lawyers' and dentists' kids at little Champaign and Urbana Country Club events and was soon killing whole summers being driven through dawns to tournaments all over Illinois, Indiana, Iowa. At fourteen I was ranked seventeenth in the United States Tennis Association's Western Section ("Western" being the creakily ancient USTA's designation for the Midwest; farther west were the Southwest, Northwest, and Pacific Northwest sections). My flirtation with tennis excellence had way more to do with the township where I learned and trained and with a weird proclivity for intuitive math than it did with athletic talent. I was, even by the standards of junior competition in which everyone's a bud of pure potential, a pretty untalented tennis player. My hand-eye was OK, but I was neither large nor quick, had a near-concave chest and wrists so thin I could bracelet them with a thumb and pinkie, and could hit a tennis ball no harder or truer than most girls in my age bracket. What I could do was "Play the Whole Court." This was a piece of tennis truistics that could mean any number of things. In my case, it meant I knew my limitations and the limitations of what I stood inside, and adjusted thusly. I was at my very best in bad conditions.

Now, conditions in Central Illinois are from a mathematical perspective interesting and from a tennis perspective bad. The summer heat and wet-mitten humidity, the grotesquely fertile soil that sends grasses and broadleaves up through the courts' surface by main force, the midges that feed on sweat and the mosquitoes that spawn in the fields' furrows and in the conferva-choked ditches that box each field, night tennis next to impossible because the moths and crap-gnats drawn by the sodium lights form a little planet around each tall lamp and the whole lit court surface is aflutter with spastic little shadows.

But mostly wind. The biggest single factor in Central Illinois' quality of outdoor life is wind. There are more local jokes than I can summon about bent weather vanes and leaning barns, more downstate sobriquets for kinds of wind than there are in Malamut for snow. The wind had a personality, a (poor) temper, and, apparently, agendas. The wind blew autumn leaves into intercalated lines and arcs of force so regular you could photograph them for a textbook on Cramer's Rule and the cross-products of curves in 3-space. It molded winter snow into blinding truncheons that buried stalled cars and required citizens to shovel out not only driveways but the sides of homes; a Central Illinois "blizzard" starts only when the snowfall stops and the wind begins. Most people in Philo didn't comb their hair because why bother. Ladies wore those plastic flags tied down over their parlor-jobs so regularly I thought they were required for a real classy coiffure; girls on the East Coast outside with their hair hanging and tossing around looked wanton and nude to me. Wind wind etc. etc.

The people I know from outside it distill the Midwest into blank flatness, black land and fields of green fronds or five-o'clock stubble, gentle swells and declivities that make the topology a sadistic exercise in plotting quadrics, highway vistas so same and dead they drive motorists mad. Those from IN/WI/Northern IL think of their own Midwest as agronomics and commodity futures and corn-detasseling and bean-walking and seed-company caps, apple-cheeked Nordic types, cider and slaughter and football games with white fogbanks of breath exiting helmets. But in the odd central pocket that is Champaign-Urbana, Rantoul, Philo, Mahomet-Seymour, Mattoon, Farmer City, and Tolono, Midwestern life is informed and deformed by wind. Weatherwise, our township is on the eastern upcurrent of what I once heard an atmospherist in brown tweed call a Thermal Anomaly. Something about southward rotations of crisp air off the Great Lakes and muggy southern stuff from Arkansas and Kentucky miscegenating, plus an odd dose of weird zephyrs from the Mississippi valley three hours west. Chicago calls itself the Windy City, but Chicago, one big windbreak, does not know from a true religious-type wind. And meteorologists have nothing to tell people in Philo, who know perfectly well that the real story is that to the west, between us and the Rockies, there is basically nothing tall, and that weird zephyrs and stirs joined breezes and gusts and thermals and downdrafts and whatever out over Nebraska and Kansas and moved east like streams into rivers and jets and military fronts that gathered like avalanches and roared in reverse down pioneer oxtrails, toward our own personal unsheltered asses. The worst was spring, boys' high school tennis season, when the nets would stand out stiff as proud flags and an errant ball would blow clear to the easternmost fence, interrupting play on the next several courts. During a bad blow some of us would get rope out and tell Rob Lord, who was our fifth man in singles and spectrally thin, that we were going to have to tie him down to keep him from becoming a projectile. Autumn, usually about half as bad as spring, was a low constant roar and the massive clicking sound of continents of dry leaves being arranged into force-curves — I'd heard no sound remotely like this megaclicking until I heard, at nineteen, on New Brunswick's Fundy Bay, my first high-tide wave break and get sucked back out over a shore of polished pebbles. Summers were manic and gusty, then often around August deadly calm. The wind would just die some August days, and it was no relief at all; the cessation drove us nuts. Each August, we realized afresh how much the sound of wind had become part of the sound-track to life in Philo. The sound of wind had become, for me, silence. When it went away, I was left with the squeak of the blood in my head and the aural glitter of all those little eardrum hairs quivering like a drunk in withdrawal. It was months after I moved to western MA before I could really sleep in the pussified whisper of New England's wind-sound.

To your average outsider, Central Illinois looks ideal for sports. The ground, seen from the air, strongly suggests a board game: anally precise squares of dun or khaki cropland all cut and divided by plumb-straight tar roads (in all farmland, roads still seem more like impediments than avenues). In winter, the terrain always looks like Mannington bathroom tile, white quadrangles where bare (snow), black where trees and scrub have shaken free in the wind. From planes, it always looks to me like Monopoly or Life, or a lab maze for rats; then, from ground level, the arrayed fields of feed corn or soybeans, fields furrowed into lines as straight as only an Allis Chalmers and sextant can cut them, look laned like sprint tracks or Olympic pools, hashmarked for serious ball, replete with the angles and alleys of serious tennis. My part of the Midwest always looks laid down special, as if planned.

The terrain's strengths are also its weaknesses. Because the land seems so even, designers of clubs and parks rarely bother to roll it flat before laying the asphalt for tennis courts. The result is usually a slight list that only a player who spends a lot of time on the courts will notice. Because tennis courts are for sun- and eye-reasons always laid length-wise north-south, and because the land in Central Illinois rises very gently as one moves east toward Indiana and the subtle geologic sum-

mit that sends rivers doubled back against their own feeders somewhere in the east of that state, the court's forehand half, for a rightie
facing north, always seems physically uphill from the backhand — at a
tournament in Richmond IN, just over the Ohio line, I noticed the tilt
was reversed. The same soil that's so full of humus farmers have to be
bought off to keep markets unflooded keeps clay courts chocked with
jimson and thistle and volunteer corn, and it splits asphalt courts open
with the upward pressure of broadleaf weeds whose pioneer-stock seeds
are unthwarted by a half-inch cover of sealant and stone. So that all
but the very best maintained courts in the most affluent Illinois dis-
tricts are their own little rural landscapes, with tufts and cracks and
underground-seepage puddles being part of the lay that one plays. A
court's cracks always seem to start off to the side of the service box and
meander in and back toward the service line. Foliated in pockets, the
black cracks, especially against the forest green that contrasts with the
barn red of the space outside the lines to signify fair territory, give
the courts the eerie look of well-rivered sections of Illinois, seen from
back aloft.

A tennis court, 78' × 27', looks, from above, with its slender rec-
tangles of doubles alleys flanking its whole length, like a cardboard carton with flaps folded back. The net, 3.5 feet high at the posts, divides
the court widthwise in half; the service lines divide each half again into
backcourt and fore-. In the two forecourts, lines that run from the base
of the net's center to the service lines divide them into 21' × 13.5' service boxes. The sharply precise divisions and boundaries, together with
the fact that — wind and your more exotic-type spins aside — balls can
be made to travel in straight lines only, make textbook tennis plane
geometry. It is billiards with balls that won't hold still. It is chess on
the run. It is to artillery and airstrikes what football is to infantry and
attrition.

Tennis-wise, I had two preternatural gifts to compensate for not
much physical talent. Make that three. The first was that I always sweated
so much that I stayed fairly ventilated in all weathers. Oversweating
seems an ambivalent blessing, and it didn't exactly do wonders for my
social life in high school, but it meant I could play for hours on a

Turkish-bath July day and not flag a bit so long as I drank water and ate salty stuff between matches. I always looked like a drowned man by about game four, but I didn't cramp, vomit, or pass out, unlike the gleaming Peoria kids whose hair never even lost its part right up until their eyes rolled up in their heads and they pitched forward onto the shimmering concrete. A bigger asset still was that I was extremely comfortable inside straight lines. None of the odd geometric claustrophobia that turns some gifted juniors into skittish zoo animals after a while. I found I felt best physically enwebbed in sharp angles, acute bisections, shaved corners. This was environmental. Philo, Illinois, is a cockeyed grid: nine north-south streets against six northeast-southwest, fifty-one gorgeous slanted-cruciform corners (the east and west intersection-angles' tangents could be evaluated integrally in terms of their secants!) around a three-intersection central town common with a tank whose nozzle pointed northwest at Urbana, plus a frozen native son, felled on the Salerno beachhead, whose bronze hand pointed true north. In the late morning, the Salerno guy's statue had a squat black shadow-arm against grass dense enough to putt on; in the evening the sun galvanized his left profile and cast his arm's accusing shadow out to the right, bent at the angle of a stick in a pond. At college it suddenly occurred to me during a quiz that the differential between the direction the statue's hand pointed and the arc of its shadow's rotation was first-order. Anyway, most of my memories of childhood — whether of furrowed acreage, or of a harvester's sentry duty along RR104W, or of the play of sharp shadows against the Legion Hall softball field's dusk — I could now reconstruct on demand with an edge and pro-tractor.

I liked the sharp intercourse of straight lines more than the other kids I grew up with. I think this is because they were natives, whereas I was an infantile transplant from Ithaca, where my dad had Ph.D.'d. So I'd known, even horizontally and semiconsciously as a baby, something different, the tall hills and serpentine one-ways of upstate NY. I'm pretty sure I kept the amorphous mush of curves and swells as a contrasting backlight somewhere down in the lizardy part of my brain, because the Philo children I fought and played with, kids who knew and had known nothing else, saw nothing stark or new-worldish in the township's planar layout, prized nothing crisp. (Except why do I think it significant that so many of them wound up in the military, performing smart right-faces in razor-creased dress blues?)

Unless you're one of those rare mutant virtuosos of raw force, you'll find that competitive tennis, like money pool, requires geometric thinking, the ability to calculate not merely your own angles but the angles of response to your angles. Because the expansion of response-possibilities is quadratic, you are required to think n shots ahead, where n is a hyperbolic function limited by the sinh of opponent's talent and the cosh of the number of shots in the rally so far (roughly). I was good at this. What made me for a while near-great was that I could also admit the differential complication of wind into my calculations; I could think and play octacally. For the wind put curves in the lines and transformed the game into 3-space. Wind did massive damage to many Central Illinois junior players, particularly in the period from April to July when it needed lithium badly, tending to gust without pattern, swirl and backtrack and die and rise, sometimes blowing in one direction at court level and in another altogether ten feet overhead. The precision in thinking required one to induct trends in percentage, thrust, and retaliatory angle — precision our guy and the other townships' volunteer coaches were good at abstracting about with chalk and board, attaching a pupil's leg to the fence with clothesline to restrict his arc of movement in practice, placing laundry baskets in different corners and making us sink ball after ball, taking masking tape and laying down Chinese boxes within the court's own boxes for drills and wind sprints — all this theoretical prep went out the window when sneakers hit actual court in a tournament. The best-planned, best-hit ball often just blew out of bounds, was the basic unlyrical problem. It drove some kids near-mad with the caprice and unfairness of it all, and on real windy days these kids, usually with talent out the bazoo, would have their first apoplectic racket-throwing tantrum in about the match's third game and lapse into a kind of sullen coma by the end of the first set, now bitterly *expecting* to get screwed over by wind, net, tape, sun. I, who was affectionately known as Slug because I was such a lazy turd in practice, located my biggest tennis asset in a weird robotic detachment from whatever unfairnesses of wind and weather I couldn't plan for. I couldn't begin to tell you how many tournament matches I won between the ages of twelve and fifteen against bigger, faster, more coordinated, and better-coached opponents simply by hitting balls unimaginatively back down the middle of the court in schizophrenic gales, letting the other kid play with more verve and panache, waiting for enough of his ambitious balls aimed near the lines to curve or slide via wind outside the green court and white stripe into the raw red territory that won me yet another ugly point. It wasn't pretty or fun to watch, and even with the Illinois wind I never could have won whole matches this way had the opponent not eventually had his small nervous breakdown, buckling under the obvious injustice of losing to a shallow-chested "pusher" because of the shitty rural courts and rotten wind that rewarded cautious automatism instead of verve and panache. I was an unpopular player, with good reason. But to say that I did not use verve or imagination was untrue. Acceptance is its own verve, and it takes imagination for a player to like wind, and I liked wind; or rather I at least felt the wind had some basic right to be there, and found it sort of interesting, and was willing to expand my logistical territory to countenace the devastating effect a 15- to 30-mph stutter-breeze swirling southwest to east would have on my best calculations as to how ambitiously to respond to Joe Perfecthair's topspin drive into my backhand corner.

The Illinois combination of pocked courts, sickening damp, and wind required and rewarded an almost Zen-like acceptance of things as they actually were, on-court. I won a lot. At twelve, I began getting entry to tournaments beyond Philo and Champaign and Danville. I was driven by my parents or by the folks of Gil Antitoi, son of a Canadian-history professor from Urbana, to events like the Central Illinois Open in Decatur, a town built and owned by the A. E. Staley processing concern and so awash in the stink of roasting corn that kids would play with bandannas tied over their mouths and noses; like the Western Closed Qualifier on the ISU campus in Normal; like the McDonald's Junior Open in the serious corn town of Galesburg, way out west by the River; like the Prairie State Open in Pekin, insurance hub and home of Caterpillar Tractor; like the Midwest Junior Clay Courts at a chichi private club in Peoria's pale version of Scarsdale.

Over the next four summers I got to see way more of the state than is normal or healthy, albeit most of this seeing was a blur of travel and crops, looking between nod-outs at sunrises abrupt and terribly candent over the crease between fields and sky (plus you could see any town you were aimed at the very moment it came around the earth's curve, and the only part of Proust that really moved me in college was the early description of the kid's geometric relation to the distant church spire at Combray), riding in station wagons' backseats through Saturday dawns and Sunday sunsets. I got steadily better; Antitoi, unfairly assisted by an early puberty, got radically better.

By the time we were fourteen, Gil Antitoi and I were the Central Illinois cream of our age bracket, usually seeded one and two at area tournaments, able to beat all but a couple of even the kids from the Chicago suburbs who, together with a contingent from Grosse Pointe MI, usually dominated the Western regional rankings. That summer the best fourteen-year-old in the nation was a Chicago kid, Bruce Brescia (whose penchant for floppy white tennis hats, low socks with bunnytails at the heel, and lurid pastel sweater vests testified to proclivities that wouldn't dawn on me for several more years), but Brescia and his henchman, Mark Mees of Zanesville OH, never bothered to play anything but the Midwestern Clays and some indoor events in Cook County, being too busy jetting off to like the Pacific Hardcourts in Ventura and Junior Wimbledon and all that. I played Brescia just once, in the quarters of an indoor thing at the Rosemont Horizon in 1977, and the results were not pretty. Antitoi actually got a set off Mees in the national Qualifiers one year. Neither Brescia nor Mees ever turned pro; I don't know what happened to either of them after eighteen.

Antitoi and I ranged over the exact same competitive territory; he was my friend and foe and bane. Though I'd started playing two years before he, he was bigger, quicker, and basically better than I by about age thirteen, and I was soon losing to him in the finals of just about every tournament I played. So different were our appearances and approaches and general gestalts that we had something of an epic rivalry from '74 through '77. I had gotten so prescient at using stats, surface, sun, gusts, and a kind of Stoic cheer that I was regarded as a kind of physical savant, a medicine boy of wind and heat, and could play just forever, sending back moonballs baroque with spin. Antitoi, uncomplicated from the get-go, hit the everliving shit out of every round object that came within his

ambit, aiming always for one of two backcourt corners. He was a Slugger;
I was a Slug. When he was "on," i.e. having a good day, he varnished the
court with me. When he wasn't at his best (and the countless hours I and
David Saboe from Bloomington and Kirk Riehagen and Steve Cassil of
Danville spent in meditation and seminar on just what variables of diet,
sleep, romance, car ride, and even sock-color factored into the equation
of Antitoi's mood and level day to day), he and I had great matches, real
marathon wind-suckers. Of eleven finals we played in 1974, I won two.

Midwest junior tennis was also my initiation into true adult sadness.
I had developed a sort of hubris about my Taoistic ability to control via
noncontrol. I'd established a private religion of wind. I even liked to bike.
Awfully few people in Philo bike, for obvious wind reasons, but I'd found
a way to sort of tack back and forth against a stiff current, holding some
wide book out at my side at about 120° to my angle of thrust — Bayne
and Pugh's *The Art of the Engineer* and Cheiro's *Language of the Hand*
proved to be the best airfoils — so that through imagination and verve
and stoic cheer I could not just neutralize but use an in-your-face gale
for biking. Similarly, by thirteen I'd found a way not just to accommodate but to *employ* the heavy summer winds in matches. No longer just
mooning the ball down the center to allow plenty of margin for error
and swerve, I was now able to use the currents kind of the way a pitcher
uses spit. I could hit curves way out into cross-breezes that'd drop the
ball just fair; I had a special wind-serve that had so much spin the ball
turned oval in the air and curved left to right like a smart slider and then
reversed its arc on the bounce. I'd developed the same sort of autonomic
feel for what the wind would do to the ball that a standard-trans driver
has for how to shift. As a junior tennis player, I was for a time a citizen of
the concrete physical world in a way the other boys weren't, I felt. And I
felt betrayed at around fourteen when so many of these single-minded
flailing boys became abruptly mannish and tall, with sudden sprays of
hair on their thighs and wisps on their lips and ropy arteries on their
forearms. My fifteenth summer, kids I'd been beating easily the year before all of a sudden seemed overpowering. I lost in two semifinals, at
Pekin and Springfield in '77, of events I'd beaten Antitoi in the finals of
in '76. My dad just about brought me to my knees after the Springfield
loss to some kid from the Quad Cities when he said, trying to console
me, that it had looked like a boy playing a man out there. And the other

boys sensed something up with me, too, smelled some breakdown in the odd détente I'd had with the elements: my ability to accommodate and fashion the exterior was being undercut by the malfunction of some internal alarm clock I didn't understand.

I mention this mostly because so much of my Midwest's communal psychic energy was informed by growth and fertility. The agronomic angle was obvious, what with my whole township dependent for tax base on seed, dispersion, height, and yield. Something about the adults' obsessive weighing and measuring and projecting, this special calculus of thrust and growth, leaked inside us children's capped and bandanna'd little heads out on the fields, diamonds, and courts of our special interests. By 1977 I was the only one of my group of jock friends with virginity intact. (I know this for a fact, and only because these guys are now schoolteachers and commoditists and insurers with families and standings to protect will I not share with you just how I know it.) I felt, as I became a later and later bloomer, alienated not just from my own recalcitrant glabrous little body, but in a way from the whole elemental exterior I'd come to see as my coconspirator. I knew, somehow, that the call to height and hair came from outside, from whatever apart from Monsanto and Dow made the corn grow, the hogs rut, the wind soften every spring and hang with the scent of manure from the plain of beanfields north between us and Champaign. My vocation ebbed. I felt uncalled. I began to experience the same resentment toward whatever children abstract as nature that I knew Steve Cassil felt when a soundly considered approach shot down the forehand line was blown out by a gust, that I knew Gil Antitoi suffered when his pretty kick-serve (he was the only top-flight kid from the slow weedy township courts to play serve-and-volley from the start, which is why he had such success on the slick cement of the West Coast when he went on to play for Cal-Fullerton) was compromised by the sun: he was so tall, and so stubborn about adjusting his high textbook service toss for solar conditions, that serving from the court's north end in early afternoon matches always filled his eyes with violet blobs, and he'd lumber around for the rest of the point, flailing and pissed. This was back when sunglasses were unheard of, on-court.

But so the point is I began to feel what they'd felt. I began, very quietly, to resent my physical place in the great schema, and this resentment

and bitterness, a kind of slow root-rot, is a big reason why I never qualified for the sectional championships again after 1977, and why I ended
up in 1980 barely making the team at a college smaller than Urbana
High while kids I had beaten and then envied played scholarship tennis
for Purdue, Fullerton, Michigan, Pepperdine, and even — in the case of
Pete Bouton, who grew half a foot and forty IQ points in 1977 — for
the hallowed U of I at Urbana-Champaign.

Alienation-from-Midwest-as-fertility-grid might be a little on the
overmetaphysical side, not to mention self-pitying. This was the time,
after all, when I discovered definite integrals and antiderivatives and
found my identity shifting from jock to math-wienie anyway. But it's
also true that my whole Midwest tennis career matured and then degenerated under the aegis of the Peter Principle. In and around my township — where the courts were rural and budgets low and conditions so
extreme that the mosquitoes sounded like trumpets and the bees like
tubas and the wind like a five-alarm fire, that we had to change shirts
between games and use our water jugs to wash blown field-chaff off our
arms and necks and carry salt tablets in Pez containers — I was truly
near-great: I could Play the Whole Court; I was In My Element. But all
the more important tournaments, the events into which my rural excellence was an easement, were played in a different real world: the courts'
surface was redone every spring at the Arlington Tennis Center, where
the National Junior Qualifier for our region was held; the green of these
courts' fair territory was so vivid as to distract, its surface so new and
rough it wrecked your feet right through your shoes, and so bare of flaw,
tilt, crack, or seam that it was totally disorienting. Playing on a perfect
court was for me like treading water out of sight of land: I never knew
where I was out there. The 1976 Chicago Junior Invitational was held
at Lincolnshire's Bath and Tennis Club, whose huge warren of thirty-six
courts was enclosed by all these troubling green plastic tarps attached to
all the fences, with little archer-slits in them at eye level to afford some
parody of spectation. These tarps were Wind-B-Gone windscreens,
patented by the folks over at Cyclone Fence in 1971. They did cut down
on the worst of the unfair gusts, but they also seemed to rob the court
space of new air: competing at Lincolnshire was like playing in the bottom of a well. And blue bug-zapper lights festooned the lightposts when
really major Midwest tournaments played into the night: no clouds of

midges around the head or jagged shadows of moths to distinguish from balls' flights, but a real unpleasant zotting and frying sound of bugs being decommissioned just overhead; I won't pause to mention the smell. The point is I just wasn't the same, somehow, without deformities to play around. I'm thinking now that the wind and bugs and chuckholes formed for me a kind of inner boundary, my own personal set of lines. Once I hit a certain level of tournament facilities, I was disabled because I was unable to accommodate the absence of disabilities to accommodate. If that makes sense. Puberty-angst and material alienation notwithstanding, my Midwest tennis career plateaued the moment I saw my first windscreen.

Still strangely eager to speak of weather, let me say that my township, in fact all of East-Central Illinois, is a proud part of what meteorologists call Tornado Alley. Incidence of tornadoes all out of statistical proportion. I personally have seen two on the ground and five aloft, trying to assemble. Aloft tornadoes are gray-white, more like convulsions in the thunderclouds themselves than separate or protruding from them. Ground tornadoes are black only because of the tons of soil they suck in and spin around. The grotesque frequency of tornadoes around my township is, I'm told, a function of the same variables that cause our civilian winds: we are a coordinate where fronts and air masses converge. Most days from late March to June there are Tornado Watches somewhere in our TV stations' viewing area (the stations put a little graphic at the screen's upper right, like a pair of binoculars for a Watch and the Tarot deck's Tower card for a Warning, or something). Watches mean conditions are right and so on and so forth, which, big deal. It's only the rarer Tornado Warnings, which require a confirmed sighting by somebody with reliable sobriety, that make the Civil Defense sirens go. The siren on top of the Philo Middle School was a different pitch and cycle from the one off in the south part of Urbana, and the two used to weave in and out of each other in a godawful threnody. When the sirens blew, the native families went to their canning cellars or fallout shelters (no kidding); the academic families in their bright prefab houses with new lawns and foundations of flat slab went with whatever good-luck tokens they could lay hands on to the very most central point on the ground floor after opening every single window to thwart implosion from precipitous pressure drops. For my family, the very most central point was a hallway between my dad's study and a linen closet, with a reproduction of a Flemish annunciation scene on one wall and a bronze Aztec sunburst hanging with guillotinic mass on the other; I always tried to maneuver my sister under the sunburst.

If there was an actual Warning when you were outside and away from home — say at a tennis tournament in some godforsaken public park at some city fringe zoned for sprawl — you were supposed to lie prone in the deepest depression you could locate. Since the only real depressions around most tournament sites were the irrigation and runoff ditches that bordered cultivated fields, ditches icky with conferva and mosquito spray and always heaving with what looked like conventions of copperheads and just basically places your thinking man doesn't lie prone in under any circumstance, in practice at Warned tournament you zipped your rackets into their covers and ran to find your loved ones or even your liked ones and just all milled around trying to look like you weren't about to lose sphincter-control. Mothers tended sometimes to wail and clutch childish heads to their bosoms (Mrs. Swearingen of Pekin was particularly popular for clutching even strange kids' heads to her formidable bosom).

I mention tornadoes for reasons directly related to the purpose of this essay. For one thing, they were a real part of Midwest childhood, because as a little kid I was obsessed with dread over them. My earliest nightmares, the ones that didn't feature mile-high robots from *Lost in Space* wielding huge croquet mallets (don't ask), were about shrieking sirens and dead white skies, a slender monster on the Iowa horizon, jutting less phallic than saurian from the lowering sky, whipping back and forth with such frenzy that it almost doubled on itself, trying to eat its own tail. Throwing off chaff and dust and chairs; it never came any closer than the horizon; it didn't have to.

In practice, Watches and Warnings both seemed to have a kind of boy-and-wolf quality for the natives of Philo. They just happened too often. Watches seemed especially irrelevant, because we could always see storms coming from the west way in advance, and by the time they were over, say, Decatur you could diagnose the basic condition by the color and height of the clouds: the taller the anvil-shaped thunderheads, the better the chance for hail and Warnings; pitch-black clouds were a happier sight than gray shot with an odd nacreous white; the shorter the interval between the sight of lightning and the sound of thunder, the faster the system was moving, and the faster the system, the worse: like most things that mean you harm, severe thunderstorms are brisk and no-nonsense.

I know why I stayed obsessed as I aged. Tornadoes, for me, were a transfiguration. Like all serious winds, they were our little stretch of plain's z coordinate, a move up from the Euclidian monotone of furrow, road, axis, and grid. We studied tornadoes in junior high: a Canadian high straight-lines it southeast from the Dakotas; a moist warm mass drawls on up north from like Arkansas: the result was not a Greek χ or even a Cartesian Γ but a circling of the square, a curling of vectors, concavation of curves. It was alchemical, Leibnizian. Tornadoes were, in our part of Central Illinois, the dimensionless point at which parallel lines met and whirled and blew up. They made no sense. Houses blew not out but in. Brothels were spared while orphanages next door bought it. Dead cattle were found three miles from their silage without a scratch on them. Tornadoes are omnipotent and obey no law. Force without law has no shape, only tendency and duration. I believe now that I knew all this without knowing it, as a kid.

The only time I ever got caught in what might have been an actual one was in June '78 on a tennis court at Hessel Park in Champaign, where I was drilling one afternoon with Gil Antitoi. Though a contemptible and despised tournament opponent, I was a coveted practice partner because I could transfer balls to wherever you wanted them with the mindless constancy of a machine. This particular day it was supposed to rain around suppertime, and a couple times we thought we'd heard the tattered edges of a couple sirens out west toward Monticello, but Antitoi and I drilled religiously every afternoon that week on the slow clayish Har-Tru of Hessel, trying to prepare for a beastly clay invitational in Chicago where it was rumored both Brescia and Mees would appear. We were doing butterfly drills — my crosscourt forehand is transferred back down the line to Antitoi's backhand, he crosscourts it to my backhand, I send it down the line to his forehand, four 45° angles, though the intersection of just his crosscourts make an X, which is four 90's and also a crucifix rotated the same quarter-turn that a swastika (which involves eight 90° angles) is rotated on Hitlerian bunting. This was the sort of stuff that went through my head when I drilled. Hessel Park was scented heavily with cheese from the massive Kraft factory at Champaign's western limit, and it had wonderful expensive soft Har-Tru courts of such a deep piney color that the flights of the fluorescent balls stayed on one's visual screen for a few extra seconds, leaving trails, is also why the angles and hieroglyphs involved in butterfly drill seem important. But the crux here is that butterflies are primarily a conditioning drill: both players have to get from one side of the court to the other between each stroke, and once the initial pain and wind-sucking are over — assuming you're a kid who's in absurd shape because he spends countless mindless hours jumping rope or running laps backward or doing star-drills between the court's corners or straight sprints back and forth along the perfect furrows of early beanfields each morning — once the first pain and fatigue of butterflies are got through, if both guys are good enough so that there are few unforced errors to break up the rally, a kind of fugue-state opens up inside you where your concentration telescopes toward a still point and you lose awareness of your limbs and the soft shush of your shoe's slide (you have to slide out of a run on Har-Tru) and whatever's outside the lines of the court, and pretty much all you know then is the bright ball and the octangled butterfly outline of its trail across the billiard green of the court. We had one just endless rally and I'd left the planet in a silent swoop inside when the court and ball and butterfly trail all seemed to surge brightly and glow as the daylight just plain went out in the sky overhead. Neither of us had noticed that there'd been no wind blowing the familiar grit into our eyes for several minutes — a bad sign. There was no siren. Later they said the C.D. alert network had been out of order. This was June 6, 1978. The air temperature dropped so fast you could feel your hairs rise. There was no thunder and no air stirred. I could not tell you why we kept hitting. Neither of us said anything. There was no siren. It was high noon; there was nobody else on the courts. The riding mower out over east at the softball field was still going back and forth. There were no depressions except a saprogenic ditch along the field of new corn just west. What could we have done? The air always smells of mowed grass before a bad storm. I think we thought it would rain at worst and that we'd play till it rained and then go sit in Antitoi's parents' station wagon. I do remember a men-

tal obscenity — I had gut strings in my rackets, strings everybody with
a high sectional ranking got free for letting the Wilson sales rep spray-
paint a *W* across the racket face, so they were free, but I liked this particular string job on this racket, I liked them tight but not real tight, 62-63
p.s.i. on a Proflite stringer, and gut becomes pasta if it gets wet, but we
were both in the fugue-state that exhaustion through repetition brings
on, a fugue-state I've decided that my whole time playing tennis was
spent chasing, a fugue-state I associated too with plowing and seeding
and detasseling and spreading herbicides back and forth in sentry duty
along perfect lines, up and back, or military marching on flat blacktop,
hypnotic, a mental state at once flat and lush, numbing and yet exquisitely felt. We were young, we didn't know when to stop. Maybe I was
mad at my body and wanted to hurt it, wear it down. Then the whole
knee-high field to the west along Kirby Avenue all of a sudden flattened
out in a wave coming toward us as if the field was getting steamrolled.
Antitoi went wide west for a forehand cross and I saw the corn get laid
down in waves and the sycamores in a copse lining the ditch point our
way. There was no funnel. Either it had just materialized and come down
or it wasn't a real one. The big heavy swings on the industrial swingsets
took off, wrapping themselves in their chains around and around the
top crossbar; the park's grass laid down the same way the field had; the
whole thing happened so fast I'd seen nothing like it; recall that Bimini
H-Bomb film of the shock wave visible in the sea as it comes toward the
ship's film crew. This all happened very fast but in serial progression:
field, trees, swings, grass, then the feel like the lift of the world's biggest
mitt, the nets suddenly and sexually up and out straight, and I seem to
remember whacking a ball out of my hand at Antitoi to watch its radical
west-east curve, and for some reason trying to run after this ball I'd just
hit, but I couldn't have tried to run after a ball I had hit, but I remember
the heavy gentle lift at my thighs and the ball curving back closer and
my passing the ball and beating the ball in flight over the horizontal net,
my feet not once touching the ground over fifty-odd feet, a cartoon, and
then there was chaff and crud in the air all over and both Antitoi and
I either flew or were blown pinwheeling for I swear it must have been
fifty feet to the fence one court over, the easternmost fence, we hit the
fence so hard we knocked it halfway down, and it stuck at 45°, Antitoi
detached a retina and had to wear those funky Jabbar retina-goggles for

the rest of the summer, and the fence had two body-shaped indentations like in cartoons where the guy's face makes a cast in the skillet that hit him, two catcher's masks of fence, we both got deep quadrangular lines impressed on our faces, torsos, legs' fronts, from the fence, my sister said we looked like waffles, but neither of us got badly hurt, and no homes got whacked — either the thing just ascended again for no reason right after, they do that, obey no rule, follow no line, hop up and down at something that might as well be will, or else it wasn't a real one. Antitoi's tennis continued to improve after that, but mine didn't.

1990

E UNIBUS PLURAM

televiาion and U.S. fiction

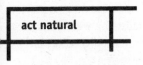

act natural

Fiction writers as a species tend to be oglers. They tend to lurk and to stare. They are born watchers. They are viewers. They are the ones on the subway about whose nonchalant stare there is something creepy, somehow. Almost predatory. This is because human situations are writers' food. Fiction writers watch other humans sort of the way gapers slow down for car wrecks: they covet a vision of themselves as *witnesses*.

But fiction writers tend at the same time to be terribly self-conscious. Devoting lots of productive time to studying closely how people come across to them, fiction writers also spend lots of less productive time wondering nervously how they come across to other people. How they appear, how they seem, whether their shirttail might be hanging out of their fly, whether there's maybe lipstick on their teeth, whether the people they're ogling can maybe size them up as somehow creepy, as lurkers and starers.

The result is that a majority of fiction writers, born watchers, tend to dislike being objects of people's attention. Dislike being watched. The exceptions to this rule — Mailer, McInerney — sometimes create the impression that most belletristic types covet people's attention. Most don't. The few who like attention just naturally get more attention. The rest of us watch.

Most of the fiction writers I know are Americans under 40. I don't know whether fiction writers under 40 watch more television than other American species. Statisticians report that television is watched over six hours a day in the average American household. I don't know any fiction writers who live in average American households. I suspect Louise Erdrich might. Actually I have never seen an average American household. Except on TV.

Right away you can see a couple of things that look potentially great, for U.S. fiction writers, about U.S. television. First, television does a lot of our predatory human research for us. American human beings are a slippery and protean bunch in real life, hard as hell to get any kind of universal handle on. But television comes equipped with just such a handle. It's an incredible gauge of the generic. If we want to know what American normality is — i.e. what Americans want to regard as normal — we can trust television. For television's whole raison is reflecting what people want to see. It's a mirror. Not the Stendhalian mirror that reflects the blue sky and mudpuddle. More like the overlit bathroom mirror before which the teenager monitors his biceps and determines his better profile. This kind of window on nervous American self-perception is simply invaluable in terms of writing fiction. And writers can have faith in television. There is a lot of money at stake, after all; and television owns the best demographers applied social science has to offer, and these researchers can determine precisely what Americans in the 1990s are, want, see — what we as Audience want to see ourselves as. Television, from the surface on down, is about desire. And, fiction-wise, desire is the sugar in human food.

The second great-seeming thing is that television looks to be an absolute godsend for a human subspecies that loves to watch people but hates to be watched itself. For the television screen affords access only one-way. A psychic ball-check valve. We can see Them; They can't see Us. We can relax, unobserved, as we ogle. I happen to believe this is why television also appeals so much to lonely people. To voluntary shut-ins. Every lonely human I know watches way more than the average U.S. six hours a day. The lonely, like the fictive, love one-way watching. For lonely people are usually lonely not because of hideous deformity or odor or obnoxiousness — in fact there exist today support- and social groups for persons with precisely these attributes. Lonely people tend, rather, to be lonely because they decline to bear the psychic costs of being around other humans. They are allergic to people. People affect them too strongly. Let's call the average U.S. lonely person Joe Briefcase. Joe Brief-case fears and loathes the strain of the special self-consciousness which seems to afflict him only when other real human beings are around, staring, their human sense-antennae abristle. Joe B. fears how he might appear, come across, to watchers. He chooses to sit out the enormously stressful U.S. game of appearance poker.

But lonely people, at home, alone, still crave sights and scenes, com-pany. Hence television. Joe can stare at Them on the screen; They remain blind to Joe. It's almost like voyeurism. I happen to know lonely people who regard television as a veritable deus ex machina for voyeurs. And a lot of the criticism, the really rabid criticism less leveled than sprayed at networks, advertisers, and audiences alike, has to do with the charge that television has turned us into a nation of sweaty, slack-jawed voyeurs. This charge turns out to be untrue, but it's untrue for interesting reasons.

What classic voyeurism is is espial, i.e. watching people who don't know you're there as those people go about the mundane but erotically charged little businesses of private life. It's interesting that so much clas-sic voyeurism involves media of framed glass — windows, telescopes, etc. Maybe the framed glass is why the analogy to television is so tempt-ing. But TV-watching is different from genuine Peeping-Tomism. Be-cause the people we're watching through TV's framed-glass screen are not really ignorant of the fact that somebody is watching them. In fact a whole *lot* of somebodies. In fact the people on television know that it is in virtue of this truly huge crowd of ogling somebodies that they are on the screen engaging in broad non-mundane gestures at all. Television does not afford true espial because television is performance, spectacle, which by definition requires watchers. We're not voyeurs here at all. We're just viewers. We are the Audience, megametrically many, though most often we watch alone: E Unibus Pluram.[1]

One reason fiction writers seem creepy in person is that by vocation they really *are* voyeurs. They need that straightforward visual theft of watching somebody who hasn't prepared a special watchable self. The only illusion in true espial is suffered by the voyee, who doesn't know he's

[1] This, and thus part of this essay's title, is from a marvelous toss-off in Michael Sorkin's "Faking It," published in Todd Gitlin, ed., *Watching Television,* Random House/Pantheon, 1987.

giving off images and impressions. A problem with so many of us fiction writers under 40 using television as a substitute for true espial, however, is that TV "voyeurism" involves a whole gorgeous orgy of illusions for the pseudo-spy, when we watch. Illusion (1) is that we're voyeurs here at all: the "voyees" behind the screen's glass are only pretending ignorance. They know perfectly well we're out there. And that we're there is also very much on the minds of those behind the second layer of glass, viz. the lenses and monitors via which technicians and arrangers apply enormous ingenuity to hurl the visible images at us. What we see is far from stolen; it's proffered — illusion (2). And, illusion (3), what we're seeing through the framed panes isn't people in real situations that do or even could go on without consciousness of Audience. I.e., what young writers are scanning for data on some reality to fictionalize is *already* composed of fictional characters in highly formalized narratives. And, (4), we're not really even seeing "characters" at all: it's not Major Frank Burns, pathetic self-important putz from Fort Wayne, Indiana; it's Larry Linville of Ojai, California, actor stoic enough to endure thousands of letters (still coming in, even in syndication) from pseudo-voyeurs berating him for being a putz from Indiana. And then (5) it's ultimately of course not even actors we're espying, not even people: it's EM-propelled analog waves and ion streams and rear-screen chemical reactions throwing off phosphenes in grids of dots not much more lifelike than Seurat's own Impressionist commentaries on perceptual illusion. Good Lord and (6) the dots are coming out of our *furniture*, all we're really spying on is our own *furniture*, and our very own chairs and lamps and bookspines sit visible but unseen at our gaze's frame as we contemplate "Korea" or are taken "live to Jerusalem" or regard the plusher chairs and classier spines of the Huxtable "home" as illusory cues that this is some domestic interior whose membrane we have (slyly, unnoticed) violated — (7) and (8) and illusions ad inf.

Not that these realities about actors and phosphenes and furniture are unknown to us. We choose to ignore them. They are part of the belief we suspend. But it's an awfully heavy load to hoist aloft for six hours a day; illusions of voyeurism and privileged access require serious complicity from the viewer. How can we be made so willingly to acquiesce to the delusion that the people on the TV don't know they're being watched, to the fantasy that we're somehow transcending privacy and feeding on unself-conscious human activity? There might be lots of reasons why these unrealities are so swallowable, but a big one is that the performers behind the glass are — varying degrees of thespian talent notwithstanding — absolute *geniuses* at seeming unwatched. Make no mistake — seeming unwatched in front of a TV camera is an art. Take a look at how non-professionals act when a TV camera is pointed at them: they often spaz out, or else they go all stiff, frozen with self-consciousness. Even PR people and politicians are, in terms of being on camera, rank amateurs. And we love to laugh at how stiff and fake non-pros appear on television. How unnatural.

But if you've ever once been the object of that terrible blank round glass stare, you know all too well how paralyzingly self-conscious it makes you feel. A harried guy with earphones and a clipboard tells you to "act natural" as your face begins to leap around on your skull, struggling for a seeming-unwatched expression that feels so impossible because "seeming unwatched" is, like "acting natural," oxymoronic. Try hitting a golf ball right after someone asks you whether you in- or exhale on your backswing, or getting promised lavish rewards if you can avoid thinking of a green rhinoceros for ten seconds, and you'll get some idea of the truly heroic contortions of body and mind that must be required for a David Duchovny or Don Johnson to act unwatched as he's watched by a lens that's an overwhelming emblem of what Emerson, years before TV, called "the gaze of millions."[2]

For Emerson, only a certain very rare species of person is fit to stand this gaze of millions. It is not your normal, hardworking, quietly desperate species of American. The man who can stand the megagaze is a walking imago, a certain type of transcendent semihuman who, in Emerson's phrase, "carries the holiday in his eye." The Emersonian holiday that television actors' eyes carry is the promise of a vacation from human self-consciousness. Not worrying about how you come across. A total unallergy to gazes. It is contemporarily heroic. It is frightening and strong. It is also, of course, an act, for you have to be just abnormally self-conscious and self-controlled to appear unwatched before cameras and lenses and men with clipboards. This self-conscious appearance

2 Quoted by Stanley Cavell in *Pursuits of Happiness*, Harvard U. Press, 1981; subsequent Emerson quotes Ibid.

of unself-consciousness is the real door to TV's whole mirror-hall of illusions, and for us, the Audience, it is both medicine and poison.

For we gaze at these rare, highly-trained, unwatched-seeming people for six hours daily. And we love these people. In terms of attributing to them true supernatural assets and desiring to emulate them, it's fair to say we sort of worship them. In a real Joe Briefcase–world that shifts ever more starkly from some community of relationships to networks of strangers connected by self-interest and technology, the people we espy on TV offer us familiarity, community. Intimate friendship. But we split what we see. The characters may be our "close friends," but the *performers* are beyond strangers: they're imagos, demigods, and they move in a different sphere, hang out with and marry only each other, seem even as actors accessible to Audience only via the mediation of tabloid, talk show, EM signal. And yet both actors and characters, so terribly removed and filtered, seem so terribly, gloriously *natural* when we watch.

Given how much we watch and what watching means, it's inevitable, for those of us fictionists or Joe Briefcases who fancy ourselves voyeurs, to get the idea that these persons behind the glass — persons who are often the most colorful, attractive, animated, *alive* people in our daily experience — are also people who are oblivious to the fact that they are watched. This illusion is toxic. It's toxic for lonely people because it sets up an alienating cycle (viz. "Why can't *I* be like that?" etc.), and it's toxic for writers because it leads us to confuse actual fiction-research with a weird kind of fiction-*consumption*. Self-conscious people's oversensitivity to real humans tends to put us before the television and its one-way window in an attitude of relaxed and total reception, rapt. We watch various actors play various characters, etc. For 360 minutes per diem, we receive unconscious reinforcement of the deep thesis that the most significant quality of truly alive persons is watchableness, and that genuine human worth is not just identical with but *rooted in* the phenomenon of watching. Plus the idea that the single biggest part of real watchableness is seeming to be unaware that there's any watching going on. Acting natural. The persons we young fiction writers and assorted shut-ins study, feel for, feel through most intently are, by virtue of a genius for feigned unself-consciousness, fit to stand people's gazes. And we, trying desperately to be nonchalant, perspire creepily on the subway.

the finger

Existentiovoyeuristic conundra notwithstanding, there's no denying the simple fact that people in the U.S.A. watch so much television basically because it's fun. I know I watch for fun, most of the time, and that at least 51% of the time I do have fun when I watch. This doesn't mean I do not take television seriously. One big claim of this essay is going to be that the most dangerous thing about television for U.S. fiction writers is that we don't take it seriously enough as both a disseminator and a definer of the cultural atmosphere we breathe and process, that many of us are so blinded by constant exposure that we regard TV the way Reagan's lame F.C.C. chairman Mark Fowler professed to see it in 1981, as "just another appliance, a toaster with pictures."[3]

It's undeniable, nevertheless, that watching television is pleasurable, and it may seem odd that so much of the pleasure my generation takes from television lies in making fun of it. But you have to remember that younger Americans grew up as much with people's disdain for TV as we did with TV itself. I knew it was a "vast wasteland" way before I knew who Newton Minow and Mark Fowler were. And it really is fun to laugh cynically at television — at the way the laughter from sitcoms' "live studio audiences" is always suspiciously constant in pitch and duration, or at the way travel is depicted on *The Flintstones* by having the exact same cut-rate cartoon tree, rock, and house go by four times. It's fun, when a withered June Allyson comes on-screen for Depend Adult Undergarments and says "If you have a bladder-control problem, you're not alone," to hoot and shout back "Well chances are you're alone *quite a bit*, June!"

Most scholars and critics who write about U.S. popular culture, though, seem both to take TV very seriously and to suffer terrible pain over what they see. There's this well-known critical litany about television's vapidity and irrealism. The litany is often even cruder and triter

[3] Bernard Nossiter, "The F.C.C.'s Big Giveaway Show," *Nation*, 10/26/85, p. 402.

than the shows the critics complain about, which I think is why most younger Americans find professional criticism of television less interesting than professional television itself. I found solid examples of what I'm talking about on the first day I even looked. The *New York Times* Arts & Leisure Section for Sunday, 8/05/90, simply bulged with bitter critical derision for TV, and some of the most unhappy articles weren't about low-quality programming so much as about how TV's become this despicable instrument of cultural decay. In a summary review of all 1990's "crash and burn" summer box-office hits in which "realism . . . seems to have gone almost entirely out of fashion," it takes Janet Maslin only a paragraph to locate her true anti-reality culprit: "We may be hearing about 'real life' only on television shows made up of fifteen-second sound bites (in which 'real people' not only speak in brief, neat truisms but actually seem to think that way, perhaps as a result of having watched too much reality-molding television themselves)."[4] And one Stephen Holden, in what starts out as a scathing assessment of the pass pop music's come to, feels he knows perfectly well what's behind what he hates: "Pop music is no longer a world unto itself but an adjunct of television, whose stream of commercial images projects a culture in which everything is for sale and the only things that count are fame, power, and the body beautiful."[5] This stuff just goes on and on, article after article, in the *Times*. The only Arts & Leisure piece I could find with anything upbeat to say about TV that morning was a breathless article on how lots of Ivy League graduates are now flying straight from school to New York and Los Angeles to become television writers and are clearing well over $200,000 to start and enjoying rapid advancement to harried clipboarded production status. In this regard, 8/05's *Times* is a good example of a strange mix that's been around for a few years now: weary contempt for television as a creative product and cultural force, combined with beady-eyed fascination about the actual behind-the-glass mechanics of making that product and projecting that force.

[4] Janet Maslin, "It's Tough for Movies to Get Real," *New York Times* Arts & Leisure Section, 8/05/90, p. 9.

[5] Stephen Holden, "Strike The Pose: When Music Is Skin-Deep," Ibid., p. 1.

Surely I'm not alone in having acquaintances I hate to watch TV with because they so clearly loathe it — they complain relentlessly about the hackneyed plots, the unlikely dialogue, the Cheez-Whiz resolutions, the bland condescension of the news anchors, the shrill wheedling of the commercials — and yet are just as clearly obsessed with it, somehow *need* to loathe their six hours a day, day in and out. Junior advertising executives, aspiring filmmakers, and grad-school poets are in my experience especially prone to this condition where they simultaneously hate, fear, and need television, and try to disinfect themselves of whatever so much viewing might do to them by watching TV with weary contempt instead of the rapt credulity most of us grew up with. (Note that most fiction writers still tend to go for the rapt credulity.)

But, since the wearily contemptuous *Times* has its own demographic thumb to the pulse of readerly taste, it's probably safe to assume that most educated, *Times*-buying Americans are wearily disgusted by television, have this weird hate-/need-/fear-6-hrs.-daily gestalt about it. Published TV-scholarship sure reflects this mood. And the numbingly dull quality to most "literary" television analyses is due less to the turgid abstraction scholars employ to make television seem an OK object of aesthetic inquiry — q.v. part of an '86 treatise: "The form of my Tuesday evening's prime-time pleasure is structured by a dialectic of elision and rift among various windows through which . . . 'flow' is more a circumstance than a product. The real output is the quantum, the smallest maneuverable broadcast bit."[6] — than to the jaded cynicism of TV-scholars who mock and revile the very phenomenon they've chosen as vocation. These scholars are like people who despise — I mean bigtime, long-term despise — their spouses or jobs, but won't split up or quit. Critical complaint seems long ago to have degenerated into plain old whining. The important question about U.S. television is no longer whether there are some truly nasty problems involved in Americans' relation to television but rather what might possibly be done about them. On this question pop critics and scholars are resoundingly mute.

The fact is that it's only in the U.S. arts, particularly in certain strands of contemporary American fiction, that the really interesting questions

[6] Sorkin, p. 163.

about fin-de-siècle TV — What exactly is it about televisual culture that we hate so much? Why are we so immersed in it if we hate it so? What implications are there in our sustained, voluntary immersion in something we hate? — are being addressed. But they are also, weirdly, being asked and answered by television itself. This is another reason why most TV criticism seems so empty. Television's managed to become its own most profitable analyst.

Midmorning, 8/05/90, as I was scanning and sneering at the sneering tone of the aforementioned *Times* articles, a syndicated episode of *St. Elsewhere* was on TV, cleaning up in a Sunday-morning Boston market otherwise occupied by televangelists, Infomercials, and the steroid- and polyurethane-ridden *American Gladiators,* itself not charmless but definitely a low-dose show. Syndication is another new area of public fascination, not only because huge cable stations like Chicago's WGN and Atlanta's TBS have upped the stakes from local to national, but because syndication is changing the whole creative philosophy of network television. Since it is in syndication deals (where the distributor gets both an up-front fee for a program and a percentage of the ad slots for his own commercials) that the creators of successful television series realize truly gross profits, many new programs are designed and pitched with both immediate prime-time and down-the-road syndication audiences in mind, and are now informed less by dreams of the ten-year-beloved-TV-institution-type run — *M*A*S*H, Cheers!* — than of a modest three-year run that will yield the 78 in-can episodes required for an attractive syndication package. By the way, I, like millions of other Americans, know this technical insider-type stuff because I saw a special three-part report about syndication on *Entertainment Tonight,* itself the first nationally syndicated "news" program and the first Infomercial so popular that TV stations were willing to pay for it.

Sunday-morning syndication is also intriguing because it makes for juxtapositions as eerily apposite as anything French surrealists could come up with. Lovable warlocks on *Bewitched* and commercially Satanic heavy-metal videos on *Top Ten Countdown* run opposite air-brushed preachers decrying demonism in U.S. culture. You can surf back and forth between a televised mass's "This is my blood" and *Gladiators'* Zap breaking a civilian's nose with a polyurethane Bataka. Or, even better, have a look at 8/05/90's *St. Elsewhere* episode 94, originally broadcast in 1988, which airs in syndication on Boston's Channel 38 immediately following two back-to-back episodes of *The Mary Tyler Moore Show*, that icon of '70s pathos. The plots of the two *Mary Tyler Moore Show*s are unimportant here. But the *St. Elsewhere* episode that followed them was partly concerned with a cameo-role mental patient who presented with the delusional belief that he was Mary Richards from *The Mary Tyler Moore Show*. He further believed that a fellow cameo-role mental patient was Rhoda, that Dr. Westphal was Mr. Grant, and that Dr. Auschlander was Murray. This psychiatric subplot was a one-shot; it was resolved by episode's end. The pseudo-Mary (a sad lumpy-looking guy, portrayed by an actor whose name I didn't catch but who I remember used to play one of Dr. Hartley's neurotic clients on the old *Bob Newhart Show*) rescues the other cameo-role mental patient, whom he believes to be Rhoda and who has been furious in his denials that he is female, much less fictional (and who is himself played by the guy who used to play Mr. Carlin, Dr. Hartley's most intractable client) from assault by a bit-part hebephrene. In gratitude, Rhoda/Mr. Carlin/mental patient declares that he'll consent to be Rhoda if that's what Mary/neurotic client/mental patient wants. At this too-real generosity, the pseudo-Mary's psychotic break breaks. The sad lumpy guy admits to Dr. Auschlander that he's not Mary Richards. He's actually just a plain old amnesiac, a guy without a meaningful identity, existentially adrift. He has no idea who he is. He's lonely. He watches a lot of TV. He says he "figured it was better to believe I was a TV character than not to believe I was anybody." Dr. Auschlander takes the penitent patient for a walk in the wintery Boston air and promises that he, the identityless guy, can someday very probably find out who he really is, provided he can dispense with "the distraction of television." Extremely grateful and happy at this prognosis, the patient removes his own fuzzy winter beret and throws it into the air. The episode ends with a freeze of the airborne hat, leaving at least one viewer credulously rapt.

This would have been just another clever low-concept '80s TV story, where the final cap-tossing coyly undercuts Dr. Auschlander's putdown of television, were it not for the countless layers of ironic, involuted TV imagery and data that whirled around this incredibly high-concept installment. Because another of this episode's cameo stars, drifting through a different subplot, is one Betty White, Sue-Ann Nivens of the old *Mary Tyler Moore Show*, here playing a tortured NASA surgeon (don't ask). It is with almost tragic inevitability, then, that Ms. White, at 32 minutes into the episode, meets up with the TV-deluded pseudo-Mary in their respective tortured wanderings through the hospital's corridors, and that she greets the mental patient's inevitable joyful cries of "Sue-Ann!" with a too-straight face as she says that he must have her confused with someone else. Of the convoluted levels of fantasy and reality and identity here — e.g. the patient simultaneously does, does not, and does have Betty White "confused" with Sue-Ann Nivens — we needn't speak in detail; doubtless a Yale Contemporary Culture dissertation is under way on Deleuze & Guattari and just this episode. But the most interesting levels of meaning here lie, and point, behind the lens. For NBC's *St. Elsewhere,* like *The Mary Tyler Moore Show* and *The Bob Newhart Show* before it, was created, produced, and guided into syndication by MTM Studios, owned by Mary Tyler Moore and overseen by her erstwhile husband, eventual NBC CEO Grant Tinker; and *St. Elsewhere*'s scripts and subplots are story-edited by Mark Tinker, Mary's stepson, Grant's heir. The deluded mental patient, an exiled, drifting veteran of one MTM program, reaches piteously out to the exiled, drifting (literally — *NASA,* for God's sake!) veteran of another MTM production, and her deadpan rebuff is scripted by MTM personnel, who accomplish the parodic undercut of MTM's Dr. Auschlander with the copyrighted MTM hat-gesture of one MTM veteran who's "deluded" he's another. Dr. A.'s Fowleresque dismissal of TV as just a "distraction" is less naïve than insane: there is nothing *but* television on this episode. Every character and conflict and joke and dramatic surge depends on involution, self-reference, metatelevision. It is in-joke within in-joke.

So then why do I get the in-joke? Because I, the viewer, outside the glass with the rest of the Audience, am *in* on the in-joke. I've seen Mary Tyler Moore's "real" toss of that fuzzy beret so often it's moved past cliché into warm nostalgia. I know the mental patient from *Bob Newhart,* Betty White from everywhere, *and* I know all sorts of intriguing irrelevant stuff about MTM Studios and syndication from *Entertainment Tonight.* I, the pseudo-voyeur, am indeed "behind the scenes," primed to get the in-joke. But it is not I the spy who have crept inside television's boundaries. It is vice versa. Television, even the mundane little businesses of its production, have become my — our — own interior. And we seem a jaded, weary, but willing and above all *knowledgeable* Audience. And this knowledgeability utterly transforms the possibilities and hazards of "creativity" in television. *St. Elsewhere*'s episode was nominated for a 1988 Emmy. For best original teleplay.

The best TV of the last five years has been about ironic self-reference like no previous species of postmodern art could ever have dreamed of. The colors of MTV videos, blue-black and lambently flickered, are the colors of television. *Moonlighting*'s David and *Bueller*'s Ferris throw asides to the viewer every bit as bald as an old melodrama villain's monologued gloat. Segments of the new late-night glitz-news *After Hours* end with a tease that features harried earphoned guys in the production booth ordering the tease. MTV's television-trivia game show, the dry-titled *Remote Control*, got so popular it burst out of its MTV-membrane and is now syndicated band-wide. The hippest commercials, with stark computerized settings and blank-faced models in mirrored shades and plastic slacks genuflecting before various forms of velocity, excitement, and prestige, seem like little more than TV's vision of how TV offers rescue to those lonely Joe Briefcases passively trapped into watching too much TV.

What explains the pointlessness of most published TV criticism is that television has become immune to charges that it lacks any meaningful connection to the world outside it. It's not that charges of nonconnection have become untrue but that they've become deeply irrelevant. It's that any such connection has become otiose. Television used to point beyond itself. Those of us born in, say, the '60s were trained by television to look where it pointed, usually at versions of "real life" made prettier, sweeter, livelier by succumbing to a product or temptation. Today's mega-Audience is way better trained, and TV has discarded what's not needed. A dog, if you point at something, will look only at your finger.

metawatching

It's not like self-reference is new to U.S. entertainment. How many old radio shows — Jack Benny, Burns and Allen, Abbott and Costello — were mostly about themselves as shows? "So, Lou, and you said I couldn't get a big star like Miss Lucille Ball to be a guest on our show, you little twerp." Etc. But once television introduces the element of watching, and once it informs an economy and culture like radio never could have, the referential stakes go way up. Six hours a day is more time than most people (consciously) do any other one thing. How human beings who absorb such high doses understand themselves will naturally change, become vastly more spectatorial, self-conscious. Because the practice of "watching" is expansive. Exponential. We spend enough time watching, pretty soon we start watching ourselves watching. Pretty soon we start to "feel" ourselves feeling, yearn to experience "experiences." And that American subspecies into fiction writing starts writing more and more about . . .

The emergence of something called Metafiction in the American '60s was hailed by academic critics as a radical aesthetic, a whole new literary form, literature unshackled from the cultural cinctures of mimetic narrative and free to plunge into reflexivity and self-conscious meditations on aboutness. Radical it may have been, but thinking that postmodern Metafiction evolved unconscious of prior changes in readerly taste is about as innocent as thinking that all those college students we saw on television protesting the Vietnam war were protesting only because they hated the Vietnam war. (They may have hated the war, but they also wanted to be seen protesting on television. TV was where they'd *seen* this war, after all. Why wouldn't they go about hating it on the very medium that made their hate possible?) Metafictionists may have had aesthetic theories out the bazoo, but they were also sentient citizens of a community that was exchanging an old idea of itself as a nation of doers and be-ers for a new vision of the U.S.A. as an atomized mass of self-conscious watchers and appearers. For Metafiction, in its ascendant and most important phases, was really nothing more than a single-order expansion of its own great theoretical nemesis, Realism: if Realism called it like it saw it, Metafiction simply called it as it saw itself seeing itself see it. This high-cultural postmodern genre, in other words, was deeply informed by the emergence of television and the metastasis of self-conscious watching. And (I claim) American fiction remains deeply informed by television . . . especially those strains of fiction with roots in postmodernism, which even at its rebellious Metafictional zenith was less a "response to" televisual culture than a kind of abiding-in-TV. Even back then, the borders were starting to come down.

It's strange that it took television itself so long to wake up to watching's potent reflexivity. Television shows about the business of television shows were rare for a long time. *The Dick van Dyke Show* was prescient, and Mary Moore carried its insight into her own decade-long exploration of local-market angst. Now, of course, there's been everything from *Murphy Brown* to *Max Headroom* to *Entertainment Tonight*. And with Letterman, Miller, Shandling, and Leno's battery of hip, sardonic, this-is-just-TV schticks, the circle back to the days of "We've just got to get Miss Ball on our show, Bud" has closed and come spiral, television's power to jettison connection and castrate protest fueled by the very ironic postmodern self-consciousness it had first helped fashion.

It will take a while, but I'm going to prove to you that the nexus where television and fiction converse and consort is self-conscious irony. Irony is, of course, a turf fictionists have long worked with zeal. And irony is important for understanding TV because "TV," now that it's gotten powerful enough to move from acronym to way of life, revolves off just the sorts of absurd contradictions irony's all about exposing. It is ironic that television is a syncretic, homogenizing force that derives much of its power from diversity and various affirmations thereof. It is ironic that an extremely canny and unattractive self-consciousness is necessary to create TV performers' illusion of unconscious appeal. That products presented as helping you express individuality can afford to be advertised on television only because they sell to enormous numbers of people. And so on.

Television regards irony sort of the way educated lonely people regard television. Television both fears irony's capacity to expose, and needs it. It needs irony because television was practically *made* for irony. For TV is a bisensuous medium. Its displacement of radio wasn't picture displacing sound; it was picture added. Since the tension between what's said and what's seen is irony's whole sales territory, classic televisual irony works via the conflicting juxtaposition of pictures and sounds. What's seen undercuts what's said. A scholarly article on network news describes a famous interview with a corporate guy from United Fruit on a CBS special about Guatemala: "I sure don't know of anybody being so-called 'oppressed,' " this guy, in a '70s leisure suit and bad comb-over, tells Ed Rabel. "I think this is just something that some reporters have thought up."[7] The whole interview is intercut with commentless footage of big-bellied kids in Guatemalan slums and union organizers lying in the mud with cut throats.

Television's classic irony function came into its own in the summer of 1974, as remorseless lenses opened to view the fertile "credibility gap" between the image of official disclaimer and the reality of high-level she-nanigans. A nation was changed, as Audience. If even the president lies to you, whom are you supposed to trust to deliver the real? Television, that summer, got to present itself as the earnest, worried eye on the real-ity behind all images. The irony that television is itself a river of image, however, was apparent even to a twelve-year-old, sitting there, rapt. After '74 there seemed to be no way out. Images and ironies all over the place. It's not a coincidence that *Saturday Night Live*, that Athens of irrever-ent cynicism, specializing in parodies of (1) politics and (2) television, premiered the next fall (on television).

I'm worried when I say things like "television fears . . ." and "televi-sion presents itself . . ." because, even though it's kind of a necessary ab-straction, talking about television as if it were an entity can easily slip into the worst sort of anti-TV paranoia, treating of TV as some autonomous diabolical corrupter of personal agency and community gumption. I am concerned to avoid anti-TV paranoia here. Though I'm convinced that television today lies, with a potency somewhere between symptom and synecdoche, behind a genuine crisis for U.S. culture and literature, I do not agree with reactionaries who regard TV as some malignancy visited on an innocent populace, sapping IQs and compromising SAT scores while we all sit there on ever fatter bottoms with little mesmerized spi-rals revolving in our eyes. Critics like Samuel Huntington and Barbara Tuchman who try to claim that TV's lowering of our aesthetic standards is responsible for a "contemporary culture taken over by commercialism directed to the mass market and necessarily to mass taste"[8] can be re-futed by observing that their Propter Hoc isn't even Post Hoc: by 1830, de Tocqueville had already diagnosed American culture as peculiarly de-voted to easy sensation and mass-marketed entertainment, "spectacles

---

[7] Daniel Hallin, "We Keep America On Top of the World," in Gitlin's anthology.

[8] Barbara Tuchman, "The Decline of Quality," *New York Times Magazine*, 11/02/80.

vehement and untutored and rude" that aimed "to stir the passions more than to gratify the taste."[9] Treating television as evil is just as reductive and silly as treating it like a toaster w/pictures.

It is of course undeniable that television is an example of Low Art, the sort of art that has to please people in order to get their money. Because of the economics of nationally broadcast, advertiser-subsidized entertainment, television's one goal — never denied by anybody in or around TV since RCA first authorized field tests in 1936 — is to ensure as much watching as possible. TV is the epitome of Low Art in its desire to appeal to and enjoy the attention of unprecedented numbers of people. But it is not Low because it is vulgar or prurient or dumb. Television is often all these things, but this is a logical function of its need to attract and please Audience. And I'm not saying that television is vulgar and dumb because the people who compose Audience are vulgar and dumb. Television is the way it is simply because people tend to be extremely similar in their vulgar and prurient and dumb interests and wildly different in their refined and aesthetic and noble interests. It's all about syncretic diversity: neither medium nor Audience is faultable for quality.

Still, for the fact that individual American human beings are consuming vulgar, prurient, dumb stuff at the astounding average perhousehold dose of six hours a day — for this both TV and we need to answer. We are responsible basically because nobody is holding any weapons on us forcing us to spend amounts of time second only to sleep doing something that is, when you come right down to it, not good for us. Sorry to be a killjoy, but there it is: six hours a day is not good.

Television's greatest minute-by-minute appeal is that it engages without demanding. One can rest while undergoing stimulation. Receive without giving. In this respect, television resembles certain other things one might call Special Treats (e.g. candy, liquor), i.e. treats that are basically fine and fun in small amounts but bad for us in large amounts and *really* bad for us if consumed in the massive regular amounts reserved for nutritive staples. One can only guess at what volume of gin or poundage of Toblerone six hours of Special Treat a day would convert to.

---

[9] M. Alexis de Tocqueville, *Democracy in America*, Vintage, 1945 edition, pp. 57 and 73.

On the surface of the problem, television is responsible for our rate of its consumption only in that it's become so terribly successful at its acknowledged job of ensuring prodigious amounts of watching. Its social accountability seems sort of like that of designers of military weapons: unculpable right up until they get a little too good at their job.

But the analogy between television and liquor is best, I think. Because (bear with me a second) I'm afraid good old average Joe Briefcase might be a teleholic. I.e., watching TV can become malignantly addictive. It may become malignantly addictive only once a certain threshold of quantity is habitually passed, but then the same is true of Wild Turkey. And by "malignant" and "addictive" I again do not mean evil or hypnotizing. An activity is addictive if one's relationship to it lies on that downward-sloping continuum between liking it a little too much and really needing it. Many addictions, from exercise to letter-writing, are pretty benign. But something is *malignantly* addictive if (1) it causes real problems for the addict, and (2) it offers itself as a relief from the very problems it causes.[10] A malignant addiction is also distinguished for spreading the problems of the addiction out and in in interference patterns, creating difficulties for relationships, communities, and the addict's very sense of self and spirit. In the abstract, some of this hyperbole might strain the analogy for you, but concrete illustrations of malignantly addictive TV-watching cycles aren't hard to come by. If it's true that many Americans are lonely, and if it's true that many lonely people are prodigious TV-watchers, and it's true that lonely people find in television's 2-D images relief from their stressful reluctance to be around real human beings, then it's also obvious that the more time spent at home alone watching TV, the less time spent in the world of real human beings, and that the less time spent in the real human world, the harder it becomes not to feel inadequate to the tasks involved in being a part of the world, thus fundamentally apart from it, alienated from it, solipsistic, lonely. It's also true that to the extent one begins to view pseudo-relationships with Bud Bundy or Jane Pauley as acceptable alternatives to relationships with real people, one will have commensurately less con-

[10] I didn't get this definition from any sort of authoritative source, but it seems pretty modest and commonsensical.

scious incentive even to try to connect with real 3-D persons, connections that seem pretty important to basic mental health. For Joe Briefcase, as for many addicts, the Special Treat begins to substitute for something nourishing and needed, and the original genuine hunger — less satisfied than bludgeoned — subsides to a strange objectless unease.

TV-watching as a malignant cycle doesn't even require special preconditions like writerly self-consciousness or neuroallergic loneliness. Let's for a second imagine Joe Briefcase as now just an average U.S. male, relatively unlonely, adjusted, married, blessed with 2.3 apple-cheeked issue, utterly normal, home from hard work at 5:30, starting his average six-hour stint in front of the television. Since Joe B. is average, he'll shrug at pollsters' questions and answer averagely that he most often watches television to "unwind" from those elements of his day and life he finds unpleasant. It's tempting to suppose that TV enables this unwinding simply because it offers an Auschlanderian "distraction," something to divert the mind from quotidian troubles. But would mere distraction ensure continual massive watching? Television offers way more than distraction. In lots of ways, television purveys and enables *dreams*, and most of these dreams involve some sort of transcendence of average daily life. The modes or presentation that work best for TV — stuff like "action," with shoot-outs and car wrecks, or the rapid-fire "collage" of commercials, news, and music videos, or the "hysteria" of prime-time soap and sitcom with broad gestures, high voices, too much laughter — are unsubtle in their whispers that, somewhere, life is quicker, denser, more interesting, more . . . well, *lively* than contemporary life as Joe Briefcase knows it. This might seem benign until we consider that what good old average Joe Briefcase does more than almost anything else in contemporary life is watch television, an activity which anyone with an average brain can see does not make for a very dense and lively life. Since television must seek to attract viewers by offering a dreamy promise of escape from daily life, and since stats confirm that so grossly much of ordinary U.S. life is watching TV, TV's whispered promises must somehow undercut television-watching in theory ("Joe, Joe, there's a world where life is lively, where nobody spends six hours a day unwinding before a piece of furniture") while reinforcing television-watching in practice ("Joe, Joe, your best and only access to this world is TV").

Well, average Joe Briefcase has an OK brain, and deep down inside he knows, as we do, that there's some kind of psychic shell-game going on in this system of conflicting whispers. But if it's so bald a delusion, why do he and we keep watching in such high doses? Part of the answer — a part which requires discretion lest it slip into anti-TV paranoia — is that the phenomenon of television somehow trains or conditions our viewership. Television has become able not only to ensure that we watch but somehow to inform our deepest responses to what's watched. Take jaded TV-critics, or our acquaintances who sneer at the numbing sameness of all the television they sit still for. I always want to grab these unhappy guys by the lapels and shake them until their teeth rattle and point to the absence of guns to their heads and ask why the hell they keep watching, then. But the truth is that there's some complex high-dose psychic transaction between TV and Audience whereby Audience gets trained to respond to and then like and then *expect* trite, hackneyed, numbing television shows, and to expect them to such an extent that when networks do occasionally abandon time-tested formulas the Audience usually punishes them for it by not watching novel shows in sufficient numbers to let them get off the ground. Hence the networks' bland response to its critics that in the majority of cases — and until the rise of hip metatelevision you could count the exceptions on one hand — "different" or "high-concept" programming simply doesn't get ratings. High-quality television cannot stand up to the gaze of millions, somehow.

Now, it is true that certain PR techniques — e.g. shock, grotesquerie, or irreverence — can ease novel sorts of shows' rise to national demographic viability. Examples here might be the "shocking" *A Current Affair,* the "grotesque" *Real People,* the "irreverent" *Married . . . with Children.* But these programs, like most of those touted by the industry as "fresh" or "outrageous," turn out to be just tiny transparent variations on old formulas.

It's not fair to blame television's shortage of originality on any lack of creativity among network talent. The truth is that we seldom get a chance to know whether anybody behind any TV show is creative, or more accurately that they seldom get a chance to show us. Despite the unquestioned assumption on the part of pop-culture critics that television's poor old Audience, deep down, "craves novelty," all available evidence suggests, rather, that the Audience *really* craves sameness but thinks, deep down, that it *ought* to crave novelty. Hence the mixture of devotion and sneer on so many viewerly faces. Hence also the weird viewer complicity behind TV's sham "breakthrough programs": Joe Briefcase needs that PR-patina of "freshness" and "outrageousness" to quiet his conscience while he goes about getting from television what we've all been trained to want from it: some strangely American, profoundly shallow, and eternally temporary *reassurance.*

Particularly in the last decade, this tension in the Audience between what we do want and what we think we ought to want has been television's breath and bread. TV's self-mocking invitation to itself as indulgence, transgression, a glorious "giving in" (again, not exactly foreign to addictive cycles) is one of two ingenious ways it's consolidated its six-hour hold on my generation's cojones. The other is postmodern irony. The commercials for *Alf*'s Boston debut in a syndicated package feature the fat, cynical, gloriously decadent puppet (so much like Snoopy, like Garfield, like Bart, like Butt-Head) advising me to "Eat a whole lot of food and stare at the TV." His pitch is an ironic permission-slip to do what I do best whenever I feel confused and guilty: assume, inside, a sort of fetal position, a pose of passive reception to comfort, escape, reassurance. The cycle is self-nourishing.

guilty fictions

Not, again, that the cycle's root conflict is new. You can trace the opposition between what persons do and ought to desire at least as far back as Plato's chariot or the Prodigal's return. But the way entertainments appeal to and work within this conflict has been transformed in televisual culture. This culture-of-watching's relation to the cycle of indulgence, guilt, and reassurance has important consequences for U.S. art, and though the parallels are easiest to see w/r/t Warhol's Pop or Elvis's Rock, the most interesting intercourse is between television and American literature.

One of the most recognizable things about this century's postmodern fiction has always been the movement's strategic deployment of pop-cultural references — brand names, celebrities, television programs — in even its loftiest High Art projects. Think of just about any example of avant-garde U.S. fiction in the last twenty-five years, from Slothrop's passion for Slippery Elm throat lozenges and his weird encounter with Micky Rooney in *Gravity's Rainbow,* to "You"'s fetish for the *New York Post*'s COMA BABY feature in *Bright Lights, Big City,* to Don DeLillo's pop-hip characters saying stuff to each other like "Elvis fulfilled the terms of the contract. Excess, deterioration, self-destructiveness, grotesque behavior, a physical bloating and a series of insults to the brain, self-delivered."[11]

The apotheosis of the pop in postwar art marked a whole new marriage between High and Low culture. For the artistic viability of postmodernism was a direct consequence, again, not of any new facts about art, but of facts about the new importance of mass commercial culture. Americans seemed no longer united so much by common beliefs as by common images: what binds us became what we stand witness to. Nobody sees this as a good change. In fact, pop-cultural references have become such potent metaphors in U.S. fiction not only because of how united Americans are in our exposure to mass images but also because of our guilty indulgent psychology with respect to that exposure. Put simply, the pop reference works so well in contemporary fiction because (1) we all recognize such a reference, and (2) we're all a little uneasy about how we all recognize such a reference.

The status of Low-cultural images in postmodern and contemporary fiction is very different from those images' place in postmodernism's artistic ancestors, e.g. the "dirty realism" of a Joyce or the ur-Dadaism of something like Duchamp's toilet sculpture. Duchamp's aesthetic display of that vulgarest of appliances served an exclusively theoretical end: it was making statements like "The Museum is the Mausoleum is the Men's Room," etc. It was an example of what Octavio Paz calls "Meta-irony,"[12] an attempt to reveal that categories we divide into superior/arty and inferior/vulgar are in fact so interdependent as to be coextensive. The use of Low references in a lot of today's High literary fiction, on the other hand, serves a less abstract agenda. It is meant (1) to help create a mood of irony and irreverence, (2) to make us uneasy and so "comment" on

11   Don DeLillo, *White Noise,* Viking, 1985, p. 72.

12   Octavio Paz, *Children of the Mire,* Harvard U. Press, 1974, pp. 103–118.

the vapidity of U.S. culture, and (3) most important, these days, to be just plain realistic.

Pynchon and DeLillo were ahead of their time. Today, the belief that pop images are basically just mimetic devices is one of the attitudes that separates most U.S. fiction writers under c. 40 from the writerly generation that precedes us, reviews us, and designs our grad-school curricula. This generation gap in conceptions of realism is, again, TV-dependent. The U.S. generation born after 1950 is the first for whom television was something to be lived with instead of just looked at. Our elders tend to regard the set rather as the flapper did the automobile: a curiosity turned treat turned seduction. For younger writers, TV's as much a part of reality as Toyotas and gridlock. We literally cannot imagine life without it. We're not different from our fathers in that television presents and defines our contemporary world. Where we are different is that we have no memory of a world without such electric definition. This is why the derision so many older fictionists heap on a "Brat Pack" generation they see as insufficiently critical of mass culture is at once understandable and misguided. It's true that there's something sad about the fact that David Leavitt's short stories' sole description of some characters is that their T-shirts have certain brand names on them. But the fact is that, for most of Leavitt's educated young readership, members of a generation raised and nourished on messages equating what one consumes with who one is, Leavitt's descriptions really do do the job. In our post-1950s, inseparable-from-TV association pool, brand loyalty really is synecdochic of character; this is simply a fact.

For those U.S. writers whose ganglia were formed pre-TV, those who are big on neither Duchamp nor Paz and who lack the oracular foresight of a DeLillo, the mimetic deployment of pop-culture icons seems at best an annoying tic and at worst a dangerous vapidity that compromises fiction's seriousness by dating it out of the Platonic Always where it ought to reside. In one of the graduate workshops I went through, a certain gray eminence kept trying to convince us that a literary story or novel should always eschew "any feature which serves to date it"[13]

---

[13] This professor was the sort of guy who used "which" when the appropriate relative pronoun was the less fancy "that," to give you an idea.

because "serious fiction must be Timeless." When we protested that, in his own well-known work, characters moved about electrically lit rooms, drove cars, spoke not Anglo-Saxon but postwar English, and inhabited a North America already separated from Africa by continental drift, he impatiently amended his proscription to those explicit references that would date a story in the "frivolous Now." When pressed for just what stuff evoked this F.N., he said of course he meant the "trendy mass-popular-media" reference. And here, at just this point, transgenerational discourse broke down. We looked at him blankly. We scratched our little heads. We didn't get it. This guy and his students simply did not conceive the "serious" world the same way. His automobiled Timeless and our MTV'd own were different.

If you read the big literary supplements, you've doubtless seen the intergenerational squabble this sort of scene typifies.[14] The plain fact is that certain things having to do with fiction production are different for young U.S. writers now. And television is at the vortex of most of the flux. Because younger writers are not only Artists probing for the nobler interstices in what Stanley Cavell calls the reader's "willingness to be pleased"; we are also, now, self-defined parts of the great U.S. Audience, and have our own aesthetic pleasure-centers; and television has formed and trained us. It won't do, then, for the literary establishment simply to complain that, for instance, young-written characters don't have very interesting dialogues with each other, that young writers' ears seem "tinny." Tinny they may be, but the truth is that, in younger Americans' experience, people in the same room don't do all that much direct conversing with each other. What most of the people I know do is they all sit and face the same direction and stare at the same thing and then structure commercial-length conversations around the sorts of questions that myopic car-crash witnesses might ask each other — "Did you just see what I just saw?" Plus, if we're going to talk about the virtues of "realism," the paucity of profound conversation in younger fiction seems accurately to reflect more than just our own generation — I mean six hours a day, in average households young and old, just how much con-

---

14 If you want to see a typical salvo in this generation war, look at William Gass's "A Failing Grade for the Present Tense" in the 10/11/87 *New York Times Book Review*.

versation can really be going on? So now whose literary aesthetic seems "dated"?

In terms of literary history, it's important to recognize the distinction between pop and televisual references, on the one hand, and the mere use of TV-like techniques, on the other. The latter have been around in fiction forever. The Voltaire of *Candide*, for instance, uses a bisensuous irony that would do Ed Rabel proud, having Candide and Pangloss run around smiling and saying "All for the best, the best of all worlds" amid war-dead, pogroms, rampant nastiness, etc. Even the stream-of-consciousness guys who fathered Modernism were, on a very high level, constructing the same sorts of illusions about privacy-puncturing and espial on the forbidden that television has found so effective. And let's not even talk about Balzac.

It was in post-atomic America that pop influences on literature became something more than technical. About the time television first gasped and sucked air, mass popular U.S. culture seemed to become High-Art-viable as a collection of symbols and myth. The episcopate of this pop-reference movement were the post-Nabokovian Black Humorists, the Metafictionists and assorted franc-and latinophiles only later comprised by "postmodern." The erudite, sardonic fictions of the Black Humorists introduced a generation of new fiction writers who saw themselves as sort of avant-avant-garde, not only cosmopolitan and polyglot but also technologically literate, products of more than just one region, heritage, and theory, and citizens of a culture that said its most important stuff about itself via mass media. In this regard one thinks particularly of the Gaddis of *The Recognitions* and *JR*, the Barth of *The End of the Road* and *The Sot-Weed Factor*, and the Pynchon of *The Crying of Lot 49*. But the movement toward treating of the pop as its own reservoir of mythopeia gathered momentum and quickly transcended both school and genre. Plucking from my shelves almost at random, I find poet James Cummins's 1986 *The Whole Truth*, a cycle of sestinas deconstructing Perry Mason. Here's Robert Coover's 1966 *A Public Burning*, in which Eisenhower buggers Nixon on-air, and his 1968 *A Political Fable*, in which the Cat in the Hat runs for president. I find Max Apple's 1986 *The Propheteers*, a novel-length imagining of Walt Disney's travails. Or here's part of poet Bill Knott's 1974 "And Other Travels":

> . . . in my hand a cat o nine tails on every tip of which was
>   Clearasil
> I was worried because Dick Clark had told the camera-
>   man
> not to put the camera on me during the dance parts
> of the show because my skirts were too tight[15]

which serves as a great example because, even though this stanza appears in the poem without anything you'd normally call context or support, it is in fact *self*-supported by a reference we all, each of us, immediately get, conjuring as it does with *Bandstand* ritualized vanity, teenage insecurity, the management of spontaneous moments. It is the perfect pop image, at once slight and universal, soothing and discomfiting.

Recall that the phenomena of watching and consciousness of watching are by nature expansive. What distinguishes another, later wave of postmodern literature is a further shift from television-images as valid objects of literary allusion to television and metawatching as themselves valid *subjects*. By this I mean certain literature beginning to locate its raison in its commentary on/response to a U.S. culture more and more of and for watching, illusion, and the video image. This involution of attention was first observable in academic poetry. See for instance Stephen Dobyns's 1980 "Arrested Saturday Night":

> This is how it happened: Peg and Bob had invited
> Jack and Roxanne over to their house to watch
> the TV, and on the big screen they saw Peg and Bob,
> Jack and Roxanne watching themselves watch
> themselves on progressively smaller TVs . . .[16]

---

[15] In Bill Knott's *Love Poems to Myself, Book One,* Barn Dream Press, 1974.

[16] In Stephen Dobyns's *Heat Death,* McLelland and Stewart, 1980.

or Knott's 1983 "Crash Course":

> I strap a TV monitor on my chest
> so that all who approach can see themselves
> and respond appropriately.[17]

The true prophet of this shift in U.S. fiction, though, was the afore-mentioned Don DeLillo, a long-underrated conceptual novelist who has made signal and image his unifying topoi the same way Barth and Pynchon had sculpted in paralysis and paranoia a decade earlier. DeLillo's 1985 *White Noise* sounded, to fledgling fictionists, a kind of televisual clarion-call. Scenelets like the following seemed especially important:

> Several days later Murray asked me about
> a tourist attraction known as the most
> photographed barn in America. We drove
> twenty-two miles into the country around
> Farmington. There were meadows and apple
> orchards. White fences trailed through the
> rolling fields. Soon the signs started appearing.
> THE MOST PHOTOGRAPHED BARN
> IN AMERICA. We counted five signs before
> we reached the site. . . . We walked along
> a cowpath to the slightly elevated spot set
> aside for viewing and photographing. All
> the people had cameras; some had tripods,
> telephoto lenses, filter kits. A man in a
> booth sold postcards and slides — pictures
> of the barn taken from the elevated spot.
> We stood near a grove of trees and watched
> the photographers. Murray maintained a
> prolonged silence, occasionally scrawling
> some notes in a little book.

---

[17] In Bill Knott's *Becos*, Vintage, 1983.

"No one sees the barn," he said finally.

A long silence followed.

"Once you've seen the signs about the barn, it becomes impossible to see the barn."

He fell silent once more. People with cameras left the elevated site, replaced at once by others.

"We're not here to capture an image. We're here to maintain one. Can you feel it, Jack? An accumulation of nameless energies."

There was an extended silence. The man in the booth sold postcards and slides.

"Being here is a kind of spiritual surrender. We see only what the others see. The thousands who were here in the past, those who will come in the future. We've agreed to be part of a collective perception. This literally colors our vision. A religious experience in a way, like all tourism."

Another silence ensued.

"They are taking pictures of taking pictures," he said.[18]

I quote this at such length not only because it's too good to edit but also to draw your attention to two relevant features. One is the Dobynsesque message here about the metastasis of watching. For not only are people watching a barn whose only claim to fame is being an object of watching, but the pop-culture scholar Murray is watching people watch a barn, and his friend Jack is watching Murray watch the watching, and we readers are pretty obviously watching Jack the narrator watch Murray watching, etc. If you leave out the reader, there's a similar regress of recordings of barn and barn-watching.

[18] *White Noise,* pp. 12–13.

But more important are the complicated ironies at work in the scene. The scene itself is obviously absurd and absurdist. But most of the writing's parodic force is directed at Murray, the would-be transcender of spectation. Murray, by watching and analyzing, would try to figure out the how and whys of giving in to collective visions of mass images that have themselves become mass images only because they've been made the objects of collective vision. The narrator's "extended silence" in response to Murray's blather speaks volumes. But it's not to be taken as implying sympathy with the sheeplike photograph-hungry crowd. These poor Joe Briefcases are no less objects of ridicule for the fact that their "scientific" critic is himself being ridiculed. The narrative tone throughout is a kind of deadpan sneer, irony's special straight face, w/ Jack himself mute during Murray's dialogue — since to speak out loud in the scene would render the narrator a part of the farce (instead of a detached, transcendent "observer and recorder") and so himself vulnerable to ridicule. With his silence, DeLillo's alter ego Jack eloquently diagnoses the very disease from which he, Murray, barn-watchers, and readers all suffer.

i do have a thesis

I want to persuade you that irony, poker-faced silence, and fear of ridicule are distinctive of those features of contemporary U.S. culture (of which cutting-edge fiction is a part) that enjoy any significant relation to the television whose weird pretty hand has my generation by the throat. I'm going to argue that irony and ridicule are entertaining and effective, and that at the same time they are agents of a great despair and stasis in U.S. culture, and that for aspiring fiction writers they pose especially terrible problems.

My two big premises are that, on the one hand, a certain subgenre of pop-conscious postmodern fiction, written mostly by young Americans, has lately arisen and made a real attempt to transfigure a world of and for appearance, mass appeal, and television; and that, on the other hand, televisual culture has somehow evolved to a point where it seems invulnerable to any such transfiguring assault. Television, in other words, has become able to capture and neutralize any attempt to change or even protest the attitudes of passive unease and cynicism that television requires of Audience in order to be commercially and psychologically viable at doses of several hours per day.

image-fiction

The particular fictional subgenre I have in mind has been called by some editors post-postmodernism and by some critics Hyperrealism. Some of the younger readers and writers I know call it Image-Fiction. Image-Fiction is basically a further involution of the relations between lit and pop that blossomed with the '60s' postmodernists. If the postmodern church fathers found pop images valid *referents* and *symbols* in fiction, and if in the '70s and early '80s this appeal to the features of mass culture shifted from use to mention — i.e. certain avant-gardists starting to treat of pop and TV-watching as themselves fertile *subjects* — the new Fiction of Image uses the transient received myths of popular culture as a *world* in which to imagine fictions about "real," albeit pop-mediated, characters. Early uses of Imagist tactics can be seen in the DeLillo of *Great Jones Street*, the Coover of *Burning*, and in Max Apple, whose '70s short story "The Oranging of America" projects an interior life onto the figure of Howard Johnson.

But in the late '80s, despite publisher unease over the legalities of imagining private lives for public figures, a real bumper crop of this behind-the-glass stuff started appearing, authored largely by writers who didn't know or cross-fertilize one another. Apple's *Propheteers*, Jay Cantor's *Krazy Kat*, Coover's *A Night at the Movies, or You Must Remember This*, William T. Vollmann's *You Bright and Risen Angels*, Stephen Dixon's *Movies: Seventeen Stories*, and DeLillo's own fictional hologram of Oswald in *Libra* are all notable post-'85 instances. (Observe too that, in another '80s medium, the arty *Zelig*, *Purple Rose of Cairo*, and *sex, lies, and videotape*, plus the low-budget *Scanners* and *Videodrome* and *Shockers*, all began to treat of mass-entertainment screens as permeable.)

It's in the last year that the Image-Fiction scene has really taken off. A. M. Homes's 1990 *The Safety of Objects* features a stormy love affair between a boy and a Barbie doll. Vollmann's 1989 *The Rainbow Stories* has Sonys as characters in Heideggerian parables. Michael Martone's 1990 *Fort Wayne Is Seventh on Hitler's List* is a tight cycle of stories about the Midwest's pop-culture giants — James Dean, Colonel Sanders, Dillinger — the whole project of which, spelled out in a preface about Image-Fiction's legal woes, involves "questioning the border between fact and fiction when in the presence of fame."[19] And Mark Leyner's 1990 campus smash *My Cousin, My Gastroenterologist,* less a novel than what the book's jacket copy describes as "a fiction analogue of the best drug you ever took," features everything from meditations on the color of Carefree Panty Shield wrappers to "Big Squirrel, the TV kiddie-show host and kung fu mercenary" to NFL instant replays in an "X-ray vision which shows leaping skeletons in a bluish void surrounded by 75,000 roaring skulls."[20]

One thing I have to insist you realize about this new subgenre is that it's distinguishable not just by a certain neo-postmodern technique but by a genuine socio-artistic agenda. The Fiction of Image is not just a use or mention of televisual culture but an actual *response* to it, an effort to impose some sort of accountability on a state of affairs in which more Americans get their news from television than from newspapers and in which more Americans every evening watch *Wheel of Fortune* than all three network news programs combined.

And please see that Image-Fiction, far from being a trendy avantgarde novelty, is almost atavistic. It is a natural adaptation of the hoary techniques of literary Realism to a '90s world whose defining boundaries have been deformed by electric signal. For one of realistic fiction's big jobs used to be to afford easements across borders, to help readers leap over the walls of self and locale and show us unseen or -dreamed-of people and cultures and ways to be. Realism made

---

19 Martone, *Fort Wayne Is Seventh on Hitler's List,* Indiana U. Press, 1990, p. ix.

20 Leyner, *My Cousin, My Ga ⬤ :nterologist,* Harmony/Crown, 1990, p. 82.

the strange familiar. Today, when we can eat Tex-Mex with chopsticks while listening to reggae and watching a Soviet-satellite newscast of the Berlin Wall's fall — i.e., when damn near *everything* presents itself as familiar — it's not a surprise that some of today's most ambitious Realist fiction is going about trying to *make the familiar strange*. In so doing, in demanding fictional access behind lenses and screens and headlines and reimagining what human life might truly be like over there across the chasms of illusion, mediation, demographics, marketing, imago, and appearance, Image-Fiction is paradoxically trying to restore what's taken for "real" to three whole dimensions, to reconstruct a univocally round world out of disparate streams of flat sights.

That's the good news.

The bad news is that, almost without exception, Image-Fiction doesn't satisfy its own agenda. Instead, it most often degenerates into a kind of jeering, surfacey look "behind the scenes" of the very televisual front people already jeer at, a front they can already get behind the scenes of via *Entertainment Tonight* and *Remote Control.*

The reason why today's Image-Fiction isn't the rescue from a passive, addictive TV-psychology that it tries so hard to be is that most Image-Fiction writers render their material with the same tone of irony and self-consciousness that their ancestors, the literary insurgents of Beat and postmodernism, used so effectively to rebel against their own world and context. And the reason why this irreverent postmodern approach fails to help the new Imagists transfigure TV is simply that TV has beaten the new Imagists to the punch. The fact is that for at least ten years now, television has been ingeniously absorbing, homogenizing, and re-presenting the very same cynical postmodern aesthetic that was once the best alternative to the appeal of Low, over-easy, mass-marketed narrative. How TV's done this is blackly fascinating to see.

A quick intermission contra paranoia. By saying that Image-Fiction aims to "rescue" us from TV, I again am not suggesting that television has diabolic designs, or wants souls, or brainwashes people. I'm just referring again to the kind of natural Audience-conditioning consequent to high daily doses, a conditioning so subtle it can be observed best obliquely, through examples. And so if a term like "conditioning" still seems hyperbolic or hysterical to you, I'll ask you to consider for a moment the exemplary issue of prettiness. One of the things that makes the people on television fit to stand the Megagaze is that they are, by ordinary human standards, extremely pretty. I suspect that this, like most television conventions, is set up with no motive more sinister than to appeal to the largest possible Audience — pretty people tend to be more appealing to look at than non-pretty people. But when we're talking about television, the combination of sheer Audience size and quiet psychic intercourse between images and oglers starts a cycle that both enhances pretty people's appeal and erodes us viewers' own security in the face of gazes. Because of the way human beings relate to narrative, we tend to identify with those characters we find appealing. We try to see ourselves in them. The same I.D.-relation, however, also means that we try to see them in ourselves. When everybody we seek to identify with for six hours a day is pretty, it naturally becomes more important to us to be pretty, to be viewed as pretty. Because prettiness becomes a priority for us, the pretty people on TV become all the more attractive, a cycle which is obviously great for TV. But it's less great for us civilians, who tend to own mirrors, and who also tend not to be anywhere near as pretty as the TV-images we want to identify with. Not only does this cause some angst personally, but the angst increases because, nationally, everybody else is absorbing six-hour doses and identifying with pretty people and valuing prettiness more, too. This very personal anxiety about our prettiness has become a national phenomenon with national consequences. The whole U.S.A. gets different about things it values and fears. The boom in diet aids, health and fitness clubs, neighborhood tanning parlors, cosmetic surgery, anorexia, bulimia, steroid-use among boys, girls throwing acid at each other because one girl's hair looks more like Farrah Fawcett's than another ... are these supposed to be unrelated to each other? to the apotheosis of prettiness in a televisual culture?

It's not paranoid or hysterical to acknowledge that television in enormous doses affects people's values and self-perception in deep ways. Nor that televisual conditioning influences the whole psychology of one's relation to himself, his mirror, his loved ones, and a world of real people and real gazes. No one's going to claim that a culture all about watching and appearing is fatally compromised by unreal standards of beauty and fitness. But other facets of TV-training reveal themselves as more ra-pacious, more serious, than any irreverent fiction writer would want to take seriously.

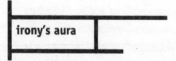

irony's aura

It's widely recognized that television, with its horn-rimmed battery of statisticians and pollsters, is awfully good at discerning patterns in the flux of popular ideologies, absorbing those patterns, processing them, and then re-presenting them as persuasions to watch and to buy. Commercials targeted at the '80s' upscale Boomers, for example, are notorious for using processed versions of tunes from the rock culture of the '60s and '70s both to elicit the yearning that accompanies nostalgia and to yoke purchase of products with what for yuppies is a lost era of genuine conviction. Ford sport-vans are advertised with "This is the dawning of the age of the Aerostar"; Ford recently litigates with Bette Midler over the theft of her old vocals on "Do You Wanna Dance"; the CA Raisin Board's claymation raisins dance to "Heard It Through the Grapevine"; etc. If the cynical re-use of songs and the ideals they used to symbolize seems distasteful, it's not like pop musicians are paragons of noncommercialism themselves, and anyway nobody ever said selling was pretty. The effects of any one instance of TV absorbing and pablumizing cultural tokens seem innocuous enough. The recycling of whole cultural trends, and the ideologies that inform them, is a different story.

U.S. pop culture is just like U.S. serious culture in that its central tension has always set the nobility of individualism against the warmth of communal belonging. For its first twenty or so years, it seemed as though television sought to appeal mostly to the Group-Belonging side of the equation. Communities and bonding were extolled on early TV, even though TV itself, and especially its advertising, has from the outset projected itself at the lone viewer, Joe Briefcase, alone. (Television commercials always make their appeals to individuals, not groups, a fact that seems curious in light of the unprecedented size of TV's Audience, until one hears gifted salesmen explain how people are always most vulnerable, hence frightened, hence persuadable, when they are approached solo.)

Classic television commercials were all about the Group. They took the vulnerability of Joe Briefcase — sitting there, watching his furniture, lonely — and capitalized on it by linking purchase of a given product with Joe B.'s inclusion in some attractive community. This is why those of us over 21 can remember all those interchangeable old commercials featuring groups of pretty people in some ecstatic context, all having just way more fun than anybody has a license to have, and all united as Happy Group by the conspicuous fact that they're holding a certain bottle of pop or brand of snack — the blatant appeal here is that the relevant product can help Joe Briefcase belong: . . . "We're the Pepsi Generation. . . ."

But since at least the '80s, the Individualist side of the great U.S. conversation has held sway in TV advertising. I'm not sure just why or how this happened. There are probably great connections to be traced — with Vietnam, youth culture, Watergate and recession and the New Right's rise — but the point is that a lot of the most effective TV commercials now make their appeal to the lone viewer in a terribly different way. Products are now most often pitched as helping the viewer "express himself," assert his individuality, "stand out from the crowd." The first instance I ever saw was a perfume vividly billed in the early '80s as reacting specially with each woman's "unique body chemistry" and creating "her own individual scent," the ad depicting a cattle-line of languid models waiting cramped and expressionless to get their wrists squirted one at a time, each smelling her moist individual wrist with a kind of biochemical revelation, then moving off in what a back-pan reveals to be different directions from the squirter. (We can ignore the obvious sexual connotations, squirting and all that; some tactics are changeless.) Or think of that recent series of over-dreary black-and-white Cherry 7-Up ads where the only characters who get to have color and stand out from their surroundings are the pink people who become pink at the exact moment they imbibe good old Cherry 7-Up. Examples of stand-apart ads are pretty much ubiquitous now.

Except for being sillier (e.g. products billed as distinguishing individuals from crowds sell to huge crowds of individuals), these ads aren't
really any more complicated or subtle than the old Join-the-Fulfilling-
Group ads that now seem so quaint. But the new Stand-Out-From-the-
Pack ads' relation to their mass of lone viewers is both complex and
ingenious. Today's best ads are still about the Group, but they now present the Group as something fearsome, something that can swallow you
up, erase you, keep you from "being noticed." But noticed by whom?
Crowds are still vitally important in the stand-apart ads' thesis on identity, but now a given ad's crowd, far from being more appealing, secure,
and alive than the individual, functions as a mass of identical feature-
less eyes. The crowd is now, paradoxically, both (1) the "herd" in contrast to which the viewer's distinctive identity is to be defined and (2)
the witnesses whose sight alone can confer distinctive identity. The lone
viewer's isolation in front of his furniture is implicitly applauded — it's
better, realer, these solipsistic ads imply, to fly solo — and yet it's also
implicated as threatening, confusing, since after all Joe Briefcase is not
an idiot, sitting here, and knows himself as a viewer to be guilty of the
two big sins the ads decry: being a passive watcher (of TV) and being
part of a great herd (of TV-watchers and Stand-Apart-product-buyers).
How odd.

The surface of Stand-Out ads still presents a relatively unalloyed Buy
This Thing, but the deep message of television w/r/t these ads looks to be
that Joe Briefcase's ontological status as just one in a reactive watching
mass is at some basic level shaky, contingent, and that true actualization
of self would ultimately consist in Joe's becoming one of the images that
are the *objects* of this great herd-like watching. That is, television's real
pitch in these commercials is that it's better to be inside the TV than to
be outside, watching.

The lonely grandeur of Stand-Apart advertising not only sells companies' products, then. It manages brilliantly to ensure — even in commercials that television gets paid to run — that ultimately it's TV, and
not any specific product or service, that will be regarded by Joe B.
as the ultimate arbiter of human worth. An oracle, to be consulted
a lot. Advertising scholar Mark C. Miller puts it succinctly: "TV has
gone beyond the explicit celebration of commodities to the implicit
reinforcement of that spectatorial posture which TV requires of

us."[21] Solipsistic ads are another way television ends up pointing at itself, keeping the viewer's relation to his furniture at once alienated and anaclitic.

Maybe, though, the relation of contemporary viewer to contemporary television is less a paradigm of infantilism and addiction than it is of the U.S.A.'s familiar relation to all the technology we equate at once with freedom and power and slavery and chaos. For, as with television, whether we happen personally to love technology, hate it, fear it, or all three, we still look relentlessly to technology for solutions to the very problems technology seems to cause — see e.g. catalysis for smog, S.D.I. for nuclear missiles, transplants for assorted rot.

And as with tech, so the gestalt of television expands to absorb all problems associated with it. The pseudo-communities of prime-time soaps like *Knots Landing* and *thirtysomething* are viewer-soothing products of the very medium whose ambivalence about the Group helps erode people's sense of connection. The staccato editing, sound bites, and summary treatment of knotty issues is network news' accommodation of an Audience whose attention span and appetite for complexity have naturally withered a bit after years of high-dose spectation. Etc.

But TV has technology-bred problems of its own. The advent of consumer cable, often with packages of over 40 channels, threatens networks and local affiliates alike. This is particularly true when the viewer is armed with a remote-control gizmo: Joe B. is still getting his six total hours of daily TV, but the amount of his retinal time devoted to any one option shrinks as he remote-scans a much wider band. Worse, the VCR, with its dreaded fast-forward and zap functions, threatens the very viability of commercials. Television advertisers' entirely sensible solution? Make the ads as appealing as the programs. Or at any rate try to keep Joe B. from disliking the commercials enough that he's willing to move his thumb to check out 2½ minutes of *Hazel* on the Superstation while NBC sells lip balm. Make the ads prettier, livelier, full of enough rapidly juxtaposed visual quanta so that Joe's attention just

---

[21] Mark Crispin Miller, "Deride and Conquer" in Gitlin's anthology.

doesn't get to wander, even if he remote-kills the volume. As one ad executive underputs it, "Commercials are becoming more like entertaining films."[22]

There's an obverse way, of course, to make commercials resemble programs. Have programs start to resemble commercials. That way the ads seem less like interruptions than like pace-setters, metronomes, commentaries on the shows' theory. Invent a *Miami Vice*, where there's little annoying plot to interrupt but an unprecedented emphasis on appearances, visuals, attitude, a certain "look."[23] Make music videos with the same amphetaminic pace and dreamy archetypal associations as ads — it doesn't hurt that videos are basically long music-commercials anyway. Or introduce the sponsor-supplied Infomercial that poses, in a lighthearted way, as a soft-news show, like *Amazing Discoveries* or those Robert Vaughn–hosted Hair-Loss Reports that haunt TV's wee cheap hours. Blur — just as postmodern lit did — the lines between genres, agendas, commercial art and arty commercials.

Still, television and its sponsors had a bigger long-term worry, and that was their shaky détente with the individual viewer's psyche. Given that television must revolve off basic antinomies about being and watching, about escape from daily life, the averagely intelligent viewer can't be all that happy about his daily life of high-dose watching. Joe Briefcase might have been happy enough *when* watching, but it was hard to think he could be too terribly happy *about* watching so much. Surely, deep down, Joe was uncomfortable with being one part of the biggest crowd in human history watching images that suggest that life's meaning consists in standing visibly apart from the crowd. TV's guilt/indulgence/reassurance cycle addresses these concerns on one level. But might there not be some deeper way to keep Joe Briefcase firmly in the crowd of watchers, by somehow associating his very viewership with transcendence of watching crowds? But that would be absurd. Enter irony.

[22] At Foote, Cone and Belding, quoted by Miller — so the guy said it in the mid-'80s.

[23] A similar point is made about *Miami Vice* in "We Build Excitement," Todd Gitlin's own essay in his anthology.

I've claimed — so far sort of vaguely — that what makes television's hegemony so resistant to critique by the new Fiction of Image is that TV has coopted the distinctive forms of the same cynical, irreverent, ironic, absurdist post-WWII literature that the new Imagists use as touchstones. The fact is that TV's re-use of postmodern cool has actually evolved as an inspired solution to the keep-Joe-at-once-alienated-from-and-part-of-the-million-eyed-crowd problem. The solution entailed a gradual shift from oversincerity to a kind of bad-boy irreverence in the Big Face that TV shows us. This in turn reflected a wider shift in U.S. perceptions of how art was supposed to work, a transition from art's being a creative instantiation of real values to art's being a creative rejection of bogus values. And this wider shift, in its turn, paralleled both the development of the postmodern aesthetic and some deep and serious changes in how Americans chose to view concepts like authority, sincerity, and passion in terms of our willingness to be pleased. Not only are sincerity and passion now "out," TV-wise, but the very idea of pleasure has been undercut. As Mark C. Miller puts it, contemporary television "no longer solicits our rapt absorption or hearty agreement, but — like the ads that subsidize it — actually flatters us for the very boredom and distrust it inspires in us."[24]

Miller's 1986 "Deride and Conquer," far and away the best essay ever published about network advertising, details vividly an example of how TV's contemporary kind of appeal to the lone viewer works. It concerns a 1985-86 ad that won Clio Awards and still occasionally runs. It's that Pepsi commercial where a special Pepsi sound-van pulls up to a packed sweltering beach and the impish young guy in the van activates a lavish PA system and opens up a Pepsi and pours it into a cup up next to the microphone. And the dense glittered sound of much carbonation goes out over the beach's heat-wrinkled air, and heads turn vanward as if pulled with strings as his gulp and refreshed-sounding spirants and gasps are broadcast. And the final shot reveals that the sound-van is also a concession truck, and the whole beach's pretty population has now collapsed to a clamoring mass around the truck, everybody hopping up and down and pleading to be served first,

[24] Miller, p. 194.

as the camera's view retreats to an overhead crowd-shot and the slogan is flatly intoned: "Pepsi: the Choice of a New Generation." Truly a stunning commercial. But need one point out — as Miller's essay does in some detail — that the final slogan is here tongue-in-cheek? There's about as much "choice" at work in this commercial as there was in Pavlov's bell-kennel. The use of the word "choice" here is a dark joke. In fact the whole 30-second spot is tongue-in-cheek, ironic, self-mocking. As Miller argues, it's not really *choice* that the commercial is selling Joe Briefcase on, "but the total negation of choices. Indeed, the product itself is finally incidental to the pitch. The ad does not so much extol Pepsi per se as recommend it by implying that a lot of people have been fooled into buying it. In other words, the point of this successful bit of advertising is that Pepsi has been advertised successfully."[25]

There are important things to realize here. First, this Pepsi ad is deeply informed by a fear of remote gizmos, zapping, and viewer disdain. An ad about ads, it used self-reference to seem too hip to hate. It protects itself from the scorn today's TV-cognoscente feels for both the fast-talking hard-sell ads Dan Aykroyd parodied into oblivion on *Saturday Night Live* and the quixotic associative ads that linked soda-drinking with romance, prettiness, and Group-inclusion, ads that today's hip viewer finds old-fashioned and "manipulative." In contrast to a blatant Buy This Thing, the Pepsi commercial pitches parody. The ad is utterly up-front about what TV ads are popularly despised for doing, viz. using primal, flim-flam appeals to sell sugary crud to people whose identity is nothing but mass consumption. This ad manages simultaneously to make fun of itself, Pepsi, advertising, advertisers, and the great U.S. watching consuming crowd. In fact the ad is uxorious in its flattery of only one person: the lone viewer, Joe B., who even with an average brain can't help but discern the ironic contradiction between the "Choice" slogan (sound) and the Pavlovian orgy around the van (sight). The commercial invites Joe to "see through" the manipulation the beach's horde is rabidly buying. The commercial invites a complicity between its own witty irony and veteran viewer Joe's cynical, nobody's-fool appreciation of that irony. It invites Joe into an in-joke the Audience is the butt of. It congratulates Joe Briefcase, in other words, on transcending the very crowd that defines him. And entire crowds of Joe B.'s responded: the ad boosted Pepsi's market share through three sales quarters.

Pepsi's campaign is not unique. Isuzu Inc. hit pay dirt in the late '80s with its series of "Joe Isuzu" spots, featuring an oily, Satanic-looking salesman who told whoppers about Isuzu's genuine llama-skin upholstery and ability to run on tapwater. Though the ads never said much of anything about why Isuzus are in fact good cars, sales and awards accrued. The ads succeeded as parodies of how oily and Satanic car commercials are. They invited viewers to congratulate Isuzu's ads for being ironic, to congratulate themselves for getting the joke, and to congratulate Isuzu Inc. for being "fearless" and "irreverent" enough to acknowledge that car ads are ridiculous and that Audience is dumb to believe them. The ads invite the lone viewer to drive an Isuzu as some sort of anti-advertising statement. The ads successfully associate Isuzu-purchase with fearlessness and irreverence and the capacity to see through deception. You can now find successful television ads that mock TV-ad conventions almost anywhere you look, from Settlemeyer's Federal Express and Wendy's spots with their wizened, sped-up burlesques of commercial characters, to those hip Doritos splices of commercial spokesmen and campy old clips of *Beaver* and *Mr. Ed.*

Plus you can see this tactic of heaping scorn on pretentions to those old commercial virtues of authority and sincerity — thus (1) shielding the heaper of scorn from scorn and (2) congratulating the patron of scorn for rising above the mass of people who still fall for outmoded pretensions — employed to serious advantage on many of the television programs the commercials support. Show after show, for years now, has been either a self-acknowledged blank, visual, postmodern allusion- and attitude-fest, or, even more common, an uneven battle of wits between some ineffectual spokesman for hollow authority and his precocious children, mordant spouse, or sardonic colleagues. Compare television's treatment of earnest authority figures on pre-ironic shows — *The FBI's* Erskine, *Star Trek's* Kirk, *Beaver's* Ward, *The Partridge Family's* Shirley, *Hawaii Five-0's* McGarrett — to TV's depiction of Al Bundy on *Married*

. . . *with Children,* Mr. Owens on *Mr. Belvedere,* Homer on *The Simpsons,* Daniels and Hunter on *Hill Street Blues,* Jason Seaver on *Growing Pains,* Dr. Craig on *St. Elsewhere.*

The modern sitcom,[26] in particular, is almost wholly dependent for laughs and tone on the *M*A*S*H*-inspired savaging of some buffoonish spokesman for hypocritical, pre-hip values at the hands of bitingly witty insurgents. As Hawkeye savaged Frank and later Charles, so Herb is savaged by Jennifer and Carlson by J. Fever on *WKRP,* Mr. Keaton by Alex on *Family Ties,* boss by typing pool on *Nine to Five,* Seaver by whole family on *Pains,* Bundy by entire planet on *Married . . . w/* (the ultimate sitcom-parody of sitcoms). In fact, just about the only authority figures who retain any credibility on post-'80 shows (besides those like *Hill Street'*s Furillo and *Elsewhere'*s Westphal, who are beset by such relentless squalor and stress that simply hanging in there week after week renders them heroic) are those upholders of values who can communicate some irony about themselves, make fun of themselves before any merciless Group around them can move in for the kill — see Huxtable on *Cosby,* Belvedere on *Belvedere, Twin Peaks'*s Special Agent Cooper, Fox TV's Gary Shandling (the theme to whose show goes "This is the theme to Ga-ry's show"), and the ironic '80s' true Angel of Death, Mr. D. Letterman.

Its promulgation of cynicism about authority works to the general advantage of television on a number of levels. First, to the extent that TV can ridicule old-fashioned conventions right off the map, it can create an authority vacuum. And then guess what fills it. The real authority on a world we now view as constructed and not depicted becomes the medium that constructs our world-view. Second, to the extent that TV can refer exclusively to itself and debunk conventional standards as hollow, it is invulnerable to critics' charges that what's on is shallow or crass or bad, since any such judgments appeal to conventional, extra-televisual standards about depth, taste, quality. Too, the ironic tone of TV's self-reference means that no one can accuse TV of trying to put anything

---

[26] Miller's "Deride . . ." has a similar analysis of sitcoms, but Miller ends up arguing that the crux is some weird Freudio-patricidal element in how TV comedy views The Father.

over on anybody. As essayist Lewis Hyde points out, self-mocking irony is always "Sincerity, with a motive."[27]

And, more to the original point, if television can invite Joe Briefcase into itself via in-gags and irony, it can ease that painful tension between Joe's need to transcend the crowd and his inescapable status as Audience-member. For to the extent that TV can flatter Joe about "seeing through" the pretentiousness and hypocrisy of outdated values, it can induce in him precisely the feeling of canny superiority it's taught him to crave, and can keep him dependent on the cynical TV-watching that alone affords this feeling.

And to the extent that it can train viewers to laugh at characters' un-ending put-downs of one another, to view ridicule as both the mode of social intercourse and the ultimate art-form, television can reinforce its own queer ontology of appearance: the most frightening prospect, for the well-conditioned viewer, becomes leaving oneself open to others' ridicule by betraying passé expressions of value, emotion, or vulnerabil-ity. Other people become judges; the crime is naïveté. The well-trained viewer becomes even more allergic to people. Lonelier. Joe B.'s exhaus-tive TV-training in how to worry about how he might come across, seem to watching eyes, makes genuine human encounters even scarier. But televisual irony has the solution: further viewing begins to seem almost like required research, lessons in the blank, bored, too-wise expression that Joe must learn how to wear for tomorrow's excruciating ride on the brightly lit subway, where crowds of blank, bored-looking people have little to look at but each other.

What does TV's institutionalization of hip irony have to do with U.S. fiction? Well, for one thing, American literary fiction tends to be about U.S. culture and the people who inhabit it. Culture-wise, shall I spend much of your time pointing out the degree to which televisual values influence the contemporary mood of jaded weltschmerz, self-mocking materialism, blank indifference, and the delusion that cyni-cism and naïveté are mutually exclusive? Can we deny connections

---

[27] Lewis Hyde, "Alcohol and Poetry: John Berryman and the Booze Talking," *American Poetry Review*, reprinted in the *Pushcart Prize* anthology for 1987.

between an unprecedentedly powerful consensual medium that suggests no real difference between image and substance, on one hand, and stuff like the rise of Teflon presidencies, the establishment of nationwide tanning and liposuction industries, the popularity of "Vogueing" to a cynical synthesized command to "Strike a Pose"? Or, in contemporary art, that televisual disdain for "hypocritical" retrovalues like originality, depth, and integrity has no truck with those recombinant "appropriation" styles of art and architecture in which "past becomes pastiche," or with the repetitive solmizations of a Glass or a Reich, or with the self-conscious catatonia of a platoon of Raymond Carver wannabes?

In fact, the numb blank bored demeanor — what one friend calls the "girl-who's-dancing-with-you-but-would-obviously-rather-be-dancing-with-somebody-else" expression — that has become my generation's version of cool is all about TV. "Television," after all, literally means "seeing far"; and our six hours daily not only helps us feel up-close and personal at like the Pan-Am Games or Operation Desert Shield but also, inversely, trains us to relate to real live personal up-close stuff the same way we relate to the distant and exotic, as if separated from us by physics and glass, extant only as performance, awaiting our cool review. Indifference is actually just the '90s' version of frugality for U.S. young people: wooed several gorgeous hours a day for nothing but our attention, we regard that attention as our chief commodity, our social capital, and we are loath to fritter it. In the same regard, see that in 1990, flatness, numbness, and cynicism in one's demeanor are clear ways to transmit the televisual attitude of stand-out-transcendence — flatness and numbness transcend sentimentality, and cynicism announces that one knows the score, was last naïve about something at maybe like age four.

Whether or not 1990's youth culture seems as grim to you as it does to me, surely we can agree that the culture's TV-defined pop ethic has pulled a marvelous touché on the postmodern aesthetic that originally sought to co-opt and redeem the pop. Television has pulled the old dynamic of reference and redemption inside-out: it is now *television* that takes elements of the *postmodern* — the involution, the absurdity, the sardonic fatigue, the iconoclasm and rebellion — and bends them to the ends of spectation and consumption. This has been going on for a while. As early as '84, critics of capitalism were warning that "What began as a mood of the avant-garde has surged into mass culture."[28]

But postmodernism didn't just all of a sudden "surge" into television in 1984. Nor have the vectors of influence between the postmodern and the televisual been one-way. The chief connection between today's television and today's fiction is historical. The two share roots. For postmodern fiction — authored almost exclusively by young white overeducated males — clearly evolved as an intellectual expression of the "rebellious youth culture" of the '60s and '70s. And since the whole gestalt of youthful U.S. rebellion was made possible by a national medium that erased communicative boundaries between regions and replaced a society segmented by location and ethnicity with what rock music critics have called "a national self-consciousness stratified by generation,"[29] the phenomenon of TV had as much to do with postmodernism's rebellious irony as it did with Peaceniks' protest rallies.

In fact, by offering young, overeducated fiction writers a comprehensive view of how hypocritically the U.S.A. saw itself circa 1960, early television helped legitimize absurdism and irony as not just literary devices but sensible responses to a ridiculous world. For irony — exploiting gaps between what's said and what's meant, between how things try to appear and how they really are — is the time-honored way artists seek to illuminate and explode hypocrisy. And the television of lone-gunman westerns, paternalistic sitcoms, and jut-jawed law enforcement circa 1960 celebrated what by then was a deeply hypocritical American self-image. Miller describes nicely how the 1960s sitcom, like the westerns that preceded them,

> negated the increasing powerlessness of
> white-collar males with images of paternal
> strength and manly individualism. Yet by
> the time these sit-coms were produced,

[28] Fredric Jameson, "Postmodernism, or the Cultural Logic of Late Capitalism," *New Left Review* #146, Summer 1984, pp. 60–66.

[29] Pat Auferhode, "The Look of the Sound," in good old Gitlin's anthology, p. 113.

> the world of small business [whose virtues
> were the Hugh Beaumontish ones of "self-
> possession, probity, and sound judgment"]
> had been . . . superseded by what C. Wright
> Mills called "the managerial demi-urge,"
> and the virtues personified by . . . Dad were
> in fact passé.[30]

In other words, early U.S. TV was a hypocritical apologist for values whose reality had become attenuated in a period of corporate ascendancy, bureaucratic entrenchment, foreign adventurism, racial conflict, secret bombing, assassination, wiretaps, etc. It's not one bit accidental that postmodern fiction aimed its ironic crosshairs at the banal, the naïve, the sentimental and simplistic and conservative, for these qualities were just what '60s TV seemed to celebrate as distinctively American.

And the rebellious irony in the best postmodern fiction wasn't just credible as art; it seemed downright socially useful in its capacity for what counterculture critics called "a *critical negation* that would make it self-evident to everyone that the world is not as it seems."[31] Kesey's black parody of asylums suggested that our arbiters of sanity were often crazier than their patients; Pynchon reoriented our view of paranoia from deviant psychic fringe to central thread in the corporo-bureaucratic weave; DeLillo exposed image, signal, data and tech as agents of spiritual chaos and not social order. Burroughs's icky explorations of American narcosis exploded hypocrisy; Gaddis's exposure of abstract capital as deforming exploded hypocrisy; Coover's repulsive political farces exploded hypocrisy.

Irony in postwar art and culture started out the same way youthful rebellion did. It was difficult and painful, and productive — a grim diagnosis of a long-denied disease. The assumptions *behind* early postmodern irony, on the other hand, were still frankly idealistic: it was

---

[30] Miller, p. 199.

[31] Greil Marcus, *Mystery Train*, Dutton, 1976.

assumed that etiology and diagnosis pointed toward cure, that a revelation of imprisonment led to freedom.

So then how have irony, irreverence, and rebellion come to be not liberating but enfeebling in the culture today's avant-garde tries to write about? One clue's to be found in the fact that irony is *still around*, bigger than ever after 30 long years as the dominant mode of hip expression. It's not a rhetorical mode that wears well. As Hyde (whom I pretty obviously like) puts it, "Irony has only emergency use. Carried over time, it is the voice of the trapped who have come to enjoy their cage."[32] This is because irony, entertaining as it is, serves an almost exclusively negative function. It's critical and destructive, a ground-clearing. Surely this is the way our postmodern fathers saw it. But irony's singularly unuseful when it comes to constructing anything to replace the hypocrisies it debunks. This is why Hyde seems right about persistent irony being tiresome. It is unmeaty. Even gifted ironists work best in sound bites. I find gifted ironists sort of wickedly fun to listen to at parties, but I always walk away feeling like I've had several radical surgical procedures. And as for actually driving cross-country with a gifted ironist, or sitting through a 300-page novel full of nothing but trendy sardonic exhaustion, one ends up feeling not only empty but somehow . . . oppressed.

Think, for a moment, of Third World rebels and coups. Third World rebels are great at exposing and overthrowing corrupt hypocritical regimes, but they seem noticeably less great at the mundane, non-negative task of then establishing a superior governing alternative. Victorious rebels, in fact, seem best at using their tough, cynical rebel-skills to avoid being rebelled against themselves — in other words, they just become better tyrants.

And make no mistake: irony tyrannizes us. The reason why our pervasive cultural irony is at once so powerful and so unsatisfying is that an ironist is *impossible to pin down*. All U.S. irony is based on an implicit "I don't really mean what I'm saying." So what *does* irony as a cultural norm mean to say? That it's impossible to mean what you say? That maybe it's too bad it's impossible, but wake up and smell the coffee already? Most likely, I think, today's irony ends up saying: "How totally *banal* of you to

[32] Hyde, op. cit.

ask what I really mean." Anyone with the heretical gall to ask an ironist what he actually stands for ends up looking like an hysteric or a prig. And herein lies the oppressiveness of institutionalized irony, the too-successful rebel: the ability to interdict the *question* without attending to its *subject* is, when exercised, tyranny. It is the new junta, using the very tool that exposed its enemy to insulate itself.

This is why our educated teleholic friends' use of weary cynicism to try to seem superior to TV is so pathetic. And this is why the fiction-writing citizen of our televisual culture is in such very deep shit. What do you do when postmodern rebellion becomes a pop-cultural institution? For this of course is the second answer to why avant-garde irony and rebellion have become dilute and malign. They have been absorbed, emptied, and redeployed by the very televisual establishment they had originally set themselves athwart.

Not that television is culpable for any evil here. Just for immoderate success. This is, after all, what TV *does:* it discerns, decocts, and re-presents what it thinks U.S. culture wants to see and hear about itself. No one and everyone is at fault for the fact that television started gleaning rebellion and cynicism as the hip upscale Baby-Boomer *imago populi.* But the harvest has been dark: the forms of our best rebellious art have become mere gestures, schticks, not only sterile but perversely enslaving. How can even the idea of rebellion against corporate culture stay meaningful when Chrysler Inc. advertises trucks by invoking "The Dodge Rebellion"? How is one to be a bona fide iconoclast when Burger King sells onion rings with "Sometimes You Gotta Break the Rules"? How can an Image-Fiction writer hope to make people more critical of televisual culture by parodying television as a self-serving commercial enterprise when Pepsi and Subaru and FedEx parodies of self-serving commercials are already doing big business? It's almost a history lesson: I'm starting to see just why turn-of-the-last-century Americans' biggest fear was of anarchists and anarchy. For if anarchy actually *wins,* if rulelessness become the *rule,* then protest and change become not just impossible but incoherent. It'd be like casting a ballot for Stalin: you are voting for an end to all voting.

So here's the stumper for the U.S. writer who both breathes our cultural atmosphere and sees himself heir to whatever was neat and valuable in avant-garde literature: how to rebel against TV's aesthetic of rebellion, how to snap readers awake to the fact that our televisual culture has become a cynical, narcissistic, essentially empty phenomenon, when television regularly *celebrates* just these features in itself and its viewers? These are the very questions DeLillo's poor schmuck of a popologist was asking back in '85 about America, that most photographed of barns:

> "What was the barn like before it was
> photographed?" he said. "What did it look
> like, how was it different from other barns,
> how was it similar to other barns? We can't
> answer these questions because we've read
> the signs, seen the people snapping the
> pictures. We can't get outside the aura.
> We're part of the aura. We're here, we're
> now."
>
> He seemed immensely pleased by this.[33]

end of the end of the line

What responses to television's commercialization of the modes of literary protest seem possible, then, today? One obvious option is for the fiction writer to become reactionary, fundamentalist. Declare contemporary television evil and contemporary culture evil and turn one's back on the whole spandexed mess and invoke instead good old pre-1960s Hugh Beaumontish virtues and literal readings of the Testaments and be pro-Life, anti-Fluoride, antediluvian. The problem with this is that Americans who've opted for this tack seem to have one eyebrow straight across their forehead and knuckles that drag on the ground and really tall hair and in general just seem like an *excellent* crowd to want to transcend. Besides, the rise of Reagan/Bush/Gingrich showed that hypocritical nostalgia for a kinder, gentler, more Christian pseudo-

[33] *White Noise,* p. 13.

past is no less susceptible to manipulation in the interests of corporate commercialism and PR image. Most of us will still take nihilism over neanderthalism.

Another option would be to adopt a somewhat more enlightened political conservatism that exempts viewer and networks alike from any complicity in the bitter stasis of televisual culture and which instead blames all TV-related problems on certain correctable defects in technology. Enter media futurologist George Gilder, a Hudson Institute senior fellow and author of *Life After Television: The Coming Transformation of Media and American Life.* The single most fascinating thing about *Life After Television* is that it's a book with *commercials.* Published in something called The Larger Agenda Series by one "Whittle Direct Books" in Federal Express Inc.'s Knoxville headquarters, the book sells for only $11.00 hard including postage, is big and thin enough to look great on executive coffee tables, and has very pretty full-page ads for Federal Express on every fifth page. The book's also largely a work of fiction, plus it's a heartrending dramatization of why anti-TV conservatives, motivated by simple convictions like "Television is at heart a totalitarian medium" whose "system is an alien and corrosive force in democratic capitalism," are going to be of little help with our ultraradical-TV problems, attached as conservative intellectuals are to their twin tired remedies for all U.S. ills, viz. the beliefs that (1) the discerning consumer-instincts of the Little Guy will correct all imbalances if only Big Systems will quit stifling his Freedom to Choose, and that (2) technology-bred problems can be resolved technologically.

Gilder's basic diagnosis runs thus. Television as we know and suffer it is "a technology with supreme powers but deadly flaws." The really fatal flaw is that the whole structure of television programming, broadcasting, and reception is still informed by the technological limitations of the old vacuum tubes that first enabled TV. The

> expense and complexity of these tubes
> used in television sets meant that most of
> the processing of signals would have to be
> done at the [networks],

a state of affairs which

> dictated that television would be a top-
> down system — in electronic terms, a
> "master-slave" architecture. A few broad-
> casting centers would originate programs
> for millions of passive receivers, or "dumb
> terminals."

By the time the transistor (which does essentially what vacuum tubes do but in less space at lower cost) found commercial applications, the top-down TV system was already entrenched and petrified, dooming viewers to docile reception of programs they were dependent on a very few networks to provide, and creating a "psychology of the masses" in which a trio of programming alternatives aimed to appeal to millions and millions of Joe B.'s. The TV signals are analog waves. Analogs are the required medium, since "With little storage or processing available at the set, the signals . . . would have to be directly displayable waves," and "analog waves directly simulate sound, brightness, and color." But analog waves can't be saved or edited by their recipient. They're too much like life: there in gorgeous toto one instant and then gone. What the poor TV viewer gets is only what he sees. This state of affairs has cultural consequences Gilder describes in apocalyptic detail. Even "High Definition Television" (HDTV), touted by the industry as the next big advance in entertainment, will, according to Gilder, be just the same vacuous emperor in a snazzier suit.

But for Gilder, TV, still clinging to the crowd-binding and hierarchical technologies of yesterdecade, is now doomed by the advances in microchip and fiber-optic technology of the last few years. The user-friendly microchip, which consolidates the activities of millions of transistors on one 49¢ wafer, and whose capacities will get even more attractive as controlled electron-conduction approaches the geodesic paradigm of efficiency, will allow receivers — TV sets — to do much of the image-processing that has hitherto been done "for" the viewer by the broadcaster. In another happy development, transporting images through glass fibers rather than via the EM spectrum will allow people's TV sets to be hooked up with each other in a kind of interactive net instead of all feeding passively at the transmitting teat of a single broadcaster. And fiber-optic transmissions have the further advantage that they conduct characters of information digitally. Since, as Gilder explains, "digital signals have an advantage over analog signals in that they can be stored and manipulated without deterioration" as well as being crisp and interferenceless as quality CDs, they'll allow the microchipped television receiver (and thus the viewer) to enjoy much of the discretion over selection, manipulation, and recombination of video images that is today restricted to the director's booth.

For Gilder, the new piece of furniture that will free Joe Briefcase from passive dependence on his furniture will be "the telecomputer, a personal computer adapted for video processing and connected by fiber-optic threads to other telecomputers around the world." The fibrous TC "will forever break the broadcast bottleneck" of television's One Over Many structure of image-dissemination. Now everybody'll get to be his own harried guy with earphones and clipboard. In the new millennium, U.S. television will finally become ideally, GOPishly democratic: egalitarian, interactive, and "profitable" without being "exploitative."

Boy does Gilder know his "Larger Agenda" audience. You can just see saliva overflowing lower lips in boardrooms as Gilder forecasts that the consumer's whole complicated fuzzy inconveniently transient world will become storable, manipulable, broadcastable, and viewable in the comfort of his own condo. "With artful programming of telecomputers, you could spend a day interacting on the screen with Henry Kissinger, Kim Basinger, or Billy Graham." Rather ghastly interactions to contemplate, perhaps, but then in Gilderland *each to his own:*

> Celebrities could produce and sell their
> own software. You could view the Super
> Bowl from any point in the stadium you
> choose, or soar above the basket with
> Michael Jordan. Visit your family on the
> other side of the world with moving pictures
> hardly distinguishable from real-life im-
> ages. Give a birthday party for Grandma
> in her nursing home in Florida, bringing
> her descendents from all over the country
> to the foot of her bed in living color.

And not just warm 2-D images of family: *any* experience will be transferrable to image and marketable, manipulable, consumable. People will be able to

> go comfortably sight-seeing from their liv-
> ing room through high-resolution screens,
> visiting Third-World countries without
> having to worry about air fares or exchange
> rates . . . , you could fly an airplane over
> the Alps or climb Mount Everest — all on
> a powerful high-resolution display.

We will, in short, be able to engineer our own dreams.

So, in sum, a conservative tech writer offers a really attractive way of looking at viewer passivity, at TV's institutionalization of irony, narcissism, nihilism, stasis, loneliness. It's not our fault! It's outmoded technology's fault! If TV-dissemination were up to date, it would be impossible for it to "institutionalize" anything through its demonic "mass-psychology." Let's let Joe B., the little lonely average guy, be his own manipulator of video-bits. Once all experience is finally reduced to marketable image, once the receiving user of user-friendly receivers can break from the coffle and choose freely, Americanly, from an Americanly infinite variety of moving images *hardly distinguishable from real-life images,* and can then choose further just how he wishes to store, enhance, edit, recombine, and present those images to himself in the privacy of his very own home and skull, then TV's ironic, totalitarian grip on the American psychic cojones will be broken. !!!

Note that Gilder's semiconducted vision of a free, orderly video future is way more upbeat than postmodernism's old view of image and data. The novels of Pynchon and DeLillo revolve metaphorically off the concept of interference: the more connections, the more chaos, and the harder it is to cull any meaning from the seas of signal. Gilder would call their gloom outmoded, their metaphor infected with the deficiencies of the transistor:

> In all networks of wires and switches,
> except for those on the microchip, com-
> plexity tends to grow exponentially as
> the number of interconnections rises,
> (but) in the silicon maze of microchip tech-
> nology . . . efficiency, not complexity,
> grows as the square of the number of inter-
> connections to be organized.

Rather than a vacuous TV-culture drowning in cruddy images, Gilder foresees a TC-culture redeemed by a whole lot more to choose from and a whole lot more control over what you choose to . . . umm . . . see? pseudo-experience? dream?

It's wildly unrealistic to think that expanded choices alone will resolve our televisual bind. The advent of cable upped choices from 4 or 5 to 40+ synchronic alternatives, with little apparent loosening of television's grip on mass attitudes. It seems, rather, that Gilder sees the '90s' impending breakthrough as U.S. viewers' graduation from passive reception of facsimiles of experience to active manipulation of facsimiles of experience. It's worth questioning Gilder's definition of televisual "passivity." His new tech would indeed end "the passivity of mere reception." But the passivity of Audience, the acquiescence inherent in a whole culture of and about watching, looks unaffected by TCs.

The appeal of watching television has always involved fantasy. And contemporary TV has gotten vastly better at enabling the viewer's fantasy that he can transcend the limitations of individual human experience, that he can be inside the set, imago'd, "anyone, anywhere."[34] Since the limitations of being one human being involve certain restrictions on the number of different experiences possible to us in a given period of time, it's arguable that the biggest TV-tech "advances" of recent years have done little but abet this fantasy of escape from the defining limits of being human. Cable expanded our choices of evening realities; hand-held gizmos let us leap instantly from one reality to another; VCRs let us commit experiences to an eidetic memory that permits re-experience

---

[34] A term Gitlin uses in "We Build Excitement."

at any time without loss or alteration. These advances sold briskly and upped average viewing-doses, but they sure haven't made U.S. televisual culture any less passive or cynical.

Of course, the downside of TV's big fantasy is that it's just a fantasy. As a Treat, my escape from the limits of genuine experience is neato. As a steady diet, though, it can't help but render my own reality less attractive (because in it I'm just one Dave, with limits and restrictions all over the place), render me less fit to make the most of it (because I spend all my time pretending I'm not in it), and render me ever more dependent on the device that affords escape from just what my escapism makes unpleasant.

It's tough to see how Gilder's soteriol vision of having more "control" over the arrangement of high-quality fantasy-bits is going to ease either the dependency that is part of my relation to TV or the impotent irony I must use to pretend I'm not dependent. Whether I'm "passive" or "active" as a viewer, I still must cynically pretend, because I'm still dependent, because my real dependency here is not on a single show or a few networks any more than the hophead's is on the Turkish florist or the Marseilles refiner. My real dependence is on the fantasies and the images that enable them, and thus on any technology that can make images both available and fantastic. Make no mistake: we *are* dependent on image-technology; and the better the tech, the harder we're hooked.

The paradox in Gilder's rosy forecast is the same as in all forms of artificial enhancement. The more enhancing the mediation — see for instance binoculars, amplifiers, graphic equalizers, or "moving pictures hardly distinguishable from real-life images" — the more direct, vivid, and real the experience *seems*, which is to say the more direct, vivid, and real the fantasy and dependence *are*. An exponential surge in the mass of televisual images, and a commensurate increase in my ability to cut, paste, magnify, and combine them to suit my own fancy, can do nothing but render my interactive TC a more powerful enhancer and enabler of fantasy, my attraction to that fantasy stronger, the real experiences of which my TC offers more engaging and controllable simulacra paler and more frustrating to deal with, and me just a *whole* lot more dependent on my furniture. Jacking the number of choices and options up with better tech will remedy exactly nothing so long as no sources of insight on comparative worth, no guides to *why* and *how* to choose among experiences, fantasies, beliefs, and predilections, are permitted serious consideration in U.S. culture. Umm, insights and guides to value used to be among literature's jobs, didn't they? But then who's going to want to take such stuff seriously in ecstatic post-TV life, with Kim Basinger waiting to be interacted with?

Oh God, I've just reread my criticisms of Gilder. That he is naïve. That he is an ill-disguised apologist for corporate self-interest. That his book has commercials. That beneath its futuristic novelty it's just the same old American same-old that got us into this televisual mess. That Gilder vastly underestimates the intractability of the mess. Its hopelessness. Our gullibility, fatigue, disgust. My attitude, reading Gilder, has been sardonic, aloof, depressed. I have tried to make his book look ridiculous (which it is, but still). My reading of Gilder is televisual. I am in the aura.

Well, but at least good old Gilder is unironic. In this respect he's like a cool summer breeze compared to Mark Leyner, the young New Jersey medical-ad copywriter whose *My Cousin, My Gastroenterologist* is the biggest thing for campus hipsters since *The Fountainhead*. Leyner's novel exemplifies a third kind of literary response to our problem. For of course young U.S. writers can "resolve" the problem of being trapped in the televisual aura the same way French poststructuralists "resolve" their hopeless enmeshment in the logos. We can resolve the problem by celebrating it. Transcend feelings of mass-defined angst by genuflecting to them. We can be *reverently ironic.*

My Cousin, My Gastroenterologist is new not so much in kind as in degree. It is a methedrine compound of pop pastiche, offhand high tech, and dazzling televisual parody, formed with surreal juxtapositions and grammarless monologues and flash-cut editing, and framed with a relentless irony designed to make its frantic tone seem irreverent instead of repellent. You want sendups of commercial culture?

> I had just been fired from McDonald's
> for refusing to wear a kilt during production
> launch week for their new McHaggis
> sandwich.

he picks up a copy of *das plumpe denken*
new england's most disreputable german-
language newsmagazine blast in egg cream
factory kills philatelist he turns the page
radioactive glow-in-the-dark semen found
in canada he turns the page modern-day
hottentots carry young in resealable sandwich bags he turns the page wayne newton
calls mother's womb single-occupancy
garden of eden morgan fairchild calls sally
struthers loni anderson

what color is your mozzarella? i asked the
waitress it's pink — it's the same color
as the top of a mennen lady speed stick
dispenser, y'know that color? no, maam
I said it's the same color they use for the
gillette daisy disposable razors for women
. . . y'know that color? nope well, it's the
same pink as pepto-bismol, y'know that
color? oh yeah, I said, well do you have
spaghetti?

You want mordant sendups of television?

Muriel got the *TV Guide,* flipped to Tues-
day 8 P.M., and read aloud: . . . There's a
show called "A Tumult of Pubic Hair and
Bobbing Flaccid Penises as Sweaty Naked
Chubby Men Run From the Sauna Scream-
ing Snake! Snake!". . . It also stars Brian
Keith, Buddy Ebsen, Nipsey Russell, and
Lesley Ann Warren

You like mocking self-reference? The novel's whole last chapter is a
parody of its own "About the Author" page. Or maybe you're into hip
identitylessness?

> Grandma rolled up a magazine and hit
> Buzz on the side of the head. . . . Buzz's
> mask was knocked loose. There was no
> skin beneath that mask. There were two
> white eyeballs protruding on stems from
> a mass of oozing blood-red musculature.

> I can't tell if she's human or a fifth-
> generation gynemorphic android and I
> don't care

Parodic meditations on the boundaryless flux of televisual mono-
culture?

> I'm stirring a pitcher of Tanqueray martinis
> with one hand and sliding a tray of frozen
> clams *oreganata* into the oven with my
> foot. God, these methedrine suppositories
> that Yogi Vithaldas gave me are good! As
> I iron a pair of tennis shorts I dictate a
> haiku into the tape recorder and then . . .
> do three minutes on the speedbag before
> making an origami praying mantis and
> then reading an article in *High Fidelity*
> magazine as I stir the coq au vin.

The decay of both the limits and the integrity of the single human self?

> There was a woman with the shrunken,
> wrinkled face of an eighty- or ninety-year-
> old. And this withered hag, this apparent
> octogenarian, had the body of a male
> Olympic swimmer. The long lean sinewy
> arms, the powerful V-shaped upper torso,
> without a single ounce of fat. . . .

> to install your replacement head place the
> head assembly on neck housing and insert
> guide pins through mounting holes . . . if,
> after installing new head, you are unable
> to discern the contradictions in capitalist
> modes of production, you have either in-
> stalled your head improperly or head is
> defective

In fact, one of *My Cousin, My Gastroenterologist*'s unifying obsessions is this latter juxtaposition of parts of selves, people and machines, human subjects and discrete objects. Leyner's fiction is, in this regard, an eloquent reply to Gilder's prediction that our TV-culture problems can be resolved by the dismantling of images into discrete chunks we can recombine however we wish. Leyner's world is a Gilderesque dystopia. The passivity and schizoid decay still endure for Leyner in his characters' reception of images and waves of data. The ability to *combine* them only adds a layer of disorientation: when all experience can be deconstructed and reconfigured, there become simply too many choices. And in the absence of any credible, noncommercial guides for living, the freedom to choose is about as "liberating" as a bad acid trip: each quantum is as good as the next, and the only standard of a particular construct's quality is its weirdness, incongruity, its ability to stand out from a crowd of other image-constructs and wow some Audience.

Leyner's own novel, in its amphetaminic eagerness to wow the reader, marks the far dark frontier of the Fiction of Image — literature's absorption of not just the icons, techniques, and phenomena of television, but of television's whole objective. *My Cousin, My Gastroenterologist*'s sole aim is, finally, to *wow*, to ensure that the reader is pleased and continues to read. The book does this by (1) flattering the reader with appeals to his erudite postmodern weltschmerz and (2) relentlessly reminding the reader that the author is smart and funny. The book itself is extremely funny, but it's not funny the way funny stories are funny. It's not that funny things happen here; it's that funny things are self-consciously imagined and pointed out, like a comedian's stock "You ever notice how . . . ?" and "You ever wonder what would happen if . . . ?"

Actually, Leyner's whole high-Imagist style most often resembles a kind of lapidary stand-up comedy:

> Suddenly Bob couldn't speak properly. He
> had suffered some form of spontaneous
> aphasia. But it wasn't total aphasia. He
> could speak, but only in a staccato tele-
> graphic style. Here's how he described
> driving through the Midwest on Interstate
> 80: "Corn corn corn corn Stuckeys. Corn
> corn corn corn Stuckeys."

> there's a bar on the highway which caters
> almost exclusively to authority figures and
> the only drink it serves is lite beer and the
> only food it serves is surf and turf and the
> place is filled with cops and state troopers
> and gym teachers and green berets and toll
> attendants and game wardens and crossing
> guards and umpires

Leyner's fictional response to television is less a novel than a piece of witty, erudite, extremely high-quality prose television. Velocity and vividness replace development. People flicker in and out; events are garishly there and then gone and never referred to. There's a brashly irreverent rejection of "outmoded" concepts like integrated plot or en-during character. Instead there's a series of dazzlingly creative parodic vignettes, designed to appeal to the 45 seconds of near-Zen concentra-tion we call the TV attention span. In the absence of a plot, unifying the vignettes are moods — antic anxiety, the overstimulated stasis of too many choices and no chooser's manual, irreverent brashness toward televisual reality. And, after the manner of films, music videos, dreams, and television programs, there are recurring "Key Images," here exotic drugs, exotic technologies, exotic foods, exotic bowel dysfunctions. And it is no accident that *My Cousin, My Gastroenterologist*'s central preoccupation is with digestion and elimination. Its mocking challenge to the reader is the same one presented by television's flood of realities and choices: ABSORB ME — PROVE YOU'RE CONSUMER ENOUGH.

Leyner's work, the best Image-Fiction yet, is both amazing and forgettable, wonderful and oddly hollow. I'm concluding by talking about it at length because, in its masterful reabsorption of the very features TV has itself absorbed from postmodern art, Leyner's book seems like the ultimate union of U.S. television and fiction. It seems also to cast the predicament of Image-Fiction itself into stark relief: the best stuff the subgenre's produced to date is hilarious, upsetting, sophisticated, and extremely shallow — doomed to shallowness by its desire to ridicule a TV-culture whose mockery of itself and all value already absorbs all ridicule. Leyner's attempt to "respond" to television via ironic genuflection is all too easily subsumed into the tired televisual ritual of mock-worship. It is dead on the page.

It's entirely possible that my plangent noises about the impossibility of rebelling against an aura that promotes and vitiates all rebellion say more about my residency inside that aura, my own lack of vision, than they do about any exhaustion of U.S. fiction's possibilities. The next real literary "rebels" in this country might well emerge as some weird bunch of *anti*-rebels, born oglers who dare somehow to back away from ironic watching, who have the childish gall actually to endorse and instantiate single-entendre principles. Who treat of plain old untrendy human troubles and emotions in U.S. life with reverence and conviction. Who eschew self-consciousness and hip fatigue. These anti-rebels would be outdated, of course, before they even started. Dead on the page. Too sincere. Clearly repressed. Backward, quaint, naïve, anachronistic. Maybe that'll be the point. Maybe that's why they'll be the next real rebels. Real rebels, as far as I can see, risk disapproval. The old postmodern insurgents risked the gasp and squeal: shock, disgust, outrage, censorship, accusations of socialism, anarchism, nihilism. Today's risks are different. The new rebels might be artists willing to risk the yawn, the rolled eyes, the cool smile, the nudged ribs, the parody of gifted ironists, the "Oh how *banal*." To risk accusations of sentimentality, melodrama. Of overcredulity. Of softness. Of willingness to be suckered by a world of lurkers and starers who fear gaze and ridicule above imprisonment without law. Who knows. Today's most engaged young fiction does seem like some kind of line's end's end. I guess that means we all get to draw our own conclusions. Have to. Are you immensely pleased.

1990

getting away from already pretty much being away from it all

08/05/93/0800h. Press Day is a week or so before the Fair opens. I'm supposed to be at the grounds' Illinois Building by like 0900 to get Press Credentials. I imagine Credentials to be a small white card in the band of a fedora. I've never been considered Press before. My main interest in Credentials is getting into rides and stuff for free.

I'm fresh in from the East Coast to go to the Illinois State Fair for a swanky East-Coast magazine. Why exactly a swanky East-Coast magazine is interested in the Illinois State Fair remains unclear to me. I suspect that every so often editors at these magazines slap their foreheads and remember that about 90% of the United States lies between the Coasts and figure they'll engage somebody to do pith-helmeted anthropological reporting on something rural and heartlandish. I think they decided to engage me for this one because I actually grew up around here, just a couple hours' drive from downstate Springfield. I never did go to the State Fair, though, growing up — I pretty much topped out at the County Fair level.

In August it takes hours for the dawn fog to burn off. The air's like wet wool. 0800h. is too early to justify the car's AC. I'm on I-55 going S/SW. The sun's a blotch in a sky that isn't so much cloudy as opaque. The corn starts just past the breakdown lanes and goes right to the sky's hem. The August corn's as tall as a tall man. Illinois corn is now knee-high by about the 4th of May, what with all the advances in fertilizers and herbicides. Locusts chirr in every field, a brassy electric sound that Dopplers oddly in the speeding car. Corn, corn, soybeans, corn, exit ramp, corn, and every few miles an outpost way off on a reach in the distance — house, tree w/ tire-swing, barn, satellite dish. Grain silos are the only real skyline. The Interstate is dull and pale. The occasional other cars all look ghostly, their drivers' faces humidity-stunned. A fog hangs just over the fields like the land's mind or something. The temperature's over 80 and already climbing with the sun. It'll be 90+ by 1000h., you can tell: there's already that tightening quality to the air, like it's drawing itself in for a long siege.

Credentials 0900h., Welcome & Briefing 0915h., Press Tour on Special Tram 0945h.

I grew up in rural Illinois but haven't been back for a long time and can't say I've missed it — the yeasty heat, the lush desolation of limitless corn, the flatness.

But it's like bike-riding, in a way. The native body readjusts automatically to the flatness, and as your calibration gets finer, driving, you can start to notice that the dead-level flatness is only apparent. There are unevennesses, ups and downs, slight but rhythmic. Straight-shot I-55 will start, ever so slightly, to rise, maybe 5° over a mile, then go just as gentle back down, and then you see an overpass bridge ahead, over a river — the Salt Fork, the Sangamon. The rivers are swollen, but nothing like out around St. Louis. These gentle rises and then dips down to rivers are glacial moraines, edges of the old ice that shaved the Midwest level. The middling rivers have their origin in glacial runoff. The whole drive is a gentle sine wave like this, but it's like sea-legs: if you haven't spent years here you'll never feel it. To people from the Coasts, rural IL's topography's a nightmare, something to hunker down and speed through — the sky opaque, the dull crop-green constant, the land flat and dull and endless, a monotone for the eyes. For natives it's different. For me, at least, it got creepy. By the time I left for college the area no longer seemed dull so much as empty, lonely. Middle-of-the-ocean lonely. You can go weeks without seeing a neighbor. It gets to you.

08/05/0900h. But so it's still a week before the Fair, and there's something surreal about the emptiness of parking facilities so huge and complex that they have their own map. The parts of the Fairgrounds that I can see, pulling in, are half permanent structures and half tents and displays in various stages of erection, giving the whole thing the look of somebody half-dressed for a really important date.

08/05/0905h. The man processing Press Credentials is bland and pale and has a mustache and a short-sleeve knit shirt. In line before me are newshounds from *Today's Agriculture,* the *Decatur Herald & Review, Illinois Crafts Newsletter, 4-H News,* and *Livestock Weekly.* Press Credentials turn out to be just a laminated mugshot with a gator-clip for your pocket; not a fedora in the house. Two older ladies from a local horticulture organ behind me engage me in shoptalk. One of these ladies describes herself as the Unofficial Historian of the Illinois State Fair: she goes around giving slide shows on the Fair at nursing homes and Rotary lunches. She begins to emit historical data at a great rate — the Fair started in 1853; there was a Fair every year during the Civil War but not during WWII, plus no Fair in 1893 for some reason; the Governor has failed to cut the ribbon personally on Opening Day only twice; etc. It occurs to me I probably ought to have brought a notebook. I also notice I'm the only person in the room in a T-shirt. It's a fluorescent-lit cafeteria in something called the Illinois Building Senior Center, uncooled. All the local TV crews have their equipment spread out on tables and are lounging against walls talking about the apocalyptic 1993 floods to the immediate west, which floods are ongoing. They all have mustaches and short-sleeve knit shirts. In fact the only other males in the room without mustaches and golf-shirts are the local TV reporters, four of them, all in Eurocut suits. They are sleek, sweatless, deeply blue-eyed. They stand together up by the dais. The dais has a podium and a flag and a banner with GIVE US A WHIRL! on it, which I deduce is probably this year's Fair's Theme, sort of the way senior proms have a Theme. There's a compelling frictionlessness about the local TV reporters, all of whom have short blond hair and vaguely orange makeup. A vividness. I keep feeling a queer urge to vote for them for something.

The older ladies behind me tell me they've bet I'm here to cover either the auto racing or the pop music. They don't mean it unkindly. I tell them why I'm here, mentioning the magazine's name. They turn toward each other, faces alight. One (not the Historian) actually claps her hands to her cheeks.

"*Love* the recipes," she says.

"*Adore* the recipes," the Unofficial Historian says.

And I'm sort of impelled over to a table of all post-45 females, am introduced as on assignment from *Harper's* magazine, and everyone looks at one another with star-struck awe and concurs that the recipes really are first-rate, top-hole, the living end. One seminal recipe involving Amaretto and something called "Baker's chocolate" is being recalled and discussed when a loudspeaker's feedback brings the Fair's official Press Welcome & Briefing to order.

The Briefing is dull. We are less addressed than rhetorically bludgeoned by Fair personnel, product spokespeople, and middle-management State politicos. The words *excited, proud,* and *opportunity* are used a total of 76 times before I get distracted off the count. I've suddenly figured out that all the older ladies I'm at the table with have confused *Harper's* with *Harper's Bazaar.* They think I'm some sort of food writer or recipe scout, here to maybe vault some of the Midwestern food competition winners into the homemaker's big time. Ms. Illinois State Fair, tiara bolted to the tallest coiffure I've ever seen (bun atop bun, multiple layers, a veritable wedding cake of hair), is proudly excited to have the opportunity to present two corporate guys, dead-eyed and sweating freely in suits, who in turn report the excited pride of McDonald's and WalMart at having the opportunity to be this year's Fair's major corporate sponsors. It occurs to me that if I allow the *Harper's-Bazaar*-food-scout misunderstanding to persist and circulate I can eventually show up at the Dessert Competition tents with my Press Credentials and they'll feed me free prize-winning desserts until I have to be carried off on a gurney. Older ladies in the Midwest can *bake.*

08/05/0950h. Under way at 4 mph on the Press Tour, on a kind of flatboat with wheels and a lengthwise bench so ridiculously high that everybody's feet dangle. The tractor pulling us has signs that say ETHANOL and AGRIPOWERED. I'm particularly keen to see the carnies setting up rides in the Fairgrounds' "Happy Hollow," but we head first to the corporate and political tents. Most every tent is still setting up. Workmen crawl over structural frames. We wave at them; they wave back;

it's absurd: we're only going 4 mph. One tent says CORN: TOUCH-ING OUR LIVES EVERY DAY. There are massive many-hued tents courtesy of McDonald's, Miller Genuine Draft, Osco, Morton Commercial Structures Corp., the Land of Lincoln Soybean Association (LOOK WHERE SOYBEANS GO! on a half-up display), Pekin Energy Corp. (PROUD OF OUR SOPHISTICATED COMPUTER-CONTROLLED PROCESSING TECHNOLOGY), Illinois Pork Producers, and the John Birch Society (we'll be checking out that tent for sure). Two tents that say REPUBLICAN and DEMOCRAT. Other smaller tents for various Illinois officeholders. It's well up in the 90s and the sky is the color of old jeans. Over a system of crests to Farm Expo — twelve acres of wicked-looking needle-teethed harrows, tractors, harvesters and seeders — and then Conservation World, 22 acres I never do get straight on the conserving purpose of.

Then back around the rear of the big permanent structures — Artisans Bldg., Illinois Bldg. Senior Center, Expo Center (it says POULTRY on the tympanum, but it's the Expo Center) — passing tantalizingly close to Happy Hollow, where half-assembled rides stand in giant arcs and rays and shirtless guys with tattoos and wrenches slouch around them, fairly oozing menace and human interest — and I want a chance to chat with them before the Hollow opens and there's pressure to actually ride the carnival rides, since I am one of those people who gets sick on Near-Death-Experience carnival rides — but on at a crawl up a blacktop path to the Livestock Buildings on the Fairgrounds' west (upwind!) side. By this time, most of the Press is off the tram and walking in order to escape the tour's PA speaker, which is tinny and brutal. Horse Complex. Cattle Complex. Swine Barn. Sheep Barn. Poultry and Goat Barns. These are all long brick barracks open down both sides of their length. Inside some are stalls; others have pens divided into squares with aluminum rails. Inside, they're gray cement, dim and pungent, huge fans overhead, workers in overalls and waders hosing everything down. No animals yet, but the smells still hang from last year — horses' odors sharp, cows' rich, sheep's oily, swine's unspeakable. No idea what the Poultry Barn smelled like because I couldn't bring myself to go in. Traumatically pecked once, as a child, at the Champaign County Fair, I have a longstanding phobic thing about poultry.

The ethanol tractor's exhaust is literally flatulent-smelling as we crawl out past the Grandstand, where there will apparently be evening concerts and harness- and auto-racing — "WORLD'S FASTEST MILE DIRT TRACK" — and head for something called the Help Me Grow tent to interface with the state's First Lady, Brenda Edgar. It occurs to me that the 366-acre terrain of the Fairgrounds is awfully hilly for downstate IL; it's either a geologic anomaly or it's been man-enhanced. The Help Me Grow tent is on a grassy ridge that overlooks Happy Hollow. I think it's near where I parked. The dismantled-looking rides out below make the view complex. The Expo Center and Coliseum across the Hollow on an opposite ridge have odd neo-Georgian facades, a lot like the older buildings at the State U. over in Champaign. Nature-wise the view is lovely. The serious flooding's well to the west of Springfield, but we've had the same rains, and the grass here is lush and deep green, the trees' leaves balloon explosively like trees in Fragonard, and everything smells juicy and highly edible and still growing here in a month when I remember everything as tired and dry. The first sign of the Help Me Grow area is the nauseous bright red of Ronald McDonald's hair. He's capering around a small plasticky playground area under candy-stripe tenting. Though the Fair's ostensibly unopen, troupes of kids mysteriously appear and engage in rather rehearsed-looking play as we approach. Two of the kids are black, the first black people I've seen anywhere on the Fairgrounds. No parents in view. Just outside the tent, the Governor's wife stands surrounded by flinty-eyed aides. Ronald pretends to fall down. The Press forms itself into a kind of ring. There are several state troopers in khaki and tan, streaming sweat under their Nelson Eddy hats. My view isn't very good. Mrs. Edgar is cool and groomed and pretty in a lacquered way, of the sort of female age that's always suffixed with "-ish." Her tragic flaw is her voice, which sounds almost heliated. The Mrs. Edgar/McDonald's Help Me Grow Program, when you decoct the rhetoric, is basically a statewide crisis line for over-the-edge parents to call and get talked out of beating up their kids. The number of calls Mrs. Edgar says the line's fielded just this year is both de- and impressive. Shiny pamphlets are distributed. Ronald McDonald, speech slurry and makeup cottage-cheeseish in the heat, cues the kids to come over for some low-rent sleight of hand and Socratic banter. Lacking a real journalist's killer instinct, I've been jostled way to the back of the ring, and my view is obscured by the towering hair of Ms. Illinois State

Fair, whose function on the Press Tour remains unclear. I don't want to asperse, but Ronald McDonald sounds like he's under the influence of something more than fresh country air. I drift away under the tent, where there's a metal watercooler. But no cups. It's hotter under the tent, and there's a reek of fresh plastic. All the toys and plastic playground equipment have signs that say COURTESY OF and then a corporate name. A lot of the photographers in the ring have on dusty-green safari vests, and they sit cross-legged in the sun, getting low-angle shots of Mrs. Edgar. There are no tough questions from the media. The tram's tractor is putting out a steady sweatsock-shape of blue-green exhaust. Right at the edge of the tent is where I notice that the grass is different: the grass under the tenting is a different grass, pine-green and prickly-looking, more like the St. Augustine grass of the deep U.S. South. Solid bent-over investigative journalism reveals that in fact it's artificial grass. A huge mat of plastic artificial grass has been spread over the knoll's real grass, under the candy-stripe tent. This may have been my only moment of complete East-Coast cynicism the whole day. A quick look under the edge of the fake grass mat reveals the real grass underneath, flattened and already yellowing.

One of the few things I still miss from my Midwest childhood was this weird, deluded but unshakable conviction that everything around me existed all and only *For Me*. Am I the only one who had this queer deep sense as a kid? — that everything exterior to me existed only insofar as it affected me somehow? — that all things were somehow, via some occult adult activity, specially arranged for my benefit? Does anybody else identify with this memory? The child leaves a room, and now everything in that room, once he's no longer there to see it, melts away into some void of potential or else (my personal childhood theory) is trundled away by occult adults and stored until the child's reentry into the room recalls it all back into animate service. Was this nuts? It was radically self-centered, of course, this conviction, and more than a little paranoid. Plus the *responsibility* it conferred: if the whole of the world dissolved and resolved each time I blinked, what if my eyes didn't open?

Maybe what I really miss now is the fact that a child's radical delusive self-centeredness doesn't cause him conflict or pain. His is the sort of regally innocent solipsism of like Bishop Berkeley's God: all things are nothing until his sight calls them forth from the void: his stimulation is the world's very being. And this is maybe why a little kid so fears the dark: it's not the possible presence of unseen fanged things in the dark, but rather the actual absence of everything his blindness has now erased. For me, at least, pace my folks' indulgent smiles, this was my true reason for needing a nightlight: it kept the world turning.

Plus maybe this sense of the world as all and only For-Him is why special ritual public occasions drive a kid right out of his mind with excitement. Holidays, parades, summer trips, sporting events. Fairs. Here the child's manic excitement is really exultation at his own power: the world will now not only exist For-Him but will present itself as *Special*-For-Him. Every hanging banner, balloon, gilded booth, clown-wig, turn of the wrench on a tent's erection — every bright bit signifies, refers. Counting down to the Special Event, time itself will alter, from a child's annular system of flashes and sweeps to a more adultish linear chronology — the concept of *looking forward to* — with successive moments ticking off toward a calendar-X'd telos, a new kind of fulfilling and apocalyptic End, the 0-hour of the Special Occasion, *Special*, of the garish and in all ways exceptional *Spectacle* which the child has made be and which is, he intuits at the same inarticulate depth as his need for a nightlight, For-Him alone, unique at the absolute center.

08/13/0925h. Official Opening. Ceremony, introductions, verbiage, bromides, really big brass shears for the ribbon across the Main Gate. It's cloudless and dry, but forehead-tighteningly hot. Noon will be a kiln. Knit-shirt Press and rabid early Fairgoers are massed from the Gate all the way out to Sangamon Avenue, where homeowners with plastic flags invite you to park on their lawn for $5.00. I gather "Little Jim" Edgar, the Governor, isn't much respected by the Press, most of whom are whispering about Michael Jordan's father's car being found but the father being missing, still. No anthropologist worth his helmet would be without the shrewd counsel of a colorful local, and I've brought a Native Companion here for the day (I can get people in free with my Press Credentials), and we're standing near the back. Governor E. is maybe fifty and greyhound-thin and has steel glasses and hair that looks carved out of feldspar. He radiates sincerity, though, after the hacks who introduced him, and speaks plainly and sanely and I think well — of both the terrible pain of

the '93 Flood and the redemptive joy of seeing the whole state pull together to help one another, and of the special importance of this year's
State Fair as a conscious affirmation of real community, of state solidar-
ity and fellow-feeling and pride. Governor Edgar acknowledges that the
state's really taken it on the chin in the last couple months, but that it's
a state that's resilient and alive and most of all, he's reminded looking
around himself here today, united, *together,* both in tough times and in
happy times, happy times like for instance this very Fair. Edgar invites
everybody to get in there and to have a really good time, and to revel in
watching everybody else also having a good time, all as a kind of reflective exercise in civics, basically. The Press seem unmoved. I thought his
remarks were kind of powerful, though.

And this Fair — the idea and now the reality of it — does seem to
have something uniquely to do with state-as-community, a grand-scale
togetherness. And it's not just the claustrophobic mash of people waiting to get inside. I can't get my finger onto just what's especially com-
munitarian about an Illinois State Fair as opposed to like a New Jersey
State Fair. I'd bought a notebook, but I left the car windows down last
night and it got ruined by rain, and Native Companion kept me waiting
getting ready to go and there wasn't time to buy a new notebook. I don't
even have a pen, I realize. Whereas good old Governor Edgar has three
different-colored pens in his knit shirt's breast pocket. This clinches it:
you can always trust a man with multiple pens.

The Fair occupies space, and there's no shortage of space in downstate
IL. The Fairgrounds take up 300+ acres on the east side of Springfield,
a depressed capital of 109,000 where you can't spit without hitting some
sort of Lincoln-site plaque. The Fair spreads itself out, and visually so.
The Main Gate's on a rise, and through the two sagged halves of cut ribbon you get a great specular vantage on the whole thing — virgin and
sun-glittered, even the tents looking fresh-painted. It seems garish and
innocent and endless and aggressively Special. Kids are having like little
like epileptic fits all around us, frenzied with a need to somehow take in
everything at once.

I suspect that part of the self-conscious-community thing here has
to do with space. Rural Midwesterners live surrounded by unpopulated
land, marooned in a space whose emptiness starts to become both physical and spiritual. It is not just people you get lonely for. You're alienated

from the very space around you, in a way, because out here the land's less an environment than a commodity. The land's basically a factory. You live in the same factory you work in. You spend an enormous amount of time with the land, but you're still alienated from it in some way. It's probably hard to feel any sort of Romantic spiritual connection to nature when you have to make your living from it. (Is this line of thinking somehow Marxist? Not when so many IL farmers still own their own land, I guess. This is a whole different kind of alienation.)

But so I theorize to Native Companion (who worked detassling summer corn with me in high school) that the Illinois State Fair's animating thesis involves some kind of structured interval of communion with both neighbor and space — the sheer *fact* of the land is to be celebrated here, its yields ogled and stock groomed and paraded, everything on decorative display. That what's Special here is the offer of a vacation from alienation, a chance for a moment to love what real life out here can't let you love. Native Companion, rummaging for her lighter, is about as interested in this stuff as she was about the child-as-empiricist-God-delusion horseshit back in the car, she apprises me.

08/13/1040h. The livestock venues are at full occupancy animal-wise, but we seem to be the only Fairgoers who've come right over from the Opening Ceremony to tour them. You can now tell which barns are for which animals with your eyes closed. The horses are in their own individual stalls, with half-height doors and owners and grooms on stools by the doors, a lot of them dozing. The horses stand in hay. Billy Ray Cyrus plays loudly on some stableboy's boom box. The horses have tight hides and apple-sized eyes that are set on the sides of their heads, like fish. I've rarely been this close to fine livestock. The horses' faces are long and somehow suggestive of coffins. The racers are lanky, velvet over bone. The draft and show horses are mammoth and spotlessly groomed and more or less odorless — the acrid smell in here is just the horses' pee. All their muscles are beautiful; the hides enhance them. Their tails whip around in sophisticated double-jointed ways, keeping the flies from mounting any kind of coordinated attack. (There really is such a thing as a horsefly.) The horses all make farty noises when they sigh, heads hanging over the short doors. They're not for petting, though. When you come close they flatten their ears and show big teeth. The grooms laugh to themselves as we jump back. These are special competitive horses, intricately bred, w/ high-strung artistic temperaments. I wish I'd brought carrots: animals can be bought, emotionally. Stall after stall of horses. Standard horse-type colors. They eat the same hay they stand in. Occasional feedbags look like gas masks. A sudden clattering spray-sound like somebody hosing down siding turns out to be a glossy chocolate stallion, peeing. He's at the back of his stall getting combed, and the door's wide open, and we watch him pee. The stream's an inch in diameter and throws up dust and hay and little chips of wood from the floor. We hunker down and have a look upward, and I suddenly for the first time understand a certain expression describing certain human males, an expression I'd heard but never truly understood till just now, prone and gazing upward in some blend of horror and awe.

You can hear the cows all the way from the Horse Complex. The cow stalls are all doorless and open to view. I don't guess a cow presents much of an escape risk. The cows in here are white-spotted dun or black, or else white with big continents of dun or black. They have no lips and their tongues are wide. Their eyes roll and they have huge nostrils. I'd always thought of swine as the really nostrily barnyard animal, but cows have some serious nostrils going on, gaping and wet and pink or black. One cow has a sort of mohawk. Cow manure smells wonderful — warm and herbal and blameless — but cows themselves stink in a special sort of rich biotic way, rather like a wet boot. Some of the owners are scrubbing down their entries for the upcoming Beef Show over at the Coliseum (I have a detailed Media Guide, courtesy of WalMart). These cows stand immobilized in webs of canvas straps inside a steel frame while ag-professionals scrub them down with a hose-and-brush thing that also oozes soap. The cows do not like this one bit. One cow we watch getting scrubbed for a while — whose face seems eerily reminiscent of former British P.M. Winston Churchill's face — trembles and shudders in its straps and makes the whole frame rock and clank, lowing, its eyes rolled almost to the whites. Native Companion and I cringe and make soft appalled noises. This cow's lowing starts all the other cows lowing, or maybe they just see what they're in for. The cow's legs keep half-buckling, and the owner kicks at them (the legs). The owner's face is intent but expressionless. White mucus hangs from the cow's snout. Other ominous dripping and gushings from elsewhere. It almost tips the steel frame over at one point, and the owner punches the cow in the ribs.

Swine have *fur!* I never thought of pigs as having fur. I've actually never been very close to a pig before, for olfactory reasons. Growing up over near Urbana, the hot days when the wind blew from the U. of I. Swine Barns just southwest of our neighborhood were very grim days indeed. The U. of I. Swine Barns were actually what made my father finally knuckle under and let us get central AC. Swine smell, Native Companion reports her own father saying, "like Death his very own self is takin' a shit." The swine in here at the State Fair Swine Barn are show hogs, a breed called Poland China, their thin fur a kind of white crewcut over pink skin. A lot of the swine are down on their sides, stuporous and throbbing in the Barn's heat. The awake ones grunt. They stand and lie on very clean large-curd sawdust in low-fenced pens. A couple of barrows are eating both the sawdust and their own excrement. Again, we're the only tourists here. It also occurs to me that I didn't see a single farmer or ag-professional at the Opening Ceremony. It's like there are two different Fairs, different populations. A bullhorn on a wall announces that the Junior Pygmy Goat judging is under way over at the Goat Barn.

Pigs are in fact fat, and a lot of these swine are frankly huge — say ⅓ the size of a Volkswagen. Every once in a while you hear about farmers getting mauled or killed by swine. No teeth in view here, though the swine's hoofs look maul-capable — they're cloven and pink and kind of obscene. I'm not sure whether they're called hoofs or feet on swine. Rural Midwesterners learn by like second grade that there's no such word as "hooves." Some of the swine have large standing fans going in front of their pens, and twelve big ceiling-fans roar, but it's still stifling in here. The smell is both vomity and excremental, like some hideous digestive disorder on a grand scale. Maybe a cholera ward would come close. The owners and swineherds all have on rubber boots nothing like L. L. Bean East-Coast boots. Some of the standing swine commune through the bars of their pens, snouts almost touching. The sleeping swine thrash in dreams, their hind legs working. Unless they're in distress, swine grunt at a low constant pitch. It's a pleasant sound.

But now one butterscotch-colored swine is screaming. Distressed swine scream. The sound is both human and inhuman enough to make your hair stand. You can hear this one distressed swine all the way across the Barn. The professional swinemen ignore the pig, but we fuss on over, Native Companion making concerned baby-talk sounds until I shush her. The pig's sides are heaving; it's sitting up like a dog with its front legs quivering, screaming horribly. This pig's keeper is nowhere in sight. A small sign on its pen says it's a Hampshire Swine. It's having respiratory trouble, clearly: I'm guessing it inhaled either sawdust or excrement. Or else maybe it's just had it with the smell in here. Its front legs now buckle so it's on its side spasming. Whenever it can get enough breath together it screams. It's unendurable, but none of the ag-professionals comes vaulting over the pens to administer aid or anything. Native Companion and I are literally wringing our hands in sympathy. We both make plangent little noises at the pig. Native Companion tells me to go get somebody instead of standing there with my thumb up my butt. I feel enormous stress — nauseous smells, impotent sympathy, plus we're behind schedule: we are currently missing the Jr. Pygmy Goats, Philatelic Judging at the Expo Building, a 4-H Dog Show at something called Club Mickey D's, the Semifinals of the Midwest Arm-Wrestling Championships at the Lincoln Stage, a Ladies Camping Seminar, and the opening rounds of the Speed Casting Tournament over at the mysterious Conservation World. A swineherd kicks her Poland China sow awake so she can add more sawdust to its pen; Native Companion utters a pained sound. There are clearly exactly two Animal Rights advocates in this Swine Barn. We both can observe a kind of sullen, callous expertise in the demeanor of the ag-pros in here. A prime example of spiritual-alienation-from-land-as-factory, I posit. Except why take all the trouble to breed and train and care for a special animal and bring it all the way to the IL State Fair if you don't care anything about it?

Then it occurs to me that I had bacon yesterday and am even now looking forward to my first corn dog of the Fair. I'm standing here wringing my hands over a distressed swine and then I'm going to go pound down a corn dog. This is connected to my reluctance to charge over to a swine-pro and demand emergency resuscitative care for this agonized Hampshire. I can sort of picture the look the farmer would give me.

Not that it's profound, but I'm struck, amid the pig's screams and wheezes, by the fact that these agricultural pros do not see their stock as pets or friends. They are just in the agribusiness of weight and meat. They are unconnected even at the Fair, this self-consciously Special occasion of connection. And why not, maybe? — even at the Fair, their products continue to drool and smell and ingest their own excrement and scream, and the work just goes on and on. I can imagine what the ag-pros must think of us, cooing at the swine: we Fairgoers don't have to deal with the business of breeding and feeding our meat; our meat simply materializes at the corn-dog stand, allowing us to separate our healthy appetites from fur and screams and rolling eyes. We tourists get to indulge our tender Animal Rights feelings with our tummies full of bacon. I don't know how keen these sullen farmers' sense of irony is, but mine's been honed East-Coast keen, and I feel like a bit of a schmuck in the Swine Barn.

08/13/1150h. Since Native Companion was lured here for the day by the promise of free access to sphincter-loosening high-velocity rides, we make a quick descent into Happy Hollow. Most of the rides aren't even twirling hellishly yet. Guys with ratchet wrenches are still cranking away at the Ring of Fire. The giant Gondola Ferris Wheel is only half-assembled, and its seat-draped lower half resembles a hideous molary grin. It's over 100° in the sun, easy.

The Happy Hollow Carnival area's a kind of rectangular basin that extends east-west from near the Main Gate out to the steep pathless hillside just below Livestock. The Midway is made of dirt and flanked by carnival-game booths and ticket booths and rides. There's a merry-go-round and a couple of sane-paced kids' rides, but most of the rides down here look like genuine Near-Death Experiences. On this first morning the Hollow seems to be open only technically, and the ticket booths are unmanned, though heartbreaking little streams of AC'd air are blowing out through money-slots in the booths' glass. Attendance is sparse, and I notice none of the ag-pros or farm people are anywhere in sight down here. What there are are carnies. A lot of them slouch and slump in awnings' shade. Every one of them seems to chain-smoke. The Tilt-a-Whirl operator's got his boots up on his control panel reading a motorcycle-and-naked-lady magazine while two guys attach enormous rubber hoses to the ride's guts. We sidle over for a chat. The operator's 24 and from Bee Branch Arkansas, and has an earring and a huge tattoo of a motorcycle w/ naked lady on his triceps. He's way more interested in chatting with Native Companion than with me. He's been at this gig five years, touring with this one here same company here. Couldn't rightly say if he liked it or not, the gig: like as compared to what? Broke in the trade on the Toss-a-Quarter-Onto-the-Plates game and got, like, transferred over to the Tilt-a-Whirl in '91. He smokes Marlboro 100's but wears a cap that says WINSTON. He wants to know if Native Companion'd like to take a quick walk back across the Hollow and see something way out of the usual range of what she's used to. All around us are booths for various carny-type games. All the carny-game barkers have headset microphones; some are saying "Testing" and reciting their pitches' lines in tentative warm-up ways. A lot of the pitches seem frankly sexual: "You got to get it up to get it in"; "Take it out and lay 'er down, only a dollar"; "Make it stand up. Two dollars five chances. Make it stand up." In the booths, rows of stuffed animals hang by their feet like game put out to cure. One barker's testing his mike by saying "Testes" instead of "Testing." It smells like machine grease and hair tonic down here, and there's already a spoiled, garbagey smell. My Media Guide says 1993's Happy Hollow is contracted to ". . . one of the largest owners of amusement attractions in the country," one Blomsness and Thebault All-Star Amusement Enterprises of Crystal Lake IL, up near Chicago. But the carnies themselves all seem to be from the middle South — Tennessee, Arkansas, Oklahoma. They are visibly unimpressed by the Press Credentials clipped to my shirt. They tend to look at Native Companion like she's food, which she ignores. There's very little of that childhood sense of all the games and rides being Special and For-Me, I have to say. I promptly lose $4.00 trying to "get it up and in" by tossing miniature basketballs into angled straw baskets in such a way that they don't bounce back out. The game's barker can toss the balls behind his back and get them to stay in, but he's right up next to the baskets. My shots carom out from eight feet away — the straw baskets look soft, but their bottoms make a suspicious steely sound when the balls hit.

It's so hot that we move in quick staggered vectors between areas of shade. I decline to take my shirt off because there'd be no way to display my Credentials. We zigzag gradually westward across the Hollow. I am keen to hit the Junior Beef Show which starts at 1300h. Then there are, of course, the Dessert Competition tents.

One of the fully assembled rides near the Hollow's west end is something called The Zipper. It's riderless but in furious motion, a kind of Ferris Wheel on amphetamines. Individual caged cars are hinged to spin on their own axes as they go around in a tight vertical ellipse. The machine looks less like a zipper than the head of a chain saw. Its off-white paint is chipped, and it sounds like a shimmying V-12, and in general it's something I'd run a mile in tight shoes to avoid riding. But Native Companion starts clapping and hopping around excitedly as we approach The Zipper. (This is a person who bungee jumps, to give you an idea.) And the operator at the controls sees her, waves back, and shouts down to Git on over and git some if she's a mind to. He claims they want to test The Zipper somehow. He's up on a kind of steel platform, elbowing a colleague next to him in a way I don't much like. We have no tickets, I point out, and none of the cash-for-ticket booths are manned. By now we're somehow at the base of the stairway up to the platform and control panel. The operator says without looking at me that the matter of tickets this early on Opening Day "Ain't no sweat off my balls." The operator's colleague conducts Native Companion up the waffled-steel steps and straps her into a cage, upping a thumb at the operator, who gives a sort of Rebel Yell and pulls a lever. Native C.'s cage begins to ascend. Pathetic little fingers appear in the cage's mesh. The Zipper operator is ageless and burnt-brown and has a mustache waxed to wicked points like steers' horns, rolling a Drum cigarette with one hand as he nudges levers upward and the ellipse speeds up and the individual cages start to spin independently on their hinges. Native Companion is a blur of color inside her cage, but the operator and colleague (whose jeans have worked down his hips to the point where the top of his butt-crack is clearly visible) watch studiously as her spinning cage and the clanking empty cages circle the ellipse approx. once a second. I have a particular longstanding fear of things that spin independently inside a larger spin. I can barely even watch this. The Zipper is the color of unbrushed teeth, with big scabs of rust. The operator and colleague sit on a little steel bench before a panel full of black-knobbed levers. Do testicles themselves sweat? They're supposed to be very temperature-sensitive. The colleague spits

Skoal into a can he holds and tells the operator to "Well then take her to Eight then you pussy." The Zipper begins to whine and the thing to spin so fast that a detached car would surely be hurled into orbit. The colleague has a small American flag folded into a bandanna around his head. The empty cages shudder and clank as they whirl, spinning independently. One long scream, wobbled by Doppler, is coming from Native C.'s cage, which is going around and around on its hinges while a shape inside tumbles like stuff in a dryer. My particular neurological makeup (extremely sensitive: carsick, airsick, heightsick; my sister likes to say I'm "lifesick") makes even just watching this an act of enormous personal courage. The scream goes on and on; it's nothing like a swine's. Then the operator stops the ride abruptly with Native C.'s car at the top, so she's hanging upside down inside the cage. I call up Is she OK, but the response is just high-pitched noises. I see the two carnies gazing upward very intently, shading their eyes. The operator's stroking his mustache contemplatively. The cage's inversion has made Native Companion's dress fall up. They're ogling her nethers, obviously. As they laugh, the sound literally sounds like "Tee hee hee hee." A less sensitive neurological specimen probably would have stepped in at this point and stopped the whole grotesque exercise. My own makeup leans more toward disassociation when under stress. A mother in shorts is trying to get a stroller up the steps of the Funhouse. A kid in a *Jurassic Park* T-shirt is licking an enormous flat lollipop with a hypnotic spiral on it. A sign at a gas station we passed on Sangamon Avenue was hand-lettered and said "BLU-BLOCK SUNGLASSES — *Like Seen On TV.*" A Shell station off I-55 near Elkhart sold cans of snuff out of a vending machine. 15% of the female Fairgoers here have their hair in curlers. 25% are clinically fat. Midwestern fat people have no compunction about wearing shorts or halter-tops. A radio reporter had held his recorder's mike up too close to a speaker during Governor E.'s opening remarks, causing hellacious feedback. Now the operator's joggling the choke-lever so The Zipper stutters back and forth, forward and backward, making N.C.'s top car spin around and around on its hinges. His colleague's T-shirt has a stoned Ninja Turtle on it, toking on a joint. There's a distended A♯ scream from the whirling cage, as if Native C.'s getting slow-roasted. I summon saliva to step in and really say something stern, but at this point they start bringing her down. The

operator is deft at his panel; the car's descent is almost fluffy. His hands
on the levers are a kind of parody of tender care. The descent takes forever — ominous silence from Native Companion's car. The two carnies
are laughing and slapping their knee. I clear my throat twice. There's
a trundly sound as Native Companion's car gets locked down at the
platform. Jiggles of movement in the cage, and the door's latch slowly
turns. I expect whatever husk of a human being emerges from the car
to be hunched and sheet-white, dribbling fluids. Instead she sort of
bounds out:

"That was fucking *great*. Joo see that? Son bitch spun that car *sixteen
times*, joo see it?" This woman is native Midwestern, from my hometown. My prom date a dozen years ago. Now married, with three children, teaches water-aerobics to the obese and infirm. Her color is high.
Her dress looks like the world's worst case of static cling. She's still
got her *chewing gum* in, for God's sake. She turns to the carnies: "You
sons bitches that was fucking *great*. Assholes." The colleague is half-
draped over the operator; they're roaring with laughter. Native Companion has her hands on her hips sternly, but she's grinning. Am I the
only one who was in touch with the manifestly overt sexual-harassment
element in this whole episode? She takes the steel stairs down three at
a time and starts up the hillside toward the food booths. There is no
sanctioned path up the incredibly steep hill on the Hollow's western side.
Behind us the operator calls out: "They don't call me King of The Zipper for nuthin', sweet thang." She snorts and calls back over her shoulder "Oh you and whose fucking *platoon?*" and there's more laughter
behind us.

I'm having a hard time keeping up on the slope. "Did you hear that?"
I ask her.

"Jesus I thought I bought it for sure at the end that was so great.
Fucking cornholers. But'd you *see* that one spin up top at the end,
though?"

"Did you hear that Zipper King comment?" I say. She has her hand
around my elbow and is helping me up the hillside's slick grass. "Did you
sense something kind of sexual-harassmentish going on through that
whole little sick exercise?"

"Oh for fuck's sake Slug it was *fun*." (Ignore the nickname.) "Son of
a bitch spun that car *eighteen times*."

"They were looking up your *dress*. You couldn't see them, maybe. They hung you upside down at a great height and made your dress fall up and *ogled* you. They shaded their eyes and made comments to each other. I saw the whole thing."

"Oh for fuck's sake."

I slip a little bit and she catches my arm. "So this doesn't bother you? As a Midwesterner, you're unbothered? Or did you just not have an accurate sense of what was going on back there?"

"So if I noticed or I didn't, why does it have to be *my* deal? What, because there's assholes in the world I don't get to ride on The Zipper? I don't get to ever spin? Maybe I shouldn't ever go to the pool or ever get all girled up, just out of fear of assholes?" Her color is still high.

"So I'm curious, then, about what it would have taken back there, say, to have gotten you to lodge some sort of complaint with the Fair's management."

"You're so fucking *innocent*, Slug," she says. (The nickname's a long story; ignore it.) "Assholes are just assholes. What's getting hot and bothered going to do about it except keep me from getting to have fun?" She has her hand on my elbow this whole time — the hillside's a bitch.

"This is potentially key," I'm saying. "This may be just the sort of regional politico-sexual contrast the swanky East-Coast magazine is keen for. The core value informing a kind of willed politico-sexual stoicism on your part is your prototypically Midwestern appreciation of fun —"

"Buy me some pork skins, you dipshit."

"— whereas on the East Coast, politico-sexual indignation *is* the fun. In New York, a woman who'd been hung upside down and ogled would go get a whole lot of other women together and there'd be this frenzy of politico-sexual indignation. They'd confront the ogler. File an injunction. Management'd find itself litigating expensively — violation of a woman's right to nonharassed fun. I'm telling you. Personal and political fun merge somewhere just east of Cleveland, for women."

Native Companion kills a mosquito without looking at it. "And they all take Prozac and stick their finger down their throat too out there. They might ought to try just climbing on and spinning and ignoring assholes and saying Fuck 'em. That's pretty much all you can do with assholes."

"This could be integral."

08/13/1235h. Lunchtime. The Fairgrounds are a St. Vitus's dance of blacktop footpaths, the axons and dendrites of mass spectation, connecting buildings and barns and corporate tents. Each path is flanked, pretty much along its whole length, by booths hawking food. There are tall Kaopectate-colored shacks that sell Illinois Dairy Council milkshakes for an off-the-scale $2.50 — though they're mindbendingly good milkshakes, silky and so thick they don't even insult your intelligence with a straw or spoon, giving you instead a kind of small plastic trowel. There are uncountable pork options: Paulie's Pork Out, the Pork Patio, Freshfried Pork Skins, the Pork Street Cafe. The Pork Street Cafe is a "One Hundred Percent All-Pork Establishment," says its loudspeaker. "Ever last thing." I'm praying this doesn't include the beverages. No way I'm eating any pork after this morning's swine stress, anyway. And it's too hot even to think about the Dessert Competitions. It's at least 95° in the shade here due east of Livestock, and the breeze is shall we say fragrant. But food is getting bought and ingested at an incredible clip all up and down the path. The booths are ubiquitous, and each one has a line in front of it. Everybody's packed in together, eating as they walk. A peripatetic feeding frenzy. Native Companion is agitating for pork skins. Zipper or no, she's *"storvin','"* she says, "to *daith*." She likes to put on a parodic hick accent whenever I utter a term like "peripatetic."

(You do not want details on what pork skins are.)

So along the path there are I.D.C. milkshakes (my lunch), Lemon Shake-Ups, Ice Cold Melon Man booths, Citrus Push-Ups, and Hawaiian Shaved Ice you can suck the syrup out of and then crunch the ice (my dessert). But a lot of what's getting bought and gobbled is to my mind not hot-weather food at all: bright-yellow popcorn that stinks of salt; onion rings big as leis; Poco Penos Stuffed Jalapeño Peppers; Zorba's Gyros; shiny fried chicken; Bert's Burritos — "BIG AS YOU'RE HEAD" (sic); hot Italian beef; hot New York City Beef (?); Jojo's Quick Fried Donuts (the only booth selling coffee, by the way); pizza by the shingle-sized slice and chitlins and Crab Rangoon and Polish sausage. (Rural

Illinois' complete lack of ethnic identity creates a kind of postmodern embarrassment of riches — foods of every culture and creed become our own, quick-fried and served on cardboard and consumed on foot.) There are towering plates of "Curl Fries," which are pubic-hair-shaped and make people's fingers shine in the sun. Cheez-Dip Hot Dogs. Pony Pups. Hot Fritters. Philly Steak. Ribeye BBQ Corral. Joanie's Original ½-lb Burgers' booth's sign says 2 CHOICES — RARE OR MOOIN'. I can't believe people eat this kind of stuff in this kind of heat. The sky is cloudless and galvanized; the sun fairly pulses. There's the green reek of fried tomatoes. (Midwesterners say "tomāto.") The sound of myriad deep fryers forms a grisly sound-carpet all up and down the gauntlet of booths. The Original 1-lb Butterfly Pork Chop booth's sign says PORK: THE OTHER WHITE MEAT, the only discernible armwave to the health-conscious so far. Non-natives note, it's the Midwest: no nachos, no chili, no Evian, nothing Cajun.

But holy mackerel are there sweets: Fried Dough; Black Walnut Taffy; Fiddlesticks; Hot Crackerjack. Caramel apples for a felonious $1.50. Angel's Breath, known also as Dentist's Delight. Vanilla fudge that breaks a kind of weird sweat the minute it leaves its booth's freezer. The crowd moves at one slow pace, eating, dense-packed between the rows of booths. No ag-pros in sight. The crowd's adults are either pale or with the pink tinge of new burn, thin-haired and big-bellied in tight jeans, some downright fat and moving by sort of shifting their weight from side to side; boys minus shirts and girls in primary-colored halters; littler boys and girls in squads; parents with strollers; terribly pale academics in Bermudas and sandals; big women in curlers; lots of people carrying shopping bags; absurd floppy hats; almost all with '80s-fashion sunglasses — all seemingly eating, crowded together, twenty abreast, moving slowly, packed in, sweating, shoulders rubbing, the air deep-fried and spicy with antiperspirant and Coppertone, jowl to jowl. Picture Tokyo's rush-hour subway on an epic scale. It's a rare grand mass of Midwest humanity, eating and shuffling and rubbing, moving toward the Coliseum and Grandstand and Expo Building and the Livestock shows beyond. It's maybe significant that nobody looks like they're feeling oppressed or claustrophobic or bug-eyed at being airlessly hemmed in by the endless crowd we're all part of. Native Companion cusses and laughs when people step on her feet. Something East-Coast in me prickles at the bovine and herdlike quality of the crowd, though, i.e. us, hundreds of hands rising from paper tray to mouth as we jostle and press toward our respective attractions. From the air we'd look like some kind of Bataan March of docile consumption. (Native Companion laughs and says the batons aren't ever till the second day.) We're Jr.-Beef-Show-bound. You do not want to know what appalling combination of high-lipid foods N. Companion lunches on as we're borne by a living river toward prize-winning beef. The booths keep rolling past. There's Ace-High All-Butter Fudge. There are Rice-Krispie-squarish things called Krakkles. Angel Hair Cotton Candy. There are Funnel Cakes, viz. cake batter quick-fried to a tornadic spiral and rolled in sugared butter. Eric's Salt Water Taffy. Something called Zak's Fried Ice Cream. Another artery-clogger: Elephant Ears. An Elephant Ear is an album-sized expanse of oil-fried dough slathered with butter and cinnamon-sugar, sort of cinnamon toast from hell, really and truly shaped like an ear, surprisingly yummy, it turns out, but sickly soft, the texture of adipose flesh, and undeniably elephant-sized — no one's in line for Ears except the morbidly obese.

One food venue we fight across the current to check out special is a huge high-tech neonated stand: DIPPIN DOTS — *"Ice Cream Of The Future."* The countergirl sits on a tall stool shrouded in dry-ice steam and is at most thirteen years old, and my Press Credentials for the first time make someone's eyes widen, and we get free samples, little cups of what seem to be tiny little ice-cream pellets, fluorescent BB's that are kept, the countergirl swears to *God,* at 55° below 0 — Oh *God* she doesn't *know* whether it's 0°C or 0°F; that wasn't in the DIPPIN DOTS training video. The pellets melt in your mouth, after a fashion. More like evaporate in your mouth. The taste is vivid, but the Dots' texture's weird, abstract. Futuristic. The stuff's intriguing but just too Jetsonian to really catch on. The countergirl spells her last name for us and wants to say Hey to someone named Jody in return for the samples.

08/13/1310h. "Here we've got as balanced in dimension as any heifer you'll see today. A high-volume heifer but also solid on mass. Good to look at in terms of rib-length to -depth. Depth of forerib. Notice the depth of flank on the front quarter. We'd like to see maybe perhaps a little more muscle mass on the rear flank. Still, an outstanding heifer."

We're in the Jr. Livestock Center. A lot of cows move in a ring around the perimeter of the dirt circle, each cow led by an ag-family kid. The "Jr." pretty clearly refers to the owners, not the animals. Each cow's kid holds a long poker with a right-angled tooth at its end. They take turns prodding their cow into the center of the ring to move in a tighter circle while its virtues and liabilities are assessed. We're up in the stands. Native Companion is smitten. The Beef Show Official at the microphone looks uncannily like the actor Ed Harris, blue-eyed and somehow sexily bald. He's dressed just like the kids in the ring — dark new stiff jeans, check shirt, bandanna around neck. On him it doesn't look goofy. Plus he's got a stunning white cowboy hat. While Ms. Illinois Beef Queen presides from a dais decked with flowers sent over from the Horticulture Show, the Beef Official stands in the arena itself, his legs apart and his thumbs in his belt, 100% man, radiating livestock savvy. N.C. seems less smitten than decapitated, frankly.

"Okay this next heifer, a lot of depth of rib but a little tighter in the foreflank. A bit tighter-flanked, if you will, from the standpoint of capacity."

The cows' owners are farm kids, deep-rural kids from back-of-beyond counties like Piatt, Moultrie, Vermilion, all County Fair winners. They are earnest, nervous, pride-puffed. Dressed rurally up. Straw-colored crewcuts. High number of freckles per capita. They're kids remarkable for a kind of classic Rockwellian U.S. averageness, the products of balanced diets, vigorous labor, and solid GOP upbringings. The Jr. Livestock Center bleachers are over half-full, and it's all ag-people, farmers, parents mostly, many with video cameras. Cowhide vests and ornate dress-boots and simply amazing hats. Illinois farmers are rural and kind of inarticulate, but they are not poor. Just the amount of re-volving credit you need to capitalize a fair-sized operation — seed and herbicide, heavy equipment, crop insurance — makes a lot of them millionaires on paper. Media dirges notwithstanding, banks are no more keen to foreclose on Midwestern farmers than they are on Third World nations; they're in that deeply. Nobody's in sunglasses or shorts; everyone's tanned in an earthtone, all-business way. And if the Fair's ag-pros are also stout, it's in a harder, squarer, somehow more *earned* way than the tourists on the paths outside. The bleachers' fathers have bushy eyebrows and simply enormous thumbs, I notice. Native C. keeps making growly throat noises about the Beef Official. The J.L.C. is cool and dim and spicy with livestock. The atmosphere's good-natured but serious. Nobody's eating any booth-food, and nobody's carrying the Fair's complimentary GOVERNOR EDGAR shopping bags.

"An excellent heifer from a profile standpoint."

"Here we have a low-volume heifer but with exceptional mass in the rear quarter."

I can't tell whose cow is winning.

"Certainly the most extreme heifer out here in terms of frame to depth."

Some of the cows looked drugged. Maybe they're just superbly trained. You can imagine these farm kids getting up every day so early they can see their breath and leading their cows in practice circles under the cold stars, then having to do all their chores. I feel good in here. The cows in the ring all have colored ribbons on their tails. The lows and snorts of other cows on deck echo under the stands' bleachers. Sometimes the bleachers shake like something's butting the struts down there.

There are baroque classifications I can't start to follow — Breed, Class, Age. A friendly ag-lady with a long tired face beside us explains the kids' pokers, though. They're called Show Sticks, used to arrange the cows' feet when they're standing, and to prod, scratch, swat, or stroke, depending. The lady's own boy took second in the "Polled Hereford" — that's him getting congratulated by Ms. IL Beef Queen for a *Livestock Weekly* photographer. Native Companion isn't crazy about the smells and bellows in here, but she says if her husband calls me up next week looking for her it'll mean she's decided to "up and follow that Ed Harris fellow home." This is even after I remark that he could use a little more depth in the forerib.

The cows are shampooed and mild-eyed and lovely, incontinence notwithstanding. They are also assets. The ag-lady beside us says her family's operation will realize maybe like $2,500 for the Hereford in the Winners Auction coming up. Illinois farmers call their farms "operations," rarely "farms" and never "spreads." The lady says $2,500 is "maybe about around half" what the family's spent on the heifer's breeding and upkeep and care. "We do this for pride," she says. This is more like it. Pride, care, selfless expense. The little boy's chest puffs out as the

Official tips his blinding hat. Farm spirit. Oneness w/ crop and stock. I'm making mental notes till my temples throb. N.C. asks about the Official fellow. The ag-lady explains he's a beef buyer for a major Peoria packing plant and that the bidders in the upcoming Winners Auction (five brown suits and three string ties on the dais) are from McDonald's, Burger King, White Castle, etc. Meaning the mild-eyed winners have been sedulously judged as meat. The ag-lady has a particular bone to pick with McDonald's, "that always come in and overbid high on the champions and don't care about anything else. Mess up the pricing." Her husband confirms that they got "screwed back to front" on last year's bidding.

We skip the Junior Swine Show.

08/13/1400–1600h. We hurtle here and there, sort of surfing on the paths' crowds. Paid attendance today is 100,000+. A scum of clouds has cut the heat, but I'm on my third shirt. Society Horse Show at Coliseum. Wheat-Weaving Demonstration in Hobby, Arts & Crafts Bldg. Peonies like supernovas in the Horticulture Tent, where some of the older ladies from the Press Tour want to talk corn chowder recipes with me. We have no time. I'm getting the sort of overload-headache I always get in museums. Native C. is also stressed. And we're not the only tourists with that pinched glazed hurry-up look. There are just too many things to experience. Arm-Wrestling Finals where bald men fart audibly with effort. Assyrian National Council in the Fairgrounds' Ethnic Village — a riot of gesturing people in sheets. Everyone's very excited, at everything. Drum and Bugle Competition in Miller Lite Tent. On the crowded path outside Farm Expo a man engages in blatant frottage. Corn-fed young ladies in overalls cut off at the pockets. Hideous tottery Ronald McD. working the crowd at Club Mickey D's' 3-on-3 Hoops Competition — three of the six basketball players are black, the first black people I've seen here since Mrs. Edgar's hired kids. Pygmy Goat Show at Goat Barn. In the Media Guide: WALK ILLINOIS!(?), then Slide Show on Prairie Reclamation back over at Conservation World, then Open Poultry Judging, which I've decided to steel myself to see.

The afternoon becomes one long frisson of stress. I'm sure we'll miss something crucial. Native C. has zinc oxide on her nose and needs to get back home to pick up her kids. Plodding, elbowing. Seas of Fairgoing flesh, all looking, still eating. These Fairgoers seem to gravitate only to the crowded spots, the ones with long lines already. No one's playing any East-Coast games of Beat the Crowd. Midwesterners lack a certain cunning. Under stress they look like lost children. But no one gets impatient. Something adult and potentially integral strikes me. Why the Fairgoing tourists don't mind the crowds, lines, noise — and why I'm getting none of that old special sense of the Fair as uniquely For-Me. The State Fair here is For-*Us*. Self-consciously so. Not For-Me or -You. The Fair's deliberately *about* the crowds and jostle, the noise and overload of sight and smell and choice and event. It's Us showing off for Us.

A theory: Megalopolitan East-Coasters' summer vacations are literally getaways, flights-from — from crowds, noise, heat, dirt, the neural wear of too many stimuli. Thus ecstatic escapes to mountains, glassy lakes, cabins, hikes in silent woods. Getting Away From It All. Most East-Coasters see more than enough stimulating people and sights M-F, thank you; they stand in enough lines, buy enough stuff, elbow enough crowds, see enough spectacles. Neon skylines. Convertibles with 110-watt sound systems. Grotesques on public transport. Spectacles at every urban corner practically grabbing you by the lapels, commanding attention. The East-Coast existential treat is thus some escape from confines and stimuli — silence, rustic vistas that hold still, a turning inward: Away. Not so in the rural Midwest. Here you're pretty much Away all the time. The land here is big. Pool-table flat. Horizons in every direction. Even in comparatively citified Springfield, see how much farther apart the homes are, how broad the yards — compare with Boston or Philly. Here a seat to yourself on all public transport; parks the size of airports; rush hour a three-beat pause at a stop sign. And the farms themselves are huge, silent, mostly vacant space: you can't see your neighbor. Thus the vacation-impulse in rural IL is manifested as a flight-*toward*. Thus the urge physically to commune, melt, become part of a crowd. To see something besides land and corn and satellite TV and your wife's face. Crowds out here are a kind of adult nightlight. Hence the sacredness out here of Spectacle, Public Event. High school football, church social, Little League, parades, Bingo, market day, State Fair. All very big, very deep deals. Something in a Midwesterner sort of *actuates* at a Public Event. You can see it here. The

faces in this sea of faces are like the faces of children released from
their rooms. Governor Edgar's state spirit rhetoric at the Main Gate's
ribbon rings true. The real Spectacle that draws us here is Us. The
proud displays and the paths between them and the special-treat booths
along the paths are less important than the greater-than-sum We that
trudge elbow to elbow, pushing strollers and engaging in sensuous
trade, expending months of stored-up attention. A neat inversion of
the East-Coast's summer withdrawal. God only knows what the West
Coast's like.

We're about 100 yards shy of the Poultry Building when I break down.
I've been a rock about the prospect of Open Poultry Judging all day,
but now my nerve totally goes. I can't go in there. Listen to the untold
thousands of sharp squawking beaks in there, I say. Native Companion
not unkindly offers to hold my hand, talk me through it. It's 93° and
I have pygmy-goat shit on my shoe and am almost weeping with fear
and embarrassment. I sit down on one of the green pathside benches to
collect myself while N.C. goes to call home about her kids. I've never
before realized that "cacophony" was onomatopoeic: the noise of the
Poultry Bldg. is cacophonous and scrotum-tightening and totally horrible. I think it's what insanity must sound like. No wonder madmen
clutch their heads and scream. There's also a thin stink, and lots of bits
of feather are floating all over. And this is *outside* the Poultry Bldg. I
hunch on the bench. When I was eight, at the Champaign County Fair,
I was pecked without provocation, flown at and pecked by a renegade
fowl, savagely, just under the right eye, the scar of which looks like a
permanent zit.

Except of course one problem with the prenominate theory is that
there's more than one Us, hence more than one State Fair. Ag-people
at the Livestock barns and Farm Expo, non-farm civilians at the food-
booths and touristy exhibits and Happy Hollow. The two groups do not
much mix. Neither is the neighbor the other pines for.

Then there are the carnies. The carnies mix with no one, never seem
to leave Happy Hollow. Late tonight, I'll watch them drop flaps to turn
their carnival booths into tents. They'll smoke cheap dope and drink
peppermint schnapps and pee out onto the Midway's dirt. I think carnies
must be the rural U.S.'s gypsies — itinerant, insular, swarthy, unclean,
not to be trusted. You are in no way drawn to them. They all have the

same hard blank eyes as people in bus terminal bathrooms. They want your money and to look up your skirt; beyond that you're just blocking the view. Next week they'll dismantle and pack and haul up to the Wisconsin State Fair, where they'll again never set foot off the Midway they pee on.

The State Fair is rural IL's moment of maximum community, but even at a Fair whose whole raison is For-Us, Us's entail Thems, apparently. The carnies make an excellent Them. And the ag-people really hate them, the carnies. While I'm sitting there on the bench disassociating and waiting for N. Companion to come back, all of a sudden an old withered guy in an Illinois Poultry Association cap careers past on one of those weird three-wheeled carts, like a turbo-charged wheelchair, and runs neatly over my sneaker. This ends up being my one unassisted interview of the day, and it's brief. The old guy keeps revving his cart's engine like a biker. "*Traish*," he calls the carnies. "Lowlifes. Wouldn't let my own kids go off down there on a goddamn bet," gesturing down the hill at the twirling rides. He raises pullets down near Olney. He has something in his cheek. "Steal you blind. Drug-addicted and such. Swindle you nekked, them games. Traish. Me I ever year we drive up, why, I carry my wallet like this here," pointing to his hip. His wallet is on a big steel clip attached to a wire on his belt; the whole thing looks vaguely electrified.

Q: "But would they want to? Your kids I mean. Would they want to hit the Hollow, ride the rides, eat all-butter fudge, test various skills, mingle a little?"

He spits brownly. "*Hail* no. We all come for the shows." He means the Livestock Competitions. "See some folks, talk stock. Drink a beer. Work all year round raising 'em for showbirds. It's for pride. And to see folks. Shows're over Tuesday, why, we go on home." He looks like a bird himself. His face is mostly nose, his skin loose and pebbly like poultry's. His eyes are the color of denim. "Rest of all this here's for city people." Spits. He means Springfield, Decatur, Champaign. "Walk around, stand in line, eat junk, buy soovners. Give their wallet to the traish. Don't even know there's folks come here to work up here," gesturing at the barns. He spits again, leaning way out to the side of the cart to do it. "We come up to work, see some folks. Drink a beer. Bring our own goddamn food. Mother packs a hamper. Hail, what they'd want to go on down there?" I think meaning his kids. "Ain't no folks they know down there." He laughs. Asks my name. "It's good to see folks," he says. "We all stayin' up to the *mo*tel. Watch your wallet, boy." And he asks after my tire-treaded foot, very politely, before peeling out toward the chicken din.

08/14/1015h. Rested, rehydrated. No Native Companion along to ask embarrassing questions about why the reverential treatment; plenty of time for the *Harper's Bazaar* rumor to metastasize: I am primed to hit the Dessert Competitions.

8/14/1025h. Dessert Competitions.

08/14/1315h. Illinois State Fair Infirmary; then motel; then Springfield Memorial Medical Center Emergency Room for distention and possible rupture of transverse colon (false alarm); then motel; incapacitated till well after sunset; whole day a washout; incredibly embarrassing, unprofessional; indescribable. Delete entire day.

08/15/0600h. Upright and moving just outside the Hollow. Still transversely distressed, unrested; shaky but resolute. Sneakers already soaked. It rained in brutal sheets last night, damaged tents, tore up corn near the motel. Midwestern thunderstorms are real Old Testament skullclutchers: Richter-Scale thunder, sideways rain, big zigzags of cartoon lightning. By the time I tottered back over last night Tammy Wynette had closed early at the Grandstand, but Happy Hollow went till midnight, a whole lot of neon in the rain.

The dawn is foggy. The sky looks like soap. An enfilade of snores from the booths-turned-tents along the Midway. Happy Hollow is a bog. Someone behind the lowered flaps of the shoot-2D-ducks-with-an-air-rifle booth is having a wicked coughing fit, obscenely punctuated. Distant sounds of dumpsters getting emptied. Twitters of various birds. The Blomsness-Thebault management trailer has a blinky electric burglar alarm on it. The goddamn cocks are at it already up in the Poultry Bldg. Thunder-mutters sound way off east over Indiana. Trees shudder and shed drops in the breeze. The blacktop paths are empty, eerie, shiny with rain.

08/15/0620h. Looking at legions of sleeping sheep. Sheep Building. I am the only waking human in here. It's cool and quiet. Sheep excrement has an evil vomity edge to it, but olfactorily it's not too bad in here. One or two sheep are upright but silent. No fewer than four ag-pros are in the pens sleeping right up next to their sheep, about which the less speculation the better as far as I'm concerned. The roof in here is leaky and most of the straw is sopped. There are little printed signs on every pen. In here are Yearling Ewes, Brood Ewes, Ewe Lambs, Fall Lambs. Breedwise we've got Corriedales, Hampshires, Dorset Horns, Columbias. You could get a Ph.D. just in sheep, from the looks of it. Rambouillets, Oxfords, Suffolks, Shropshires, Cheviots, Southdowns. And these are just like the major classes. I've forgotten to say you can't see the actual sheep. The actual corporeal sheep themselves are all in tight white bodysuits, cotton maybe, with eye- and mouth-holes. Like Superhero suits. Sleeping in them. Presumably to keep their wool clean until it's judged. No fun later when the temperature starts climbing, though, I bet.

Back outside. Floating protean ghosts of fog and evap on the paths. The Fairgrounds are creepy with everything set up but no one about. A creepy air of hasty abandonment, a feeling like you run home from kindergarten and the whole family's up and moved, left you. Plus no-where dry to sit down and test out the notebook. (More like a tablet, purchased along w/ Bic ballpoint last night at the S.M.M.C. Card, Gift & Greeting shop. All they had was a little kid's tablet with that weird soft gray paper and some kind of purple brontosaurus-type character named Barney on the cover.

08/15/0730h. Pentacostal Sunday Services in Twilight Ballroom. Services joyless, humorless, worshippers lean and starchy and dour like characters from Hals portraits. Not one person smiles the whole time, and there's no little interval where you get to go around shaking people's hands and wishing them Peace. It's already 80° but so damp that people's breath hangs in front of their face.

08/15/0820h. Press Room, 4th Floor, Illinois Bldg. I'm pretty much the only credentialed Press without a little plywood cubbyhole for mail and Press Releases. Two guys from an ag-newspaper are trying to hook a fax machine up to a rotary-phone jack. Michael Jordan's father's body has been found, and the wire services are going nuts in one corner. Wire service teletypes really do sound exactly like the background on old TV newscasts from childhood. Also, the East St. Louis levee's given way; National Guardsmen are being mobilized. (East St. Louis needs Guardsmen even when it's dry, from my experience.) A State Fair PR guy arrives for the daily Press Briefing. Coffee and unidentifiable muffinish things courtesy of WalMart. I am hunched and pale. This P.M.'s highlights: Midwest Truck and Tractor Pull, the "Bill Oldani 100" U.S.A.C. auto race. Tonight's Grandstand Show's to be the poor old doddering Beach Boys, who I suspect now must make their entire living from State Fairs. The Beach Boys' "Special Guest" warm-up is to be America, another poor old doddering band. The PR guy cannot give away all his free Press Passes to the concert. Plus I learn I missed some law-and-order dramatics yesterday, apparently: two minors from Carbondale arrested riding The Zipper last night when a vial of cocaine fell out of one of their pockets and direct-hit a state trooper alertly eating a Lemon Push-Up on the Midway below; a reported rape or date-rape in Parking Lot 6; assorted bunkos and D&D's. Plus two separate reporters vomited on from a great height in two separate incidents under two separate Near-Death-Experience rides, trying to cover the Hollow.

08/15/0840h. A Macy's-float-sized inflatable Ronald, seated and eerily Buddha-like, presides over the north side of the Club Mickey D's tent. A family is having their picture taken in front of the inflatable Ronald, arranging their little kids in a careful pose. Notebook entry: *Why?*

08/15/0842h. Fourth trip to the bathroom in three hours. Elimination can be a dicey undertaking here. The Fair has scores of Midwest

Pottyhouses brand portable toilets at various strategic sites. Midwest Pottyhouses are man-sized plastic huts, reminiscent of Parisian *pissoirs* but also utilized for *numero deux,* clearly. Each Midwest Pottyhouse has its own undulating shroud of flies, plus your standard heavy-use no-flush outhouse smell, and I for one would rather succumb to a rupture than use a Pottyhouse, though the lines for them are long and sanguine. The only real restrooms are in the big exhibit buildings. The Coliseum's is like a grade school boys' room, especially the long communal urinal, a kind of huge porcelain trough. Performance- and other anxieties abound here, with upwards of twenty guys all flanking and facing each other, each with his unit out. All the men's rooms have hot-air blowers instead of paper towels, meaning you can't wash your face, and all have annoying faucet controls you have to keep a grip on to operate, meaning toothbrushing is a contorted affair. The highlight is watching Midwestern ag-guys struggle with suspenders and overall straps as they exit the stalls.

08/15/0847h. A quick scan of the Draft Horse Show. The Coliseum's interior is the size of a blimp hangar, with an elliptical dirt arena. The stands are permanent and set in cement and go on and up forever. The stands are maybe 5% full. Echoes are creepy, but the smell of the arena's moist earth is lush and nice. The draft horses themselves are enormous, eight feet high and steroidically muscled. I think they were originally bred to pull things; God only knows their function now. There are two- and three-year-old Belgian Stallions, Percherons, and the Bud-famous Clydesdales with their bellbottoms of hair. The Belgians are particularly thick through the chest and rear quarter (I'm starting to develop an eye for livestock). Again, the Official wears a simply bitching white cowboy hat and stands at ease, legs well apart. This one has a weak chin and something wrong with one of his eyelids, though, at least. All the competitors are again shampooed and combed, black and gunpowder-gray and the dull white of sea-foam, their tails cropped and the stumps decorated with girlish bows that look obscene against all this muscle. The horses' heads bob when they walk, rather like pigeons' heads. They're led in the now familiar concentric circles by their owners, big-bellied men in brown suits and string ties. At obscure PA commands, the owners break their animals into thundering canter, holding their bridles and running just under the head, stomachs bouncing around (the men's). The horses' hoofs throw up big clods of earth as they run, so that it sort of rains dirt for several yards behind them. They look mythic when they run. Their giant hoofs are black and have shiny age-striations like a tree-stump's rings.

It's something of a relief to see no fast-food buyers on the dais awaiting Auction. As with Beef, though, a young beauty queen in a tiara presides from a flower-decked throne. It's unclear just who she is: "Ms. Illinois Horseflesh" sounds unlikely, as does "Ms. Illinois Draft Horse." (Though there is a 1993 Illinois Pork Queen, over in Swine.)

08/15/0930h. Sun erumpent, mid-90s, puddles and mud trying to evaporate into air that's already waterlogged. Every smell just hangs there. The general sensation is that of being in the middle of an armpit. I'm once again at the capacious McDonald's tent, at the edge, the titanic inflatable clown presiding. (Why is there no WalMart tent?) There's a fair-sized crowd in the basketball bleachers at one side and rows of folding chairs at the other. It's the Illinois State Jr. Baton-Twirling Finals. A metal loudspeaker begins to emit disco, and little girls pour into the tent from all directions, twirling and gamboling in vivid costume. There's a symphony of zippers from the seats and stands as video cameras come out by the score, and I can tell it's pretty much just me and a thousand parents.

The baroque classes and divisions, both team and solo, go from age three (!) to sixteen, with epithetic signifiers — e.g. the four-year-olds compose the Sugar 'N' Spice division, and so on. I'm in a chair right up front (but in the sun) behind the competition's judges, introduced as "Varsity Twirlers from the [why?] University of Kansas." They are four frosted blondes who smile a lot and blow huge grape bubbles.

The twirler squads are all from different towns. Mount Vernon and Kankakee seem especially rich in twirlers. The twirlers' spandex costumes, differently colored for each team, are paint-tight and really brief in the legs. The coaches are grim, tan, lithe-looking women, clearly twirlers once, on the far side of their glory now and very serious-looking, each with a clipboard and whistle. It's all a little like figure skating. The teams go into choreographed routines, each routine with a title and a

designated disco or show tune, full of compulsory baton-twirling maneuvers with highly technical names. A mom next to me is tracking
scores on what looks almost like an astrology chart, and is in no mood
to explain anything to a novice baton-watcher. The routines are wildly
complex, and the loudspeaker's play-by-play is mostly in code. All I can
determine for sure is that I've bumbled into what has to be the single
most spectator-hazardous event at the Fair. Missed batons go all over,
whistling wickedly. The three-, four-, and five-year-olds aren't that dangerous, though they do spend most of their time picking up dropped
batons and trying to hustle back into place — the parents of especially
fumble-prone twirlers howl in fury from the stands while the coaches
chew gum grimly — but the littler girls don't have the arm-strength to
really endanger anybody, although one of the judges does take a Sugar
'N' Spice's baton across the bridge of the nose and has to be helped from
the tent.

But when the seven- and eight-year-olds hit the floor for a series of
"Armed Service Medleys" (spandex with epaulets and officers' caps and
batons over shoulders like M-16s), errant batons start pinwheeling into
the tent's ceiling, sides, and crowd with real force. I myself duck several
times. A man just down the row takes one in the plexus and falls over in
his metal chair with a horrid crash. The batons (one stray I picked up
had REGULATION LENGTH embossed down the shaft) have white
rubber stoppers on each end, but it's that dry hard kind of rubber, and
the batons themselves are not light. I don't think it's an accident that
police nightsticks are also called service batons.

Physically, even within same-age teams, there are marked incongru-
ities in size and development. One nine-year-old is several heads taller
than another, and they're trying to do an involved back-and-forth duet
thing with just one baton, which ends up taking out a bulb in one of the
tent's steel hanging lamps and showering part of the stands with glass.
A lot of the younger twirlers look either anorexic or gravely ill. There
are no fat baton-twirlers. The enforcement of this no-endomorph rule is
probably internal: a fat person'd have to get exactly one look at herself in
tight sequinned spandex to abandon all twirling ambitions for all time.

Ironically, it's the botched maneuvers that allow one to see how
baton-twirling (which to me had always seemed sleight-of-handish and
occult) works in terms of mechanics. It seems to consist not in twirling
so much as sort of spinning the baton on your knuckle while the fin-

gers underneath work and writhe furiously for some reason, maybe sup-
plying torque. Some serious kinetic force is coming from somewhere,
clearly. A sort of attempted sidearm-twirl sends a baton Xing out and
hitting a big woman's kneecap with a ringing clang, and her husband
puts his hand on her shoulder as she sits up very rigid and white, pop-
eyed, her mouth a little bloodless hyphen. I miss good old Native
Companion, who's the sort of person who can elicit conversation even
from the recently baton-struck.

A team of ten-year-olds from the Gingersnap class have little cotton bunnytails on their costumes' bottoms and rigid papier-mâché ears,
and they can do some serious twirling. A squad of eleven-year-olds
from Towanda does an involved routine in tribute to Operation Desert
Storm. To most of the acts there's either a cutesy ultrafeminine aspect
or a stern butch military one; there's little in between. Starting with the
twelve-year-olds — one team in black spandex that looks like cheesecake leotards — there is, I'm afraid, a frank sexuality that begins to get
uncomfortable. You can already see some of the sixteen-year-olds out
under the basketball hoop doing little warm-up twirls and splits, and
they're disturbing enough to make me wish there was a copy of the state's
criminal statutes handy and prominent. Also disturbing is that in an
empty seat next to me is a gun, a rifle, real-looking, with a white wood
stock, which who knows whether it's really real or part of an upcoming
martial routine or what, that's been sitting here ownerless ever since the
competition started.

Oddly, it's the cutesy feminine routines that result in the really serious casualties. A dad standing up near the stands' top with a Toshiba
viewfinder to his eye takes a tomahawking baton directly in the groin
and falls forward onto somebody eating a Funnel Cake, and they take out
good bits of several rows below them, and there's an extended halt to the
action, during which I decamp — steering way clear of the sixteen-year-
olds on the basketball court — and as I clear the last row yet another
baton comes *wharp-wharp*ing cruelly right over my shoulder, caroming
viciously off big R.'s inflated thigh.

08/15/1105h. A certain swanky East-Coast organ is unfortunately
denied journalistic impressions of the Illinois Snakes Seminar, the
Midwestern Birds of Prey Demonstration, the Husband-Calling Contest,

and something the Media Guide calls "The Celebrity 'Moo-Moo' Classic" — all of these clearly must-sees — because they're all also in venues right near the Food and Dessert Tent Grotto, which even the abstract thought of another proffered wedge of Chocolate Silk Triple-Layer Cake in the shape of Lincoln's profile produces a pulsing ache in the bulge I've still got on the left side of my abdomen. So right now I'm five acres and six hundred food-booths away from midday's must-see events, in the slow stream of people entering the Expo Bldg.

I'd planned on skipping the Expo Bldg., figuring it was full of like home-furniture-refinishing demos and futuristic mockups of Peoria's skyline. I'd had no idea it was . . . *air-conditioned*. Nor that it comprises a whole additional different IL State Fair with its own separate pros and patrons. It's not just that there are no carnies or ag-people in here. The place is jammed with people I've seen literally nowhere else on the Fairgrounds. It's a world and gala unto itself, self-sufficient: the fourth Us of the Fair.

The Expo Bldg.'s a huge enclosed mallish thing, AC'd down to 80°, with a cement floor and a hardwood mezzanine overhead. Every interior inch here is given over to adversion and commerce of a very special and lurid sort. Just inside the big east entrance a man with a headset mike is slicing up a block of wood and then a tomato, standing on a box in a booth that says *SharpKut,* hawking these spinoffs of Ginsu knives, "AS SEEN ON TV." Next door is a booth offering personalized pet-I.D. tags. Another's got the infamous mail-order-advertised Clapper, which turns on appliances automatically at the sound of two hands clapping (but also at the sound of a cough, sneeze, or sniff, I discover — caveat emp.). There's booth after booth, each with an audience whose credulity is heartrending. The noise in the Expo Bldg. is apocalyptic and complexly echoed, sound-carpeted by crying children and ceiling-fans' roar. A large percentage of the booths show signs of hasty assembly and say AS SEEN ON TV in bright brave colors. The booths' salesmen all stand raised to a slight height; all have headset microphones and speakers with built-in amps and rich neutral media voices.

It turns out these franchised Expo vendors, not unlike the Blomsness carnies (any comparison to whom makes the vendors show canine teeth, though), go from State Fair to State Fair all summer. One young man demonstrating QUICK 'N' BRITE — "A WHOLE NEW CONCEPT IN CLEANING" — was under the persistent impression that he was in Iowa.

There's a neon-bordered booth for something called a RAINBOW-VAC, a vacuum cleaner whose angle is that it uses water in its canister instead of a bag, and the canister is clear Lucite, so you get a graphic look at just how much dirt it's getting out of a carpet sample. People in polyester slacks and/or orthopedic shoes are clustered three-deep around this booth, greatly moved, but all I can think of is that the thing looks like the world's biggest heavy-use bong, right down to the water's color. There's a predictably strong odor surrounding the Southwestern Leatherworx booth. Likewise at Distressed Leather Luggage (missing hyphen? misplaced mod?). I'm not even halfway down one side of the Expo's main floor, list-wise. The mezzanine has still more booths. There's a booth that offers clock-faces superimposed on varnished photorealist paintings of Christ, John Wayne, Marilyn Monroe. There's a Computerized Posture Evaluation booth. A lot of the headsetted vendors are about my age or younger. Something ever so slightly over-groomed about them suggests a Bible-college background. It's just cool enough in here for a sweat-soaked shirt to get clammy. One vendor recites a pitch for Ms. Suzanne Somers's THIGHMASTER while a lady in a leotard lies on her side on the fiberboard counter and demonstrates the product. I'm in the Expo Bldg. almost two hours, and every time I look up the poor lady's still at it with the THIGHMASTER. Most of the Expo vendors won't answer questions and give me beady looks when I stand there making notes in the Barney tablet. But the THIGHMASTER lady — friendly, garrulous, violently cross-eyed, in (understandably) phenomenal physical condition — informs me she gets an hour off for lunch at 1400 but is back on her side all the way to closing at 2300. I remark that her thighs must be pretty well Mastered by now, and her leg sounds like a bannister when she raps her knuckle against it, and we have a good laugh together until her vendor finally makes her ask me to scram.

The Copper Kettle All-Butter Fudge booth does brisk air-conditioned business. There's something called a Full Immersion Body Fat Analysis for $8.50. A certain CompuVac Inc. offers a $1.50 Computerized Personality Analysis. Its booth's computer panel's tall and full of blinking lights and reel-to-reel tapes, like an old bad sci-fi-film computer. My own Personality Analysis, a slip of paper that protrudes like a tongue from a red-lit slot, says "Your Boldness of Nature is Ofset With The Fear Of Taking Risk" (sic[2]). My suspicion that there's a guy hunched behind the blinking panel feeding its slot recycled fortune-cookie slips is overwhelming but unverifiable.

Booth after booth. A Xanadu of chintzola. Obscure non-stick cookware. "EYE GLASSES CLEANED FREE." A booth with anti-cellulite sponges. More DIPPIN DOTS futuristic ice cream. A woman with Velcro straps on her shoes gets fountain-pen ink out of a linen tablecloth with a Chapsticky-looking spot remover whose banner says "AS SEEN ON 'AMAZING DISCOVERIES,' " a wee-hour infomercial I'm kind of a fan of. A plywood booth that for $9.95 will take a photo and superimpose your face on either an FBI Wanted poster or a *Penthouse* cover. An MIA — BRING THEM HOME! booth staffed by women playing Go Fish. An anti-abortion booth called LIFESAVERS that lures you over with free candy. Sand Art. Shredded-Ribbon Art. Therm-L-Seal Double Pane Windows. An indescribable booth for "LATEST ADVANCE ROTARY NOSE HAIR CLIPPERS" whose other sign reads (I kid you not) *"Do Not Pull Hair From Nose, May Cause Fatal Infection."* Two different booths for collectible sports cards, "Top Ranked Investment Of The Nineties." And tucked way back on one curve of the mezzanine's ellipse: *yes:* black velvet paintings, including several of Elvis in pensive poses.

And people are buying this stuff. The Expo's unique products are targeted at a certain type of Midwestern person I'd all but forgotten. I'd somehow not noticed these persons' absence from the paths and exhibits. This is going to sound not just East-Coastish but elitist and snotty. But facts are facts. The special community of shoppers in the Expo Bldg. are a Midwestern subphylum commonly if unkindly known as Kmart People. Farther south they'd be a certain fringe-type of White Trash. Kmart People tend to be overweight, polyestered, grim-faced, toting glazed unhappy children. Toupees are the movingly obvious shiny square-cut kind, and the women's makeup is garish and often asymmetrically applied, giving many of the female faces a kind of demented look. They are sharp-voiced and snap at their families. They're the type you see slapping their kids in supermarket checkouts. They are people who work at like Champaign's Kraft and Decatur's A. E. Staley and think pro wrestling is real. I'm sorry, but this is all true. I went to high school with

Kmart People. I know them. They own firearms and do not hunt. They aspire to own mobile homes. They read the *Star* without even a pretense of contempt and have toilet paper with little off-color jokes printed on it. A few of these folks might check out the Tractor Pull or U.S.A.C. race, but most are in the Expo to stay. This is what they've come for. They couldn't give one fat damn about ethanol exhibits or carnival rides whose seats are hard to squeeze into. Agriculture shmagriculture. And Gov. Edgar's a closet pinko: they heard it on Rush. They plod up and down, looking put out and intensely puzzled, as if they're sure what they've come for's got to be here someplace. I wish Native C. were here; she's highly quotable on the subject of Kmart People. One big girl with tattoos and a heavy-diapered infant wears a T-shirt that says "WARNING: I GO FROM 0 TO HORNEY IN 2.5 BEERS."

Have you ever wondered where these particular types of unfunny T-shirts come from? the ones that say things like "HORNEY IN 2.5" or "Impeach President Clinton . . . AND HER HUSBAND TOO!!"? Mystery solved. They come from State Fair Expos. Right here on the main floor's a monster-sized booth, more like an open bodega, with shirts and laminated buttons and license-plate borders, all of which, for this subphylum, Testify. This booth seems integral, somehow. The seamiest fold of the Midwestern underbelly. The Lascaux Caves of a certain rural mentality. "40 Isn't Old . . . IF YOU'RE A TREE" and "The More Hair I Lose, The More Head I Get" and "Retired: No Worries, No Paycheck" and "I Fight Poverty . . . I WORK!!" As with *New Yorker* cartoons, there's an elusive sameness about the shirts' messages. A lot serve to I.D. the wearer as part of a certain group and then congratulate that group for its sexual dynamism — "Coon Hunters Do It All Night" and "Hairdressers Tease It Till It Stands Up" and "Save A Horse: Ride A Cowboy." Some presume a weird kind of aggressive relation between the shirt's wearer and its reader — "We'd Get Along Better . . . If You Were A BEER" and "Lead Me Not Into Temptation, I Know The Way MYSELF" and "What Part Of NO Don't You Understand?" There's something complex and compelling about the fact that these messages are not just uttered but *worn*, like they're a badge or credential. The message compliments the wearer somehow, and the wearer in turn endorses the message by spreading it across his chest, which fact is then in further turn supposed to endorse the wearer as a person of plucky or risqué wit. It's also meant to cast the wearer as an Individual, the sort of person who not only makes but wears a Personal Statement. What's depressing is that the T-shirts' statements are not only preprinted and mass-produced, but so dumbly unfunny that they serve to place the wearer squarely in that large and unfortunate group of people who think such messages not only Individual but funny. It all gets tremendously complex and depressing. The lady running the booth's register is dressed like a '68 Yippie but has a hard carny face and wants to know why I'm standing here memorizing T-shirts. All I can manage to tell her is that the "HORNEY" on these "2.5 BEERS"-shirts is misspelled; and now I really feel like an East-Coast snob, laying judgments and semiotic theories on these people who ask of life only a Republican in the White House and a black velvet Elvis on the woodgrain mantel of their mobile home. They're not hurting anybody. A good third of the people I went to high school with now probably wear these T-shirts, and proudly.

And I'm forgetting to mention the Expo Bldg.'s other nexus of commerce — church booths. The populist evangelism of the rural Midwest. An economy of spirit. It's not your cash they want. A Church of God booth offers a Computerized Bible Quiz. Its computer is CompuVac-ish in appearance. I go eighteen for twenty on the Quiz and am invited behind a chamois curtain for a "person-to-person faith exploration," which thanks anyway. The conventional vendors get along fine with the Baptists and Jews for Jesus who operate booths right near them. They all laugh and banter back and forth. The SharpKut guy sends all the vegetables he's microsliced over to the LIFESAVERS booth, where they put them out with the candy. The scariest spiritual booth is right up near the west exit, where something called Covenant Faith Triumphant Church has a big hanging banner that asks "WHAT IS THE *ONE* MAN MADE THING IN HEAVEN?" and I stop to ponder, which with charismatics is instant death, because a breastless bushy-browed woman is out around the booth's counter like a shot and in my personal space. She says "Give up? Give up do you?" I tell her I'll go ahead and bite. She's looking at me very intensely, but there's something off about her gaze: it's like she's looking *at* my eyes rather than *into* them. What one man-made thing, I ask. She puts her finger to her palm and makes screwing motions. Signifying coitus? (I don't say "coitus" out loud, though.) "Not but one thing," she says. "The holes in Christ's palms," screwing her finger in. It's scary. Except isn't it pretty well known that Roman crucifees were nailed at the wrists, since palm-flesh won't support weight? So but now I've been drawn into an actual dialogue, going so far as to let the lady take my arm and pull me toward the booth's counter. "Lookee here for a second now," she says. She has both hands around my arm. I feel a sinking in my gut; I'm programmed from childhood to know that I've made a serious error. A Midwestern child of academics gets trained early on to avoid these weird-eyed eager rural Christians who accost your space, to say Not Interested at the front door and No Thanks to mimeoed leaflets, to look right through streetcorner missionaries as if they were NYC panhandlers. I have erred. The woman more or less throws me up against the Covenant Faith counter, on which counter is a fine oak box, yay big, with a propped sign: "Where Will YOU Be When YOU Look Like THIS?" "Take you a look-see in here." The box has a hole in the top. Inside the box is a human skull. I'm pretty sure it's plastic. The interior lighting's tricky. But I'm pretty sure the skull isn't genuine. I haven't inhaled for over a minute now. The woman is looking at the side of my face. "Are you *sure* is the question," she says. I manage to make my straightening-up motion lead right into a backing-away motion. "Are you a hundred percent *sure*." Overhead, on the mezzanine, the THIGHMASTER lady's still at it, on her side, head on her arm, smiling cross-eyed into space.

08/15/1336h. I'm on a teetery stool watching the Prairie State Cloggers Competition in a Twilight Ballroom that's packed with ag-folks and well over 100°. An hour ago I'd nipped in here to get a bottle of soda-pop on my way to the Truck and Tractor Pull. By now the Pull's got to be nearly over, and in half an hour the big U.S.A.C. dirt-track auto race starts, which I've already reserved a ticket for. But I can't tear myself away from the scene in here. This is far and away the funnest, most emotionally intense thing at the Fair. Run, don't walk, to your nearest clogging venue.

I'd imagined goony Jed Clampett types in tattered hats and hobnail boots, a-stompin' and a-whoopin', etc. Clogging, Scotch-Irish in origin and the dance of choice in Appalachia, I guess did used to involve actual clogs and boots and slow stomps. But clogging has now miscegenated with square dancing and honky-tonk boogie to become a kind of intricately synchronized, absolutely kick-ass country tap dance.

There's teams from Pekin, Leroy, Rantoul, Cairo, Morton. They each do three numbers. The music is up-tempo country or 4/4 dance-pop. Each team has anywhere from four to ten dancers. They're 75% women. Few of the women are under 35, fewer still under 175 lbs. They're country mothers, red-cheeked gals with bad dye jobs and big pretty legs. They wear Westernwear tops and midiskirts with multiple ruffled slips underneath; and every once in a while they'll grab handfuls of cloth and flip the skirts up like cancan dancers. When they do this they either yip or whoop, as the spirit moves them. The men all have thinning hair and cheesy rural faces, and their skinny legs are rubberized blurs. The men's Western shirts have piping on the chest and shoulders. The teams are all color-coordinated — blue and white, black and red. The white shoes all the dancers wear look like golf shoes with metal taps clamped on.

Their numbers are to everything from shitkicker Waylon and Tammy to Aretha, Miami Sound Machine, Neil Diamond's "America." The routines have some standard tap-dance moves — sweep, flare, chorus-line kicking. But it's fast and sustained and choreographed down to the last wrist-flick. And square dancing's genes can be seen in the upright, square-shouldered postures on the floor, a kind of florally enfolding tendency to the choreography, some of which features high-speed promenades. But it's adrenaline-dancing, meth-paced and exhausting to watch because your own feet move; and it's erotic in a way that makes MTV look lame. The cloggers' feet are too fast to be seen, really, but they all tap out the exact same rhythm. A typical routine's is something like: *ta*tatata*ta*tatata*tatata*. The variations around the basic rhythm are baroque. When they kick or spin, the two-beat absence of tap complexifies the pattern.

The audience is packed in right to the edge of the portable hardwood flooring. The teams are mostly married couples. The men are either rail-thin or have big hanging guts. A couple of the men are great fluid Astaire-like dancers, but mostly it's the women who compel. The males have constant sunny smiles, but the women look orgasmic; they're the really serious ones, transported. Their yips and whoops are involuntary, pure exclamation. They are arousing. The audience claps savvily on the backbeat and whoops when the women do. It's almost all folks from the ag and livestock shows — the flannel shirts, khaki pants, seed caps, and freckles. The spectators are soaked in sweat and extremely happy. I think this is the ag-community's Special Treat, a chance here to cut loose a little while their animals sleep in the heat. The psychic transactions between cloggers and crowd seem representative of the Fair as a whole: a culture talking to itself, presenting credentials for its own inspection. This is just a smaller and specialized rural Us — bean farmers and herbicide brokers and 4-H sponsors and people who drive pickup trucks because they really need them. They eat non-Fair food from insulated hampers and drink beer and pop and stomp in perfect time and put their hands on neighbors' shoulders to shout in their ear while the cloggers twirl and fling sweat on the crowd.

There are no black people in the Twilight Ballroom. The looks on the younger ag-kids' faces have this awakened astonished aspect, like they didn't realize their own race could dance like this. Three married couples from Rantoul, wearing full Western bodysuits the color of raw coal, weave an incredible filigree of high-speed tap around Aretha's "R-E-S-P-E-C-T," and there's no hint of racial irony in the room; the song has been made these people's own, emphatically. This '90s version of clogging does have something sort of pugnaciously white about it, a kind of performative nose-thumbing at Jackson and Hammer. There's an atmosphere in the room — not racist, but aggressively white. It's hard to describe. The atmosphere's the same at a lot of rural Midwest public events. It's not like if a black person came in he'd be ill-treated; it's more like it would just never occur to a black person to come in here.

I can barely hold the tablet to scribble journalistic impressions, the floor's rumbling under so many boots and sneakers. The record player's old-fashioned and the loudspeakers are shitty and it all sounds fantastic. Two little girls are playing jacks under the table I'm next to. Two of the dancing Rantoul wives are fat, but with great legs. Who could practice this kind of dancing as much as they must and stay fat? I think maybe rural Midwestern women are just congenitally big. But these people clogging get *down*. And they do it as a troupe, a collective, with none of the narcissistic look-at-me grandstanding of great dancers in rock clubs. They hold hands and whirl each other around and in and out, tapping like mad, their torsos upright and almost formal, as if only incidentally attached to the blur of legs below. It goes on and on. I'm rooted to my stool. Each team seems the best yet. On the crowd's other side across the floor I can see the old poultry farmer, he of the carny-hatred and electrified wallet. He's still got his billed poultry cap on, making a megaphone of his hands to whoop with the women, leaning way forward in his geriatric scooter, body bobbing like he's stomping in time while his little black boots stay clamped in their stays.

08/15/1636h. Trying to hurry to Grandstand; trapped in masses on central path out past FoodaRama. I'm eating a corn dog cooked in 100% soybean oil. I can hear the hornety engines of the U.S.A.C. 100 race, which must have started quite a while ago. Huge plume of track-dust hanging over Grandstand. Distant tinny burble of excited PA announcer. The corn dog tastes strongly of soybean oil, which itself tastes like corn oil that's been strained through an old gym towel. Tickets for the race are an obscene $13.50. Baton-twirling is *still* under way in the McD.'s tent. A band called Captain Rat and the Blind Rivets is playing at the Lincoln Stage, and as the path's mass goes by I can see dancers in there. They look jagged and arrhythmic and blank, bored in that hip young East-Coast-taught way, facing in instead of out, not touching their partners. The people not dancing don't even look at them, and after the clogging the whole thing looks unspeakably lonely and numb.

08/15/1645h. The official name of the race is the William "Wild Bill" Oldani Memorial 100 Sprint Car Race of the Valvoline-U.S.A.C. Silver Crown Series' Tru-Value Championship Circuit. The Grandstand seats 9800 and is packed. The noise is beyond belief. The race is nearly over: the electric sign on the infield says LAP 92. The board says the leader is #26, except his black-and-green SKOAL car's in the middle of the pack. Apparently he's lapped people. The crowd's mostly men, very tan, smoking, mustaches, billed caps with automotive associations. Most of the spectators wear earplugs; the ones in the real know wear those thick airline-worker noise-filter earmuffs. The seventeen-page program is mostly impenetrable. There are either 49 or 50 cars, called either Pro Dirt or Silver Crown cars, and they're basically go-carts from hell, with a soapbox-derby chassis and huge dragster tires, gleaming tangles of pipes and spoilers jutting out all over, and unabashedly phallic bulges

up front, where I suspect the engines are. What I know about auto racing could be inscribed with a dry Magic Marker on the lip of a Coke
bottle. The program says these models are what they used to race at
Indy in the 1950s. It's unclear whether that means these specific cars
or this genre of car or what. I'm pretty sure "Indy" refers to the Indianapolis 500. The cars' cockpits are open and webbed in straps and
roll bars; the drivers wear helmets the same color as their cars, with
white ski-masky things over their faces to keep out the choking dust.
The cars come in all hues. Most look to be sponsored by either Skoal or
Marlboro. Pit crews in surgical white lean out into the track and flash
obscure commands written on little chalkboards. The infield is clot-
ted with trailers and tow trucks and Officials' stands and electric signs.
Women in skimpy tops stand on different trailers, seeming very partisan
indeed. It's all very confusing. Certain facts in the program just don't
add up — like the Winner's Purse is only $9200, yet each car supposedly
represents a six-figure annual investment for various sponsors. Whatever they invest in, it isn't mufflers. I can barely take my hands off my
ears long enough to turn the program's pages. The cars sound almost
like jets — that insectile whine — but with a diesely, lawn-mowerish
component you can feel in your skull. Part of the problem is the raw
concrete of the Grandstand's seating; another's the fact that the seating's on just one side of the Grandstand, on the straightaway. When
the main mass of cars passes it's unendurable; your very skeleton hurts
from the noise, and your ears are still belling when they come around
again. The cars go like mad bats on the straightaways and then shift
down for the tight turns, their rear tires wobbling in the dirt. Certain
cars pass other cars, and some people cheer when they do. Down at the
bottom of my section of seats a little boy held up on a cement fence-
support by his father is rigid, facing away from the track, his hands
clamped over his ears so hard his elbows stick way out, and his face
is a rictus of pain as the cars go by. The little boy and I sort of rictus
at each other. A fine dirty dust hangs in the air and coats everything,
tongues included. Then all of a sudden binoculars come out and everyone stands as there's some sort of screeching slide and crash on a far
turn, all the way across the infield; and firemen in full-length slickers
and hats go racing out there in fire trucks, and the PA voice's pitch goes
way up but is still incomprehensible, and a man with those airline

earmuffs in the Officials' stands leans out and flails at the air with a bright-yellow flag, and the go-carts throttle down to autobahn speed, and the Official Pace Car (a Trans Am) comes out and leads them around, ahd everybody stands up, and I stand too. It's impossible to see anything but a swizzle stick of smoke above the far turn, and the engine noise is endurable and the PA silent, and the relative quiet hangs there while we all wait for news, and I look around hard at all the faces below the raised binoculars, but it's not at all clear what sort of news we're all hoping for.

08/15/1730h. Ten-minute line for an I.D.C. milkshake. Oily blacktop stink on heated paths. I ask a little kid to describe the taste of his Funnel Cake and he runs away. Ears still mossily ringing — everything sounds kind of car-phonish. Display of a 17.6-lb zucchini squash outside the Agri-Industries Pavilion. One big zucchini, all right. Several of the Dessert Tent ladies are at the Tupperware Retrospective (no kidding) right nearby, though, and I make myself scarce in a hurry. In the Coliseum, the only historical evidence of the Tractor Pull is huge ideograms of tire tracks, mounds of scored dirt, dark patches of tobacco juice, smells of burnt rubber and oil. Two buildings over is a curiously non-State-Pride-related exhibit, by the Harley Davidson Corporation, of "Motorcycles Of Distinction." Also a deltiology exhibit — card after card, some back from the 1940s, mostly of crops, thunderclouds massing at horizons, flat sweeps of very black land. In a broad tent next door's the "Motorsport Spectacular Exhibition," which is kind of surreal: a whole lot of really shiny and fast-looking sports cars in utter stasis, just sitting there, hoods up, innards exposed, clusters of older men in berets studying the cars with great intensity, some with white gloves and jeweler's loupes. Between two minor corporate tents is the serendipitous snout of the "Sertoma Mobile Hearing Test Trailer," inside which a woman with a receding hairline scores me overdecibeled but aurally hale. Fifteen whole minutes both in- and outside the huge STATE COMPTROLLER ROLAND BURRIS tent fails to uncover the tent's function. Next door, though, is a bus on display from the city of Peoria's All-Ethanol Bus System; it is painted to resemble a huge ear of corn. I don't know whether actual fleets of green-and-yellow corn-buses are deployed in Peoria or whether this is just a stunt.

08/15/1800h. Back again at the seemingly inescapable Club Mickey D's. All signs of baton-twirlers and fallen spectators have been erased. The tent's now set up for Illinois Golden Gloves Boxing. Out on the floor is a kind of square made up of four boxing rings. The rings are made out of clothesline and poles anchored by cement-filled tires, one ring per age division — Sixteens, Fourteens, Twelves, Tens(!). Here's another unhyped but riveting spectacle. If you want to see genuine interhuman violence, go check out a Golden Gloves tourney. None of your adult pros' silky footwork or Rope-a-Dope defenses here. Here asses are thoroughly kicked in what are essentially playground brawls with white-tipped gloves and brain-shaped headguards. The combatants' tank tops say things like "Rockford Jr. Boxing" and "Elgin Fight Club." The rings' corners have stools for the kids to sit on and get worked over by their teams' coaches. The coaches look like various childhood friends of mine's abusive fathers — florid, blue-jawed, bull-necked, flinty-eyed, the kind of men who bowl, watch TV in their underwear, and oversee sanctioned brawls. Now a fighter's mouthguard goes flying out of the Fourteens' ring, end over end, trailing strings of spit, and the crowd around that ring howls. In the Sixteens' ring is a Springfield kid, a local hero, one Darrell Hall, against a slim fluid Latino named Sullivano from Joliet. Hall outweighs Sullivano by a good twenty pounds. Hall also looks like just about every kid who ever beat me up in high school, right down to the wispy mustache and upper lip's cruel twist. The crowd around the Sixteens' ring is all his friends — guys with muscle shirts and varsity gym shorts and gelled hair, girls in cutoff overalls and complex systems of barrettes and scrunchies. There are repeated shouts of "Kick his *ass* Darrell!" The Latino sticks and moves. Somebody in this tent is smoking a joint, I can smell. The Sixteens can actually box. The ceiling's lights are bare bulbs in steel cones, hanging cockeyed from a day of batons. Everybody here pours sweat. A few people look askance at the little clicker I carry. The reincarnation of every high school cheerleader I ever pined for is in the Sixteens' crowd. The girls cry out and sort of frame their face in their hands whenever Darrell Hall gets hit. I do not know why cutoff overall shorts have evaded the East Coast's fashion ken; they are devastating. The fight in Fourteens is stopped for a moment to let the ref wipe a gout of blood from one kid's glove. Sullivano glides and jabs, sort of orbiting Hall. Hall is implacable, a hunched and feral fighter, boring in. Air explodes through his nose when he lands a blow. He keeps trying to back the Latino against the clothesline. People fan themselves with wood-handled fans from the Democratic Party. Mosquitoes work the crowd. The refs keep slapping at their necks. The rains have been bad, and the mosquitoes this August are the bad kind, big and vaguely hairy, field-bred, rapacious, the kind that can swarm on a calf overnight and the farmer finds his calf in the morning splay-legged and bled kosher. This actually happens. Mosquitoes are not to be fucked with out here. (East-Coast friends laugh at my dread of mosquitoes, and they make fun of the little battery-powered box I carry whenever I'm outside at night. Even in like NYC or Boston I carry it. It's from an obscure catalogue and produces a sound like a dragonfly — a.k.a. *odonata anisoptera,* sworn eternal foe to all mosquitoes everywhere — a faint high-speed clicking that sends any right-thinking mosquito out of its mind with fear. On East 55th, carrying the little box is maybe a bit neurotic; here, with me ripe and sweaty and tall in this crowd, the good old trusty clicker saves more than just my ass.) I can also see the Tens from this vantage, a vicious free-for-all between two tiny kids whose headguards make their heads look too big for their bodies. Neither ten-year-old has any interest in defense. Their shoes' toes touch as they windmill at each other, scoring at will. Scary dads chew gum in their corners. One kid's mouthguard keeps falling out. Now the Sixteens' crowd explodes as their loutish Darrell catches Sullivano with an uppercut that puts him on his bottom. Sullivano gamely rises, but his knees wobble and he won't face the ref. Hall raises both arms and faces the crowd, disclosing a missing incisor. The girls betray their cheerleading backgrounds by clapping and jumping up and down at the same time. Hall shakes his gloves at the ceiling as several girls call his name, and you can feel it in the air's very ions: Darrell Hall is going to get laid before the night's over.

The digital thermometer in the Ronald-god's big left hand reads 93° at 1815h. Behind him, big ominous scoop-of-coffee-ice-cream clouds are piling up at the sky's western reef, but the sun's still above them and very much a force. People's shadows on the paths are getting pointy. It's the part of the day when little kids go into jagged crying fits from what their parents naïvely call exhaustion. Cicadas chirr in the grass by the tent. The ten-year-olds stand literally toe to toe and whale the living shit out of each other. It's the sort of implausibly savage mutual beating you see in fight-movies. Their ring now has the largest crowd. The fight'll be all but impossible to score. But then it's over in an instant at the second intermission when one of the little boys, sitting on his stool, being whispered to by a coach with tattooed forearms, suddenly throws up. Prodigiously. For no apparent reason. It's kind of surreal. Vomit flies all over. Kids in the crowd go "Eeeyuuu." Several partially digested food-booth items are identifiable — maybe that's the apparent reason. The sick fighter starts to cry. His scary coach and the ref wipe him down and help him from the ring, not ungently. His opponent tentatively puts up his arms.

08/15/1930h. And there is, in this state with its origin and reason in food, a strong digestive subtheme running all through the '93 Fair. In a way, we're all here to be swallowed up. The Main Gate's maw admits us, slow tight-packed masses move peristaltically along complex systems of branching paths, engage in complex cash-and-energy transfers at the villi alongside the paths, and are finally — both filled and depleted — expelled out of exits designed for heavy flow. And there are the exhibits of food and of the production of food, the unending food-booths and the peripatetic consumption of food. The public Potties and communal urinals. The moist body-temp heat of the Fairgrounds. The livestock judged and applauded as future food while the animals stand in their own manure, chewing cuds.

Plus there are those great literalizers of all metaphor, little kids — boxers and fudge-gluttons, sunstroke-casualties, those who overflow just from the adrenaline of the Specialness of it all — the rural Midwesterners of tomorrow, all throwing up.

And so the old heavo-ho is the last thing I see at Golden Gloves Boxing and then the first thing I see at Happy Hollow, right at sunset. Standing with stupid Barney tablet on the Midway, looking up at the Ring of Fire — a set of flame-colored train cars sent around and around the inside of a 100-foot neon hoop, the operator stalling the train at the top and hanging the patrons upside down, jackknifed over their seatbelts, with loose change and eyeglasses raining down — looking up, I witness a single thick coil of vomit arc from a car; it describes a 100-foot spiral and lands with a meaty splat between two young girls whose T-shirts say something about volleyball and who look from the ground to each with expressions of slapstick horror. And when the flame-train finally brakes at the ramp, a mortified-looking little kid totters off, damp and green, staggering over toward a Lemon Shake-Up stand.

I am basically scribbling impressions as I jog. I've put off a real survey of the Near-Death Experiences until my last hour, and I want to get everything catalogued before the sun sets. I've had some distant looks at the nighttime Hollow from up on the Press Lot's ridge and have an idea that being down here in the dark, amid all this rotating neon and the mechanical clowns and plunging machinery's roar and piercing screams and barkers' amplified pitches and high-volume rock, would be like every bad Sixties movie's depiction of a bum acid trip. It strikes me hardest in the Hollow that I am not spiritually Midwestern anymore, and no longer young — I do not like crowds, screams, loud noise, or heat. I'll endure these things if I have to, but they're no longer my idea of a Special Treat or sacred Community-interval. The crowds in the Hollow — mostly high school couples, local toughs, and kids in single-sex packs, as the demographics of the Fair shift to prime time — seem radically gratified, vivid, actuated, sponges for sensuous data, feeding on it all somehow. It's the first time I've felt truly lonely at the Fair.

Nor, I have to say, do I understand why some people will pay money to be careened and suspended and dropped and whipped back and forth at high speeds and hung upside down until they vomit. It seems to me like paying to be in a traffic accident. I do not get it; never have. It's not a regional or cultural thing. I think it's a matter of basic neurological makeup. I think the world divides neatly into those who are excited by the managed induction of terror and those who are not. I do not find terror exciting. I find it terrifying. One of my basic life goals is to subject my nervous system to as little total terror as possible. The cruel paradox of course is that this kind of makeup usually goes hand in hand with a delicate nervous system that's extremely easy to terrify. I'm pretty sure I'm more frightened looking up at the Ring of Fire than the patrons are riding it.

Happy Hollow has not one but two Tilt-a-Whirls. An experience called Wipe Out straps customers into fixed seats on a big lit disc that spins with a wobble like a coin that won't quite lie down. The infamous Pirate Ship puts forty folks in a plastic galley and swings it in a pendulous arc until they're facing straight up and then down. There's vomit on the sides of the Pirate Ship, too. The carny operating the P. Ship is made to wear an eyepatch and parrot and hook, on the tip of which hook burns an impaled Marlboro.

The operator of the Funhouse is slumped in a plastic control booth that reeks of sinsemilla.

The 104-foot Giant Gondola Wheel is a staid old Ferris wheel that puts you facing your seatmate in a kind of steel teacup. Its rotation is stately, but the cars at the top look like little lit thimbles, and you can hear thin female screams from up there as their dates grab the teacups' sides and joggle.

The lines are the longest for the really serious Near-Death Experiences: Ring of Fire, The Zipper, Hi Roller — which latter runs a high-speed train around the inside of an ellipse that is itself spinning at right angles to the train's motion. The crowds are dense and reek of repellent. Boys in fishnet shirts clutch their dates as they walk. There's something intensely *public* about young Midwestern couples. The girls have tall teased hair and bee-stung lips, and their eye makeup runs in the heat and gives them a vampirish aspect. The overt sexuality of modern high school girls is not just a Coastal thing. There's a Midwestern term, "drape," for the kind of girl who hangs onto her boyfriend in public like he's a tree in a hurricane. A lot of the girls on the Midway are drapes. I swing my trusty dragonfly-clicker before me in broad censerish arcs as I jog. I'm on a strict and compressed timetable. The Amour Express sends another little train at 60+ mph around a topologically deformed ring, half of which is enclosed in a fiberglass tunnel with neon hearts and arrows. Bug zappers up on the lightpoles are doing a brisk business. A fallen packet of Trojans lies near the row of Lucite cubes in which slack-jawed cranes try to pick up jewelry. The Hollow's basically an east-west vector, but I jog in rough figure-eights, passing certain venues several times. The Funhouse operator's sneakers are sticking out of his booth; the rest of him is out of view. Kids are running into the Funhouse for free. For a moment I'm convinced I've spotted Alan Thicke, of all celebrities, shooting an air rifle at a row of 2-D cardboard Iraqis for a *Jurassic Park* stuffed animal.

It seems journalistically irresponsible to describe the Hollow's rides without experiencing at least one of them firsthand. The Kiddie Kopter is a carousel of miniature Sikorsky prototypes rotating at a sane and dignified clip. The propellers on each helicopter rotate as well. My copter is admittedly a bit snug, even with my knees drawn up to my chest. I get kicked off the ride when the whole machine's radical tilt reveals that I weigh quite a bit more than the maximum 100 pounds, and I have to say that both the carny in charge and the other kids on the ride were unnecessarily snide about the whole thing. Each ride has its own PA speaker with its own charge of adrenalizing rock; the Kiddie Kopter's speaker is playing George Michael's "I Want Your Sex" as the little bastards go around. The late-day Hollow itself is an enormous sonic mash from which different sounds take turns protruding — mostly whistles, sirens, calliopes, mechanized clown-cackles, heavy-metal tunes, human screams hard to distinguish from recorded screams.

It isn't Alan Thicke, on closer inspection.

Both the Thunderboltz and the Octopus hurl free-spinning modular cars around a topologically complex plane. The Thunderboltz's north side and entrance ramp show still more evidence of gastric distress. Then there's the Gravitron, an enclosed, top-shaped structure inside which is a rubberized chamber that spins so fast you're mashed against the wall like a fly on a windshield. It's basically a centrifuge for the centrifugal separation of people's brains from those brains' blood supply. Watching people come out of the Gravitron is not a pleasant experience at all, and you do not want to know what the ground around the exit looks like. A small boy stands on one foot tugging the operator's khaki sleeve, crying that he lost a shoe in there. The best description of the carnies' tan is that they're somehow *sinisterly* tan. I notice that many of them have the low brow and prognathous jaw typically associated with Fetal Alcohol Syndrome. The carny operating the Scooter — bumper cars, fast, savage, underinsulated, a sure trip to the chiropractor — has been slumped in the same position in the same chair every time I've seen him, staring past the frantic cars and tearing up used ride-tickets with the vacant intensity of someone on a Locked Ward. I lean casually against his platform's railing so that my Credentials dangle prominently and ask him in a neighborly way how he keeps from going out of his freaking mind with the boredom of his job. He turns his head very slowly, revealing a severe facial tic: "The fuck you talking bout."

The same two carnies as before are at The Zipper's controls, in the exact same clothes, looking up into the full cars and elbowing each other. The Midway smells of machine oil and fried food, smoke and Cutter repellent and mall-bought adolescent perfume and ripe trash in the bee-swarmed cans. The very Nearest-to-Death ride looks to be the Kamikaze, way down at the western end near the Zyklon roller coaster. Its neon sign has a grinning skull with a headband and says simply KAMIKAZE. It's a 70-foot pillar of white-painted iron with two 50-foot hammer-shaped arms hanging down, one on either side. The cars are at the end of these arms, twelve-seaters enclosed in clear plastic. The two arms swing ferociously around, as in 360°, vertically, and in opposite directions, so that at the top and bottom of every rotation it looks like your car is going to get smashed up against the other car and you can see faces in the other car hurtling toward you, gray with fright and squishy with G's. An eight-ticket, four-dollar waking nightmare.

No. Now I've found the worst one. It wasn't even here yesterday. It must have been brought in special. It may not even be part of the carnival proper. It's the SKY COASTER. The SKY COASTER stands regally aloof at the Hollow's far western edge, just past the Uphill-Bowling-for-Dinnerware game, in a kind of grotto formed by Blomsness-Thebault trailers and dismantled machinery. At first all you can see is the very-yellow of some piece of heavy construction equipment, then after a second there's some other, high-overhead stuff that from the east is just a tangle of Expressionist shadows against the setting sun. A small but steady stream of Fairgoers leads into the SKY COASTER grotto.

It's a 175-foot construction crane, a BRH-200, one of the really big mothers, with a tank's traction belts instead of wheels, a canary-yellow cab, and a long proboscis of black steel, 200 feet long, canted upward at maybe 70°. This is half of the SKY COASTER. The other half is a 100-foot+ tower assembly of cross-hatched iron that's been erected a couple hundred yards north of the crane. There's a folding table in front of the clothesline cordoning off the crane, and there's a line of people at the table. The woman taking their money is fiftyish and a compelling advertisement for sunscreen. Behind her on a vivid blue tarp are two meaty blond guys in SKY COASTER T-shirts helping the next customer strap himself into what looks like a combination straitjacket and utility belt, bristling with hooks and clips. It's not yet entirely clear what's going on. From here the noise of the Hollow behind is both deafening and muffled, like high tide behind a dike. My Media Guide, sweated into the shape of a buttock from my pocket, says: "If you thought bungee jumping was a thrill, wait until you soar high above the Fairgrounds on SKY COASTER. The rider is fastened securely into a full-body harness that hoists them [sic, hopefully] onto a tower and releases them to swing in a pendulum-like motion while taking in a spectacular view of the Fairgrounds below." The hand-printed signs at the folding table are more telling: "$40.00. AMEX Visa MC. NO REFUNDS. NO STOPPING HALF WAY UP." The two guys are leading the customer up the stairs of a construction platform maybe ten feet high. One guy's at each elbow, and I realize they're helping hold the customer up. Who would pay $40.00 for an experience you have to be held up even to walk toward? Why pay money to cause something to occur you will be grateful to survive? I simply do not get it. Plus there's also something slightly off about this customer, odd. For one thing, he's wearing tinted aviator glasses. No one in the rural Midwest wears aviator glasses, tinted or otherwise. Then I see what it really is. He's wearing $400 Banfi loafers. Without socks. This guy, now lying prone on the platform below the crane, is *from the East Coast*. He's a *ringer*. I almost want to shout it. A woman's on the blue tarp, already in harness, rubber-kneed, waiting her turn. A steel cable descends from the tip of the crane's proboscis, on its end a fist-sized clip. Another cable leads from the crane's cab along the ground to the tower, up through ring-tipped pitons all up the tower's side, and over a pulley right at the top, another big clip on the end. One of the blond guys waves the tower's cable down and brings it over to the platform. Both the crane's and tower's cables' clips are attached to the back of the East-Coast man's harness, fastened and locked. The man's trying to look around behind him to see what-all's attached to him as the two big blonds leave the platform. Yet another blond man in the crane's cab throws a lever, and the tower's cable pulls tight in the grass and up the tower's side and down. The crane's cable stays slack as the man is lifted into the air by the tower's cable. The harness covers his shorts and shirt, so he looks babe-naked as he rises. The one cable sings with tension as the East-Coaster is pulled slowly to the top of the tower. He's still stomach-down, limbs wriggling. At a certain height he starts to look like livestock in a sling. You can tell he's trying to swallow until his face gets too small to see. Finally he's all the way up at the top of the tower, his ass against the cable's pulley, trying not to writhe. I can barely take notes. They cruelly leave him up there awhile, slung, a smile of slack cable between him and the crane's tip. The grotto's crowd mutters and points, shading eyes against the red sun. One teenage boy describes the sight to another teenage boy as "Harsh." I myself am constructing a mental list of the violations I would undergo before I'd let anyone haul me ass-first to a great height and swing me like high-altitude beef. One of the blond guys has a bullhorn and is playing to the crowd's suspense, calling up to the slung East-Coaster: "Are. You. Ready." The East-Coaster's response-noises are more bovine than human. His tinted aviator glasses hang askew from just one ear; he doesn't bother to fix them. I can see what's going to happen. They're going to throw a lever and detach the tower-cable's clip, and the man in sockless Banfis will free-fall for what'll seem forever, until the crane's cable's slack is taken up and the line takes his weight and goes tight behind him and swings him way out over the grounds to the south, his arc's upward half almost as high as the tower was, and then he'll fall all over again, back, and get caught and swung the other way, back and forth, the man prone at the arc's trough and seeming to stand at either apex, swinging back and forth and erect and prone against a rare-meat sunset. And just as the crane's cab's blond reaches for his lever and the crowd mightily inhales, just then, I lose my nerve, in my very last moment at the Fair — I recall my childhood's serial nightmare of being swung or whipped in an arc that threatens to come full circle — and I decline to be part of this, even as witness — and I find, again, in extremis, access to childhood's other worst nightmare, the only sure way to obliterate all; and the sun and sky and plummeting Yuppie go out like a light.

1993

greatly exaggerated

In the 1960s the poststructuralist metacritics came along and turned literary aesthetics on its head by rejecting assumptions their teachers had held as self-evident and making the whole business of interpreting texts way more complicated by fusing theories of creative discourse with hardcore positions in metaphysics. Whether you're a fan of Barthes, Foucault, de Man, and Derrida or not, you at least have to credit them with this fertile miscegenation of criticism and philosophy: critical theory is now a bona fide area of study for young American philosophers interested in both Continental poetics and Anglo-American analytic practice. H. L. Hix is one of these young (judging by his author photo, about twelve) U.S. philosophers, and I'm pretty sure that his 1992 *Morte d'Author: An Autopsy* is a Ph.D. dissertation that was more than good enough to see print as part of Temple University Press's "The Arts and Their Philosophies" series.

One of the wickedly fun things about following literary theory in the 1990s is going to be watching young critics/philosophers now come along and attack their poststructuralist teachers by criticizing assumptions those teachers have held as self-evident. This is just what Professor Hix is doing with one of the true clarion-calls that marked the shift from New Criticism and structuralism to deconstruction, Roland Barthes' 1968 announcement of "The Death of the Author." Barthes' seminal essay has prompted twenty-three years of vigorous interjournal debate among European theorists (pro-death) and U.S. philosophers (anti-death, mostly), a debate that Hix has impressively compiled and arranged between two covers, and a debate that he has, rather less impressively, sought to resolve by accusing all parties of not being nearly complicated enough in their understanding of the term "author"'s in- and extensions.

If you're not a critical-theory jockey, then to appreciate why the metaphysical viability of the author is a big deal you have to recognize the difference between a writer — the person whose choices and actions account for a text's features — and an author — the entity whose intentions are taken to be responsible for a text's meaning. Hix, paraphrasing the ever-limpid Alexander Nehamas, uses the old saw about monkeys and typewriters to illustrate the distinction: "It is surely possible, though obviously unlikely, that a thousand monkeys at a thousand typewriters could by sheer chance produce an encyclopedia. If they did, they would be able to account for all the features of the text: Everything in the text was put there . . . by monkeys at Smith-Coronas. But . . . there would be no way to account for the meaning of the text's features, because . . . the monkeys could not have meant anything by their typing." Authors are monkeys who mean.

And for Romantic and early-twentieth-century critics, textual interpretation was author-based. For Wordsworth, the critic regards a text as the creative instantiation of a writer's very self. Rather more clinically, I. A. Richards saw criticism as all and only an effort to nail down the "relevant mental condition" of a text's creator. Axiomatic for both schools was the idea of a real *author*, an entity for whose definition most critics credit Hobbes's *Leviathan*, which describes real authors as persons who, first, accept responsibility for a text and, second, "own" that text, i.e. retain the right to determine its meaning. It's just this definition of "author" that Barthes in '68 was trying to refute, arguing with respect to the first criterion that a writer cannot determine his text's consequences enough to be really responsible (Salinger wasn't hauled into court as an accessory when John Lennon was shot), and with respect to the second that the writer's not the text's owner in Hobbes's sense because it is really critical *readers* who decide and thus determine what a piece of writing means.

It's Barthes' second argument here that's the real poststructural death certificate, and this line is really just an involution of the New Critics' WWII-era reaction against Richards and the Romantics. The New Critics, rather level-headedly at first, sought to dethrone the author by attacking what they called "the Intentional Fallacy." Writers are sometimes wrong about what their texts mean, or sometimes have no idea what they really mean. Sometimes the text's meaning even changes for the writer. It doesn't matter what the writer means, basically, for the New Critics; it matters only what the text says. This critical overthrow of creative intent set the stage for the poststructural show that opened a couple decades later. The deconstructionists ("deconstructionist" and "poststructuralist" mean the same thing, by the way: "poststructuralist" is what you call a deconstructionist who doesn't want to be called a deconstructionist), explicitly following Husserl and Brentano and Heidegger the same way the New Critics had co-opted Hegel, see the debate over the ownership of meaning as a skirmish in a larger war in Western philosophy over the idea that presence and unity are ontologically prior to expression. There's been this long-standing deluded presumption, they think, that if there is an utterance then there must exist a unified, efficacious presence that causes and owns that utterance. The poststructuralists attack what they see as a post-Platonic prejudice in favor of presence over absence and speech over writing. We tend to trust speech over writing because of the immediacy of the speaker: he's right there, and we can grab him by the lapels and look into his face and figure out just exactly what one single thing he means. But the reason why the poststructuralists are in the literary theory business at all is that they see writing, not speech, as more faithful to the metaphysics of true expression. For Barthes, Derrida, and Foucault, writing is a better animal than speech because it is iterable; it is iterable because it is abstract; and it is abstract because it is a function not of presence but of absence: the reader's absent when the writer's writing, and the writer's absent when the reader's reading.

For the deconstructionist, then, a writer's circumstances and intentions are indeed a part of the "context" of a text, but context imposes no real cinctures on the text's meaning, because meaning in language requires a cultivation of absence rather than presence, involves not the imposition but the erasure of consciousness. This is so because these guys — Derrida following Heidegger and Barthes Mallarmé and Foucault God knows who — see literary language as not a tool but an environment. A writer does not wield language; he is subsumed in it.

Language speaks us; writing writes; etc. Hix makes little mention of Heidegger's *Poetry, Language, Thought* or Derrida's *Margins of Philosophy*, where all this stuff is set out most clearly, but he does quote enough Barthes — "To write is . . . to reach that point where only language acts, 'performs,' and not 'me'" — so you get the idea that author-as-owner is not just superfluous but contradictory, and enough Foucault — "The writing of our day has freed itself from the necessity of 'expression'; [it is] an interplay of signs, regulated less by the content it signifies than by the very nature of the signifier" — so you can see that even the New Critics' Holy Text disappears as the unitary lodestone of meaning and value. For Hix's teachers, trying to attribute writing's meaning to a static text or a human author is like trying to knit your own body, your own *needles*. Hix has an even better sartorial image: "Previously, the text was a cloth to be unraveled by the reader; if the cloth were unwound all the way, the reader would find the author holding the other end. But Barthes makes the text a shroud, and no one, not even a corpse, is holding the other end."

Hix himself is a good weaver; *Morte d'Author* is a tight piece of work. Its first half is a critical overview of some of the major positions on authorial vital signs. Not only is there Hobbes and Frye on what an author is, there's Foucault v. Nehamas on just how to recognize what an author is, and Barthes v. William Gass on whether to even bother trying to find an author. There are also brief critical summaries of Derrida, Culler, Stecker, Booth, and Burke. Hix's discussion isn't comprehensive, quite: Heidegger and Hegel are scarcely mentioned, Husserl (a major influence on Derrida) is absent, as are such important contemporary figures in the debate as Stanley Cavell (whose *Must We Mean What We Say?* is at least as important to Hix's subject as Booth's *Rhetoric of Fiction*), Paul de Man, Edward Said, and Gayatri Spivak. And Hix's analysis of the players he does cover suffers from the scholarly anality that's so common to published dissertations, an obsession with the jots and tittles of making excruciatingly clear what he's saying and where he's going. Wearying t-crossings like "I will isolate three of his claims in particular, disagreeing with two of them and agreeing with the other," and microprecise critiques like "Wimsatt and Beardsley's error may be hidden behind the passive voice; Cain's is hidden behind the present tense" make the reader wish Hix's editor had helped him delete gestures that seem directed at thesis committees rather than paying customers.

Hix's obsessive attention to detail is perhaps justified, though, by the fact that *Morte d'Author* aims to be more than just a compendium of views on the dead-author controversy. Hix promulgates his own theory of authorship, one that he claims clears up the debate and lays the foundation for a more sophisticated approach to literary criticism in the wake of deconstructionism's plumeocide. Though his solution to the problem isn't the universal solvent he leads the reader to expect, his project is still a neat example of that modern commissure where Continental theory and analytic practice fuse. What Hix offers as a resolution to the debate is a combination of a Derridean metaphysics that rejects assumptions of unified causal presence and a Wittgensteinian analytic method of treating actual habits of discourse as a touchstone for figuring out what certain terms really mean and do.

Hix, early in his summary of modern theories about the author, divides the extant views into two opposed camps. The anti-death guys still see the author as the "origin" / "cause" of a text, and the pro-death guys see the author as the "function" / "effect" of a text. Hix posits that both sides of the debate "mistake . . . one aspect of the author for the whole." All the debaters have oversimplified what "author" really means. They've done this because they've made what Hix calls "the assumption of homogeneity," simplistically regarding "author" as referring to "a unitary entity or phenomenon." If we examine the way "author" is really used in critical discourse, Hix argues, we are forced to see the word's denotation as really a complex interaction of the activities of the "historical writer" (the guy with the pencil), that writer's influences and circumstances, the narrative persona adopted in a text, the extant text itself, the critical atmosphere that surrounds and informs the interpretation of the text, the individual reader's actual interpretations of the text, and even the beliefs and actions consequent to that interpretation. In other words, the entire post-1968 squabble has been pointless, because the theorists involved haven't bothered to consider what "author" truly means and embraces before they set about interring or resuscitating the patient.

The wicked fun here is to watch how Hix uses the deconstructionists' own instruments against them. Derrida's attack on the presumption of metaphysical presence in literary expression forms Hix's blueprint for attacking the assumption of homogeneity, and Hix's attempt to "undermine" and "overturn" an essentially binary opposition of author-as-cause v. author-as-effect is a textbook poststructural move. What's more original and more interesting is Hix's use of a kind of Austin/Wittgenstein ordinary-language analysis on the extension of the predicate "author." Instead of joining his teachers in the metaphysical stratosphere they zoom around in, Hix quite plausibly suggests that we examine how smart readers really do use the term "author" in various kinds of critical discourse in order to figure out what the nature of the beast is before we whip out the spade or the de-fib paddles. His project, as he outlines it, seems both sensible and fun to watch.

Hix's actual analysis of author-ity is way less sensible and way *way* less fun. For one thing, his actual argumentation is wildly uneven. In the same breath, he'll recommend identification as necessary for determining viability, then say that a thorough definition of "author" is prima facie important because no satisfactory theory of text and reading is possible until there's a solid theory of the author, which begs the poststructuralists' whole question of whether a text even requires an author in order to be and to mean. Hix clearly *does* think a text requires an author, and so what pretends to be a compromise between the Bury-Him and the Save-Him camps is really a sneaky pro-life apology.

But the incredibly baroque definition of "author" Hix comes up with by the book's final chapter, "Post-Mortem," seems finally to commit the very homicide Barthes called for. The difference is that where Barthes simply argued that the idea of an author is now for critical purposes otiose, Hix so broadens the denotation of "author" that the word ceases really to identify anything. Nouns, after all, are supposed to pick things out. But while Hix claims that "to deny the assumption of homogeneity, though it entails that the historical writer is not the exclusive locus of meaning, does not entail that meaning has no locus," he ends up preserving the idea of a meaning-locus by making that locus such a swirling soup of intricate actions and conditions and relations that he essentially erases the author by making the de-

notation of his signifier vacuous. It ends up being a kind of philosophical Westmorelandism: Hix destroys the author in order to save
him.

Though his conclusions do not resolve the problem they address,
Hix's attempts to organize and defend them yield some impressive
scholarly writing. He has a rare gift for the neat assembly of different
sides of questions, and his complex theory has the virtue of being able
to account for many of the ambiguities in the way we do in a fact make
such claims as that Luke is the author of the third Gospel, Jefferson is the
author of the Declaration of Independence, George Eliot is the author of
Middlemarch, and Franklin W. Dixon is the author of *The Hardy Boys at
Skeleton Cove.* His section on "Schizoscription" is a fascinating discussion of the "implied author" in first-person persona-lit like Browning's
"My Last Duchess" and Swift's "A Modest Proposal," and it affords, believe it or not, a genuinely intelligible theory of how irony works. And ingenious examples, like that of the brain-damaged patient in A. R. Luria's
The Man with the Shattered World who could write but not read what he
wrote, not only help Hix argue against the notion that the writer is the
ultimate "insider" with respect to his own work, they're also just plain
cool.

It's Hix's flair for images and examples that may make *Morte d'Author*
of interest to general lit.-lovers. His prose is often witty and conversational, and his talent for constructing test cases offers a welcome relief from the painstaking academic detail he tends to fall into. I'm not
sure just how much familiarity with twentieth-century literary theory
the book requires. Hix does, roundaboutly, give most of the background to the dead-author conundrum. But a reader who's not comfortable with ghastly jargon like Foucault's "The conception of *écriture*
sustains the privileges of the author through the safeguard of the *a
priori*" is going to get flummoxed, because Hix tends to toss quota-
tions like this around without much gloss. It's finally hard for me to
predict just whom, besides professional critics and hardcore theory-
wienies, 226 dense pages on whether the author lives is really going to interest. For those of us civilians who know in our gut that
writing is an act of communication between one human being and
another, the whole question seems sort of arcane. As William (anti-
death) Gass observes in *Habitations of the Word,* critics can try to

erase or over-define the author into anonymity for all sorts of technical, political, and philosophical reasons, and "this 'anonymity' may mean many things, but one thing which it cannot mean is that *no one did it*."

1992

David Lynch keeps his head

1   what movie this article is about

David Lynch's *Lost Highway*, written by Lynch and Barry Gifford, featuring Bill Pullman, Patricia Arquette, Balthazar Getty. Financed by CIBY 2000, France. ©1996 by one Asymmetrical Productions, Lynch's company, whose offices are right next door to Lynch's own house in the Hollywood Hills and whose logo, designed by Lynch, is a very cool graphic that looks like this:

Lost Highway is set in Los Angeles and the desertish terrain immediately inland from it. Actual shooting goes from December '95 through February '96. Lynch normally runs a Closed Set, with redundant security arrangements and an almost Masonic air of secrecy around his movies' productions, but I am allowed onto the *Lost Highway* set on 8–10 January 1996. This is not just because I'm a fanatical Lynch fan from way back, though I did make my pro-Lynch fanaticism known when the Asymmetrical people were trying to decide whether to let a writer onto the set. The fact is I was let onto *Lost Highway*'s set because of *Premiere* magazine's industry juice, and because there's rather a lot at stake for

Lynch and Asymmetrical on this movie (see Section 5), and they probably feel like they can't afford to indulge their allergy to PR and the Media Machine quite the way they have in the past.

2 what David Lynch is really like

I have absolutely no idea. I rarely got closer than five feet away from him and never talked to him. One of the minor reasons Asymmetrical Productions let me onto the set is that I don't even pretend to be journalist and have no idea how to interview somebody and saw no real point in trying to interview Lynch, which turned out perversely to be an advantage, because Lynch emphatically didn't want to be interviewed while *Lost Highway* was in production, because when he's shooting a movie he's incredibly busy and preoccupied and immersed and has very little attention or brain-space available for anything other than the movie. This may sound like PR bullshit, but it turns out to be true — e.g.:

The first time I lay actual eyes on the real David Lynch on the set of his movie, he's peeing on a tree. I am not kidding. This is on 8 January in West LA's Griffith Park, where some of *Lost Highway*'s exteriors and driving scenes are being shot. Lynch is standing in the bristly underbrush off the dirt road between the Base Camp's trailers and the set, peeing on a stunted pine. Mr. David Lynch, a prodigious coffee-drinker, apparently pees hard and often, and neither he nor the production can afford the time it'd take him to run down the Base Camp's long line of trailers to the trailer where the bathrooms are every time he needs to pee. So my first sight of Lynch is only from the back, and (understandably) from a distance. *Lost Highway*'s cast and crew pretty much ignore Lynch's urinating in public, and they ignore it in a relaxed rather than a tense or uncomfortable way, sort of the way you'd ignore a child's alfresco peeing.

> *trivia tidbit:* **what movie people on location sets call the special trailer that houses the bathrooms**

"The Honeywagon."

3   entertainments David Lynch has created/directed that are mentioned in this article

Eraserhead (1977), *The Elephant Man* (1980), *Dune* (1984), *Blue Velvet* (1986), *Wild at Heart* (1989), two televised seasons of *Twin Peaks* (1990–92), *Twin Peaks: Fire Walk with Me* (1992), and the mercifully ablated TV program *On the Air* (1992).

4   other renaissance-mannish things he's done

Has directed music videos for Chris Isaak; has directed the theater-teaser for Michael Jackson's lavish 30-minute "Dangerous" video; has directed commercials for Klein's Obsession, Saint-Laurent's Opium, Alka-Seltzer, the National Breast Cancer Campaign,[1] and New York City's new Garbage Collection Program. Has produced *Into the Night*, an album by Julee Cruise of songs cowritten by Lynch and Angelo Badalamenti, songs that include the *Twin Peaks* theme and *Blue Velvet*'s "Mysteries of Love."[2] Had for a few years a weekly *L.A. Reader* comic strip, "The Angriest Dog in the World." Has cowritten with Badalamenti (who's also doing the original music for *Lost Highway*) *Industrial Symphony #1*, the 1990 video of which features Nicolas Cage and Laura Dern and Julee Cruise and the hieratic dwarf from *Twin Peaks* and top-less cheerleaders and a flayed deer, and which sounds pretty much like the title suggests it would — *IS# 1* was also performed live at the Brooklyn Academy of Music in 1992, to somewhat mixed reviews. Has had a bunch of gallery shows of his Abstract Expressionist paintings, reviews of which have been rather worse than mixed. Has codirected, with James Signorelli, 1992's[3] *Hotel Room*, a feature-length video of vignettes all

---

[1]   (I haven't yet been able to track down clips of the N.B.C.C. spots, but the mind reels at the possibilities implicit in the conjunction of D. Lynch and radical mastectomy. . . .)

[2]   "M.o.L.," only snippets of which are on *BV*'s soundtrack, has acquired an underground reputation as one of the great make-out tunes of all time — well worth checking out.

[3]   ('92 having been a year of simply manic creative activity for Lynch, apparently)

set in one certain room of a NYC railroad hotel, a hoary mainstream conceit ripped off from Neil Simon and sufficiently Lynchianized in *Hotel Room* to be then subsequently rip-offable by Tarantino *et posse* in 1995's *Four Rooms*. Has published *Images* (Hyperion, 1993, $40.00), a sort of coffee-table book consisting of movie stills, prints of Lynch's paintings, and some of Lynch's art photos (some of which art photos are creepy and moody and sexy and cool and some of which are just photos of spark plugs and dental equipment and seem kind of dumb[4]).

5   **this article's special focus or "angle" w/r/t *Lost Highway*, suggested (not all that subtly) by certain editorial presences at *Premiere* magazine**

With the smash *Blue Velvet*, a Palme d'Or at Cannes for *Wild at Heart*, and then the national phenomenon of *Twin Peaks*'s first season, David Lynch clearly established himself as the U.S.A.'s foremost avant-garde / commercially viable avant-garde / "offbeat" director, and for a while there it looked like he might be able single-handedly to broker a new marriage between art and commerce in U.S. movies, opening formula-frozen Hollywood to some of the eccentricity and vigor of art film.

Then 1992 saw *Twin Peaks*'s unpopular second season, the critical and commercial failure of *Fire Walk with Me*, and the bottomlessly horrid *On the Air*, which was euthanized by ABC after six very long-seeming weeks. This triple whammy had critics racing back to their PC's to re-evaluate Lynch's whole oeuvre. The former subject of a *Time* cover-story

---

[4] Dentistry seems to be a new passion for Lynch, by the way — the photo on the title page of *Lost Highway*'s script, which is of a guy with half his face normal and half unbelievably distended and ventricose and gross, was apparently culled from a textbook on extreme dental emergencies. There's great enthusiasm for this photo around Asymmetrical Productions, and they're looking into the legalities of using it in *Lost Highway*'s ads and posters, which if I was the guy in the photo I'd want a truly astronomical permission fee.

in 1990 became the object of a withering ad hominem backlash, stuff like the *L.A. Weekly*'s: "Hip audiences assume Lynch must be satiric, but nothing could be further [sic] from the truth. He isn't equipped for critiquing [*sic*] anything, satirically or otherwise; his work doesn't pass through any intellectual checkpoints. One reason so many people say 'Huh?' to his on-screen fantasies is that the director himself never does."

So the obvious "Hollywood Insider"-type question w/r/t *Lost Highway* is whether the movie is going to rehabilitate Lynch's reputation. This is a legitimately interesting question, although, given the extreme unpredictability of the sorts of forces that put people on *Time* covers, it's probably more realistic to shoot for whether *LH ought* to put Lynch back on top of whatever exactly it was he was on top of. For me, though, a more interesting question ended up being whether David Lynch really gives much of a shit about whether his reputation is rehabilitated or not. The impression I get from rewatching his movies and from hanging around his latest production is that he doesn't, much. This attitude — like Lynch himself, like his work — seems to me to be both admirable and sort of nuts.

6   what *Lost Highway* is apparently about

According to Lynch's own blurb on the title page of the script's circulating copy, it's

> *A 21st Century Noir Horror Film*
> *A graphic investigation into parallel identity crises*
> *A world where time is dangerously out of control*
> *A terrifying ride down the lost highway*

which is a bit overheated, prose-wise, maybe, but was probably put there as a High-Concept sound-bite for potential distributors or something. The spiel's second line is what comes closest to describing *Lost Highway*, though "parallel identity crises" seems like kind of an uptown way of saying the movie is about somebody literally turning into somebody else. And this, despite the many new and different things about *Lost Highway*, makes the movie almost classically Lynchian — the theme of multiple/ambiguous identity has been almost as much a Lynch trademark as ominous ambient noises on his soundtracks.

7 **last bit of (6) used as a segue into a quick sketch of Lynch's genesis as a heroic auteur**

However concerned with fluxes in identity his movies are, David Lynch has remained remarkably himself throughout his filmmaking career. You could probably argue it either way — that Lynch hasn't compromised/sold out, or that he hasn't grown all that much in twenty years of making movies — but the fact remains that Lynch has held fast to his own intensely personal vision and approach to filmmaking, and that he's made significant sacrifices in order to do so. "I mean come on, David could make movies for anybody," says Tom Sternberg, one of *Lost Highway*'s producers. "But David's not part of the Hollywood Process. He makes his own choices about what he wants. He's an *artist*."

This is essentially true, though like most artists Lynch has not been without patrons. It was on the strength of *Eraserhead* that Mel Brooks's production company hired Lynch to make *The Elephant Man* in 1980, and that movie earned Lynch an Oscar nomination and was in turn the reason that no less an ur-Hollywood-Process figure than Dino De Laurentiis picked Lynch to make the film adaptation of Frank Herbert's *Dune*, offering Lynch not only big money but a development deal for future projects with De Laurentiis's production company.

1984's *Dune* is unquestionably the worst movie of Lynch's career, and it's pretty darn bad. In some ways it seems that Lynch was miscast as its director: *Eraserhead* had been one of those sell-your-own-plasma-to-buy-the-film-stock masterpieces, with a tiny and largely unpaid cast and crew. *Dune*, on the other hand, had one of the biggest budgets in Hollywood history, and its production staff was the size of a small Caribbean nation, and the movie involved lavish and cutting-edge special effects (half the fourteen-month shooting schedule was given over to miniatures and stop-action). Plus Herbert's novel itself is incredibly long and complex, and so besides all the headaches of a major commercial production financed by men in Ray-Bans Lynch also had trouble making cinematic sense of the plot, which even in the novel is convoluted to the point of pain. In short, *Dune*'s direction called for a combination technician and administrator, and Lynch, though as good a technician as anyone in film,[5] is more like the type of bright child you sometimes see who's ingenious at structuring fantasies and gets totally immersed in them but will let other kids take part in them only if he retains complete imaginative control over the game and its rules and appurtenances — in short very definitely *not* an administrator.

Watching *Dune* again on video you can see that some of its defects are clearly Lynch's responsibility, e.g. casting the nerdy and potato-faced Kyle MacLachlan as an epic hero and the Police's resoundingly unthespian Sting as a psycho villain, or — worse — trying to provide plot exposition by having characters' thoughts audibilized (w/ that slight thinking-out-loud reverb) on the soundtrack while the camera zooms in on the character making a thinking-face, a cheesy old device that *Saturday Night Live* had already been parodying for years when *Dune* came out. The overall result is a movie that's funny while it's trying to be deadly serious, which is as good a definition of a flop as there is, and *Dune* was indeed a huge, pretentious, incoherent flop. But a good part of the incoherence is the responsibility of De Laurentiis's producers, who cut thousands of feet of film out of Lynch's final print right before the movie's release, apparently already smelling disaster and wanting to get the movie down to more like a normal theatrical running-time. Even on video, it's not hard to see where a lot of these cuts were made; the movie looks gutted, unintentionally surreal.

In a strange way, though, *Dune* actually ended up being Lynch's "big break" as a filmmaker. The version of *Dune* that finally appeared in the theaters was by all reliable reports heartbreaking for him, the kind of debacle that in myths about Innocent, Idealistic Artists In The

---

[5] (And *Dune* really is visually awesome, especially the desert planet's giant worm-monsters, who with their tripartately phallic snouts bear a weird resemblance to the mysterious worm Henry Spencer keeps in the mysterious thrumming cabinet in *Eraserhead*.)

Maw Of The Hollywood Process signals the violent end of the artist's Innocence — seduced, overwhelmed, fucked over, left to take the public heat and the mogul's wrath. The experience could easily have turned Lynch into an embittered hack (though probably a rich hack), doing f/x-intensive gorefests for commercial studios.[6] Or it could have sent him scurrying to the safety of academe, making obscure plotless 16mm.'s for the pipe-and-beret crowd. The experience did neither. Lynch both hung in and, on some level, gave up. *Dune* convinced him of something that all the really interesting independent filmmakers — Campion, the Coens, Jarmusch, Jaglom — seem to steer by. "The experience taught me a valuable lesson," he told an interviewer years later. "I learned I would rather not make a film than make one where I don't have final cut."

And this, in an almost Lynchianly weird way, is what led to *Blue Velvet*. *BV*'s development had been one part of the deal under which Lynch had agreed to do *Dune,* and the latter's huge splat caused two years of rather chilly relations between Dino & Dave while the latter complained about the final cut of *Dune* and wrote *BV*'s script and the former wrathfully clutched his head and the De Laurentiis Entertainment Group's accountants did the postmortem on a $40,000,000 stillbirth. Then, sort of out of nowhere, De Laurentiis offered Lynch a deal for making *BV,* a very unusual sort of arrangement that I'll bet anything was inspired by Lynch's bitching over *Dune*'s final cut and De Laurentiis's being amused and pissed off about that bitching. For *Blue Velvet,* De Laurentiis offered Lynch a tiny budget and an absurdly low directorial fee, but 100% control over the film. It seems clear that the offer was a kind of punitive bluff on the mogul's part, a kind of Be-Careful-What-You-Publicly-Pray-For thing. History unfortunately hasn't recorded what De Laurentiis's reaction was when Lynch jumped at the deal. It seems that Lynch's Innocent Idealism had survived *Dune,* and that he cared less about money and production budgets than about regaining control of the fantasy. Lynch

[6] Anybody who wants to see how the Process and its inducements destroy what's cool and alive in a director should consider the recent trajectory of Richard Rodriguez, from the plasma-financed vitality of *El Mariachi* to the gory pretension of *Desperado* to the empty and embarrassing *From Dusk to Dawn.* Very sad.

not only wrote and directed *Blue Velvet,* he cast it,[7] edited it, even cowrote the original music with Badalamenti. The sound and cinematography were done by Lynch's cronies Alan Splet and Frederick Elmes. *Blue Velvet* was, again, in its visual intimacy and sure touch, a distinctively homemade film (the home being, again, D. Lynch's skull), and it was a surprise hit, and it remains one of the '80s' great U.S. films. And its greatness is a direct result of Lynch's decision to stay in the Process but to rule in small personal films rather than to serve in large corporate ones. Whether you believe he's a good auteur or a bad one, his career makes it clear that he is indeed, in the literal *Cahiers du Cinema* sense, an auteur, willing to make the sorts of sacrifices for creative control that real auteurs have to make — choices that indicate either raging egotism or passionate dedication or a childlike desire to run the whole sandbox, or all three.

trivia tidbit

Like Jim Jarmusch's, Lynch's films are immensely popular overseas, especially in France and Japan. It's not an accident that the financing for *Lost Highway* is French. It's primarily because of foreign sales that no Lynch movie has ever lost money (though it took a long time for *Dune* to clear the red).

6a more specifically — judging by the script and rough-cut footage — what *Lost Highway* is apparently about

In its rough-cut incarnation, the movie opens in motion, driving, with the kind of frenetic behind-the-wheel perspective we know from *Blue Velvet* and *Wild at Heart.* It's a nighttime highway, a minor two-laner, and we're moving down the middle of the road, the divided centerline

---

[7] (using MacLachlan perfectly this time — since the role of Jeffrey actually calls for potato-faced nerdiness — plus *Eraserhead*'s Jack Nance and *Dune*'s Dean Stockwell and Brad Dourif, none of whom has ever been creepier, plus using *Dallas*'s Priscilla Pointer and everything's Hope Lange as scary moms . . .)

flashing strobishly just below our perspective. The sequence is beautifully lit and shot at "half time," six frames per second, so that it feels like
we're going very fast indeed.[8] Nothing is visible in the headlights; the car
seems to be speeding in a void; the shot is thus hyperkinetic and static
at the same time. Music is always vitally important to Lynch films, and
Lost Highway may break new ground for Lynch because its title song is
actually post-'50s; it's a dreamy David Bowie number called "I'm De-
ranged." A way more appropriate theme song for the movie, though, in
my opinion, would be the Flaming Lips' recent "Be My Head," because
get a load of this:

Bill Pullman is a jazz saxophonist whose relationship with his wife,
a brunette Patricia Arquette, is creepy and occluded and full of unspoken tensions. They start getting incredibly mysterious videotapes in the
mail that are of them sleeping or of Bill Pullman's face looking at the
camera with a grotesquely horrified expression, etc.; and they're wig-
ging out, understandably, because they regard it as pretty obvious that
somebody's breaking into their house at night and videotaping them;
and they call the cops, which cops show up at their house and turn
out in best Lynch fashion to be just ineffectual blowholes of *Dragnet*-era
clichés.

Anyway, while the creepy-video thing is under way there are also
some scenes of Pullman looking very natty and East Village in all-black
and jamming on his tenor sax in front of a packed dance floor (only in
a David Lynch movie would people dance ecstatically to abstract jazz),

---

[8] TIDBIT: HOW LYNCH AND HIS CINEMATOGRAPHER FOR *BV*
FILMED THAT HELLACIOUS FORCED "JOYRIDE" IN FRANK BOOTH'S
CAR, THE SCENE WHERE FRANK AND JACK NANCE AND BRAD DOURIF
HAVE KIDNAPPED JEFFREY BEAUMONT AND ARE MENACING HIM IN-
SIDE THE CAR WHILE THEY'RE GOING WHAT LOOKS LIKE 100+ DOWN
A DISMAL RURAL TWO-LANER: The reason it looks like the car's going so fast
is that lights outside the car are going by so fast. In fact the car wasn't even moving.
A burly grip was bouncing madly up and down on the back bumper to make the car
jiggle and roll, and other crewpeople with hand-held lamps were sprinting back and
forth outside the car to make it look like the car was whizzing past streetlights. The
whole scene's got a claustrophobia-in-motion feel that they never could have gotten
if the car'd actually been moving (the production's insurance wouldn't have allowed
that kind of speed in a real take), and the whole thing was done for about $8.95.

and of Patricia Arquette seeming restless and unhappy in a kind of narcotized, disassociated way and generally being creepy and mysterious
and making it clear that she has a kind of double life involving decadent,
lounge-lizardy men, men of whom Bill Pullman would doubtless not
approve one bit. One of the creepier scenes in the movie's first act takes
place at a decadent Hollywood party held by one of Patricia Arquette's
mysterious lizardy friends. At the party Bill Pullman is approached by
somebody the script identifies only as "The Mystery Man," who claims
not only that he's been in Bill Pullman and Patricia Arquette's house but
that he's actually there at their house *right now,* and he apparently is, because he pulls out a cellular (the movie's full of great LA touches, like
everybody having a cellular) and invites Bill Pullman to call his house,
and Bill Pullman has an extremely creepy three-way conversation with
the Mystery Man at the party and the same Mystery Man's voice there
at his house. (The Mystery Man is played by Robert Blake, which by the
way get ready for Robert Blake in this movie — see below.)

But so then, driving home from the party, Bill Pullman criticizes Patricia Arquette's decadent friends but doesn't say anything specific about
the creepy and metaphysically impossible conversation he just had with
one guy in two places, which I think is supposed to reinforce our impression that Bill Pullman and Patricia Arquette are not exactly confiding in-
timately in each other at this stage of their relationship. This impression
is further reinforced in some creepy sex scenes in which Bill Pullman has
frantic wheezing sex with a Patricia Arquette who just lies there blank
and inert and all but looking at her watch.[9]

But then so the thrust of *Lost Highway*'s first act is that a final and
climactic mysterious video comes in the mail, and it shows Bill Pullman
standing over the mutilated corpse of Patricia Arquette — we see it only
on the video. And then Bill Pullman's arrested and convicted and put on
Death Row.

Then there are some scenes of Bill Pullman on a penal institution's
Death Row, looking about as tortured and uncomprehending as any *noir*
protagonist ever in the history of film has looked, and part of his torment

[9] (sex scenes that are creepy in part because they're exactly what the viewer himself
imagines having sex with Patricia Arquette would be like)

is that he's having terrible headaches and his skull is starting to bulge out in different places and in general to look really painful and weird.

Then there's this scene where Bill Pullman's head turns into Balthazar Getty's head. As in the Bill Pullman character in *Lost Highway* turns into somebody completely else, somebody played by *Lord of the Flies*'s Balthazar Getty, who's barely out of puberty and looks nothing like Bill Pullman. The scene is indescribable, and I won't even try to describe it except to say that it's as ghastly and riveting and totally indescribable as anything I've seen in a U.S. movie.

The administration of the penal institution is understandably non-plussed when they see Balthazar Getty in Bill Pullman's cell instead of Bill Pullman. Balthazar Getty is no help in explaining how he got there, because he's got a huge hematoma on his forehead and his eyes are rolling around and he's basically in the sort of dazed state you can imagine somebody being in when somebody else's head has just changed painfully into his own head. The penal authorities ID Balthazar Getty as a 24-year-old LA auto mechanic who lives with his parents, who are apparently a retired biker and biker-chick. Meaning he's a whole other valid IDable human being, with an identity and a history, instead of just being Bill Pullman with a new head.

No one's ever escaped from this prison's Death Row before, apparently, and the penal authorities and cops, being unable to figure out how Bill Pullman escaped, and getting little more than dazed winces from Balthazar Getty, decide (in a move whose judicial realism may be a bit shaky) to let Balthazar Getty just go home. Which he does.

Balthazar Getty goes home to his room full of motorcycle parts and Snap-On Tool cheesecake posters and slowly gets his wits back, though he still has what now looks like a wicked carbuncle on his forehead and has no idea what happened or how he ended up in Bill Pullman's cell, and he wanders around his parents' seedy house with a facial expression that looks the way a bad dream feels. There are a few scenes of him doing stuff like watching a lady hang up laundry while an ominous low-register noise sounds, and his eyes look like there's some timelessly horrific fact that's slipped his mind and he both wants to recall it and doesn't want to. His parents — who smoke dope and watch huge amounts of TV and engage in a lot of conspiratorial whispering and creepy looks, like they know important stuff Balthazar Getty and we don't know — don't ask Balthazar Getty what happened ... and again we get the feeling that relationships in this movie are not what you would call open and sharing, etc.

But it turns out that Balthazar Getty is an incredibly gifted professional mechanic who's been sorely missed at the auto shop where he works — his mother has apparently told Balthazar Getty's employer, who's played by Richard Pryor, that Balthazar Getty's absence has been due to a "fever." At this point we're still not sure whether Bill Pullman has really and truly metamorphosized into Balthazar Getty or whether this whole turning-into-Balthazar-Getty thing is taking place in Bill Pullman's head, a sort of prolonged extreme-stress pre-execution hallucination à la Gilliam's *Brazil* or Bierce's "Occurrence at Owl Creek Bridge." But the evidence for literal metamorphosis mounts in the movie's second act, because Balthazar Getty has a fully valid life and history, including a girlfriend who keeps looking suspiciously at Balthazar Getty's hellacious forehead-carbuncle and saying he "doesn't seem himself," which with repetition stops being an arch pun and becomes genuinely frightening. Balthazar Getty also has a loyal clientele at Richard Pryor's auto shop, one of whom, played by Robert Loggia, is an extremely creepy and menacing crime-boss-type figure with a thuggish entourage and a black Mercedes 6.9 with esoteric troubles that he'll trust only Balthazar Getty to diagnose and fix. Robert Loggia clearly has a history with Balthazar Getty and treats Balthazar Getty with a creepy blend of avuncular affection and patronizing ferocity. And so on this one day, when Robert Loggia pulls into Richard Pryor's auto shop with his troubled Mercedes 6.9, sitting in the car alongside Robert Loggia's thugs is an unbelievably gorgeous gun-moll-type girl, played by Patricia Arquette and clearly recognizable as same, i.e. as Bill Pullman's wife, except now she's a platinum blond. (If you're thinking *Vertigo* here, you're not far astray. Lynch has a track record of making allusions and homages to Hitchcock — e.g. *BV*'s first shot of Kyle MacLachlan spying on Isabella Rosselini through the louvered slots of her closet door is identical in every technical particular to the first shot of Anthony Perkins spying on Janet Leigh's ablutions in *Psycho* — that are more like intertextual touchstones than outright allusions, and are always taken in weird and creepy and uniquely Lynchian directions. Anyway, the *Vertigo* allusion here seems less important than the way Patricia Arquette's Duessa-like doubleness acts as a counterpoint to the movie's other "identity crisis": here are two different women (for a while) portrayed by what is recognizably the same actress, while two totally different actors portray what are simultaneously the same "person" (for a while) and two different "identities.")

And but so when Balthazar Getty's new blue-collar incarnation of Bill Pullman and Patricia Arquette's apparent blond incarnation of Bill Pullman's wife make eye-contact, sparks are generated on a scale that lends the hackneyed "I-feel-I-know-you-from-somewhere" component of erotic attraction whole new fresh layers of creepy literality. Then there are some scenes that fill in the new blond Patricia Arquette incarnation's seedy history, and some scenes showing how deeply and ferociously attached to the blond Patricia Arquette Robert Loggia is, and some scenes that make it abundantly clear that Robert Loggia is a total psychopath who is most definitely not to be fucked around with or snuck around behind the back of with the girlfriend of. And then we get some scenes showing that Balthazar Getty and the blond Patricia Arquette are — Getty's forehead-carbuncle notwithstanding, apparently — instantly and ferociously attracted to one another, and then some more scenes where they consummate this attraction with all the heavily stilted affectless vigor Lynch's sex scenes are famous for.[10]

And then there are some more scenes that reveal that Robert Loggia's character *also* has more than one identity in the movie, and that at least one of these identities knows both the decadent, lounge-lizardy, mysterious friend of Bill Pullman's deceased wife *and* the Mephistophelian Mystery Man, with whom Loggia begins making creepy and ambiguous threatening phone calls to Balthazar Getty's home, which Balthazar Getty has to listen to and try to interpret while his parents (who are played by Gary Busey and an actress named Lucy Dayton) smoke pot and exchange mysterious significant looks in front of the TV.

It's probably better not to give away too much of *Lost Highway*'s

---

[10] (a stilted, tranced quality that renders the sex scenes both sexually "hot" and aesthetically "cold," a sort of meta-erotic effect you could see Gus Van Sant trying to emulate when he had the sex scenes in *My Own Private Idaho* rendered as series of complexly postured stills, which instead of giving them Lynch's creepy tranced quality made them look more like illustrations from the *Kama-Sutra*)

final act, though you maybe ought to be apprised: that the blond Patricia Arquette's intentions toward Balthazar Getty turn out to be less than honorable; that Balthazar Getty's carbuncle all but completely heals up; that Bill Pullman does reappear in the movie; that the brunette Patricia Arquette also reappears, but not in the (so to speak) flesh; that both the blond and the brunette P. Arquette turn out to be involved (via lizardy friends) in the world of porn, as in hardcore, an involvement whose video fruits are shown (at least in the rough cut) in so much detail that I don't see how Lynch's movie is going to escape an NC-17 rating; and that *Lost Highway*'s ending is by no means an "upbeat" or "feel-good" ending. Also that Robert Blake, while a good deal more restrained and almost *effete* than Dennis Hopper was in *Blue Velvet*, is at least as riveting and creepy and unforgettable as Hopper's Frank Booth was, and that his Mystery Man is pretty clearly the devil, or at least somebody's very troubling idea of the devil, a kind of pure floating spirit of malevolence à la *Twin Peaks*'s Leland/"Bob"/Scary Owl.

6b approximate number of ways *Lost Highway* seems like it can be interpreted

Roughly 37. The big interpretive fork, as mentioned, looks to be whether we are meant to take the sudden unexplained shift in Bill Pullman's identity straight (i.e. as literally real within the movie), or as some Kafkaesque metaphor for guilt and denial and psychic evasion, or whether we're to see the whole thing — from invasive videos through Death Row through metamorphosis into mechanic, etc. — as one long hallucination on the part of a natty jazz saxophonist who could very much benefit from some professionally dispensed medication. The least interesting possibility seems to be to the last, and I'd be very surprised if anybody at Asymmetrical will want *Lost Highway* interpreted as one long psychotic dream.

Or the movie's plot could, on still another hand, simply be incoherent and make no rational sense and not be conventionally interpretable at all. This won't necessarily make it a bad David Lynch movie: *Eraserhead*'s dream-logic makes it a "narrative" only in a very loose, nonlinear way, and large parts of *Twin Peaks* and *Fire Walk with Me* make no real sense and yet are compelling and meaningful and just plain cool. Lynch seems to run into trouble only when his movies seem to the viewer to *want* to have a point — i.e. when they set the viewer up to expect some kind of coherent connection between plot elements — and then fail to deliver any such point. Examples here include *Wild at Heart* — where the connections between Santos and Mr. Reindeer (the Colonel Sandersish–looking guy who commissions hits by pushing silver dollars through hit men's mail slots) and the Harry Dean Stanton character and the death of Lula's father are intricately set up and then don't go anywhere either visually or narratively — and the first half hour of *Fire Walk with Me,* which concerns the FBI investigation of the pre-Palmer murder of another girl, and sets us up to think it's going to have important connections to the Palmer case, and instead is full of odd cues and clues that go nowhere, and is the part of the movie that even pro-Lynch critics singled out for special savagery.

Since it might bear on the movie's final quality, be apprised that *Lost Highway* is the most expensive movie Lynch has ever made on his own. Its budget is something like sixteen million dollars, which is three times *Blue Velvet*'s and at least 50% more than either *Wild at Heart*'s or *Fire Walk with Me*'s.

But so it is, at this point, probably impossible to tell whether *Lost Highway* is going to be a *Dune*-level turkey or a *Blue Velvet*–caliber masterpiece or something in-between or what. The one thing I feel I can say with total confidence is that the movie will be: *Lynchian.*

8   what *Lynchian* means and why it's important

An academic definition of *Lynchian* might be that the term "refers to a particular kind of irony where the very macabre and the very mundane combine in such a way as to reveal the former's perpetual containment within the latter." But like *postmodern* or *pornographic, Lynchian* is one of those Potter Stewart–type words that's definable only ostensively — i.e. we know it when we see it. Ted Bundy wasn't particularly Lynchian, but good old Jeffrey Dahmer, with his victim's various anatomies neatly separated and stored in his fridge alongside his chocolate milk and

Shedd Spread, was thoroughgoingly Lynchian. A recent homicide in Boston, where the deacon of a South Shore church gave chase to a vehicle that had cut him off, forced the car off the road, and shot the driver with a high-powered crossbow, was borderline-Lynchian.

A domestic-type homicide, on the other hand, could fall on various points along the continuum of Lynchianism. Some guy killing his wife in and of itself doesn't have much of a Lynchian tang to it, though if it turns out the guy killed his wife over something like a persistent failure to refill the ice-cube tray after taking the last ice cube or an obdurate refusal to buy the particular brand of peanut butter the guy was devoted to, the homicide could be described as having Lynchian elements. And if the guy, sitting over the mutilated corpse of his wife (whose retrograde '50s bouffant is, however, weirdly unmussed) with the first cops on the scene as they all wait for the boys from Homicide and the M.E.'s office, begins defending his actions by giving an involved analysis of the comparative merits of Jif and Skippy, and if the beat cops, however repelled by the carnage on the floor, have to admit that the guy's got a point, that if you've developed a sophisticated peanut-butter palate and that palate prefers Jif there's simply no way Skippy's going to be anything like an acceptable facsimile, and that a wife who fails repeatedly to grasp the importance of Jif is making some very significant and troubling statements about her empathy for and commitment to the sacrament of marriage as a bond between two bodies, minds, spirits, and palates . . . you get the idea.

For me, Lynch's movies' deconstruction of this weird "irony of the banal" has affected the way I see and organize the world. I've noted since 1986 that a good 65% of the people in metropolitan bus terminals between the hours of midnight and 6:00 A.M. tend to qualify as Lynchian figures — flamboyantly unattractive, enfeebled, grotesque, freighted with a woe out of all proportion to evident circumstances. Or we've all seen people assume sudden and grotesque facial expressions — e.g. like when receiving shocking news, or biting into something that turns out to be foul, or around small kids for no particular reason other than to be weird — but I've determined that a sudden grotesque facial expression won't qualify as a really *Lynchian* facial expression unless the expression is held for several moments longer than the circumstances could even possibly warrant, is just held there, fixed and grotesque, until it starts to signify about seventeen different things at once.[11]

trivia tidbit

Bill Pullman's distended and long-held expression of torment as he screams over Patricia Arquette's body in *Lost Highway* is nearly identical to the scream-face Jack Nance wears during *Eraserhead*'s opening's conception montage.

9   Lynchianism's ambit in contemporary movies

In 1995, PBS ran a lavish ten-part documentary called *American Cinema* whose final episode was devoted to "The Edge of Hollywood" and the increasing influence of young independent filmmakers — the Coens, Jim Jarmusch, Carl Franklin, Q. Tarantino et al. It was not just unfair but bizarre that David Lynch's name was never once mentioned in the episode, because his influence is all over these directors. The Band-Aid on the neck of *Pulp Fiction*'s Marcellus Wallace — unexplained, visually incongruous, and featured prominently in three separate set-ups — is textbook Lynch. So are the long, self-consciously mundane dialogues on pork, foot massages, TV pilots, etc. that punctuate *Pulp Fiction*'s violence, a violence whose creepy/comic stylization is also resoundingly Lynchian. The peculiar narrative tone of Tarantino's films — the thing that makes them seem at once strident and obscure, not-quite-clear in a haunting way — is Lynch's tone; Lynch invented this tone. It seems to

[11]   (And as an aside, but a true aside, I'll add that I have had since 1986 a personal rule w/r/t dating, which is that any date where I go to a female's residence to pick her up and have any kind of conversation with parents or roommates that's an even remotely Lynchian conversation is automatically the only date I ever have with that female, regardless of her appeal in other areas. And that this rule, developed after seeing *Blue Velvet*, has served me remarkably well and kept me out of all kinds of hair-raising entanglements and jams, and that friends to whom I've promulgated the rule but who have willfully ignored it and have continued dating females with clear elements of Lynchianism in their characters or associations have done so to their regret.)

me fair to say that the commercial Hollywood phenomenon that is Mr. Quentin Tarantino would not exist without David Lynch as a touchstone, a set of allusive codes and contexts in the viewer's deep-brain core. In a way, what Tarantino's done with the French New Wave and with Lynch is what Pat Boone did with Little Richard and Fats Domino: he's found (rather ingeniously) a way to take what is ragged and distinctive and menacing about their work and homogenize it, churn it until it's smooth and cool and hygienic enough for mass consumption. *Reservoir Dogs*, for example, with its comically banal lunch-chatter, creepily otiose code names, and intrusive soundtrack of campy pop from decades past, is Lynch made commercial, i.e. faster, linearer, and with what was idiosyncratically surreal now made fashionably (i.e. "hiply") surreal.

In Carl Franklin's powerful *One False Move*, the director's crucial decision to focus only on the faces of witnesses during violent scenes — i.e. to have the violence played out on watching faces, to render its effect as affect — is thoroughgoingly Lynchian. So is the relentless, *noir*-parodic use of chiaroscuro lighting in the Coens' *Blood Simple* and *The Hudsucker Proxy* and in all Jim Jarmusch's films, especially Jarmusch's 1984 *Stranger Than Paradise*, which, in terms of cinematography, blighted setting, wet-fuse pace, heavy dissolves between scenes, and a Bressonian style of acting that is at once manic and wooden, is all but an homage to Lynch's early work. Other homages you've maybe seen include Gus Van Sant's use of a quirky superstition about hats on beds as an ironic plot engine in *Drugstore Cowboy*, Mike Leigh's use of incongruous parallel plots in *Naked*, Todd Haynes's use of a creepy ambient industrial-thrum score in *Safe*, and Van Sant's use of surreal dream scenes to develop River Phoenix's character in *My Own Private Idaho*. In this same *M.O.P. Idaho*, the German john's creepy Expressionist lip-synch number, where he uses a hand-held lamp as a microphone, is a more or less explicit reference to Dean Stockwell's unforgettable lamp-synch scene in *Blue Velvet*.

Or take the granddaddy of in-your-ribs *Blue Velvet* references: the scene in *Reservoir Dogs* where Michael Madsen, dancing to a cheesy '70s tune, *cuts off a hostage's ear*. This just isn't subtle at all.

None of this is to say that Lynch himself doesn't owe debts — to Hitchcock, to Cassavetes, to Bresson and Deren and Wiene. But it is to say that Lynch has in many ways cleared and made arable the contemporary "anti-Hollywood" territory that Tarantino et al. are cash-cropping right now.[12] Recall that both *The Elephant Man* and *Blue Velvet* came out in the 1980s, that metastatic decade of cable, VCRs, merchandising tie-ins and multinational blockbusters, all the big-money stuff that threatened to empty the American film industry of everything that wasn't High Concept. Lynch's moody, creepy, obsessive, unmistakeably personal movies were to High Concept what the first great '40s *noir* films were to toothy musicals: unforeseen critical and commercial successes that struck a nerve with audiences and expanded studios' and distributors' idea of what would sell. It is to say that we owe Lynch a lot.

And it is also to say that David Lynch, at age 50, is a better, more complex, more interesting director than any of the hip young "rebels" making violently ironic films for New Line and Miramax today. It is particularly to say that — even without considering recent cringers like *Four Rooms* or *From Dusk to Dawn* — D. Lynch is an exponentially better filmmaker than Q. Tarantino. For, unlike Tarantino, D. Lynch knows that an act of violence in an American film has, through repetition and desensitization, lost the ability to refer to anything but itself. This is why violence in Lynch's films, grotesque and coldly stylized and symbolically heavy as it may be, is qualitatively different from Hollywood's or even anti-Hollywood's hip cartoon-violence. Lynch's violence always tries to *mean* something.

---

[12] Lynch's influence extends into mainstream Hollywood movies, too, by the way. The surfeit of dark dense machinery, sudden gouts of vented steam, ambient industrial sounds, etc., in Lynch's early stuff has clearly affected James Cameron and Terry Gilliam, and Gilliam has taken to the limit Lynch's preoccupation with blatantly Freudian fantasies (*Brazil*) and interpenetrations of ancient myth and modern psychoses (*The Fisher King*).

And across the spectrum, in the world of caviar-for-the-general art films, one has only to look at Atom Egoyan or Guy Maddin's abstruse, mood-lit, slow-moving angst-fests, or at the Frenchman Arnaud DesPlechin's 1992 *La Sentinelle* (which the director describes as "a brooding, intuitive study in split consciousness" and which is actually about a disassociated med-student's relationship with a severed head), or actually at just about anything recent that's directed by a French male under 35, to see Lynch's sensibility stamped like an exergue on art cinema's hot young Turks, too.

9a a better way to put what i just tried to say

Quentin Tarantino is interested in watching somebody's ear getting cut off; David Lynch is interested in the ear.

10   re the issue of whether and in what way David Lynch's movies are "sick"

Pauline Kael has a famous epigram to her 1986 *New Yorker* review of *Blue Velvet*: she quotes somebody she left the theater behind as saying to a friend "Maybe I'm sick, but I want to see that again." And Lynch's movies are indeed — in all sorts of ways, some more interesting than others — "sick." Some of them are brilliant and unforgettable; others are jejune and incoherent and bad. It's no wonder that Lynch's critical reputation over the last decade has looked like an EKG: it's sometimes hard to tell whether the director's a genius or an idiot. This is part of his fascination.

If the word *sick* seems excessive to you, simply substitute the word *creepy*. Lynch's movies are inarguably creepy, and a big part of their creepiness is that they seem so *personal*. A kind way to put it is that Lynch seems to be one of these people with unusual access to their own unconscious. A less kind way to put it would be that Lynch's movies seem to be expressions of certain anxious, obsessive, fetishistic, Oedipally arrested, borderlinish parts of the director's psyche, expressions presented with very little inhibition or semiotic layering, i.e. presented with something like a child's ingenuous (and sociopathic) lack of self-consciousness. It's the psychic intimacy of the work that makes it hard to sort out what you are feeling about one of David Lynch's movies and what you are feeling about David Lynch. The ad hominem impression one tends to carry away from a *Blue Velvet* or a *Fire Walk with Me* is that they're really powerful movies but that David Lynch is the sort of person you really hope you don't get stuck next to on a long flight or in line at the DMV or something. In other words a *creepy* person.

Depending on whom you talk to, Lynch's creepiness is either enhanced or diluted by the odd distance that seems to separate his movies from the audience. Lynch's movies tend to be both extremely personal and extremely remote. The absence of linearity and narrative logic, the heavy multivalence of the symbolism, the glazed opacity of the characters' faces, the weird ponderous quality of the dialogue, the regular deployment of grotesques as figurants, the precise, painterly way scenes are staged and lit, and the overlush, possibly voyeuristic way that violence, deviance, and general hideousness are depicted — these all give Lynch's movies a cool, detached quality, one that some cinéastes view as more like cold and clinical.

Here's something that's unsettling but true: Lynch's best movies are also his creepiest/sickest. This is probably because his best movies, however surreal, tend to be anchored by strongly developed main characters — *Blue Velvet*'s Jeffrey Beaumont, *Fire Walk with Me*'s Laura, *The Elephant Man*'s Merrick and Treeves. When his characters are sufficiently developed and human to evoke our empathy, it tends to cut the distance and detachment that can keep Lynch's films at arm's length, and at the same time it makes the movies creepier — we're way more easily disturbed when a disturbing movie has characters in whom we can see parts of ourselves. For example, there's way more general ickiness in *Wild at Heart* than there is in *Blue Velvet*, and yet *Blue Velvet* is a far creepier/sicker/nastier film, simply because Jeffrey Beaumont is a sufficiently 3-D character for us to feel about/for/with. Since the really disturbing stuff in *Blue Velvet* isn't about Frank Booth or anything Jeffrey discovers about Lumberton but about the fact that a part of Jeffrey himself gets off on voyeurism and primal violence and degeneracy, and since Lynch carefully sets up his film both so that we feel a/f/w Jeffrey and so that we (I, anyway) find some parts of the sadism and degeneracy he witnesses compelling and somehow erotic, it's little wonder that I find Lynch's movie "sick" — nothing sickens me like seeing on-screen some of the very parts of myself I've gone to the movies to try to forget about.

Wild at Heart's characters, on the other hand, aren't "round" or 3-D. (This was apparently by design.) Sailor and Lula are inflated parodies of Faulknerian passion; Santo and Marietta and Bobby Peru are cartoon ghouls, collections of wicked grins and Kabuki hysterics. The movie itself is incredibly violent (horrible beatings, bloody auto wrecks, dogs stealing amputated limbs, Willem DaFoe's head blown off by a shotgun and flying around the set like a pricked balloon), but the violence comes off less as sick than as empty, a stream of stylized gestures. And empty not because the violence is gratuitous or excessive but because none of it involves a living character through whom our capacities for horror or shock could be accessed. *Wild at Heart,* though it won at Cannes, didn't get very good reviews in the U.S., and it wasn't an accident that the most savage attacks came from female critics, nor that they particularly disliked the film's coldness and emotional poverty. See for just one example *Film Comment*'s Kathleen Murphy, who saw *Wild at Heart* as little more than "a litter of quotation marks. As voyeurs, we're encouraged to twitch and giggle at a bracketed reality: well-known detritus from pop-culture memory, a kind of cinematic vogue-ing that passes for the play of human emotions." (This was not the only pan-job along these lines, and to be honest most of them had a point.)

The thing is that Lynch's uneven oeuvre presents a whole bunch of paradoxes. His best movies tend to be his sickest, and they tend to derive a lot of their emotional power from their ability to make us feel complicit in their sickness. And this ability in turn depends on Lynch's defying a historical convention that has often served to distinguish avant-garde, "nonlinear" art film from commercial narrative film. Nonlinear movies, i.e. ones without a conventional plot, usually reject the idea of strong individual characterization as well. Only one of Lynch's movies, *The Elephant Man,* has had a conventional linear narrative.[13] But most of them (the best) have devoted quite a lot of energy to character. I.e. they've had human beings in them. It may be that Jeffrey, Merrick, Laura et al. function for Lynch as they do for audiences, as nodes of identification and engines of emotional pain. The extent (large) to which Lynch seems to identify with his movies' main characters is one more thing that makes the films so disturbingly "personal." The fact that he doesn't seem to identify much with his *audience* is what makes the movies "cold," though the detachment has some advantages as well.

trivia tidbit w/ respect to (10)

Wild at Heart, starring Laura Dern as Lula and Nicolas Cage as Sailor, also features Diane Ladd as Lula's mother. The actress Diane Ladd hap-

---

[13] (This isn't counting *Dune,* which was in the dreadful position of looking like it wanted to have one but not in fact having one.)

pens to be the actress Laura Dern's real mother. *Wild at Heart* itself, for all its heavy references to *The Wizard of Oz,* is actually a pomo-ish remake of Sidney Lumet's 1959 *The Fugitive Kind,* which starred Anna Magnani and Marlon Brando. The fact that Cage's performance in *Wild at Heart* strongly suggests either Brando doing an Elvis imitation or vice versa is not an accident, nor is the fact that both *Wild at Heart* and *The Fugitive Kind* use fire as a key image, nor is the fact that Sailor's beloved snakeskin jacket — "a symbol of my belief in freedom and individual choice" — is just like the snakeskin jacket Brando wore in *The Fugitive Kind. The Fugitive Kind* happens to be the film version of Tennessee Williams's little-known *Orpheus Descending,* a play which in 1960, enjoying a new vogue in the wake of Lumet's film adaptation, ran Off-Broadway in NYC and featured Bruce Dern and Diane Ladd, Laura Dern's parents, who met and married while starring in this play.

The extent to which David Lynch could expect a regular civilian viewer of *Wild at Heart* to know about any of these textual and organic connections is: 0; the extent to which he cares whether anybody got it or not is apparently: also 0.

11 last bit of (10) used as a segue into the issue of what exactly David Lynch seems to *want* from you

Movies are an authoritarian medium. They vulnerabilize you and then dominate you. Part of the magic of going to a movie is surrendering to it, letting it dominate you. The sitting in the dark, the looking up, the tranced distance from the screen, the being able to see the people on the screen without being seen by the people on the screen, the people on the screen being so much bigger than you, prettier than you, more compelling than you, etc. Film's overwhelming power isn't news. But different kinds of movies use this power in different ways. Art film is essentially teleological: it tries in various ways to "wake the audience up" or render us more "conscious." (This kind of agenda can easily degenerate into pretentiousness and self-righteousness and condescending horsetwaddle, but the agenda itself is large-hearted and fine.) Commercial film doesn't seem like it cares very much about an audience's instruction or enlightenment. Commercial film's goal is to "entertain," which usually means enabling various fantasies that allow the movie-goer to pretend he's somebody else and that life is somehow bigger and more coherent and more compelling and attractive and in general just more entertaining than a moviegoer's life really is. You could say that a commercial movie doesn't try to wake people up but rather to make their sleep so comfortable and their dreams so pleasant that they will fork over money to experience it — this seduction, a fantasy-for-money transaction, is a commercial movie's basic point. An art film's point is usually more intellectual or aesthetic, and you usually have to do some interpretive work to get it, so that when you pay to see an art film you're actually paying to do work (whereas the only work you have to do w/r/t most commercial film is whatever work you did to afford the price of the ticket).

David Lynch's movies are often described as occupying a kind of middle ground between art film and commercial film. But what they really occupy is a whole third different kind of territory. Most of Lynch's best films don't really *have* much of a point, and in lots of ways they seem to resist the film-interpretive process by which movies' (certainly avant-garde movies') central points are understood. This is something the British critic Paul Taylor seems to get when he says that Lynch's movies are "to be experienced rather than explained." Lynch's movies are indeed susceptible to a variety of sophisticated interpretations, but it would be a serious mistake to conclude from this that his movies' point is "film-interpretation is necessarily multivalent" or something — they're just not that kind of movie.

Nor are they *seductive,* though, at least in the commercial senses of being comfortable or linear or High-Concept or "feel-good." You almost never in a Lynch movie get the sense that the point is to "entertain" you, and never that the point is to get you to fork over money to see it. This is one of the unsettling things about a Lynch movie: you don't feel like you're entering into any of the standard unspoken/unconscious contracts you normally enter into with other kinds of movies. This is unsettling because in the absence of such an unconscious contract we lose some of the psychic protections we normally (and necessarily) bring to bear on a medium as powerful as film. That is, if we know on some level what a movie *wants* from us, we can erect certain internal defenses that let us choose how much of ourselves we give away to it.[14] The absence of point or recognizable agenda in Lynch's films, though, strips these subliminal defenses and lets Lynch get inside your head in a way movies normally don't. This is why his best films' effects are often so emotional and nightmarish (we're defenseless in our dreams, too).

This may, in fact, be Lynch's true and only agenda: just to get inside your head.[15] He sure seems to care more about penetrating your head than about what he does once he's in there. Is this "good" art? It's hard to say. It seems — once again — either ingenious or psychopathic.

12   one of the relatively picayune *Lost Highway* scenes I got to be on the set of

Given his movies' penchant for creepy small towns, Los Angeles might seem an unlikely place for Lynch to set *Lost Highway,* and at first I'm thinking its choice might represent either a cost-cutting move or a grim sign of Lynch having finally Gone Hollywood.

LA in January, though, turns out to be plenty Lynchian in its own right. Surreal/banal juxtapositions and interpenetrations are everyplace you look. The cab from LAX has a DDS machines attached to the meter so you can pay the fare by major credit card. Or there's my hotel's[16] lobby, which is filled with beautiful Steinway piano music, except when you go over to put a buck in the piano player's snifter or whatever it turns out there's nobody playing, the piano's playing itself, but it's not a player

[14] I know I'm not putting this well; it seems too complicated to be put well. It has something to do with the fact that some movies are too scary or intense for younger viewers: a little kid, whose psychic defenses aren't yet developed, can be terribly frightened by a horror movie that you or I would regard as cheesy and dumb.

[15] The way *Lost Highway* makes the idea of head-entry literal is not an accident.

[16] (*Premiere* magazine puts its writers in extremely snazzy hotels, by the way. I strongly doubt all hotels in LA are like this.)

piano, it's a regular Steinway with a weird computerized box attached to the underside of its keyboard; the piano plays 24 hours a day and never once repeats a song. My hotel's in what's either West Hollywood or the downscale part of Beverly Hills; two clerks at the registration desk start arguing the point when I ask where exactly in LA we are. The argument goes on for an absurdly long time with me just standing there.

My hotel room has unbelievably fancy and expensive French doors that open out onto a balcony, except the balcony's exactly ten inches wide and has an iron fence with decorations so sharp-looking you don't want to get anywhere near it. I don't think the French doors and balcony are meant to be a joke. There's an enormous aqua-and-salmon mall across the street, very upscale, with pricey futuristic escalators slanting up across the mall's exterior, and yet I never in three days see a single person a- or descend the escalator; the mall is all lit up and open and seems totally deserted. The winter sky seems smogless but unreal, its blue the same supersaturant blue as *Blue Velvet*'s opening's famous sky.

LA has a big city's street musicians, but here the musicians play on median strips instead of on the sidewalk or subway, and patrons throw change and fluttering bills at them from their speeding cars, many with the casual accuracy of long practice. On the median strips between the hotel and David Lynch's sets, most of the street musicians were playing instruments like finger-cymbals and citterns.

Fact: in my three days here for *Premiere* magazine I will meet two (2) different people named Balloon.

The major industry around here seems to be valet parking; even some of the fast food restaurants here have valet parking; I'd love to have the West Hollywood/Beverly Hills concession on maroon valet sportcoats. A lot of the parking attendants have long complicated hair and look sort of like the Italian male model who's on Harlequin Romance covers. In fact pretty much everybody on the street seems ridiculously good-looking. Everybody is also extremely well- and fashionably dressed; by the third day I figure out that the way to tell poor and homeless people is that they look like they dress off the rack.[17] The only even marginally ravaged-

---

[17] I know things like this sound like a cheap gag, but I swear I'm serious. The incongruous realism of cheap gags is what made the whole thing Lynchian.

looking persons in view are the hard-faced Latin guys selling oranges out of grocery carts on whatever median strips aren't already taken by cittern players. Supermodels can be seen running across four-lane roads against the light and getting honked at by people in fuchsia Saabs and tan Mercedeses.

And it's true, the big stereotype: from any given vantage at any given time there are about four million cars to be seen on the roads, and none of them seems to be unwaxed. People here have got not only vanity license plates but vanity license-plate *frames*. And just about everybody talks on the phone as they drive; after a while you get the crazy but unshakable feeling that they're all talking to each other, that whoever's talking on the phone as they drive is talking to somebody else who's driving.

On the first night's return from the set, a Karmann-Ghia passed us on Mulholland with its headlights off and an older woman behind the wheel holding a paper plate between her teeth and *still* talking on a phone.

So the point is Lynch isn't as out of his filmic element in LA as one might have initially feared.

Plus the location helps make this movie "personal" in a new way, because LA is where Lynch and his S.O., Ms. Mary Sweeney,[18] make their home. Corporate and technical headquarters for Asymmetrical Productions is the house right next door to theirs. Two houses down on the same street is the house Lynch has chosen to use for the home of Bill Pullman and brunette Patricia Arquette in *Lost Highway*'s first act. It's a house that looks rather a lot like Lynch's own, a house whose architecture could be called Spanish in roughly the same way Goya could be called Spanish.

A film's director usually has a number of Assistant Directors, whose various responsibilities are firmly established by Hollywood convention. The First Assistant Director's responsibility is the maximally smooth ordered flow of the set. He's in charge of coordinating details, shouting for quiet on the set, worrying, and yelling at people and being disliked for it. This allows the director himself to be kind of a benign and unhassled monarch, occupied mostly with high-level creative concerns and popu-

---

[18] Mary Sweeney is one of *Lost Highway*'s three producers. Her main responsibilities seem to be the daily rushes and the rough cut and its storage and organization. She was Lynch's editor on *Fire Walk with Me*.

lar with the crew in a kind of grandfatherly way. *Lost Highway*'s First Assistant Director is a veteran 1st A.D. named Scott Cameron, who wears khaki shorts and has stubble and is good-looking in a kind of unhappy way.[19] The Second Assistant Director is in charge of scheduling and is the person who makes up the daily Call Sheet, which outlines the day's production schedule and says who has to show up where and when. There's also a Second Second Assistant Director,[20] who's in charge of interfacing with the actors and actresses and making sure their makeup and costumes are OK and going to summon them from their trailers when the stand-ins are done blocking off the positions and angles for a scene and everything's ready for the first string to come on.

Part of the 2nd A.D.'s daily Call Sheet is a kind of charty-looking précis of the scenes to be shot that day; it's called a "One Line Schedule" or "One Liner." Here is what January 8's One Liner looks like:

(1) Scs 112   *INT MR. EDDY'S MERCEDES* /DAY/ 1 *pgs*
     MR. EDDY[21] DRIVES MERCEDES, PETE[22] LISTENS FOR CAR TROUBLE.

---

[19] (One *Lost Highway* crewperson described Scott Cameron as "the Mozart of stress," whatever that's supposed to mean.)

[20] (not "Third Assistant," for some firmly established reason)

[21] (= Robert Loggia)

[22] (= Balthazar Getty, about whom the less said the better, probably, except maybe to say that he looks sort of like Tom Hanks and John Cusack and Charlie Sheen all mashed together and then emptied of some vital essence. He's not particularly tall, but he looks tall in *Lost Highway*'s footage because he has extremely poor posture and David Lynch has for some reason instructed him to exaggerate the poor posture. As a Hot Young Male Actor, Balthazar Getty is to Leonardo DiCaprio roughly what a Ford Escort is to a Lexus. His breakthrough role was as Ralph in the latest *Lord of the Flies*, in which he was bland and essenceless but not terrible. He was miscast and misdirected as a homeless kid in *Where the Day Takes You* (like how does a homeless kid manage to have fresh mousse in his hair every day?) and really good in a surly bit part in *Mr. Holland's Opus*.

    To be frank, it's almost impossible for me to separate predictions about how good Balthazar Getty's going to be in *Lost Highway* from my impressions of him as a human being around the set, which latter impressions were so uniformly negative that it's probably better not to say too much about it. For just one thing, he'd annoy hell out

(2) Scs 113   *EXT MULHOLLAND DRIVE* /DAY/ ⅛ pgs
MR. EDDY TAKES THE CAR FOR A CRUISE, INFINITI MOVES UP FAST BEHIND THEM

(3) Scs 114   *EXT MR. EDDY'S MERCEDES* /DAY/ ⅛ pgs
MR. EDDY LETS INFINITI PASS AND FORCES IT OFF ROAD

These car-intensive scenes are, as was mentioned, being shot in Griffith Park, a roughly Delaware-sized expanse out in the foothills of the Santa Monicas. Imagine a kind of semi-arid Yellowstone, full of ridges and buttes and spontaneous little landslides of dirt and gravel. Asymmetrical's advance team has established what's called a Base Camp of about a dozen trailers along one of the little roads between Mulholland and the San Diego freeway,[23] and Security has blocked off areas of sev-

---

of everybody between takes by running around trying to borrow everybody's cellular phone for an "emergency." I'll confess that I eavesdropped on some of his emergency cellular phone conversations, and in one of them he said to somebody "But what did she say about *me?*" three times in a row. For another thing, he was a heavy smoker but never had his own cigarettes and was always bumming cigarettes from crewpeople who you could tell were making about 1% of what he was making on this movie. I admit that none of these are exactly capital offenses, but they added up. Getty also suffered from comparison with his stand-in, who was apparently his friend and who always stood right near him, wearing an identical auto-shop jumpsuit with *"Pete"* sewn in cursive on the breast and an identically gruesome ersatz carbuncle on his forehead, and who was laid back and cool and very funny — e.g. when I expressed surprise that so much time on a movie set was spent standing around waiting with nothing to do, Balthazar Getty's stand-in was the one who said "We actually work for free; it's the waiting around we get paid for," which maybe you had to be there but in the context of the mind-shattering boredom of standing around the set all day seemed incredibly funny.

OK, fuck it: the single most annoying thing about Balthazar Getty was that whenever David Lynch was around Getty would be very unctuous and over-respectful and asskissy, but when Lynch wasn't around Getty would make fun of him and do an unkind imitation of his distinctive speaking voice (w/r/t which see below) that wasn't a very good imitation but was clearly intended to be disrespectful and mean.)

[23] Eleven trailers, actually, most of them from Foothill Studio Equipment Rentals of Glendale and Transcord Mobile Studios of Burbank. All the trailers are detached and up on blocks. The Honeywagon is the fourth trailer in the line. There are trailers for Lights, Props, F/X, Wardrobe, Grippish stuff, and some for the bigger stars in the cast, though the stars' trailers don't have their names or a gold star on the door or anything. The F/X trailer flies a Jolly Roger. Hard grunge issues from the Lighting trailer, and

eral other roads for the driving scenes, burly guys with walkie-talkies and roadie-black T-shirts forming barricades at various places to keep joggers and civilian drivers from intruding into the driving shots or exposing the production to insurance liability during stunts. LA civilians are easygoing about being turned back from the barricades and seem as blasé as New Yorkers about movies being filmed on their turf.

Griffith Park, though lovely in a kind of desiccated, lunar way, turns out to be a thoroughgoingly Lynchian filming environment, with perfusive sunshine and imported-beer-colored light but a weird kind of subliminal ominousness about it. This ominousness is hard to put a finger on or describe in any sensuous way. It turns out that there's a warning out that day for a Santa Ana Wind, a strange weather phenomenon that causes fire hazards[24] and also a weird but verifiable kind of high-ion anxiety in man and beast alike. LA's murder rate is apparently higher

---

outside a couple other trailers tough-looking crewpeople sit in canvas chairs reading *Car Action* and *Guns and Ammo*. Some portion of the movie's crew spends just about all their time in Base Camp doing various stuff in trailers, though it's hard to figure out just what they're doing, because these crewpeople have the kind of carny-esque vibe about them of people who spend a lot of time with their trailers and regard the trailers as their special territory and aren't particularly keen on having you climb up in there and see what they're doing. But a lot of it is highly technical. The area closest to daylight in the back of the Lighting and/or Camera-Related trailer, for example, has tripods and lightpoles and attachments of all lengths and sizes lined up very precisely, like ordnance. Shelves near the tripods have labeled sections for "2 × MIGHTY," "2 × 8 JUNIOR," "2 × MICKEY MOLES," "2 × BABY BJs," on and on. Boxes of lenses in rows have labels like

LONG PRIMES	A FILTS/4 × 5/DIOPS	WIDEPRIMES
50mm "E" T2 4'	SPC 200-108A	30mm "C" T3 4'
75mm "E" T2 4'	B FILTS 4×5	40mm "E" T2 3.5'
100mm "E" T2 4'		

---

[24] LAFD inspectors were all over the set, glaring at you if you lit a cigarette, and nicotinic conditions were pretty rugged because Scott Cameron decreed that people could smoke only if they were standing near the sand-filled butt can, of which there was apparently only one, and David Lynch, a devoted smoker of American Spirit All-Natural cigarettes, tended to commandeer the butt can, and people who wanted to smoke and were not near Lynch pretty much had to chew their knuckle and wait for him to turn his back so they could steal the can.

during Santa Ana Wind periods than any other time, and in Griffith Park it's easy to confirm that something's up atmospherically: sounds sound harsher, smells smell stronger, breathing tastes funny, the sunlight has a way of diffracting into spikes that penetrate all the way to the back of the skull, and overall there's a weird leathery stillness to the air, the West-Coast equivalent of the odd aquarial stillness that tends to precede Midwestern thunderstorms. The air smells of sage and pine and dust and distant creosote. Wild mustard, yucca, sumac, and various grasses form a kind of five-o'clock shadow on the hillsides, and scrub oak and pine jut at unlikely angles, and some of the trees' trunks are creepily curved and deformed, and there are also a lot of obstreperous weeds and things with thorns that discourage much hiking around. The texture of the site's flora is basically that of a broom's business end. A single red-tailed hawk circles overhead through the whole first day of shooting, just one hawk, and always the same circle, so that after a while the circle seemed etched. The road where the set is is like a kind of small canyon between a butte on one side and an outright cliff on the other. The cliff affords both a good place to study the choreography of the set and, in the other direction, a spectacular view of Hollywood to the right and to the left the S.F. Valley and the Santa Monicas and the distant sea's little curved rind of blue. It's hard to get straight on whether Asymmetrical chose this particular bit of Griffith Park or whether it was simply assigned to them by the LA office that grants location-licenses to movies, but it's good tight cozy site. The whole thing forms a rough triangle, with the line of Base Camp trailers extending down one small road and the catering trailer and salad bars and picnic tables for lunch spread out along a perpendicular road and a hypotenusally-angled larger road between them that's where the actual location set is; it's the c^2 road with the set that's got the great hill and cliff for viewing.

Basically what happens all morning is that Robert Loggia's sinister black Mercedes 6.9 and the tailgating Infiniti and the production's big complicated camera truck will go off and be gone for long stretches of time, tooling back and forth along the same barricaded mile of what is ostensibly Mulholland Drive while Lynch and his Director of Photography try to capture whatever particular combinations of light and angle and speed add up to a distinctively Lynchian shot of people driving. While the car-filming is going on, the other 60 or so members of

the location crew and staff all perform small maintenance and prepara-
tory tasks and lounge around and shoot the shit and basically kill enormous amounts of time. There are, on location today, grips, propmasters,
sound people, script people, dialogue coaches, camera people, electricians, makeup and hair people, a First Aid guy, production assistants, stand-ins, stunt doubles, producers, lighting technicians, on-set
dressers, set decorators, A.D.'s, unit publicists, location managers, costume people with rollable racks of clothes like you see in NYC's Garment
District, continuity people, script people, special effects coordinators
and technicians, LAFD cigarette-discouragers, a representative of the
production's insurance underwriter, a variety of personal assistants and
factota and interns, and a substantial number of persons with no discernible function at all. The whole thing is tremendously complex and
confusing, and a precise census is hard to take because a lot of the crew
look generally alike and the functions they perform are extremely technical and complicated and performed with high-speed efficiency, and
when everybody's in motion the set's choreography is the visual equivalent of an Altman group-dialogue, and it takes a while even to start picking up on the various distinguishing cues in appearance and gear that
allow you to distinguish one species of crew personnel from another, so
that the following rough taxonomy doesn't start emerging until late on
9 January:

Grips tend to be large beefy blue-collar guys with walrus mustaches
and baseball caps and big wrists and beer-guts but extremely alive alert
intelligent eyes — they look like very bright professional movers, which
is basically what they are. The production's electricians, lighting guys,
and F/X guys, who are also as a rule male and large, are distinguished
from the grips via their tendency to have long hair in a ponytail and to
wear T-shirts advertising various brands of esoteric hi-tech gear. None
of the grips wear earrings, but over 50% of the technical guys wear earrings, and a couple have beards, and four of the five electricians for some
reason have Fu Manchu mustaches, and with their ponytails and pallor
they all have the distinctive look of guys who work in record- or head-
shops; plus in general the recreational-chemical vibe around these more
technical blue-collar guys is very decidedly not a beer-type vibe.

The male camera operators, for some reason, tend to wear pith
helmets, and the Steadicam operator's pith helmet in particular looks

authentic and armed-combat-souvenirish, with a fine mesh of coir all over it for camouflage and a jaunty feather in the band.

A majority of the camera and sound and makeup crew are female, but a lot of these, too, have a similar look: 30ish, makeupless, insouciantly pretty, wearing faded jeans and old running shoes and black T-shirts, and with lush well-conditioned hair tied carelessly out of the way so that strands tend to escape and trail and have to be chuffed out of the eyes periodically or brushed away with the back of a ringless hand — in sum, the sort of sloppily pretty tech-savvy young woman you can just tell smokes pot and owns a dog. Most of these hands-on technical females have that certain expression around the eyes that communicates the exact same attitude communicated by somebody's use of the phrase "Been there, done that." At lunch several of them won't eat anything but bean curd, and they make it clear that they don't regard certain grips' comments about what bean curd looks like as in any way worthy of response. One of the technical women, the production's still-photographer — whose name is Suzanne and is fun to talk to about her dog — has on the inside of her forearm a tattoo of the Japanese character for "strength," and she can manipulate her forearm's muscles in such a way as to make the ideogram bulge Nietzscheanly out and then recede.

A lot of the script people and wardrobe people and production assistants are also female, but they're of a different genus — younger, less lean and more vulnerable, without the technically savvy self-esteem of the camera/sound women. As opposed to the hands-on women's weltschmerzian cool, the script and P.A. females all have the same pained "I-went-to-a-really-good-college-and-what-am-I-doing-with-my-life" look in their eyes, the sort of look where you know that if they're not in twice-a-week therapy it's only because they can't afford it.

Another way to distinguish different crewpeople's status and function is to look at what kind of personal communication gear they have. The rank-and-file grips are pretty much the only people without any kind of personal communicative gear. The rest of the hands-on and technical crew carry walkie-talkies, as do the location manager, the people in touch with the camera truck, and the burly guys manning the road's barricades. Many of the other crew carry cellular phones in snazzy hip-side holsters, and the amount of cellular-phone talking going on more than lives up to popular stereotypes about LA and cellulars.[25] The Second A.D., a young black lady named Simone whom I get to interact with a lot because she's always having to inform me that I'm in the way of something and need to move (though she isn't ever crabby or impolite about it), has an actual cellular *headset* instead of just a holstered cellular phone, though with Simone the headset isn't an affectation: the poor lady spends more time conferring on the phone than any non-teenage human being I've ever seen, and the headset leaves her hands free to write stuff on the various clipboards she carries around in an actual clipboard-*holder*.

The set's true executive class — line producer, unit publicist, underwriter, D.P. — have personal pagers that sometimes will all sound at

---

[25] After absorbing so much about it from the media, actually visiting Los Angeles in person produces a curious feeling of relief at finding a place that actually confirms your stereotyped preconceptions instead of confounding them and making you loathe your own ignorance and susceptibility to media stereotype: viz. stuff like cellular phones, rampant pulchritude, the odd ambient blend of New Age gooeyness and right-wing financial acumen. (E.g., one of the two prenominate people named Balloon, a guy who wore Birkenstocks and looked like he subsisted entirely on cellulose, had worked out an involved formula for describing statistical relationships between margin-calls on certain kinds of commodity futures and the market value of certain types of real estate, and had somehow gotten the impression that I and/or *Premiere* magazine ought to be interested in describing the formula in this article in such a way as to allow Balloon to start up a kind of pricey newsletter-type thing where people would for some reason pay large amounts of money for access to this formula, and for the better part of an afternoon he was absolutely unshakable, his obtuseness almost Zen — like a Lynchian bus-station wacko with an advanced degree from the L.S.E. — and the only way to peel him off me was to promise on my honor to find some way to work him and his formula into this article, an honor-obligation I've now fulfilled, though if *Premiere* wants to take the old editorial machete to it there's not really any way I can be held responsible.

(By the way, in case you think I'm lying or exaggerating about having met two unconnected persons named Balloon on this visit, the other Balloon was part of a rather unaccomplished banjo-and-maraca street duo on the median strip just outside the lavish deserted mall across the street from the gorgeous balcony that was too narrow and hazardously fenced to step onto, and the reason I approached this Balloon was that I wanted to know whether the wicked welts on his face-and-neck-area were by any chance from errant quarters or half-dollars thrown at him from speeding cars, which they turned out not to be.))

once but just slightly out of synch, producing in the weird ionized Santa Ana air a sound-blend that fully qualifies as Lynchian. And that's how you can tell people apart telecommunicationally. (The exception to every rule is Scott Cameron, the 1st A.D., who bears with Sisyphean resignation the burden of two walkie-talkies, a cellular phone, a pager, and a very serious battery-powered bullhorn all at the same time.)

But then so about like once an hour everybody's walkie-talkie starts crackling, and then a couple minutes later Lynch and the actual shooting team and cars come hauling back in to Base and everybody on the crew springs into frantic but purposeful action so that from the specular vantage of the roadside cliff the set resembles an anthill that's been stirred with a stick. Sometimes the shooting team comes back just to change cars for a shot: the production has somehow acquired two identical black Mercedes 6.9's, and each is now embellished with different kind of filmmaking attachments and equipment. For a particular shot inside the moving Mercedes, some of the grips construct a kind of platform out of reticulate piping and secure it to the hood of the car with clamps and straps, and then various other technicians attach a 35mm Panavision camera, several different complicatedly angled mole and Bambino lights, and a 3' × 5' bounce[26] to various parts of the hood's platform. This stuff is locked down tight, and the 2nd Asst. Cameraperson, a breathtaking and all-business lady everyone addresses as "Chesney,"[27] fiddles complexly with the camera's anamorphic lens and various filters. When sunlight off the Mercedes's windshield becomes a problem,[28] the Director of Photography and the camera guy in the especially authentic-looking pith helmet and Chesney all huddle and

[26] (looks like a blank canvas or stunted sail, helps concentrate light where they want it)

[27] It's unclear whether this is her first name or her last name or a diminutive or what. Chesney is dressed in standard grunge flannel and dirty sneakers, has about 8 feet of sun-colored hair piled high on her head and held (tenuously) in place with sunglasses, and can handle an anamorphic lens like nobody's business.

[28] (There's one young guy on the crew whose entire function seems to be going around with a bottle of Windex and a roll of paper towels and Windexing every glass surface blindingly clean.)

confer and decide to brace a gauzy diffusion filter between the camera and the windshield.

The camera truck is a complex green pickup whose side door says it's the property of *Camera Trucks, Unltd*. The back part has three tiers for gear, lights, a Steadicam, a video monitor and sound feed, and then little seats for David Lynch and the Director of Photography and a camera operator. When it's back at Base, technical crewpeople converge on the truck in clusters of entomological-looking avidity and efficiency.

During the crews' frantic activity — all of it punctuated with loud bullhorn commands from Scott Cameron — the technicians from the camera truck and the stand-ins from the cars take their own turns standing around and talking on cellulars and rooting through the baskets of corporate snacks on the snack table looking for stuff they like; i.e. it's their turn to stand around and kill time. The exterior driving-shots all have stand-ins in the cars, but usually when the shooting team returns to Base the actual name actors will emerge from their trailers and join the roil. Robert Loggia in particular likes to come out and stand around chatting with his stand-in, who's of the same meaty build and olive complexion and has the same strand-intensive balding pattern and craggy facial menace as Loggia, and of course is identically dressed in mobster Armani, so that from the distance of the roadside cliff their conversation looks like its own surreal metacommentary on parallel identity crises.

David Lynch himself uses the down-time between takes to confer with A.D.'s and producers and to drink coffee and/or micturate into the undergrowth, and to smoke American Spirits and walk pensively around the Mercedeses and camera truck's technical fray, sometimes holding one hand to his cheek in a way that recalls Jack Benny. Now 50 years old, Lynch still looks like an adult version of the kind of kid who gets beat up a lot at recess. He's large, not exactly fat but soft-looking, and is far and away the palest person anywhere in view, his paleness dwarfing even the head-shop pallor of the lighting and F/X guys. He wears a black long-sleeved dress shirt with every possible button buttoned, baggy tan Chinos that are too short and flap around his ankles, and a deep-sea fisherman's cap with a very long bill. The tan cap matches his pants, and his socks match both each other and his shirt, suggesting an extremely nerdy costume that's been chosen and coordinated with care — a suggestion that with Lynch seems somehow endearing rather than pathetic. The sunglasses he wears on the camera truck are the cheap bulgey wrap-around kind that villains in old Japanese monster movies used to wear. The overstiff quality of his posture suggests either an ultradisciplinarian upbringing or a back brace. The general impression is that of a sort of geeky person who doesn't especially care whether people think he's geeky or not, an impression which equals a certain kind of physical dignity.

Lynch's face is the best thing about him, and I spend a lot of time staring at it from a variety of perspectives as he works the set. In photos of Lynch as a young man, he looks rather uncannily like James Spader, but he doesn't look like James Spader anymore. His face is now full in the sort of way that makes certain people's faces square, and it's pale and soft-looking — the cheeks you can tell are close-shaved daily and then moisturized afterward — and his eyes, which never once do that grotesque looking-in-opposite-directions-at-once thing they were doing on the 1990 *Time* cover, are large and mild and kind. In case you're one of the people who figure that Lynch must be as "sick" as his films, know that he doesn't have the beady or glassy look one associates with degeneracy-grade mental trouble. His eyes are good eyes: he looks at his set with very intense interest, but it's a warm and full-hearted interest, sort of the way you look when you're watching somebody you love doing something you also love. He doesn't fret or intrude on any of the technicians, though he will come over and confer when somebody needs to know what exactly he wants for the next set-up. He's the sort who manages to appear restful even in activity; i.e. he looks both very alert and very calm. There might be something about his calm that's a little creepy — one tends to think of really high-end maniacs being oddly calm, e.g. the way Hannibal Lecter's pulse rate stays under 80 as he bites somebody's tongue out.

13 what several different members of the crew and production staff, some of whom have been to film school, have to say about *Lost Highway*

"David's idea is to do this like dystopic vision of LA. You could do a dystopic vision of New York, but who'd care? New York's been done before."

"It's about deformity. Remember *Eraserhead?* This guy's going to be the ultimate Penishead."

"This is a movie that explores psychosis subjectively."

"I'm sure not going to go see it, I know that."

"It's a reflection on society as he sees it."

"This is a sort of a middle ground between an art film and a major studio release. This is a hard niche to work in. It's an economically fragile niche, you could say."

"This is his territory. This is taking us deeper into a space he's already carved out in previous work already — subjectivity and psychosis."

"He's doing a *Diane Arbus* number on LA, showing the *slimy undersection* of a dream-city. *Chinatown* did it, but it did it in a *historical* way, as a type of *noir-history.* David's film's about *madness;* it's *subjective,* not *historical.*"

"It's like, if you're a doctor or a nurse, are you going to go buy tickets to go see an operation for fun in your spare time, when you're done working?"

"This film represents schizophrenia *performatively,* not just *representationally.* This is done in terms of *loosening of identity, ontology,* and *continuity in time.*"

"Let me just say I have utmost respect — for David, for the industry, for what David means to this industry. Let me say for the record I'm excited. That I'm thrilled and have the utmost respect."

"It's a specialty film. Like *The Piano,* say. I mean it's not going to open in a thousand theaters."

" 'Utmost' is one word. There is no hyphen in 'utmost.' "

"It's about LA as hell. This is not unrealistic, if you want my opinion."

"It's a product like any other in a business like any other."

"It's a Negative Pick-Up. Fine Line, New Line, Miramax — they're all interested."

"David is the Id of the Now. If you quote me, say I quipped it. Say ' "David is the Id of the Now," quipped _____, who is the film's _____.' "

"David, as an artist, makes his own choices about what he wants. He makes a film when he feels he has something to say. The people who are interested in his films . . . some [of his films] are better than others.

Some are perceived as better than others. David does not look at this as his area of concern."

"He's a genius. You have to understand this. In these areas he's not like you and me."

"The head-changings are being done with makeup and lights. No CGIs."[29]

"Read *City of Quartz*. That's what this film's about right there in a nutshell."

"Some of [the producers] were talking about Hegel, whatever the hell *that* has to do with it."

"Let me just say I hope you're not planning to compromise him or us or the film in any way."

trivia tidbit

Laura Dern's soft blond hairstyle as Sandy in *Blue Velvet* is identical to Charlotte Stewart's soft blond hairstyle as Mary in *Eraserhead*.

14   a section that's a mix of extrapolations from other sections and is impossible to come up with a unified heading for

The word *postmodern* is admittedly overused, but the incongruity between the peaceful health of his mien and the creepy ambition of his films is something about David Lynch that is resoundingly postmodern. Other postmodern things about him are his speaking voice — which can be described only as sounding like Jimmy Stewart on acid — and the fact that it's literally impossible to know how seriously to take what he says. This is a genius auteur whose vocabulary in person consists of things like "Okey-doke" and "Marvy" and "Terrif" and "Gee." After the last car-filming run and then the return to Base Camp, as people are dismantling cameras and bounces and the unbelievably alluring Chesney is putting the afternoon's unused film under a reflective NASA blanket, Lynch three times in five minutes says "Golly!" Not one of these times does he utter "Golly!" with any evident irony or disingenuity or even

[29]   (= "Computer-Generated Images," as in *Jumanji*)

the flattened affect of somebody who's parodying himself. (Let's also remember that this is a man with every button on his shirt buttoned and highwater pants: it's like the only thing missing is a pocket protector.) During this same tri-"Golly!" interval, though, about fifty yards down the little hypotenal road the catering trailer's on Mr. Bill Pullman, who's sitting in a big canvas director's chair getting interviewed for his E.P.K.,[30] is leaning forward earnestly and saying of David Lynch both: "He's so truthful — that's what you build your trust on as an actor, with a director" and: "He's got this kind of *modality* to him, the way he speaks, that lets him be very open and honest and at the same time very sly. There's an irony about the way he speaks."

Whether *Lost Highway* is a smash hit or not, its atmosphere of tranced menace is going to be really good for Bill Pullman's career. From movies like *Sleepless in Seattle* and *While You Were Sleeping* and (ulp) *Casper*, I formed this view of Pullman the actor as a kind of good and decent but basically ineffectual guy, an *edgeless* guy; I always thought of him as kind of a watered-down version of the already pretty watery Jeff Daniels.[31] *Lost Highway* — for which Pullman has either lost weight or done Nautilus or both (he has, at any rate, somehow grown a set of cheekbones), and in which he's creepy and tormented and plays jagged, haunting jazz saxophone under a supersatured red-and-blue spot, and in which his face contorts in agony over the mutilated corpse of Patricia Arquette and then changes more than once into somebody else's face — is going to reveal edges and depths in Pullman that I believe will make him a true Star. For the E.P.K. he's in a tight all-black jazz musician's costume, and his makeup, already applied for a night scene

---

[30] I.e. "Electronic Press Kit," a bite-intensive interview that *Lost Highway*'s publicists can then send off to *Entertainment Tonight*, local TV stations that want Pullman-bites, etc. If the movie's a huge hit, the E.P.K.'s can then apparently be woven together into one of those *Behind the Scenes at the Making of Thus-and-Such* documentaries that HBO seems to be so fond of. Apparently all name stars have to do an E.P.K. for every movie they make; it's in their contract or something. I watched everybody's E.P.K. except Balthazar Getty's.

[31] (Pullman's turn as the jilted con man in *The Last Seduction* had some edge to it, but Pullman seems to have done such a good acting job in that one that few people realized it was him.)

in a couple hours, gives his face a creepily Reaganesque ruddiness, and while various kinds of crepuscular bugs plague the E.P.K. interviewer and cameraman and sound guy these bugs don't seem to come anywhere near Pullman, as if he's already got the aura of genuine stardom around him, the kind you can't quite define but that even insects can sense — it's like he's not even quite *there,* in his tall chair, or else simultaneously there and somewhere primally else.

Ms. Patricia Arquette has been bad in everything since *True Romance* without this fact seeming to have hurt her career any. It's hard to predict how audiences will react to her in *Lost Highway.* This is a totally new role(s) for her, as far as I can see. Her most credible performances to date have been as ingenues, plucky characters somehow in over their head, whereas in *Lost Highway* she herself is a part of the over-the-head stuff Bill Pullman and Balthazar Getty get plunged into. *Lost Highway*'s female lead is the kind of languid smoky narrow-eyed Incredibly-Sexy-But-Dangerous-Woman-With-Mindblowing-Secrets *noir*-type role that in recent years only *Body Heat*'s Kathleen Turner and *Miller's Crossing*'s Marcia Gay Harden have pulled off without falling into parody or camp. From the footage I saw, Arquette is OK but not great in *Lost Highway.* She vamps a lot, which is apparently the closest she can come to Sexy But Dangerous. The big problem is that her eyes are too opaque and her face too set and rigid to allow her to communicate effectively without dialogue, and so a lot of the long smoky silences Lynch requires of her come off stiff and uncomfortable, as if Arquette's forgotten her lines and is worrying about it. Even so, the truth is that Patricia Arquette is so out-landishly pretty in the film's rough-cut footage that at the time I didn't notice a whole lot aside from how she looked, which, seeing as how her Duessa-like character basically functions as an object in the film, seems OK, though I'm still a little uncomfortable saying it.[32]

Lost Highway will also, I predict, do huge things for the career of

---

[32] *Premiere* magazine's industrial juice or no, I wasn't allowed to watch footage of the porn videos both her characters frolic in, so I can't evaluate the harder-core parts of her performance in *Lost Highway.* It'll be interesting to see how much of the porn videos survives the final cut and the M.P.A.A.'s humorless review. If much of what the videos are rumored to contain appears in the final *Lost Highway,* Arquette may win a whole new kind of following.

Mr. Robert Blake,[33] who's been cast seemingly out of nowhere here as The Mystery Man. The choice of Blake shows in Lynch the same sort of genius for spotting villain-potential that led to his casting Hopper as Frank Booth in *Blue Velvet* and Willem DaFoe as Bobby Peru in *Wild at Heart*, an ability to detect and resurrect menacing depths in actors who seemed long ago to have lost any depths they'd ever had.[34] Gone, in *Lost Highway*, is the sensitive tough-guy of *Baretta* and the excruciating self-parody of Blake's stoned appearances on *The Tonight Show*; it's like Lynch has somehow reawakened the venomous charisma that made Blake's 1967 performance in *In Cold Blood* such a sphincter-loosener. Blake's Mystery Man is less over-the-top than was Frank Booth: The M.M. is himself velvety, almost effete, more reminiscent of Dean Stockwell's horrific cameo than of Hopper's tour de force. Blake is also here virtually unrecognizable as the steroidic cop who said things like "Dat's the name of dat tune" on '70s TV. Lynch has him many pounds lighter, hair shorn, creamed and powdered to a scotophilic pallor that makes him look both ravaged and Satanic — Blake here looks like a cross between the Klaus Kinski of *Nosferatu* and Ray Walston on some monstrous dose of PCP.

The most controversial bit of casting in *Lost Highway* is going to be Richard Pryor as Balthazar Getty's boss at the auto shop. Meaning Richard Pryor as in the Richard Pryor who's got the multiple sclerosis that's stripped him of 75 pounds and affects his speech and causes his eyes to bulge and makes him seem like a cruel child's parody of a damaged person. In *Lost Highway*, Richard Pryor's infirmity is meant to be grotesque and to jar against all our old memories of the "real" Pryor. Pryor's scenes are the parts of *Lost Highway* where I like David Lynch least: Pryor's painful to watch, and not painful in a good way or a way that has anything to do with the business of the movie, and I can't help thinking that Lynch is exploiting Pryor the same way John Waters likes to exploit

[33] R. Blake, born 1933 as Michael James Gubitosi in Nutley, New Jersey, was one of the child stars of *Our Gang*, was unforgettable as one of the killers in *In Cold Blood*, etc.

[34] Dennis Hopper's last powerful role before *Blue Velvet* had been the 1977 *Apocalypse Now*, and he'd become a kind of Hollywood embarrassment. DaFoe had been sort of typecast as Christ after *Platoon* and *Last Temptation*, though it's true that his sensualist's lips had whispered menace even on the cross.

Patricia Hearst, i.e. letting the actor think he's been hired to act when he's really been hired to be a spectacle, an arch joke for the audience to congratulate themselves on getting. And yet at the same time Pryor's symbolically perfect in this movie, in a way: the dissonance between the palsied husk on-screen and the vibrant man in our memory means that what we see in *Lost Highway* both is and is not the "real" Richard Pryor. His casting is thematically intriguing, then, but coldly, meanly so, and watching his scenes I again felt that I admired Lynch as an artist and from a distance but would have no wish to hang out in his trailer or be his friend.

15   addendum to (14) re Lynch and race

Except now for Richard Pryor, has there ever been even like *one* black person in a David Lynch movie?[35] There've been plenty of dwarves and amputees and spastics and psychotics, but have there been any other, more shall we say culturally significant minorities? Latins? Hasidim? Gay people?[36] Asian-Americans? . . . There was that sultry oriental sawmill owner in *Twin Peaks,* but her ethnicity was, to say the least, overshadowed by her sultriness.[37]

I.e. why are Lynch's movies all so *white?*

The likely answer involves the fact that Lynch's movies are essentially apolitical. Let's face it: get white people and black people together on the

---

[35]   And Richard Pryor's in the movie as Richard-Pryor-the-celebrity-who's-now-neurologically-damaged, not as a black person.

[36]   Dean Stockwell's Ben in *Blue Velvet* was probably technically gay, but what was relevant about Ben was his creepy effeminacy, which Frank called Ben's "*suaveness.*" The only homoerotic subcurrent in *Blue Velvet* is between Jeffrey and Frank, and neither of them are what you'd call gay.

[37]   (There were also, come to think of it, those two black hardware store employees (both named Ed) in *Blue Velvet,* but, again, their blackness was incidental to the comic-symbolic issue of one Ed's blindness and the other Ed's dependence on the blind Ed's perfect memory for hardware-prices. I'm talking about characters who are, like, *centrally* minorityish in Lynch's movies.)

screen and there's going to be an automatic political voltage. Ethnic and cultural and political tensions. And Lynch's films are in no way about ethnic or cultural or political tensions. The films are all about tensions, but these tensions are always in and between individuals. There are, in Lynch's movies, no real groups or associations. There are sometimes alliances, but these are alliances based on shared obsessions. Lynch's characters are essentially alone (Alone): they're alienated from pretty much everything except the particular obsessions they've developed to help ease their alienation (. . . or is their alienation in fact a consequence of their obsessions? and does Lynch really hold an obsession or fantasy or fetish to be any kind of true anodyne for human alienation? does the average fetishist have any kind of actual *relationship* with the fetish?) Anyway, *this* kind of stuff is Lynch's movies' only real politics, viz. the primal politics of Self/Exterior and Id/Object. It's a politics all about religions, darknesses, but for Lynch these have nothing to do with testaments or skin.

interconnected trivia tidbits: what kind of car Patricia Arquette has, whom she's married to, etc.

Patricia Arquette owns a brand-new maroon Porsche, which Porsche must be very special to her because she seems to be in the freaking thing all the time, even driving it the 200 feet between her trailer and the set in Griffith Park, so that the crew always has to move carts full of equipment out of the way to let her pass, yelling at one another to be careful of Patricia Arquette's beautiful car's paint job. Plus Arquette always has her stand-in with her in the car — they're apparently close friends and go everyplace together in the maroon Porsche, from a distance looking eerily identical. Patricia Arquette's husband is Mr. Nicolas Cage, who worked with Lynch on both *Wild at Heart* and the video of *Industrial Symphony #1*.

16 Patricia Arquette's description of the central challenge for
Bill Pullman and Balthazar Getty w/r/t the "motivation"
of *Lost Highway*'s metamorphosing protagonist (whose
name when he's Bill Pullman is "Fred" and when he's
Balthazar Getty is "Pete")

"The question for Bill and Balthazar is what kind of woman-hater is
Fred[-dash-Pete]? Is he the kind of woman-hater who goes out with a
woman and fucks her and then never calls her again, or is he the kind
who goes out with a woman and fucks her and then kills her? And the
real question to explore is: how different are these kinds?"

11a why what David Lynch wants from you might be a good thing

If you will keep in mind the outrageous kinds of moral manipulation we suffer at the hands of most contemporary directors,[38] it will
be easier to convince you that something in Lynch's own clinically detached filmmaking is not only refreshing but redemptive. It's not that
Lynch is somehow "above" being manipulative; it's more like he's just
not interested. Lynch's movies are about images and stories in his head
that he wants to see made external and complexly real. (His most illuminating statement about the making of *Eraserhead* involves "the ex-
hilaration he felt standing in the set of Mr. and Mrs. X's apartment
and realizing that what he had pictured in his mind had been exactly
recreated").

---

[38] (Wholly random examples:) Think of the way Parker's *Mississippi Burning*
fumbled at our consciences like a freshman at a coed's brassiere, or of *Dances with
Wolves'* crude, smug reversal of old westerns' "White=Good & Indian=Bad" equation. Or think of movies like *Fatal Attraction* and *Unlawful Entry* and *Die Hard I–III*
and *Copycat*, etc., where we're so relentlessly set up to approve the villains' bloody
punishment in the climax that we might as well be wearing togas. (The formulaic in-
exorability of these villains' defeat does give the climaxes an oddly soothing, ritualistic
quality, and it makes the villains martyrs in a way, sacrifices to our desire for black-
and-white morality and comfortable judgment . . . I think it was during the original
Die Hard that I first rooted consciously for the villain.)

It's already been observed that Lynch brings to his art the sensibility of a very bright child immersed in the minutiae of his own fantasies. This kind of approach has disadvantages: his films are not especially sophisticated or intelligent; there is little critical judgment or quality-control-type checks on ideas that do not work; things tend to be hit-or-miss. Plus the films are, like a fantasy-prone little kid, self-involved to an extent that's pretty much solipsistic. Hence their coldness.[39]

But part of the involution and coldness derives from the fact that David Lynch seems truly to possess the capacity for detachment from response that most artists only pay lip-service to: he does pretty much what he wants and appears not to give much of a shit whether you like it or even *get* it. His loyalties are fierce and passionate and almost entirely to himself.

I don't mean to make it sound like this kind of thing is wholly good or that Lynch is some kind of paragon of integrity. His passionate inwardness is refreshingly childlike, but I notice that very few of us choose to make small children our friends. And as for Lynch's serene detachment from people's response, I've noticed that, while I can't help but respect and sort of envy the moral nerve of people who truly do not care what others think of them, people like this also make me nervous, and I tend to do my admiring from a safe distance. On (again) the other hand, though, we need to acknowledge that in this age of Hollywood "message" films and focus-group screenings and pernicious Nielsenism — Cinema By Referendum, where we vote with our entertainment-dollar either for spectacular effects to make us feel something or for lalations of moral clichés that let us remain comfortable in our numbness — Lynch's rather sociopathic disinterest in our approval seems refreshing/redemptive (if also creepy).

[39] (solipsism being not exactly the cheery crackling hearth of psychophilosophical orientations)

17   **the only part of this article that's really in any way "behind the scenes"**

Asymmetrical Productions' headquarters is, as mentioned, the house next door to Lynch's house. It really is a house. In the yard outside the door are a department store swingset and a Big Wheel on its side. I don't think anybody really lives there; I think it gets treated as an annex to Lynch's own house and that Lynch's children's play spills over. You enter A.P.HQ through a sliding glass door into what is the house's kitchen, with a Mannington tile floor and a dishwasher and a fridge with witty magnets on it, plus there's a kitchen table where a college-age kid is sitting working diligently at a laptop, and at first it all looks like some ur-domestic scene of a college kid home at his folks' house for the weekend or something, except when you come closer you start to notice that the kid's got a scary haircut and a serious facial tic, and what he's doing on the laptop is cueing a still-frame shot of the brunette Patricia Arquette's mutilated corpse against some set of coded specs on a clipboard that's propped against his Boynton mug of coffee. It's unclear who the kid is or just what he's doing or whether he even gets paid to do it.[40]

As in much of the Hollywood Hills, Asymmetrical's street is more

---

[40] For somebody whose productions are supposed to be top-secret, Lynch and Asymmetrical seem awfully tolerant about having functionless interns and weird silent young people hanging around the *Lost Highway* set. Isabella Rossellini's cousin is here, "Alesandro," a 25ish guy ostensibly taking photos of the production for an Italian magazine but in fact mostly just walking around with his girlfriend in a leather miniskirt (the girlfriend) and grooming his crewcut and smoking nowhere near the butt can. Plus there's also "Rolande" (pronounced as an iamb: "Ro*lande*"; my one interchange with Rolande consisted mostly of Rolande emphasizing this point). Rolande is an incredibly creepy French kid with a forehead about three feet high who somehow charmed Lynch into taking him on as an intern and lurks on the set constantly and does nothing but stand around with a little spiral notebook taking notes in a dense crabbed psychotically neat hand. Pretty much the whole crew and staff agrees that Rolande's creepy and unpleasant to be around and that God only knows what the tiny precise notes really concern, but Lynch apparently actually likes the kid, and claps him avuncularly on the shoulder whenever the kid's within reach, at which the kid smiles very widely and then afterward walks away rubbing his shoulder and muttering darkly.

like a canyon, and people's yards are 80° slopes with ice-plant lawns, and the HQ's entry/kitchen is actually on the house's top level, so that if you want access to the rest of the house you have to go down a vertiginous spiral staircase. This and various other stuff satisfies reasonable expectations of Lynchianism w/r/t the director's working environment. The HQ's bathroom's Cold knob doesn't work and the toilet seat won't stay up, but on the wall next to the toilet is an incredibly advanced and expensive Panasonic XDP phone with what looks like a fax device attached. Asymmetrical's receptionist, Jennifer, a statutorily young female who'd be gorgeous if she didn't have Nosferatic eyeshadow and cadet-blue nail polish on, blinks so slowly you have to think she's putting you on, and she declines to say for the record what music she's listening to on her headphones, and on her desk next to the computer and phones is one copy of Deleuze and Guittarri's *Anti-Oedipus* and one copy each of *Us* and *Wrestling World*. Lynch's own office — way below ground, so that its windows must look out on solid earth — has a big solid gray door that's closed and looks not only locked but somehow *armed*, such that only a fool would try the knob, but attached to the wall right outside the office door are two steel boxes labeled OUT and IN. The OUT box is empty, and the IN contains, in descending order: a 5,000-count box of Swingline-brand staples; a large promotional envelope, with Dick Clark's and Ed McMahon's pointillist faces on it, from the Publisher's Clearinghouse Sweepstakes, addressed directly to Lynch at Asymmetrical's address; and a fresh shrink-wrapped copy of Jack Nicklaus's instructional video *Golf My Way*. Your guess here is as good as mine.

Premiere's industry juice (plus the niceness of Mary Sweeney) means that I am allowed to view a lot of *Lost Highway*'s rough-cut footage in the actual Asymmetrical Productions editing room, where the movie itself is going to be edited. The editing room is off the kitchen and living room on the house's top level, and it clearly used to be either the master bedroom or a really ambitious study. It has gray steel shelves filled with complexly coded canisters of *Lost Highway*'s exposed film. One wall is covered with rows of index cards listing each scene of *Lost Highway* and detailing technical stuff about it. There are also two separate KEM-brand flatbed viewing and editing machines, each with its own monitor and twin reel-to-reel devices for cueing up both film and sound. I am actually allowed to pull up a padded desk chair and sit there right in front of one of the KEMs's monitor while an assistant editor loads various bits of footage. The chair is old and much-used, its padded seat beaten over what has clearly been thousands of hours into the form-fitting mold of a bottom, a bottom quite a lot larger than mine — the bottom, in fact, of a combination workaholic and inveterate milkshake-drinker — and for an epiphanic moment I'm convinced I'm sitting in Mr. David Lynch's own personal film-editing chair.

The editing room is dark, understandably, its windows first blacked out and then covered with large Abstract Expressionist paintings. These paintings, in which the color black predominates, are by David Lynch, and with all due respect are not very interesting, somehow both derivative-seeming and amateurish, like stuff you could imagine Francis Bacon doing in jr. high.[41]

Far more interesting are some paintings by David Lynch's ex-wife that are stacked canted against the wall of Mary Sweeney's office downstairs. It's unclear whether Lynch owns them or has borrowed them from his ex-wife or what, but in *Lost Highway*'s first act, three of these paintings are on the wall above the couch where Bill Pullman and Patricia Arquette sit watching creepy invasive videos of themselves asleep. This is just one of David Lynch's little personal flourishes in the movie. The most interesting of the paintings, done in bright primaries with a blunt blocky style that's oddly affecting, is of a lady in a tank-top sitting at a table reading a note from her child. Superimposed above this scene in the painting is the text of the note, on what is rendered as wide-rule notebook paper and in a small child's hand, w/ reversed e's and so on:

---

[41] Lynch's best-known painting, entitled *Oww, God, Mom, the Dog He Bited Me*, is described by Lynch in his *Time* cover-story this way: "There's a clump of Band-Aids in the bottom corner. A dark background. A stick figure whose head is a blur of blood. Then a very small dog made out of glue. There is a house, a little black bump. It's pretty crude, pretty primitive and minimal. I like it." The painting itself, which is oddly absent from the book *Images* but has been published as a postcard, looks like the sort of diagnostic House-Tree-Person drawing that gets a patient institutionalized in a hurry.

> Dear Mom I keep having my fish
> dream. They bite my face!
> Tell dad I dont take naps. The
> fishes are skinny an mad
> I miss you. His wife makes me
> eat trouts and anchovys The
> fishes make nosis they blow
> bubbels. How are you [unreadable] you
> fine? don't forget to lock
> the doors the fishes [unreadable]
> me they hate me.
>   Love form
>   DANA

In the painting, what's moving is that the text of the note is superimposed such that parts of the mother's head obscure the words — those are the "[unreadable]" parts. I do not know whether Lynch has a child named Dana, but considering who the artist is, plus the painting's child's evident situation and pain, it seems both deeply moving and sort of sick that Lynch would display this piece on a wall in his movie. Anyway, now you know the text of one of Bill Pullman's *objets,* and you can get the same kind of chill I got if you squint hard enough in the movie's early interior scenes to make the picture out. And you'll be even more chilled in a later interior scene in Bill Pullman and Patricia Arquette's house, a post-murder scene, in which the same three paintings hang above the sofa but are now, without any discernible reason or explanation, upside down. The whole thing's not just creepy but *personally* creepy.

trivia tidbit

When *Eraserhead* was a surprise hit at festivals and got a distributor, David Lynch rewrote the cast and crew's contracts so they would all get a share of the money, which they still do, every fiscal quarter, in perpetuity. Lynch's A.D. and P.A. and everything else on *Eraserhead* was Catherine Coulson, who was later the Log Lady on *Twin Peaks.* Plus Coulson's son, Thomas, played the little boy who brings Henry's ablated head into the pencil factory. Lynch's loyalty to actors and his homemade, co-op-style productions make his oeuvre a veritable pomo-anthill of interfilm connections.

trivia tidbit

It is very hard for a hot director to avoid what Hollywood mental-health specialists term "Tarantino's Disorder," which involves the sustained delusion that being a good movie director entails that you will also be a good movie actor. In 1988 Lynch actually starred, with Ms. Isabella Rossellini, in Tina Rathbone's *Zelly and Me*, which if you've never heard of it you can probably figure out why.

9a the cinematic tradition it's curious that nobody seems to have observed Lynch comes right out of (w/ an epigraph)

> It has been said that the admirers of
> *The Cabinet of Doctor Caligari* are usually
> painters, or people who think and remember
> graphically. This is a mistaken conception.
> — Paul Rotha, "The German Film"

Since Lynch was originally trained as a painter (an Ab-Exp painter at that), it seems curious that no film critics or scholars[42] have ever treated of his movies' clear relation to the classical Expressionist cinema tradition of Wiene, Kobe, early Lang, etc. And I am talking here about the very simplest and most straightforward sort of definition of *Expressionist,* viz. "Using objects and characters not as representations but as transmitters for the director's own internal impressions and moods."

Certainly plenty of critics have observed, with Kael, that in Lynch's movies "There's very little art between you and the filmmaker's psyche

---

[42] (not even the Lynch-crazy French film pundits who've made his movies the subject of more than two dozen essays in *Cahiers du Cinéma* — the French apparently regard Lynch as God, though the fact that they also regard Jerry Lewis as God might salt the compliment a bit . . .)

. . . because there's less than the usual amount of inhibition." They've noted the preponderance of fetishes and fixations in Lynch's work, his characters' lack of conventional introspection (an introspection which in film equals "subjectivity"), his sexualization of everything from an amputated limb to a bathrobe's sash, from a skull to a "heart plug,"[43] from split lockets to length-cut timber. They've noted the elaboration of Freudian motifs that tremble on the edge of parodic cliché — the way Marietta's invitation to Sailor to "fuck Mommy" takes place in a bathroom and produces a rage that's then displaced onto Bob Ray Lemon; the way Merrick's opening dream-fantasy of his mother supine before a rampaging elephant has her face working in what's interpretable as either terror or orgasm; the way Lynch structures *Dune*'s labrynthian plot to highlight Paul Eutrades's "escape" with his "witch-mother" after Paul's father's "death" by "betrayal." They have noted with particular emphasis what's pretty much Lynch's most famous scene, *Blue Velvet*'s Jeffrey Beaumont peering through a closet's slats as Frank Booth rapes Dorothy while referring to himself as "Daddy" and to her as "Mommy" and promising dire punishments for "looking at me" and breathing through an unexplained gas mask that's overtly similar to the O_2-mask we'd just seen Jeffrey's own dying Dad breathing through.

They've noted all this, critics have, and they've noted how, despite its heaviness, the Freudian stuff tends to give Lynch's movies an enormous psychological power; and yet they don't seem to make the obvious point that these very heavy Freudian riffs are powerful instead of ridiculous because they're deployed Expressionistically, which among other things means they're deployed in an old-fashioned, pre-postmodern way, i.e. nakedly, *sincerely*, without postmodernism's abstraction or irony. Jeffrey Beaumont's interslat voyeurism may be a sick parody of the Primal Scene, but neither he (a "college boy") nor anybody else in the movie ever shows any inclination to say anything like "Gee, this is sort of like a sick parody of the good old Primal Scene" or even betrays any awareness that a lot of what's going on is — both symbolically and psychoanalytically — heavy as hell. Lynch's movies, for all their unsubtle archetypes and symbols and intertextual references and c., have about them the remarkable unself-consciousness that's kind of

43 (q.v. Baron Harkonen's "cardiac rape" of the servant boy in *Dune*'s first act)

the hallmark of Expressionist art — nobody in Lynch's movies analyzes or metacriticizes or hermeneuticizes or anything,[44] including Lynch himself. This set of restrictions makes Lynch's movies fundamentally unironic, and I submit that Lynch's lack of irony is the real reason some cinéastes — in this age when ironic self-consciousness is the one and only universally recognized badge of sophistication — see him as a naïf or a buffoon. In fact, Lynch is neither — though nor is he any kind of genius of visual coding or tertiary symbolism or anything. What he is is a weird hybrid blend of classical Expressionist and contemporary postmodernist, an artist whose own "internal impressions and moods" are (like ours) an olla podrida of neurogenic predisposition and phylogenic myth and psychoanalytic schema and pop-cultural iconography — in other words, Lynch is sort of G. W. Pabst with an Elvis ducktail.

This kind of contemporary Expressionist art, in order to be any good, seems like it needs to avoid two pitfalls. The first is a self-consciousness of form where everything gets very mannered and refers cutely to itself.[45] The second pitfall, more complicated, might be called "terminal idiosyncrasy" or "antiempathetic solipsism" or something: here the artist's own perceptions and moods and impressions and obsessions come off as just too particular to him alone. Art, after all, is supposed to be a kind of communication, and "personal expression" is cinematically interesting only to the extent that what's expressed finds and strikes chords within the viewer. The difference between experiencing art that succeeds as communication and art that doesn't is rather like the difference between being sexually intimate with a person and watching that person

---

[44] Here's one reason why Lynch's characters have this weird *opacity* about them, a narcotized over-earnestness that's reminiscent of lead-poisoned kids in Midwestern trailer parks. The truth is that Lynch needs his characters stolid to the point of retardation; otherwise they'd be doing all this ironic eyebrow-raising and finger-steepling about the overt symbolism of what's going on, which is the very last thing he wants his characters doing.

[45] Lynch did a one-and-a-half-gainer into this pitfall in *Wild at Heart*, which is one reason the movie comes off so pomo-cute, another being the ironic intertextual self-consciousness (q.v. *Wizard of Oz, Fugitive Kind*) that Lynch's better Expressionist movies have mostly avoided.

masturbate. In terms of literature, richly communicative Expressionism is epitomized by Kafka, bad and onanistic Expressionism by the average Graduate Writing Program avant-garde story.

It's the second pitfall that's especially bottomless and dreadful, and Lynch's best movie, *Blue Velvet*, avoided it so spectacularly that seeing the movie when it first came out was a kind of revelation for me. It was such a big deal that ten years later I remember the date — 30 March 1986, a Wednesday night — and what the whole group of us MFA Program[46] students did after we left the theater, which was to go to a coffeehouse and talk about how the movie was a revelation. Our Graduate MFA Program had been pretty much of a downer so far: most of us wanted to see ourselves as avant-garde writers, and our professors were all traditional commercial Realists of the *New Yorker* school, and while we loathed these teachers and resented the chilly reception our "experimental" writing received from them, we were also starting to recognize that most of our own avant-garde stuff really was solipsistic and pretentious and self-conscious and masturbatory and bad, and so that year we went around hating ourselves and everyone else and with no clue about how to get experimentally better without caving in to loathsome commercial-Realistic pressure, etc. This was the context in which *Blue Velvet* made such an impression on us. The movie's obvious "themes" — the evil flip side to picket-fence respectability, the conjunctions of sadism and sexuality and parental authority and voyeurism and cheesy '50s pop and Coming of Age, etc. — were for us less revelatory than the way the movie's surrealism and dream-logic *felt*: they felt *true, real*. And the couple things just slightly but marvelously off in every shot — the Yellow Man literally dead on his feet, Frank's unexplained gas mask, the eerie industrial thrum on the stairway outside Dorothy's apartment, the weird dentate-vagina sculpture[47] hanging on an otherwise bare wall over Jeffrey's bed at home, the dog drinking from the hose in the stricken dad's hand — it wasn't just that these touches seemed

---

[46] (= Master of Fine Arts Program, which is usually a two-year thing for graduate students who want to write fiction or poetry professionally)

[47] (I'm hoping now in retrospect this wasn't something Lynch's ex-wife did . . .)

eccentrically cool or experimental or arty, but that they communicated things that felt *true*. *Blue Velvet* captured something crucial about the way the U.S. present acted on our nerve endings, something crucial that couldn't be analyzed or reduced to a system of codes or aesthetic principles or workshop techniques.

This was what was epiphanic for us about *Blue Velvet* in grad school, when we saw it: the movie helped us realize that first-rate experimentalism was a way not to "transcend" or "rebel against" the truth but actually to *honor* it. It brought home to us — via images, the medium we were suckled on and most credulous of — that the very most important artistic communications took place at a level that not only wasn't intellectual but wasn't even fully conscious, that the unconscious's true medium wasn't verbal but imagistic, and that whether the images were Realistic or Postmodern or Expressionistic or Surreal or what-the-hellever was less important than whether they *felt true*, whether they rang psychic cherries in the communicatee.

I don't know whether any of this makes sense. But it's basically why David Lynch the filmmaker is important to me. I felt like he showed me something genuine and important on 3/30/86. And he couldn't have done it if he hadn't been thoroughly, nakedly, unpretentiously, unsophisticatedly himself, a self that communicates primarily itself — an Expressionist. Whether he is an Expressionist naïvely or pathologically or ultra-pomo-sophisticatedly is of little importance to me. What is important is that *Blue Velvet* rang cherries, and it remains for me an example of contemporary artistic heroism.

10a (w/ an epigraph)

> All of Lynch's work can be described as
> emotionally infantile. . . . Lynch likes to ride
> his camera into orifices (a burlap hood's eyehole
> or a severed ear), to plumb the blackness beyond.
> There, id-deep, he fans out his deck of dirty pictures . . .
> — Kathleen Murphy of *Film Comment*

One reason it's sort of heroic to be a contemporary Expressionist is that it all but invites people who don't like your art to make an ad hominem move from the art to the artist. A fair number of critics[48] object to David Lynch's movies on the grounds that they are "sick" or "dirty" or "infantile," then proceed to claim that the movies are themselves revelatory of various deficiencies in Lynch's own character,[49] troubles that range from developmental arrest to misogyny to sadism. It's not just the fact that twisted people do hideous things to one another in Lynch's films, these critics will argue, but rather the "moral attitude" implied by the way Lynch's camera records hideous behavior. In a way, his detractors have a point. Moral atrocities in Lynch movies are never staged to elicit outrage or even disapproval. The directorial attitude when hideousness occurs seems to range between clinical neutrality and an almost voyeuristic ogling. It's not an accident that Frank Booth, Bobby Peru, and Leland /"Bob" steal the show in Lynch's last three films, that there is almost a tropism about our pull toward these characters, because Lynch's camera is obsessed with them, loves them; they are his movies' heart.

Some of the ad hominem criticism is harmless, and the director himself has to a certain extent dined out on his "Master of Weird"/"Czar of Bizarre" image, see for example Lynch making his eyes go in two different directions for the cover of *Time*. The claim, though, that because Lynch's movies pass no overt "judgment" on hideousness/evil/sickness and in fact make the stuff riveting to watch, the movies are themselves

---

[48] (e.g.: Kathleen Murphy, Tom Carson, Steve Erickson, Laurent Vachaud)

[49] This critical two-step, a blend of New Criticism and pop psychology, might be termed the Unintentional Fallacy.

a- or immoral, even evil — this is bullshit of the rankest vintage, and not just because it's sloppy logic but because it's symptomatic of the impoverished moral assumptions we seem now to bring to the movies we watch.

I'm going to claim that evil is what David Lynch's movies are essentially about, and that Lynch's explorations of human beings' various relationships to evil are, if idiosyncratic and Expressionistic, nevertheless sensitive and insightful and true. I'm going to submit that the *real* "moral problem" a lot of us cinéastes have with Lynch is that we find his truths morally uncomfortable, and that we do not like, when watching movies, to be made uncomfortable. (Unless, of course, our discomfort is used to set up some kind of commercial catharsis — the retribution, the bloodbath, the romantic victory of the misunderstood heroine, etc. — i.e. unless the discomfort serves a conclusion that flatters the same comfortable moral certainties we came into the theater with.)

The fact is that David Lynch treats the subject of evil better than just about anybody else making movies today — better and also differently. His movies aren't anti-moral, but they are definitely anti-formulaic. Evil-ridden though his filmic world is, please notice that responsibility for evil never in his films devolves easily onto greedy corporations or corrupt politicians or faceless serial kooks. Lynch is not interested in the devolution of responsibility, and he's not interested in moral judgments of characters. Rather, he's interested in the psychic spaces in which people are capable of evil. He is interested in Darkness. And Darkness, in David Lynch's movies, *always wears more than one face.* Recall, for example, how *Blue Velvet*'s Frank Booth is both Frank Booth and "the Well-Dressed Man." How *Eraserhead*'s whole postapocalyptic world of demonic conceptions and teratoid offspring and summary decapitations is evil . . . yet how it's "poor" Henry Spencer who ends up a baby-killer. How in both TV's *Twin Peaks* and cinema's *Fire Walk with Me,* "Bob" is also Leland Palmer, how they are, "spiritually," both two and one. *The Elephant Man*'s sideshow barker is evil in his exploitation of Merrick, but so too is good old kindly Dr. Treeves — and Lynch very carefully has Treeves admit this aloud. And if *Wild at Heart*'s coherence suffered because its myriad villains seemed fuzzy and interchangeable, it was because they were all basically the same thing, i.e. they were all in the service of the same force or spirit. Characters are not themselves evil in Lynch movies — evil wears them.

This point is worth emphasizing. Lynch's movies are not about *monsters* (i.e. people whose intrinsic natures are evil) but about *hauntings*, about evil as environment, possibility, force. This helps explain Lynch's constant deployment of *noir*ish lighting and eerie sound-carpets and grotesque figurants: in his movies' world, a kind of ambient spiritual antimatter hangs just overhead. It also explains why Lynch's villains seem not merely wicked or sick but ecstatic, transported: they are, literally, *possessed.* Think here of Dennis Hopper's exultant "I'LL FUCK ANY-THING THAT MOVES" in *Blue Velvet,* or of the incredible scene in *Wild at Heart* when Diane Ladd smears her face with lipstick until it's devil-red and then screams at herself in the mirror, or of "Bob"'s look of total demonic ebullience in *Fire Walk with Me* when Laura discovers him at her dresser going through her diary and just about dies of fright. The bad guys in Lynch movies are always exultant, orgasmic, most fully present at their evilest moments, and this in turn is because they are not only actuated by evil but literally *inspired*[50]: they have yielded themselves up to a Darkness way bigger than any one person. And if these villains are, at their worst moments, riveting for both the camera and the audience, it's not because Lynch is "endorsing" or "romanticizing" evil but because he's *diagnosing* it — diagnosing it without the comfortable carapace of disapproval and with an open acknowledgment of the fact that one reason why evil is so powerful is that it's hideously vital and robust and usually impossible to look away from.

Lynch's idea that evil is a force has unsettling implications. People can be good or bad, but forces simply *are.* And forces are — at least potentially — everywhere. Evil for Lynch thus moves and shifts,[51] *pervades;* Darkness is in everything, all the time — not "lurking below" or "lying

[50] (i.e. "in-spired," = "affected, guided, aroused by divine influence," from the Latin *inspirare,* "breathed into")

[51] It's possible to decode Lynch's fetish for floating/flying entities — witches on broomsticks, sprites and fairies and Good Witches, angels dangling overhead — along these lines. Likewise his use of robins=Light in *BV* and owl=Darkness in *TP:* the whole point of these animals is that they're mobile.

in wait" or "hovering on the horizon": evil is *here*, right now. And so are Light, love, redemption (since these phenomena are also, in Lynch's work, forces and spirits), etc. In fact, in a Lynchian moral scheme it doesn't make much sense to talk about either Darkness or about Light in isolation from its opposite. It's not just that evil is "implied by" good or Darkness by Light or whatever, but that the evil stuff is contained within the good stuff, *encoded* in it.

You could call this idea of evil Gnostic, or Taoist, or neo-Hegelian, but it's also Lynchian, because what Lynch's movies[52] are all about is creating a narrative space where this idea can be worked out in its fullest detail and to its most uncomfortable consequences.

And Lynch pays a heavy price — both critically and financially —for trying to explore worlds like this. Because we Americans like our art's moral world to be cleanly limned and clearly demarcated, neat and tidy. In many respects it seems we *need* our art to be morally comfortable, and the intellectual gymnastics we'll go through to extract a black-and-white ethics from a piece of art we like are shocking if you stop and look closely at them. For example, the supposed ethical structure Lynch is most applauded for is the "Seamy Underside" structure, the idea that dark forces roil and passions seethe beneath the green lawns and PTA potlucks of Anytown, USA.[53] American critics who like Lynch applaud his "genius for penetrating the civilized surface of everyday life to discover the strange, perverse passions beneath" and his movies for providing "the password to an inner sanctum of horror and desire" and "evocations of the malevolent forces at work beneath nostalgic constructs."

It's little wonder that Lynch gets accused of voyeurism: critics have to make Lynch a voyeur in order to approve something like *Blue Velvet* from within a conventional moral framework that has Good on top/outside and Evil below/within. The fact is that critics grotesquely misread Lynch when they see this idea of perversity "*beneath*" and horror "*hidden*" as central to his movies' moral structure.

---

[52] (with the exception of *Dune*, in which the good and bad guys practically wear color-coded hats — but *Dune* wasn't really Lynch's film anyway)

[53] This sort of interpretation informed most of the positive reviews of both *Blue Velvet* and *Twin Peaks*.

Interpreting *Blue Velvet*, for example, as a film centrally concerned with "a boy discovering corruption in the heart of a town"[54] is about as obtuse as looking at the robin perched on the Beaumonts' window-sill at the movie's end and ignoring the writhing beetle the robin's got in its beak.[55] The fact is that *Blue Velvet* is basically a coming-of-age movie, and, while the brutal rape Jeffrey watches from Dorothy's closet might be the movie's most horrifying scene, the *real* horror in the movie surrounds discoveries that Jeffrey makes about himself — for example, the discovery that a part of him is excited by what he sees Frank Booth do to Dorothy Vallens.[56] Frank's use, during the rape, of the words "Mommy" and "Daddy," the similarity between the gas mask Frank breathes through in extremis and the oxygen mask we've just seen Jeffrey's dad wearing in the hospital — this kind of stuff isn't there just to reinforce the Primal Scene aspect of the rape. The stuff's also there clearly to suggest that Frank Booth is, in a certain deep way, Jeffrey's "father," that the Darkness inside Frank is also encoded in Jeffrey. Gee-whiz Jeffrey's discovery not of dark Frank but of his own dark affinities with Frank is the engine of the movie's anxiety. Note for example that the long and somewhat heavy angst-dream Jeffrey suffers in the film's

54 (which most admiring critics did — the quotation is from a 1/90 piece on Lynch in the *New York Times Magazine*)

55 (Not to mention ignoring the fact that Frances Bay, as Jeffrey's Aunt Barbara, stand-ing right next to Jeffrey and Sandy at the window and making an icky-face at the robin and saying "Who could eat a bug?" then — as far as I can tell, and I've seen the movie like eight times — proceeds to PUT A BUG IN HER MOUTH. Or at least if it's not a bug she puts in her mouth it's a tidbit sufficiently buggy-looking to let you be sure Lynch means *something* by having her do it right after she's criticized the robin for its diet. (Friends I've surveyed are evenly split on whether Aunt Barbara eats a bug in this scene — have a look for yourself.))

56 As, to be honest, is a part of us, the audience. Excited, I mean. And Lynch clearly sets the rape scene up to be both horrifying and exciting. This is why the colors are so lush and the *mise en scène* so detailed and sensual, why the camera lingers on the rape, fetishizes it: not because Lynch is sickly or naïvely excited by the scene but be-cause he — like us — is humanly, complexly excited by the scene. The camera's ogling is designed to implicate Frank and Jeffrey and the director and the audience all at the same time.

second act occurs not after he has watched Frank brutalize Dorothy but after he, Jeffrey, has consented to hit Dorothy during sex.

There are enough heavy clues like this to set up, for any marginally attentive viewer, what is *Blue Velvet*'s real climax, and its point. The climax comes unusually early,[57] near the end of the film's second act. It's the moment when Frank turns around to look at Jeffrey in the back seat of the car and says *"You're like me."* This moment is shot from Jeffrey's visual perspective, so that when Frank turns around in the seat he speaks both to Jeffrey and to us. And here Jeffrey — who's whacked Dorothy and liked it — is made exceedingly uncomfortable indeed; and so — if we recall that we too peeked through those closet-vents at Frank's feast of sexual fascism, and regarded, with critics, this scene as the film's most riveting — are we. When Frank says *"You're like me,"* Jeffrey's response is to lunge wildly forward in the back seat and punch Frank in the nose — a brutally primal response that seems rather more typical of Frank than of Jeffrey, notice. In the film's audience, I, to whom Frank has also just claimed kinship, have no such luxury of violent release; I pretty much just have to sit there and be uncomfortable.[58]

And I emphatically do not like to be made uncomfortable when I go to see a movie. I like my heroes virtuous and my victims pathetic and my villains' villainy clearly established and primly disapproved by both plot and camera. When I go to movies that have various kinds of hideousness in them, I like to have my own fundamental *difference* from sadists and fascists and voyeurs and psychos and Bad People unambiguously confirmed and assured by those movies. I like to judge. I like to be allowed to root for Justice To Be Done without the slight squirmy suspicion

---

[57] (prematurely!)

[58] I don't think it's an accident that of the grad-school friends I first saw *Blue Velvet* with in 1986, the two who were most disturbed by the movie — the two who said they felt like either the movie was really sick or they were really sick or both they and the movie were really sick, the two who acknowledged the movie's artistic power but declared that as God was their witness you'd never catch them sitting through *that* particular sickness-fest again — were both male, nor that both singled out Frank's smiling slowly while pinching Dorothy's nipple and looking out past Wall 4 and saying *"You're like me"* as possibly the creepiest and least pleasant moment in their personal moviegoing history.

(so prevalent and depressing in real moral life) that Justice probably wouldn't be all that keen on certain parts of *my* character, either.

I don't know whether you are like me in these regards or not . . . though from the characterizations and moral structures in the U.S. movies that do well at the box-office I deduce that there must be rather a lot of Americans who are exactly like me.

I submit that we also, as an audience, really like the idea of secret and scandalous immoralities unearthed and dragged into the light and exposed. We like this stuff because secrets' exposure in a movie creates in us impressions of epistemological privilege, of "penetrating the civilized surface of everyday life to discover the strange, perverse passions beneath." This isn't surprising: knowledge is power, and we (I, anyway) like to feel powerful. But we also like the idea of "secrets," "of malevolent forces at work *beneath* . . ." so much because we like to see confirmed our fervent hope that most bad and seamy stuff really *is* secret, "locked away" or "under the surface." We hope fervently that this is so because we need to be able to believe that our own hideousnesses and Darknesses are secret. Otherwise we get uncomfortable. And, as part of an audience, if a movie is structured in such a way that the distinction between surface/Light/good and secret/Dark/evil is messed with — in other words, not a structure whereby Dark Secrets are winched *ex machina* up to the Lit Surface to be purified by my judgment, but rather a structure in which Respectable Surfaces and Seamy Undersides are mingled, integrated, literally *mixed up* — I am going to be made acutely uncomfortable. And in response to my discomfort I'm going to do one of two things: I'm either going to find some way to punish the movie for making me uncomfortable, or I'm going to find a way to interpret the movie that eliminates as much of the discomfort as possible. From my survey of published work on Lynch's films, I can assure you that just about every established professional reviewer and critic has chosen one or the other of these responses.

I know this all looks kind of abstract and general. Consider the specific example of *Twin Peaks*'s career. Its basic structure was the good old murder-whose-investigation-opens-a-can-of-worms formula that's right out of *Noir* 101 — the search for Laura Palmer's killer yields postmortem revelations of a double life (Laura Palmer = Homecoming Queen by Day & Laura Palmer = Tormented Coke-Whore by Night) that mirrored a whole town's moral schizophrenia. The show's first season, in which the plot movement consisted mostly of more and more sub-surface hideousnesses being uncovered and exposed, was a huge smash. By the second season, though, the mystery-and-investigation structure's own logic began to compel the show to start getting more focused and explicit about who or what was actually responsible for Laura's murder. And the more explicit *Twin Peaks* tried to get, the less popular the series became. The mystery's final "resolution," in particular, was felt by critics and audiences alike to be deeply unsatisfying. And it was. The "Bob"/Leland/Evil Owl stuff was fuzzy and not very well rendered,[59] but the really deep dissatisfaction — the one that made audiences feel screwed and betrayed and fueled the critical backlash against the idea of Lynch as Genius Auteur — was, I submit, a moral one. I submit that Laura Palmer's exhaustively revealed "sins" required, by the moral logic of American mass entertainment, that the circumstances of her death turn out to be causally related to those sins. We as an audience have certain core certainties about sowing and reaping, and these certainties need to be affirmed and massaged.[60] When they were not, and as

---

[59] Worse, actually. Like most storytellers who use mystery as a structural device and not a thematic device, Lynch is way better at deepening and complicating mysteries than he is at wrapping them up. And the series' second season showed that he was aware of this and that it was making him really nervous. By its thirtieth episode, the show had degenerated into tics and shticks and mannerisms and red herrings, and part of the explanation for this was that Lynch was trying to divert our attention from the fact that he really had no idea how to wrap the central murder case up. Part of the reason I actually preferred *Twin Peaks*'s second season to its first was the fascinating spectacle of watching a narrative structure disintegrate and a narrative artist freeze up and try to shuck and jive when the plot reached a point where his own weaknesses as an artist were going to be exposed (just imagine the fear: this disintegration was happening on *national TV*).

[60] This is inarguable, axiomatic. In fact what's striking about most U.S. mystery and suspense and crime and horror films isn't these films' escalating violence but their enduring and fanatical allegiance to moral verities that come right out of the nursery: the virtuous heroine will not be serial-killed; the honest cop, who will not know his partner is corrupt until it's too late to keep the partner from getting the drop on him, will nevertheless somehow turn the tables and kill the partner in a wrenching confrontation; the predator stalking the hero/hero's family will, no matter how rational and ingenious he's been in his stalking tactics throughout the film, nevertheless turn

it became increasingly clear that they were not going to be, *Twin Peaks*'s ratings fell off the shelf, and critics began to bemoan this once "daring" and "imaginative" series' decline into "self-reference" and "mannered incoherence."

And then *Twin Peaks: Fire Walk with Me*, Lynch's theatrical "prequel" to the TV series, and his biggest box-office bomb since *Dune*, committed a much worse offense. It sought to transform Laura Palmer from dramatic object to dramatic subject. As a dead person, Laura's existence on the television show had been entirely verbal, and it was fairly easy to conceive her as a schizoid black/white construct — Good by Day, Naughty by Night, etc. But the movie, in which Ms. Sheryl Lee as Laura is on-screen more or less constantly, attempts to present this multivalent system of objectified personas — plaid-skirted coed/barebreasted roadhouse slut/tormented exorcism-candidate/molested daughter — as an integrated and living whole: these different identities were all, the movie tried to claim, the same person. In *Fire Walk with Me*, Laura was no longer "an enigma" or "the password to an inner sanctum of horror." She now embodied, in full view, all the Dark Secrets that on the series had been the stuff of significant glances and delicious whispers.

This transformation of Laura from object/occasion to subject/person was actually the most morally ambitious thing a Lynch movie has ever tried to do — maybe an impossible thing, given the psychological context of the series and the fact that you had to be familiar with the series to make even marginal sense of the movie — and it required complex and contradictory and probably impossible things from Ms. Lee, who in my opinion deserved an Oscar nomination just for showing up and trying.

---

into a raging lunatic at the end and will mount a suicidal frontal assault; etc. etc. etc. etc. etc. The truth is that a major component of the felt suspense in contemporary U.S. suspense movies concerns how the filmmaker is going to manipulate various plot and character elements in order to engineer the required massage of our moral certainties. This is why the discomfort we feel at "suspense" movies is perceived as a pleasant discomfort. And this is why, when a filmmaker fails to wrap his product up in the appropriate verity-confirming fashion, we feel not disinterest or even offense but anger, a sense of betrayal — we feel that an unspoken but very important covenant has been violated.

The novelist Steve Erickson, in a 1992 review of *Fire Walk with Me*, is one of the few critics who gave any indication of even trying to understand what the movie was trying to do: "We always knew Laura was a wild girl, the homecoming femme fatale who was crazy for cocaine and fucked roadhouse drunks less for the money than the sheer depravity of it, but the movie is finally not so much interested in the titillation of that depravity as [in] her torment, depicted in a performance by Sheryl Lee so vixenish and demonic it's hard to know whether it's terrible or a tour de force. [But not trying too terribly hard, because now watch:] Her fit of the giggles over the body of a man whose head has just been blown off might be an act of innocence or damnation [get ready:] or both." *Or* both? Of *course* both. This is what Lynch is *about* in this movie: *both* innocence and damnation; *both* sinned-against and sinning. Laura Palmer in *Fire Walk with Me* is *both* "good" and "bad," and yet also neither: she's complex, contradictory, real. And we hate this possibility in movies; we hate this "*both*" shit. "*Both*" comes off as sloppy characterization, muddy filmmaking, lack of focus. At any rate that's what we criticized *Fire Walk with Me*'s Laura for.[61] But I submit that the real reason we criticized and disliked Lynch's Laura's muddy *both*ness is that it required of us an empathetic confrontation with the exact same muddy *both*ness in ourselves and our intimates that makes the real world of moral selves so tense and uncomfortable, a *both*ness we go to the movies to get a couple hours' fucking relief from. A movie that requires that these features of ourselves and the world not be dreamed away or judged away or massaged away but *acknowledged,* and not just acknowledged but *drawn upon* in our emotional relationship to the heroine herself — this movie is going to make us feel uncomfortable, pissed off; we're going to feel, in *Premiere* magazine's own head editor's word, "Betrayed."

I am not suggesting that Lynch entirely succeeded at the project he set for himself in *Fire Walk with Me*. (He didn't.) What I am suggesting is that the withering critical reception the movie received (this movie, whose director's previous film had won the Palme d'Or, was *booed* at the 1992 Cannes Film Festival) had less to do with its failing in the project

---

[61] (not to mention for being (from various reviews) "overwrought," "incoherent," "*too much*")

than with its attempting it at all. And I am suggesting that if *Lost High-way* gets similarly savaged — or, worse, ignored — by the American art-assessment machine of which *Premiere* magazine is a wonderful working part, you might want to keep all this in mind.

1995

tennis player Michael Joyce's professional artistry as a paradigm of certain stuff about choice, freedom, limitation, joy, grotesquerie, and human completeness

When Michael Joyce of Los Angeles serves, when he tosses the ball and his face rises to track it, it looks like he's smiling, but he's not really smiling — his face's circumoral muscles are straining with the rest of his body to reach the ball at the top of the toss's rise. He wants to hit it fully extended and slightly out in front of him; he wants to be able to hit emphatically down on the ball, to generate enough pace to avoid an ambitious return from his opponent. Right now it's 1:00 Saturday, 22 July 1995, on the Stadium Court of the Stade Jarry tennis complex in Montreal. It's the first of the qualifying rounds for the Canadian Open, one of the major stops on the ATP's "hard-court circuit,"[1] which starts right after Wimbledon and climaxes at NYC's U.S. Open. The tossed ball rises and seems for a second to hang, waiting, cooperating, as balls always seem to do for great players. The opponent, a Canadian college star named Dan Brakus, is a very good tennis player. Michael Joyce, on the other hand, is a world-class tennis player. In 1991 he was the top-ranked junior in the United States and a finalist at Junior Wimbledon,[2]

---

[1] Comprising Washington, Montreal, LA, Cincinnati, Indianapolis, New Haven, and Long Island, this is possibly the most grueling part of the Association of Tennis Professionals' yearly tour, with three-digit temperatures and the cement courts shimmering like Moroccan horizons and everyone wearing a hat and even the spectators carrying sweat towels.

[2] Joyce lost that final to Thomas Enqvist, now ranked in the ATP's top twenty and a potential superstar and in high-profile attendance here at Montreal.

is now in his fourth year on the ATP tour, and is as of this day the 79th best tennis player on planet earth.

A tacit rhetorical assumption here is that you have very probably never heard of Michael Joyce of Brentwood/LA. Nor of Florida's Tommy Ho. Nor of Vince Spadea, nor of Jonathan Stark or Robbie Weiss or Steve Bryan — all American men in their twenties, all ranked in the world's top 100 at one point in 1995. Nor of Jeff Tarango, 68th in the world, unless you remember his unfortunate psychotic break in full public view during last year's Wimbledon.[3]

You are invited to try to imagine what it would be like to be among the hundred best in the world at something. At anything. I have tried to imagine; it's hard.

Stade Jarry's Stadium Court facility can hold slightly over 10,000 souls. Right now, for Michael Joyce's qualifying match, there are 93 people in the crowd, 91 of whom appear to be friends and relatives of Dan Brakus. Michael Joyce doesn't seem to notice whether there's a crowd or not. He has a way of staring intently at the air in front of his face between points. During points he looks only at the ball.

The acoustics in the near-empty Stadium are amazing — you can hear every breath, every sneaker's squeak, the authoritative *pang* of the ball against very tight strings.

Professional tennis tournaments, like professional sports teams, have distinctive traditional colors. Wimbledon's is green; the Volvo International's is light blue. The Canadian Open's is — emphatically — red.

---

[3] Tarango, 27, who completed three years at Stanford, is regarded as something of a scholar by Joyce and the other young Americans on tour. His little bio in the *1995 ATP Player Guide* lists his interests as including "philosophy, creative writing, and bridge," and his slight build and receding hairline do in fact make him look more like an academic or a tax attorney than a world-class tennis player. Also a native Californian, Tarango's a friend and something of a mentor to Michael Joyce, whom he practices with regularly and addresses as "Grasshopper." Joyce — who seems to like pretty much everybody — likes Jeff Tarango and won't comment on his on-court explosion at Wimbledon except to say that Tarango is "a very intense guy, very intellectual, that gets kind of paranoid sometimes."

The tournament's "title sponsor," du Maurier cigarettes,[4] has ads and logos all over the place in red and black. The Stadium Court is surrounded by a red tarp festooned with corporate names in black capitals, and the tarp composes the base of a grandstand that is itself decked out in red-and-black bunting, so that from any kind of distance the place looks like either a Kremlin funeral or a really elaborate brothel. The match's umpire and linesmen and ballboys all wear black shorts and red shirts emblazoned with the name of a Quebec clothing company.[5] The big beach umbrella that's spread and held over each seated player at end-change breaks has a lush red head and a black stem that looks hot to hold.

Stade Jarry's Stadium Court is adjoined on the north by the Grandstand Court, a slightly smaller venue with seats on only one side and a capacity of 4800. A five-story scoreboard lies just west of the Grandstand, and by late afternoon both courts are rectangularly shadowed. There are also eight nonstadium courts in canvas-fenced enclosures scattered across the grounds. Professional matches are under way on all ten Stade

---

[4] Title sponsors are as important to ATP tournaments as they are to collegiate bowl games. This year the Canadian Open is officially called the "du Maurier Omnium Ltée." But everybody still refers to it as the Canadian Open. There are all types and levels of sponsors for big tennis tournaments — the levels of giving and of commensurate reward are somewhat similar to PBS fundraising telethons. Names of sponsors are all over the Canadian Open's site (with variations in size and placement corresponding to levels of fiscal importance to the tournament), from the big FedEx signs over the practice courts to the RADO trademark on the serve-speed radar display on the show courts. On the scarlet tarp and the box seats all around the Stadium and Grandstand Courts are the names of other corporate sponsors: TANDEM COMPUTERS/APG INC., BELL SYGMA, BANQUE LAURENTIENNE, IMASCO LIMITÉE, EVANS TECHNOLOGIES INC., MOBILIA, BELL CANADA, ARGO STEEL, etc.

[5] Another way to be a sponsor: supply free stuff to the tournament and put your name on it in really big letters. All the courts' tall umpire-chairs have a sign that says they're supplied by TROPICANA; all the bins for fresh and unfresh towels say WAMSUTTA; the drink coolers at courtside (the size of trash barrels, with clear plastic lids) say TROPICANA and EVIAN. The players who don't individually endorse a certain brand of drink tend as a rule to drink Evian, orange juice being a bit heavy for on-court rehydration.

Jarry courts today, but they are not exactly Canadian Open matches, and for the most part they are unwatched.

The Stade Jarry grounds are all spruced up, and vendors' tents are up, and Security is in place at all designated points. Big TV trailers line the walkway outside the stadium, and burly men keep pulling complicated nests of cable out of ports in the trailers' sides.

There are very few paying customers on the grounds on Saturday, but there are close to a hundred world-class players: big spidery French guys with gelled hair, American kids with peeling noses and Pac-10 sweats, lugubrious Germans, bored-looking Italians. There are blank-eyed Swedes and pockmarked Colombians and cyberpunkish Brits. There are malevolent Slavs with scary haircuts. There are Mexican players who spend their spare time playing two-on-two soccer in the gravel outside the Players' Tent. With few exceptions, all the players have similar builds: big muscular legs, shallow chests, skinny necks, and one normal-sized arm and one monstrously huge and hypertrophic arm. They tend to congregate in the Players' Tent or outside the Transportation Trailer awaiting rides in promotional BMWs back to the Radisson des Gouverneurs, the tournament's designated hotel. Many of these players in the "Qualies," or qualifying rounds, have girlfriends in tow, sloppily beautiful European girls with sandals and patched jeans and leather backpacks, girlfriends who set up cloth lawnchairs and sun themselves next to their players' practice courts.[6] At the Radisson des Gouverneurs the players tend to congregate in the lobby, where there's a drawsheet for the Qualies up on a cork bulletin board and a multilingual tournament official behind a long desk, and the players stand around in the air-conditioning in wet hair and sandals and employ about 40 languages and wait for results of matches to go up on the board and for their own next matches' schedules to get posted. Some of the players listen to personal stereos; none seem to read. They all have the unhappy self-enclosed look of people who spend huge amounts of time on planes and waiting around in hotel lobbies, the look of people who have to create an envelope of privacy around them

---

[6] Most of the girlfriends have something indefinable about them that suggests extremely wealthy parents whom the girls are trying to piss off by hooking up with an obscure professional tennis player.

with just their expressions. Most of these players seem either extremely young — new guys trying to break onto the Tour — or conspicuously older, like over 30, with tans that look permanent and faces lined from years in the trenches of tennis's minor leagues.

The Canadian Open, one of the ATP Tour's "Super 9" tournaments that weigh most heavily in the calculation of world ranking, officially starts on Monday, 24 July. What's going on for the two days right before it is the Qualies. This is essentially a competition to determine who will occupy the eight slots in the Canadian Open's main draw designated for "qualifiers." It is a pre-tournament tournament. A qualifying tourney precedes just about every big-money ATP event, and money and prestige and lucrative careers are often at stake in Qualie rounds, and often they feature the best matches of the whole tournament, and it's a good bet you haven't heard of Qualies.

The realities of the men's professional tennis tour bear about as much resemblance to the lush finals you see on TV as a slaughterhouse does to a well-presented cut of restaurant sirloin. For every Sampras-Agassi final we watch, there's been a week-long tournament, a pyramidical single-elimination battle between 32, 64, or 128 players, of whom the finalists are the last men standing. You probably know that already. But a player has to be eligible to enter that tournament in the first place. Eligibility is determined by ATP computer ranking. Each tournament has a cutoff, a minimum ranking required to get entered in the main draw. Players below that ranking who want to get in have to compete in a kind of pre-tournament. That's the easiest way to explain what Qualies are. In actual practice the whole thing's quite a bit messier, and I'll try to describe the logistics of the Canadian Open's Qualies in just enough detail to suggest their complexity without boring you mindless.

The du Maurier Omnium Ltée has a draw of 64. The sixteen entrants with the highest ATP rankings get "seeded," which means their names are strategically dispersed in the draw so that (barring upsets) they won't have to meet each other until the latter rounds.[7] Of the seeds, the top

---

[7] The term "seeding" comes from British horticulture and is pretty straightforward. A player seeded First is expected statistically to win, Second to reach the finals, Third

eight — here Agassi, Sampras, Chang, the Russian Yevgeny Kafelnikov, Croatia's Goran Ivanisevic, South Africa's Wayne Ferreira, Germany's Michael Stich, and Switzerland's Marc Rosset, respectively — get "byes," or automatic passes into the tournament's second round. This means that there is actually room for 56 players in the main draw. The cutoff for the 1995 Canadian Open isn't 56, however, because not all of the top 56 players in the world are here.[8] Here the cutoff is 85. You'd think that this meant anybody with an ATP ranking of 86 or lower would have to play the Qualies, but here too there are exceptions. The du Maurier Omnium Ltée, like most other big tournaments, has five "wild card" entries into

---

and Fourth the semis, etc. A player who reaches the round his seed designates is said to have "justified his seed," a term that seems far more rich in implications and entendres. Serious tennis is full of these multisemiotic terms — "love," "hold" and "break," "fault," "let" as a noun, "heat," "moon," "spank," "coming in," "playing unconscious," and so on.

[8]   Except for the four Grand Slams, no tournament draws all the top players, although every tournament would obviously like to, since the more top players are entered, the better the paid attendance and the more media exposure the tournament gets for itself and its sponsors. Players ranked in the world's top twenty or so, though, tend to play a comparatively light schedule of tournaments, taking time off not only for rest and training but to compete in wildly lucrative exhibitions that don't affect ATP ranking. (We're talking *wildly* lucrative, like millions of dollars per annum for the top stars.) Given the sharp divergence of interests between tournaments and players, it's not surprising that there are Kafkanly complex rules for how many ATP tournaments a player must enter each year to avoid financial or ranking-related penalties, and commensurately complex and crafty ways players have for getting around these rules and doing pretty much what they want. These will be passed over. The thing to realize is that players of Michael Joyce's station tend to take way less time off; they try to play just about every tournament they can squeeze in unless they're forced by injury or exhaustion to sit out a couple weeks. They play so much because they need to, not just financially but because the ATP's (very complex) set of algorithms for determining ranking tends to reward players for entering as many tournaments as they can.

And so even though several of the North American hard-court circuit's tournaments are Super 9's, a fair number of top players skip them, especially European clay-court players, who hate DecoTurf and tend to stick to their own summer clay-court circuit, which is European and comprises smaller and less lucrative tournaments (like the Dutch Open, which is concurrent with the Canadian and has four of the world's top twenty entered this year). The clay-courters tend to pay the price for this at the U.S. Open, which is played on hard sizzling DecoTurf courts.

the main draw. These are special places given either to high-ranked players who entered after the required six-week deadline but are desirable to have in the tournament because they're big stars (like Ivanisevic, #6 in the world but a notorious flakeroo who "*forgot*" to enter till a week ago and got a last-minute wild card) or to players ranked lower than 85 whom the tournament wants because they are judged "uniquely deserving" (read "Canadian" — the other four players who get wild cards here are all Canadian, and two are Quebecois).

By the way, if you're interested, the ATP Tour updates and publishes its world rankings weekly, and the rankings constitute a nomological orgy that makes for truly first-rate bathroom reading. As of this writing, Mahesh Bhupathi is 284, Luis Lobo 411. There's Martin Sinner and Guy Forget. There's Adolf Musil and Jonathan Venison and Javier Frana and Leander Paes. There's — no kidding — Cyril Suk. Rodolfo Ramos-Paganini is 337, Alex Lopez-Moron 174. Gilad Bloom is 228 and Zoltan Nagy is 414. Names out of some postmodern Dickens: Udo Riglewski and Louis Gloria and Francisco Roig and Alexander Mronz. The 29th-best player in the world is named Slava Dosedel. There's Claude N'Goran and Han Shin (276 but falling fast) and Haracio de la Pensa and Marcus Barbosa and Amos Mansdorf and Mariano Hood. Andres Zingman is currently ranked two places above Sander Groen. Horst Skoff and Kris Goossens and Thomas Hagstedt are all ranked higher than Martin Zumpft. One more reason the tournament industry sort of hates upsets is that the ATP press liaisons have to go around teaching journalists how to spell and pronounce new names.

So, skipping a whole lot more complication, the point is that eight slots in the Canadian Open's main draw are reserved for qualifiers, and the Qualies is the tournament held to determine who'll get those eight slots. The Qualies itself has a draw of 64 world-class players — the cutoff for qualifying for the Qualies is an ATP ranking of 350.[9] The Qualies

---

[9]   There is here no qualifying tournament for the Qualies itself, though some particularly huge tournaments have meta-Qualies. The Qualies also have tons of wild-

won't go all the way through to the finals, only to the quarters: the eight quarterfinalists of the Qualies will receive first-round slots in the Canadian Open.[10] This means that a player in the Qualies will need to win three rounds — round of 64, round of 32, round of 16 — in two days to get into the first round of the main draw.[11]

The eight seeds in the Qualies are the eight players whom the Canadian Open officials expect will make the quarters and thus get into the main draw. The top seed this weekend is Richard Krajicek,[12] a 6′5″ Dutchman who wears a tiny white billed hat in the sun and rushes the net like it owes him money and in general plays like a rabid crane. Both his knees are bandaged. He's in the top twenty and hasn't had to play Qualies for years, but for this tournament he missed the entry deadline, found all the wild cards already given to uniquely deserving Canadians, and with phlegmatic Low Country cheer decided to go ahead and play the weekend Qualies for the match practice. The Qualies' second seed is Jamie Morgan, an Australian journeyman, around 100th in the world, whom Michael Joyce beat in straight sets last week in the second round of the main draw at the Legg Mason Tennis Classic in Washington. Michael Joyce is seeded third.

If you're wondering why Joyce, who's ranked above the #85 cutoff,

---

card berths, most of whom here are given to Canadian players, e.g. the collegian that Michael Joyce is beating up on right now in the first round.

[10] These slots are usually placed right near the top seeds, which is the reason why in the televised first rounds of major tournaments you often see Agassi or Sampras smearing some totally obscure guy — that guy's usually a qualifier. It's also part of why it's so hard for somebody low-ranked enough to have to play the Qualies of tournaments to move up in the rankings enough so that he doesn't have to play Qualies anymore — he usually meets a high-ranked player in the very first round and gets smeared.

[11] Which is another reason why qualifiers usually get smeared by the top players they face in the early rounds — the qualifier is playing his fourth or fifth match in three days, while the top players usually have had a couple days with their masseur and creative-visualization consultant to get ready for the first round. If asked, Michael Joyce will detail all these asymmetries and stacked odds the same way a farmer will speak of poor weather, with an absence of emotion that seems deep instead of blank.

[12] (pronounced KRY-chek)

is having to play the Canadian Open Qualies at all, gird yourself for one more bit of complication. The fact is that six weeks ago Joyce's ranking was *not* above the cutoff, and that's when the Canadian entry deadline was, and that's the ranking the tournament committee went on when they made up the main draw. Joyce's ranking jumped from 119 to around 80 after this year's Wimbledon, where he beat Marc Rosset (ranked 11 in the world) and reached the round of sixteen. Despite a bout of mono-nucleosis that kept him in bed through part of the spring, Joyce is having his best year ever as a pro and has jumped from 140 in the world to 79.[13] But he was not in the world's top 85 as of early June, and so he has to qualify in Montreal. It seems to me that Joyce, like Krajicek, might be excused for brooding darkly on the fact that four wild cards in the Canadian's main draw have been dispensed to Canadians ranked substantially lower than 85, but Joyce is stoic about it.[14]

The Qualie circuit is to professional tennis sort of what AAA base-ball is to the major leagues: somebody playing the Qualies in Montreal is undeniably a world-class tennis player, but he's not quite at the level where the serious TV and money are. In the main draw of the du Maurier Omnium Ltée, a first-round loser will earn $5,400 and a second-round loser $10,300. In the Montreal Qualies, a player will receive $560 for los-ing in the second round and an even $0.00 for losing in the first. This might not be so bad if a lot of the entrants for the Qualies hadn't flown thousands of miles to get here. Plus there's the matter of supporting themselves in Montreal. The tournament pays the hotel and meal ex-penses of players in the main draw but not in the Qualies.[15] The eight

---

[13] At a certain point this summer his ranking will be as high as 62.

[14] It turns out that a portion of the talent required to survive in the trenches of the ATP Tour is emotional: Joyce is able to keep from getting upset about stuff that struck me as hard not to get upset about. When he points out that there's "no point" getting exercised about unfairnesses you can't control, I think what he's really saying is that you either learn how not to get upset about it or you disappear from the Tour. The temperamental behavior of many of the game's top players — which gives the public the distorted idea that most pro players are oversensitive brats — is on a qualifier's view easily explainable: top players are temperamental because they can afford to be.

[15] The really top players not only have their expenses comped but often get paid out-right for agreeing to enter a tournament. These fees are called "guarantees" and are

survivors of the Qualies, however, will get their weekend expenses retro-actively picked up by the tournament. So there's rather a lot at stake: some of the players in the Qualies are literally playing for their supper, or for the money to make airfare home or to the site of the next Qualie.

You could think of Michael Joyce's career as now kind of on the cusp between the major leagues and AAA ball. He still has to qualify for some tournaments, but more and more often he gets straight into the main draw. The move up from qualifier to main-draw player is a huge boost, both financially and psychically, but it's still a couple plateaux away from true fame and fortune. The main draw's 64 or 128 players are still mostly the supporting cast for the stars we see in televised finals. But they are also the pool from which superstars are drawn. McEnroe, Sampras, and even Agassi had to play Qualies at the start of their careers, and Sampras

---

technically advances against prize money: in effect, an Agassi/Sampras/Becker will re-ceive a "guarantee" of the champion's prize money (usually a couple hundred thou-sand) just for competing, whether he wins the tournament or not. This means that if top seed Agassi wins the Canadian Open, he wins $254,000 U.S., but if he loses, he gets the money anyway. (This is another reason why tournaments tend to hate upsets, and, some qualifiers complain, why all sorts of intangibles from match scheduling to close line-calls tend to go the stars' way.) Not all tournaments have guarantees — the Grand Slams don't, because the top players will show up for Wimbledon and the French, Australian, and U.S. Opens on their own incentive — but most have them, and the less established and prestigious a tournament, the more it needs to guarantee money to get the top players to come and attract spectators and media (which is what the tournament's title sponsor wants, very much).

Guarantees used to be against ATP rules and were under the table; they've been le-gal since the early '90s. There's great debate among tennis pundits about whether legal guarantees have helped the game by making the finances less shady or have hurt the game by widening the psychological gap between the stars and all the other players and by upping the pressure on tournaments to make it as likely as possible that the stars don't get upset by an unknown. It is impossible to get Michael Joyce to give a straight answer on whether he thinks guarantees are good or bad — it's not like Joyce is muddled or Nixonianly evasive about it, but rather that he can't afford to think in good/bad terms, to nurture resentment or bitterness or frustration. My guess is that he avoids these feelings because they make it even harder to play against Agassi and the rest, and he cares less about what's "right" in the grand scheme than he does about maximizing his own psychological chances against other players. This seems totally understandable, though I'm kind of awed by Joyce's evident ability to shut down lines of thinking that aren't to his advantage.

spent a couple years losing in the early rounds of main draws before he suddenly erupted in the early '90s and started beating everybody.

Still, most main-draw players are obscure and unknown. An example is Jacob Hlasek[16], a Czech who is working out with Switzerland's Marc Rosset on one of the practice courts this morning when I first arrive at Stade Jarry.[17] I notice them and come over to watch only because Hlasek and Rosset are so beautiful to see; at this point I have no idea who they are. They are practicing groundstrokes down the line — Rosset's forehand and Hlasek's backhand — each ball plumb-line straight and within centimeters of the corner, the players moving with the compact nonchalance I've since come to recognize in pros when they're working out: the suggestion is one of a very powerful engine in low gear. Jacob Hlasek is 6'2" and built like a halfback, his blond hair in a short square East European cut, with icy eyes and cheekbones out to here: he looks like either a Nazi male model or a lifeguard in hell and seems in general just way too scary ever to try to talk to. His backhand's a one-hander, rather like Lendl's, and watching him practice it is like watching a great artist casually sketch something. I keep having to remember to blink. There are a million little ways you can tell that somebody's a great player — details in his posture, in the way he bounces the ball with his racquet-head to pick it up, in the casual way he twirls the racquet while waiting for the ball. Hlasek wears a plain gray T-shirt and some kind of very white European shoes. It's midmorning and already at least 90° and he isn't sweating. Hlasek turned pro in 1982, six years later had one year in the top ten, and for the last decade has been ranked in the 60s and 70s, getting straight into the main draw of all the big tournaments and usually losing in the first couple rounds. Watching Hlasek practice is prob-

[16] (pronounced YAkob hLAsick)

[17] It took forever to get there from the hotel because I didn't yet know that press can, with some wangling, get rides in the courtesy cars with the players, if there's room. Tennis journalism is apparently its own special world, and it takes a little while to learn the ins and outs of how media can finagle access to some of the services the tournament provides: courtesy cars, VIP treatment in terms of restaurant reservations, even free laundry service at the hotel. Most of this stuff I learned about just as I was getting ready to come home.

ably the first time it really strikes me how good these professionals are, because even just fucking around, Hlasek is the most impressive tennis player I've ever seen.[18] I'd be surprised if anybody reading this has ever heard of Jåcob Hlasek. By the distorted standards of TV's obsession with Grand Slam finals and the world's top five, Hlasek is merely an also-ran. But last year he made $300,000 on the tour (that's just in prize money, not counting exhibitions and endorsement contracts), and his career winnings are over $4,000,000 U.S., and it turns out his home base for a long time was Monte Carlo, where lots of European players with tax issues end up living.

Michael Joyce is listed in the ATP Player Guide as 5'11" and 165 pounds, but in person he's more like 5'9". On the Stadium Court he looks compact and stocky. The quickest way to describe him would be to say that he looks like a young and slightly buff David Caruso. He is fair-skinned and has reddish hair and the kind of patchy, vaguely pubic goatee of somebody who isn't quite able yet to grow real facial hair. When he plays in the heat he wears a hat.[19] He wears Fila clothes and uses Yonex racquets and is paid to do so. His face is childishly full, and while it isn't freckled it somehow seems like it *ought* to be freckled. A lot of professional tennis players look like lifeguards — that kind of extreme tan that looks like it's penetrated to the subdermal layer and will be retained to the grave — but Joyce's fair skin doesn't tan or even burn, though he does get red in the face when he plays, from effort.[20] His on-court expres-

---

[18] Joyce is even more impressive, but I hadn't seen Joyce yet. And Enqvist is even more impressive than Joyce, and Agassi live is even more impressive than Enqvist. After the week was over, I truly understand why Charlton Heston looks gray and ravaged on his descent from Sinai: past a certain point, impressiveness is corrosive to the psyche.

[19] During his two daily one-hour practice sessions he wears the hat backwards, and also wears boxy plaid shorts that look for all the world like swimtrunks. His favorite practice T-shirt has FEAR: THE ENEMY OF DREAMS on the chest. He laughs a lot when he practices. You can tell just by looking at him out there that he's totally likable and cool.

[20] If you've played only casually, it is probably hard to understand how physically demanding really serious tennis is. Realizing that these pros can move one another from

sion is grim without being unpleasant; it communicates the sense that Joyce's attentions on-court have become very narrow and focused and intense — it's the same pleasantly grim expression you see on, say, working surgeons and jewelers. On the Stadium Court, Joyce seems boyish and extremely adult at the same time. And in contrast to the Canadian opponent, who has the varnished good looks and Pepsodent smile of the stereotypical tennis player, Joyce looks terribly *real* out there playing: he sweats through his shirt,[21] gets flushed, whoops for breath after a

---

one end of the 27' baseline to the other pretty much at will, and that they hardly ever end a point early by making an unforced error, might stimulate your imagination. A close best-of-three-set match is probably equivalent in its demands to a couple hours of basketball, but we're talking full-court basketball.

[21] Something else you don't get a good sense of on television: tennis is a very sweaty game. On ESPN or whatever, when you see a player walk over to the ballboy after a point and request a towel and quickly wipe off his arm and hand and toss the wet towel back to the (rather luckless) ballboy, most of the time the towel thing isn't a stall or a meditative pause — it's because sweat is running down the inside of the player's arm in such volume that it's getting all over his hand and making the racquet slippery. Especially on the sizzling North American summer junket, players sweat through their shirts early on, and sometimes also their shorts. (Sampras always wears light-blue shorts that sweat through everyplace but his jockstrap, which looks funny and kind of endearing, like he's an incontinent child — Sampras is surprisingly childlike and cute on the court, in person, in contrast to Agassi, who's about as cute as a Port Authority whore.)

And they drink enormous amounts of water, staggering amounts. I thought I was seeing things at first, watching matches, as players seemed to go through one of those skinny half-liter Evian bottles every second side-change, but Michael Joyce confirmed it. Pro-grade tennis players seem to have evolved a metabolic system that allows rapid absorption of water and its transformation into sweat. I myself — who am not pro-grade, but do sweat like a pig — drink a lot of water a couple hours before I play but don't drink anything during a match. This is because a couple swallows of water usually just makes me want more, and if I drink as much as I want I end up with a protruding tummy and a sloshing sound when I run.

(Most players I spoke with confirm, by the way, that Gatorade and All-Sport and Boost and all those pricey electrolytic sports drinks are mostly bullshit, that salt and carbs at table and small lakes of daily H_2O are the way to go. The players who didn't confirm this turned out to be players who had endorsement deals with some pricey-sports-drink manufacturer, but I personally saw at least one such player dumping out his bottle's pricey electrolytic contents and replacing them with good old water, for his match.)

long point. He wears little elastic braces on both ankles, but it turns out they're mostly prophylactic.

It's 1:30 P.M. Joyce has broken Brakus's serve once and is up 3–1 in the first set and is receiving. Brakus is in the multibrand clothes of somebody without an endorsement contract. He's well over six feet tall, and like many large male collegians his game is built around his serve.[22] At 0–15, his first serve is flat and 118 mph and way out to Joyce's backhand, which is a two-hander and hard to lunge effectively with, but Joyce lunges plenty effectively and sends the ball back down the line to the Canadian's forehand, deep in the court and with such flat pace that Brakus has to stutter-step a little and backpedal to get set up — clearly he's used to playing guys for whom 118 mumps out wide would be an outright ace or at least produce such a weak return that he could move up easily and put the ball away — and Brakus now sends the ball back up the line high over the net, loopy with topspin, not all that bad a shot considering the fierceness of the return, and a topspin shot that'd back most tennis players up and put them on the defensive, and but Michael Joyce, whose level of tennis is such that he moves *in* on balls hit with topspin and hits them on the rise,[23] moves in and takes the ball on the rise and hits a backhand cross so tightly angled that nobody alive could get to it. This is kind of a typical Joyce–Brakus point. The match is carnage of a particular high-level sort: it's like watching an extremely large and powerful predator get torn to pieces by an even larger and more powerful predator. Brakus looks pissed off after Joyce's winner, makes some berating-himself-type noises, but the anger seems kind of pro forma: it's

---

[22] The taller you are, the harder you can serve (get a protractor and figure it out), but the less able to bend and reverse direction you are. Tall guys tend to be serve-and-volleyers, and they live and die by their serves. Bill Tilden, Stan Smith, Arthur Ashe, Roscoe Tanner, and Goran Ivanisevic were/are all tall guys with serve-dependent games.

[23] This is mind-bogglingly hard to do when the ball's hit hard. If we can assume you've played Little League or sandlot ball or something, imagine the hardest-hit grounder of all time coming at you at shortstop, and then you not standing waiting to try to knock it down but actually of your own free will running forward *toward* the grounder, then trying not just to catch it in a big soft glove but to strike it hard and reverse its direction and send it someplace frightfully specific and far away.

not like there's anything Brakus could have done much better, not given what he and the 79th-best player in the world have in their respective arsenals.

Michael Joyce — whose realness and approachability and candor are a big reason why he's whom I end up spending the most time watching and talking to — will later say, in response to my dry observation that a rather disproportionate number of unranked Canadians seem to have gotten wild cards into the Montreal Qualies, that Brakus "had a big serve, but the guy didn't belong on a pro court." Joyce didn't mean this in an unkind way. Nor did he mean it in a kind way. It turns out that what Michael Joyce says rarely has any kind of spin or slant on it; he mostly just reports what he sees, rather like a camera. You couldn't even call him sincere, because it's not like it seems ever to occur to him to *try* to be sincere or nonsincere. For a while I thought that Joyce's rather bland candor was a function of his not being very bright. This judgment was partly informed by the fact that Joyce didn't go to college and was only marginally involved in his high school academics (stuff I know because he told me it right away).[24] What I discovered as the tour-

---

[24] Something else that's hotly debated by tennis authorities is the trend of players going pro at younger and younger ages and skipping college and college tennis and plunging into the stress and peripatetic loneliness of the Tour, etc. Michael Joyce skipped college and went directly onto the pro tour because at 18 he'd just won the U.S. National Juniors, and this created a set of overwhelming inducements to turn pro. The winner at the National 18-and-Under Singles automatically gets a wild card into the U.S. Open's main draw for that year. In addition, a year's top junior comes to the powerful but notoriously fickle and temporary attention of major clothing and racquet companies. Joyce's victory over the 128-man National field at Kalamazoo MI in 1991 resulted in endorsement offers from Fila and Yonex worth around $100,000. $100,000 is about what it takes to finance three years on the Tour for a very young player who can't reasonably expect to earn a whole lot of prize-money.

Joyce could have turned down that offer of a three-year subsidy and gone to college, but if he'd gone to college it would have been primarily to play tennis. Coaches at major universities apparently offered Joyce inducements to come play for them so literally outrageous and incredible that I wouldn't repeat them here even if Joyce hadn't asked me not to.

The reason why Michael Joyce would have gone to college primarily to play tennis is that his interest in the academic and social aspects of collegiate life interest him about as much as hitting 2500 crosscourt forehands while a coach yells at you in foreign languages would interest you. Tennis is what Michael Joyce loves and lives for

nament wore on was that I can be kind of a snob and an asshole, and that Michael Joyce's affectless openness is a sign not of stupidity but of something else.

Advances in racquet technology and conditioning methods over the last decade have dramatically altered men's professional tennis. For much of the twentieth century, there were two basic styles of top-level play.

---

and *is*. He sees little point in telling anybody anything different. It's the only thing he's devoted himself to, and he's given massive amounts of himself to it, and as far as he understands it it's all he wants to do or be. Because he started playing at age two and competing at age seven, however, and had the first half-dozen years of his career directed rather shall we say *forcefully* and *enthusiastically* by his father (who Joyce estimates spent probably around $250,000 on lessons and court-time and equipment and travel during Michael's junior career), it seemed reasonable to ask Joyce to what extent he "*chose*" to devote himself to tennis. Can you "*choose*" something when you are forcefully and enthusiastically immersed in it at an age when the resources and information necessary for choosing are not yet yours?

Joyce's response to this line of inquiry strikes me as both unsatisfactory and marvelous. Because of course the question is unanswerable, at least it's unanswerable by a person who's already — as far as he understands it — "*chosen*." Joyce's answer is that it doesn't really matter much to him whether he originally "*chose*" serious tennis or not; all he knows is that he loves it. He tries to explain his feelings at the Nationals in 1991: "You get there and look at the draw, it's a 128 draw, there's so many guys you have to beat. And then it's all over and you've won, you're the National Champion — there's nothing like it. I get chills even talking about it." Or how it was just the previous week in Washington: "I'm playing Agassi, and it's great tennis, and there's like thousands of fans going nuts. I can't describe the feeling. Where else could I get that?"

What he says aloud is understandable, but it's not the marvelous part. The marvelous part is the way Joyce's face looks when he talks about what tennis means to him. He loves it; you can see this in his face when he talks about it: his eyes normally have a kind of Asiatic cast because of the slight epicanthic fold common to ethnic Irishmen, but when he speaks of tennis and his career the eyes get round and the pupils dilate and the look in them is one of love. The love is not the love one feels for a job or a lover or any of the loci of intensity that most of us choose to say we love. It's the sort of love you see in the eyes of really old people who've been happily married for an incredibly long time, or in religious people who are so religious they've devoted their lives to religious stuff: it's the sort of love whose measure is what it has cost, what one's given up for it. Whether there's "*choice*" involved is, at a certain point, of no interest . . . since it's the very surrender of choice and self that informs the love in the first place.

The "offensive"[25] style is based on the serve and the net game and is ideally suited to slick (or "fast") surfaces like grass and cement. The "defensive" or "baseline" style is built around foot-speed, consistency, and groundstrokes accurate enough to hit effective passing shots against a serve-and-volleyer; this style is most effective on "slow" surfaces like clay and Har-Tru composite. John McEnroe and Bjorn Borg are probably the modern era's greatest exponents of the offensive and defensive styles, respectively.

There is now a third way to play, and it tends to be called the "power-baseline" style. As far as I can determine, Jimmy Connors[26] more or less invented the power-baseline game back in the '70s, and in the '80s Ivan Lendl raised it to a kind of brutal art. In the '90s, the majority of young players on the ATP Tour now have a P.B.-type game. This game's cornerstone is groundstrokes, but groundstrokes hit with incredible pace, such that winners from the baseline are not unusual.[27] A power-baseliner's net game tends to be solid but uninspired — a P.B.er is more

[25] (aka serve-and-volley; see Note 22)

[26] I don't know whether you know this, but Connors had one of the most eccentric games in the history of tennis — he was an aggressive "power" player who rarely came to net, had the serve of an ectomorphic girl, and hit everything totally spinless and flat (which is inadvisable on groundstrokes because the absence of spin makes the ball so hard to control). His game was all the stranger because the racquet he generated all his firepower from the baseline with was a Wilson T2000, a weird steel thing that's one of the single shittiest tennis racquets ever made and is regarded by most serious players as useful only for home defense or prying large rocks out of your backyard or something. Connors was addicted to this racquet and kept using it even after Wilson stopped making it, forfeiting millions in potential endorsement money by doing so. Connors was eccentric (and kind of repulsive) in lots of others ways, too, none of which are germane to this article.

[27] In the yore days before wide-body ceramic racquets and scientific strength-training, the only two venues for hitting winners used to be the volley — where your decreased distance from the net allowed for greatly increased angle (get that protractor out) — and the defensive passing shot . . . i.e., in the tactical language of boxing, "punch" v. "counterpunch." The new power-baseline game allows a player, in effect, to punch his opponent all the way from his stool in the corner; it changes absolutely everything, and the analytic geometry of these changes would look like the worst calculus final you ever had in your life.

apt to hit a winner on the approach shot and not need to volley at all. His serve is competent and reasonably forceful, but the really inspired part of a P.B.er's game is usually his return of serve.[28] He usually has incredible reflexes and can hit winners right off the return. The P.B.er's game requires both the power and aggression of an offensive style and the speed and calculated patience of a defensive style. It is adjustable both to slick grass and to slow clay, but its most congenial surface is DecoTurf,[29] the type of slow abrasive hard-court surface now used at the U.S. Open and at all the broiling North American tournaments leading up to it, including the Canadian Open.

Boris Becker and Stefan Edberg are contemporary examples of the classic offensive style. Serve-and-volleyers are often tall,[30] and tall Americans like Pete Sampras and Todd Martin and David Wheaton are also offensive players. Michael Chang is an exponent of the pure defensive style, as are Mats Wilander, Carlos Costa, and a lot of the Tour's Western Europeans and South Americans, many of whom grew up exclusively on clay and now stick primarily to the overseas clay-court circuits. Americans Jim Courier, Jimmy Arias, and Aaron Krickstein all play a power-baseline game. So does just about every young new male player on the Tour. But the style's most famous and effective post-Lendl avatar is Andre Agassi, who on 1995's summer circuit is simply kicking everyone's ass.[31]

[28] This is why the phenomenon of "breaking serve" in a set is so much less important when a match involves power-baseliners. It is one reason why so many older players and fans no longer like to watch pro tennis as much: the structural tactics of the game are now wholly different from when they played.

[29] © Wichita KS's Koch Materials Company, "A Leader in Asphalt-Emulsions Technology."

[30] John McEnroe wasn't all that tall, and he was arguably the best serve-and-volley man of all time, but then McEnroe was an exception to pretty much every predictive norm there was. At his peak (say 1980 to 1984), he was the greatest tennis player who ever lived — the most talented, the most beautiful, the most tormented: a genius. For me, watching McEnroe don a polyester blazer and do stiff lame truistic color commentary for TV is like watching Faulkner do a Gap ad.

[31] One answer to why public interest in men's tennis has been on the wane in recent years is an essential and unpretty *thuggishness* about the power-baseline style that's

Michael Joyce's style is power-baseline in the Agassi mold: Joyce is short and right-handed and has a two-handed backhand, a serve that's just good enough to set up the baseline attack, and a great return of serve that's the linchpin of his game. Like Agassi, Joyce takes the ball early, on the rise, so it always looks like he's moving forward in the court even though he rarely comes to net. Joyce's first serve usually comes in around 95 mph,[32] and his second serve is in the low 80s, but it has so much spin on it that the ball turns weird shapes in the air and bounces high and wide to the first-round Canadian's backhand. Brakus stretches for the ball and floats a slice return, the sort of weak return that a serve-and-volleyer'd be rushing up to the net to put away on the fly. Joyce does move up, but only to midcourt, right around his own service line, where he lets the floater land and bounce up all ripe, and he winds up his forehand and hits a winner crosscourt into the deuce corner, very flat and hard, so that the ball makes an emphatic sound as it hits the scarlet tarp behind Brakus's end of the court. Ballboys move for the ball and reconfigure complexly as Joyce walks back to serve another point. The applause of the tiny crowd is so small and sad and shabby-sounding that it'd almost be better if people didn't clap at all.

As with Lendl and Agassi and Courier and many P.B.ers, Joyce's strongest shot is his forehand, a weapon of near-Wagnerian aggression and power. Joyce's forehand is particularly lovely to watch. It's more spare and textbook than Lendl's whip-crack forehand or Borg's great swooping loop; by way of decoration there's only a small loop of flourish[33] on the backswing. The stroke itself is completely horizontal, so

---

come to dominate the Tour. Watch Agassi closely sometime — for so small a man and so great a player, he's amazingly devoid of finesse, with movements that look more like a Heavy Metal musician's than an athlete's.

The power-baseline game itself has been compared to Metal or Grunge. But what a top P.B.er really resembles is film of the old Soviet Union putting down a rebellion. It's awesome, but brutally so, with a grinding, faceless quality about its power that renders that power curiously dull and empty.

[32] (compare Ivanisevic's at 130 mph or Sampras's at 125, or even this Brakus kid's at 118).

[33] The loop in a pro's backswing is kind of the trademark flourish of excellence and consciousness of same, not unlike the five-star chef's quick kiss of his own fingertips

Joyce can hit through the ball while it's still well out in front of him. As with all great players, Joyce's side is so emphatically to the net as the ball approaches that his posture is a classic contrapposto.

As Joyce on the forehand makes contact with the tennis ball, his left hand behind him opens up, as if he were releasing something, a decorative gesture that has nothing to do with the mechanics of the stroke. Michael Joyce doesn't know that his left hand opens up at impact on forehands: it is unconscious, some aesthetic tic that started when he was a child and is now inextricably hardwired into a stroke that is itself unconscious for Joyce, now, at 22, after years of hitting more forehands over and over than anyone could ever count.[34]

Agassi, who is 25 (and of whom you have heard and then some), is kind of Michael Joyce's hero. Just last week, at the Legg Mason Tennis Classic in Washington D.C., in wet-mitten heat that had players vomiting on-court and defaulting all over the place, Agassi beat Joyce in the third round of the main draw, 6–2 6–2. Every once in a while now during this Qualie match Joyce will look over at his coach next to me in the player-guest section of the Grandstand and grin and say something like "Agassi'd have killed me on that shot." Joyce's coach will

---

as he presents a pièce or the magician's hand making a French curl in the air as he directs our attention to his vanished assistant.

[34] All serious players have these little extraneous tics, stylistic fingerprints, and the pros even more so because of years of repetition and ingraining. Pros' tics have always been fun to note and chart, even just e.g. on the serve. Watch the way Sampras's lead foot rises from the heel on his toss, as if his left foot's toes got suddenly hot. The odd Tourettic way Gerulaitis used to whip his head from side to side while bouncing the ball before his toss, as if he were having a small seizure. McEnroe's weird splayed stiff-armed service stance, both feet parallel to the baseline and his side so severely to the net that he looked like a figure on an Egyptian frieze. The odd sudden shrug Lendl gives before releasing his toss. The way Agassi shifts his weight several times from foot to foot as he prepares for the toss like he needs desperately to pee. Or, here at the Canadian Open, the way the young star Thomas Enqvist's body bends queerly back as he tosses, limboing back away from the toss, as if for a moment the ball smelled very bad — this tic derives from Enqvist's predecessor Edberg's own weird spinal arch and twist on the toss. Edberg also has this strange sudden way of switching his hold on the racquet in mid-toss, changing from an Eastern forehand to an extreme backhand grip, as if the racquet were a skillet.

adjust the set of his sunglasses and say nothing — coaches are forbidden to say anything to their players during a match. Joyce's coach,
Sam Aparicio,[35] a protégé of Pancho Gonzalez, is based in Las Vegas,
which is also Agassi's home town, and Joyce has several times been flown
to Las Vegas at Agassi's request to practice with him, and is apparently
regarded by Agassi as a friend and peer — these are facts Michael Joyce
will mention with as much pride as he evinces in speaking of victories
and world ranking.

There are big differences between Agassi's and Joyce's games, though.
Though Joyce and Agassi both use the Western forehand grip and two-
handed backhand that are distinctive of topspinners, Joyce's groundstrokes are very "flat" — i.e. spinless, passing low over the net, driven
rather than brushed — because the actual motion of his strokes is
so levelly horizontal. Joyce's balls actually look more like Jimmy
Connors's balls than like Agassi's.[36] Some of Joyce's groundstrokes look

[35] Who looks rather like a Hispanic Dustin Hoffman and is an almost unbelievably
nice guy, with the sort of inward self-sufficiency of truly great teachers and coaches
everywhere, the Zen-like blend of focus and calm developed by people who have to
spend enormous amounts of time sitting in one place watching closely while somebody else does something. Sam gets 10% of Joyce's gross revenues and spends his
downtime reading dense tomes on Mayan architecture and is one of the coolest people
I've ever met either inside the tennis world or outside it (so cool I'm kind of scared of
him and haven't called him once since the assignment ended, if that makes sense). In
return for his 10%, Sam travels with Joyce, rooms with him, coaches him, supervises
his training, analyzes his matches, and attends him in practice, even to the extent of
picking up errant balls so that Joyce doesn't have to spend any of his tightly organized practice time picking up errant balls. The stress and weird loneliness of pro tennis — where everybody's in the same community, sees each other every week, but is
constantly on the diasporic move, and is each other's rival, with enormous amounts
of money at stake and life essentially a montage of airports and bland hotels and
non-home-cooked food and nagging injuries and staggering long-distance bills, and
people's families back home tending to be wackos, since only wackos will make the
financial and temporal sacrifices necessary to let their offspring become good enough
at something to turn pro at it — all this means that most players lean heavily on their
coaches for emotional support and friendship as well as technical counsel. Sam's role
with Joyce looks to me to approximate what in the latter century was called that of
"companion," one of those older ladies who traveled with nubile women when they
went abroad, etc.

[36] Agassi's balls look more like Borg's balls would have looked if Borg had been on
a year-long regimen of both steroids and methamphetamines and was hitting every

like knuckleballs going over the net, and you can actually see the ball's seams just hanging there, not spinning. Joyce also has a hitch in his backhand that makes it look stiff and slightly awkward, though his pace and placement are lethal off that side; Agassi's own backhand is flowing and hitchless.[37] And while Joyce is far from slow, he lacks Agassi's other-worldly foot-speed. Agassi is every bit as fast as Michael Chang, and watch A.A. on TV sometime as he's walking between points: he takes these tiny, violently pigeon-toed steps, the stride of a man whose feet weigh basically nothing.

Michael Joyce also — in his own coach's opinion — doesn't "see" the ball in the same magical way that Andre Agassi does, and so Joyce can't take the ball as early or generate quite the same amount of pace off his groundstrokes. This business of "seeing" is important enough to explain. Except for the serve, power in tennis is a matter not of strength but of timing. This is one reason why so few top tennis players are muscular.[38] Any normal adult male can hit a tennis ball with pro pace; the trick is being able to hit the ball both hard and accurately. If you can get your body in just the right position and time your stroke so you hit the ball

---

single fucking ball just as hard as he could — Agassi hits his groundstrokes as hard as anybody who's ever played tennis, so hard you almost can't believe it if you're right there by the court.

[37] But Agassi does have this exaggerated follow-through where he keeps both hands on the racquet and follows through almost like a hitter in baseball, which causes his shirtfront to lift and his hairy tummy to be exposed to public view — in Montreal I find this repellent, though the females in the stands around me seem ready to live and die for a glimpse of Agassi's tummy. Agassi's S.O. Brooke Shields is in Montreal, by the way, and will end up highly visible in the player-guest box for all Agassi's matches, wearing big sunglasses and what look to be multiple hats. This may be the place to insert that Brooke Shields is rather a lot taller than Agassi, and considerably less hairy, and that seeing them standing together in person is rather like seeing Sigourney Weaver on the arm of Danny DeVito. The effect is especially surreal when Brooke is wearing one of the plain classy sundresses that make her look like a deb summering in the Hamptons and Agassi's wearing his new Nike on-court ensemble, a blue-black horizontally striped outfit that together with his black sneakers make him look like somebody's idea of a French Resistance fighter.

[38] (Though note that very few of them wear eyeglasses, either.)

in just the right spot — waist-level, just slightly out in front of you, with your weight moving from your back leg to your front leg as you make contact — you can both cream the ball and direct it. And since ". . . just the right . . ." is a matter of millimeters and microseconds, a certain kind of vision is crucial.[39] Agassi's vision is literally one in a billion, and it allows him to hit his groundstrokes as hard as he can just about every time. Joyce, whose hand-eye coordination is superlative, in the top 1% of all athletes everywhere (he's been exhaustively tested), still has to take some incremental bit of steam off most of his groundstrokes if he wants to direct them.

I submit that tennis is the most beautiful sport there is,[40] and also the most demanding. It requires body control, hand-eye coordination, quickness, flat-out speed, endurance, and that strange mix of caution and abandon we call courage. It also requires smarts. Just one single shot in one exchange in one point of a high-level match is a nightmare of mechanical variables. Given a net that's three feet high (at the center) and two players in (unrealistically) a fixed position, the efficacy of one single shot is determined by its angle, depth, pace, and spin. And each of these determinants is itself determined by still other variables — for example, a shot's depth is determined by the height at which the ball passes over the net combined with some integrated function of pace and spin, with the ball's height over the net *itself* determined by the player's body position, grip on the racquet, degree of backswing, angle of racquet face, and the 3-D coordinates through which the racquet face moves during that

[39] A whole other kind of vision — the kind attributed to Larry Bird in basketball, sometimes, when he made those incredible surgical passes to people who nobody else could even see were open — is required when you're hitting: this involves seeing the other side of the court, i.e. where your opponent is and which direction he's moving in and what possible angles are open to you in consequence of where he's going. The schizoid thing about tennis is that you have to use both kinds of vision — ball and court — at the same time.

[40] Basketball comes close, but it's a team sport and lacks tennis's primal mano a mano intensity. Boxing might come close — at least at the lighter weight-divisions — but the actual physical damage the fighters inflict on each other makes it too concretely brutal to be really beautiful: a level of abstraction and formality (i.e. "play") is probably necessary for a sport to possess true metaphysical beauty (in my opinion).

interval in which the ball is actually on the strings. The tree of variables and determinants branches out, on and on, and then on even farther when the opponent's own positions and predilections and the ballistic features of the ball he's sent you to hit are factored in.[41] No CPU yet existent could compute the expansion of variables for even a single exchange — smoke would come out of the mainframe. The sort of thinking involved is the sort that can be done only by a living and highly conscious entity, and then only *un*consciously, i.e. by combining talent with repetition to such an extent that the variables are combined and controlled without conscious thought. In other words, serious tennis is a kind of art.

If you've played tennis at least a little, you probably think you have some idea of how hard a game it is to play really well. I submit to you that you really have no idea at all. I know I didn't. And television doesn't really allow us to appreciate what real top-level players can do — how hard they're actually hitting the ball, and with what control and tactical imagination and artistry. I got to watch Michael Joyce practice several times, right up close, like six feet and a chain-link fence away. This is a man who, at full run, can hit a fast-moving tennis ball into a one-foot-square area 78 feet away over a yard-high net, hard. He can do this something over 90% of the time. And this is the world's 79th-best player, one who has to play the Montreal Qualies.

It's not just the athletic artistry that compels interest in tennis at the professional level. It's also what this level requires — what it's taken for the 100th-ranked player in the world to get there, what it takes to stay, what it would take to rise even higher against other men who've paid the same price he's paid.

Bismarck's epigram about diplomacy and sausage applies also to the way we Americans seem to feel about professional athletes. We revere athletic excellence, competitive success. And it's more than attention we

---

[41] For those of you into business stats, the calculus of a shot in tennis would be rather like establishing a running compound-interest expansion in a case where not only is the rate of interest itself variable, and not only are the determinants of that rate variable, and not only is the interval in which the determinants influence the interest rate variable, but the principal *itself* is variable.

pay; we vote with our wallets. We'll spend large sums to watch a truly great athlete; we'll reward him with celebrity and adulation and will even go so far as to buy products and services he endorses.

But we prefer not to countenance the kinds of sacrifices the professional-grade athlete has made to get so good at one particular thing. Oh, we'll pay lip service to these sacrifices — we'll invoke lush clichés about the lonely heroism of Olympic athletes, the pain and analgesia of football, the early rising and hours of practice and restricted diets, the privations, the prefight celibacy, etc. But the actual facts of the sacrifices repel us when we see them: basketball geniuses who cannot read, sprinters who dope themselves, defensive tackles who shoot up bovine hormones until they collapse or explode. We prefer not to consider the shockingly vapid and primitive comments uttered by athletes in postcontest interviews, or to imagine what impoverishments in one's mental life would allow people actually to think in the simplistic way great athletes seem to think. Note the way "up-close and personal profiles" of professional athletes strain so hard to find evidence of a rounded human life — outside interests and activities, charities, values beyond the sport. We ignore what's obvious, that most of this straining is farce. It's farce because the realities of top-level athletics today require an early and total commitment to one pursuit. An almost ascetic focus.[42] A subsumption of almost all other features of human life to their one chosen talent and pursuit. A consent to live in a world that, like a child's world, is very serious and very small.

Playing two professional singles matches on the same day is unheard of, except in Qualies.[43] Michael Joyce's second qualifying round is at 7:30

[42] Sex- and substance-issues notwithstanding, professional athletes are in many ways our culture's holy men: they give themselves over to a pursuit, endure great privation and pain to actualize themselves at it, and enjoy a relationship to perfection that we admire and reward (the monk's begging bowl, the RBI-guru's eight-figure contract) and love to watch even though we have no inclination to walk that road ourselves. In other words they do it "for" us, sacrifice themselves for our (we imagine) redemption.

[43] In the Qualies for Grand Slams like Wimbledon and the U.S. Open, players sometimes have to play two three-out-of-five-set matches in one day; it is little wonder that

Saturday night. He's playing an Austrian named Julian Knowle, a tall and cadaverous guy with pointy Kafkan ears. Knowle uses two hands off both sides[44] and throws his racquet when he's mad. The match takes place on Stade Jarry's Grandstand Court, which seems more like a theater than an arena because it has seats and bleachers only on the east side. But the Grandstand's also more intimate: the box seats start just a few yards from the court surface, and you're close enough to see a wen on Joyce's cheek or the abacus of sweat on Herr Knowle's forehead. It's not as hot here at night, but it's humid, and the high-power lights all have those curious rainbow globes of diffraction around them, plus orbiting bugs. The Grandstand can hold maybe 1500 people, and tonight there are exactly four human beings in the audience as Michael Joyce basically beats the everliving shit out of Julian Knowle, who will be at the Montreal airport tonight at 1:30 to board the red-eye for a kind of minor-league clay tournament in Poznan, Poland.

During this afternoon's match Joyce wore a white Fila shirt with two different-colored sleeves. Onto his sleeve was sown a patch that says POWERBAR; Joyce is paid $1000 each time he wears this patch in play. Plus, this afternoon, a hat — in the afternoon sun, pretty much all the players in the Qualies wear hats. For tonight's match Joyce wears a pin-stripe Jim Courier–model Fila shirt with one red sleeve and one blue sleeve. The patch is on the blue sleeve. He has a red bandanna around his head, and as he begins to perspire in the humidity his face turns the same color as the bandanna. It is hard not to find this endearing. Julian Knowle has an abstract pastel shirt whose brand is unrecognizable. He has very tall hair, Knowle does, that towers over his head at near-Beavis altitude and doesn't diminish or lose its gelled integrity as he perspires.[45] Knowle's shirt, too, has sleeves of different colors. This seems

---

the surviving qualifiers often look like concentration-camp survivors by the time they get to the main draw and you see them getting annihilated by a healthy and rested top seed in the televised first round.

44 Meaning a two-handed forehand, whose pioneer was a South African named Frew McMillan and whose most famous practitioner today is Monica Seles.

45 The idea of what it would be like to perspire heavily with large amounts of gel in your hair is sufficiently horrific to me that I approached Knowle after the match to

to be the fashion constant this year among the qualifiers: sleeve-color asymmetry.

The Joyce-Knowle match takes slightly more than an hour. This is including delays caused when Knowle throws his racquet and has to go retrieve it or when he walks around in aimless circles muttering blackly to himself in some High-German dialect. Knowle's tantrums seem a little contrived and insincere to me, though, because he rarely loses a point as a result of doing anything particularly wrong. Here's a typical point in this match: it's 1–4 and 15–30 in the sixth game. Knowle hits a 110-mph slice serve to Joyce's forehand; Joyce hits a very flat and penetrating drive crosscourt, so that Knowle has to stretch and hit his forehand on the run, something that's not particularly easy to do with a two-handed forehand. Knowle gets to the forehand and hits a thoroughly respectable shot, loopy with topspin and landing maybe only a little bit short, a few feet behind the service line, whereupon he reverses direction and starts scrambling back to get in the middle of the baseline to get ready for his next shot. Joyce, as is SOP, has moved in on the slightly short ball and takes the ball on the rise just after it's bounced, driving a backhand even flatter and harder into the exact same place he hit his last shot, the spot Knowle is scrambling away from. Knowle is now forced to reverse direction and get back to where he was.[46] This he does, and he gets his racquet on the ball, but only barely, and sends back a weak little USDA Prime loblet that Joyce, now in the actual vicinity of the net, has little trouble blocking into the open court for a winner. The four people clap, Knowle's racquet goes spinning into the blood-colored tarp, and Joyce walks expressionlessly back to the deuce court to receive again whenever Knowle gets around to serving. Knowle has slightly more firepower than the first round's Brakus: his groundstrokes are formidable, probably even lethal if he has sufficient time to get to the ball and get set up. Joyce simply denies him that time. Joyce will later admit that he wasn't working all

---

ask him about it, only to discover that neither he nor his coach spoke enough English or even French to be able to determine who I was, and the whole sweat-and-gel issue will, I'm afraid, remain a matter for your own imagination.

[46] What Joyce has done is known as "wrong-footing" his opponent, though the intransigent Francophone press here keep calling the tactic a "contre-pied."

that hard in this match, and he doesn't need to. He hits few spectacular winners, but he also makes very few unforced errors, and his shots are designed to make the somewhat clumsy Knowle move a lot and to deny him the time and the peace ever to set up his game. This strategy is one that Knowle cannot solve or interdict: he hasn't got the tools for it. This may be one reason why Joyce is unaffronted by having to play the Qualies for Montreal: barring some kind of injury or neurological dysfunction, he's not going to lose to somebody like Austria's Julian Knowle — Joyce is simply on a different plateau from the mass of these Qualie players.

The idea that there can be wholly distinct levels to competitive tennis — levels so distinct that what's being played is in essence a whole different game — might seem to you weird and hyperbolic. I have played probably just enough tennis to understand that it's true. I have played against men who were on a whole different, higher plateau than I, and I have understood on the deepest and most humbling level the impossibility of beating them, of "solving their game." Knowle is technically entitled to be called a professional, but he is playing a fundamentally different grade of tennis from Michael Joyce's, one constrained by limitations Joyce does not have. I feel like I could get on a tennis court with Julian Knowle. He would beat me, perhaps badly, but I don't feel like it would be absurd for me to occupy the same 78×27–foot rectangle as he. But the idea of me playing Joyce — or even hitting around with him, which was one of the ideas I was entertaining on the flight to Montreal, to hit around with a hot young U.S. pro — is now revealed to me to be absurd and in a certain way obscene, and during this night match I resolve not even to let Joyce[47] know that I used to play competitive tennis, to play seriously and (I'd presumed) rather well. This makes me sad.

Sunday, the second day of the Qualies, is mostly a rainout. It rains off and on all day. The umpire, courtside in his tall chair, decides when the rain's falling hard enough to suspend play. A second-round match between the

---

[47] Who is clearly such a fundamentally nice guy that he would probably hit around with me for a little while just out of politeness, since for him it would be at worst somewhat dull. For me, though, it would be obscene.

world's 219th- and 345th-ranked players gets suspended four different times and takes most of the day to complete. What happens when it rains is reminiscent of baseball. The players are hustled off back to the Players' Tent but can't leave because it could stop raining any minute; they have to just sit there, match-ready. The spectators (there are slightly more on the second day) stay where they are, but little fungal domes of umbrella start appearing all over the stands. The local Quebec reporters up in the Press Box curse in French and bring out newspapers or hand-held video games or begin telling one another long sexual-adventure stories that my French is just good enough to establish as tiresome.

When it stops raining and stays stopped long enough for the umpire to give the old raised thumb, there's suddenly a flurry of custodial activity down on the Stadium Court, a Chinese fire drill of ballboys and linesmen turned groundskeepers. Strange and expensive-looking machinery appears from nowhere and is brought to bear: huge riding-mowerish forced-air machines go over the court, bludgeoning the pooled rainwater and spreading it out; then a platoon of squeegees goes over every cm of the surface; then portable blowers — rather like leaf-blowers, with an over-the-shoulder strap and a wand attachment — are applied to the persistent individual wet spots that always beset a drying court.

This article is about Michael Joyce and the untelevised realities of the Tour, not me. But since a big part of my experience of the Canadian Open and its players was one of sadness, it might be worthwhile to spend a little time letting you know where I'm coming from w/r/t these players. As a young person I played competitive tennis, traveling to tournaments all over the Midwest. Most of my best friends were also tennis players, and on a regional level we were fairly successful, and we thought of ourselves as extremely good players. Tennis and our proficiency at it were tremendously important to us — a serious junior gives up a lot of his time and freedom to develop his game,[48] and it can very easily come to

---

[48] The example of Michael Joyce's own childhood, though, shows that my friends and I were comparative sluggards, dilettantes. He describes his daily schedule thusly: "I'd be in school till 2:00. Then, after, I'd go [driven by father] to the [West End Tennis] Club [in Torrance CA] and have a lesson with [legendary, wildly expensive, and

constitute a big part of his identity and self-worth. The other fourteen-year-old Midwest hotshots and I knew that our fishpond was somehow limited; we knew that there was a national level of play and that there existed hotshots and champions at that level. But levels and plateaux beyond our own seemed abstract, somehow unreal — those of us who were the hotshots in our region literally could not imagine players our own age who were substantially better than we.

A child's world turns out to be very small. If I'd been just a little bit better, an actual regional champion, I would have qualified for national-level tournaments, and I would have gotten to see that there were fourteen-year-olds in the United States who were playing tennis on a level I knew nothing about.

My own game as a junior was a particular type of the classic defensive style, a strategy Martin Amis describes as "craven retrieval." I didn't hit the ball all that hard, but I rarely made unforced errors, and I was fast, and my general approach was simply to keep hitting the ball back to the opponent until the kid screwed up and either made an unforced error or hit a ball so short and juicy that even I could hit a winner off it. It doesn't look like a very glamorous or even interesting way to play, now that I see it here in bald retrospective print, but it was interesting to me, and you'd be surprised how effective it was (on the level at which I was competing, at least). At age twelve, a good competitive player will still generally miss after four or five balls (mostly because he'll get impatient or grandiose). At age sixteen, a good player will keep the ball in play for more like maybe seven or eight shots before he misses. At the collegiate level, too (at least in Division III), opponents were stronger than junior players but not

---

unbelievably hard-ass Robert] Lansdorp [former childhood coach of, among others, Tracy Austin] from 3:00 to 4:00. Then I'd have drills from 4:00 to 6:00, then we'd drive all the way home — it's like half an hour — and I'm like, 'Thank God, I can watch TV or go up and talk with [friends] on the phone or something,' but Dad is like, 'You didn't practice your serve yet.' At twelve or thirteen [years old], you're not going to want to do it. [No lie, since two hours of serious drills alone were usually enough to put your correspondent in a fetal position for the rest of the day.] You need somebody to make you do it. [This is one way of looking at it.] But then, after like a hundred or so serves, I start to get into [standing by himself out on the Joyces' tennis court in their backyard with a huge bucket of balls and hitting serve after serve to no one in what must by then have been the gathering twilight], I like it, I'm glad I'm doing it."

markedly more consistent, and if I could keep a rally going to seven or eight shots, I could usually win the point on the other guy's mistake.[49]

[49] An important variable I'm skipping is that children are (not surprisingly) immature and tend to get angry with themselves when they screw up, and so a key part of my strategy involved putting the opponent in a position where he made a lot of unforced errors and got madder and madder at himself, which would ruin his game. Feelings of self-disgust at his errors, or (even better for me) bitter grievance at the universe for making him have "bad luck" or an "off day" would mount until usually by sometime in the second set he'd sink into a kind of enraged torpor and *expect* to miss, or occasionally he'd even have a kind of grand Learesque tantrum, complete with racquet-hurling and screamed obscenities and sometimes tears. This happened less and less as I got older and opponents got more mature, and by the time I was in college only genuine head-cases could be counted on to get so mad that they'd basically make themselves lose to an inferior player (viz. me). It's something of a shock, then, to watch Joyce do to his third-round Qualies opponent what I used to do to twelve-year-old rich kids, which is essentially to retrieve and avoid errors and wait for this opponent to have a temper tantrum. Because Sunday was a rainout, Joyce's third round is played Monday at 10:00 A.M., at the same time that some of the main draw's first rounds are beginning. Joyce's opponent is a guy named Mark Knowles, 25, the 1986 U.S. Junior Indoor Champion, a native of the Bahamas, now known primarily as a doubles player but still a serious opponent, ranked in the world's top 200, somebody on Joyce's plateau.

Knowles is tall and thin, muscular in the corded way tall thin people are muscular, and has an amazing tan and tight blond curls and from a distance is an impressive-looking guy, though up close he has a kind of squished, buggy face and the slightly bulging eyes of a player who, I can tell, is spring-loaded on a tantrum. There's a chance to see Knowles up close because he and Joyce play their match on one of the minor courts, where spectators stand and lean over a low fence only a few yards from the court. I and Joyce's coach and Knowles's coach and beautiful girlfriend are the only people really seriously standing and watching, though a lot of spectators on their way to more high-profile matches pass by and stop and watch a few points before moving on. The constant movement of civilians past the court aggrieves Knowles no end, and sometimes he shouts caustic things to people who've started walking away while a point is still in progress.

"Don't worry about it!" is one thing Knowles shouted at someone who moved. "We're only playing for money! We're only professionals! Don't give it a second thought!" Joyce, preparing to serve, will stare affectlessly straight ahead while he waits for Knowles to finish yelling, his expression sort of like the one Vegas dealers have when a gambler they're cleaning out is rude or abusive, a patient and unjudging look whose expression is informed by the fact that they're extremely well compensated for being patient and unjudging.

Sam Aparicio describes Knowles as "brilliant but kind of erratic," and I think the coach is being kind, because Knowles seems to me to belong on a Locked Ward for people with serious emotional and personality disorders. He rants and throws racquets

I still play — not competitively, but seriously — and I should confess that deep down somewhere inside I still consider myself an extremely good tennis player, real hard to beat. Before coming to Montreal, I'd seen professional tennis only on television, which as has been noted does not give the viewer a very accurate picture of how good pros are. I thus further confess that I arrived in Montreal with some dim unconscious expectation that these professionals — at least the obscure ones, the nonstars — wouldn't be all *that* much better than I. I don't mean to imply that I'm insane: I was ready to concede that age, a nasty ankle injury in '91 that I haven't bothered to get surgically fixed yet, and a penchant for nicotine (and worse) meant that I wouldn't be able to compete physically with a young unhurt professional; but on TV (while eating junk and smoking) I'd seen pros whacking balls at each other that didn't look to be moving substantially faster than the balls I hit. In other words, I arrived at my first professional tournament with the pathetic deluded pride that attends ignorance. And

---

and screams scatological curses I haven't heard since junior high. If one of his shots hits the top of the net-cord and bounces back, Knowles will scream "I must be the luckiest guy in the world!", his eyes protruding and mouth twisted. For me he's an eerie echo of all the rich and well-instructed Midwest kids I used to play and beat because they'd be unable to eat the frustration when things didn't go their way. He seems not to notice that Joyce gets as many bad breaks and weird bounces as he, or that passing spectators are equally distracting to both players. Knowles seems to be one of these people who view the world's inconveniences as specific and personal, and it makes my stomach hurt to watch him. When he hits a ball against the fence so hard it seems to damage the ball, the umpire gives him a warning, but in the sort of gentle compassionate voice of a kindergarten teacher to a kid who's known to have A.D.D. I have a hard time believing that someone this off-the-wall could rise to a serious pro plateau, though it's true that when Knowles isn't letting his attention get scattered he's a gorgeous player, with fluid strokes and marvelous control over spin and pace. His read on Joyce is that Joyce is a slugger (which is true), and his tactic is to try to junk him up — change pace, vary spins, hit drop shots to draw Joyce in, deny Joyce pace or rhythm — and because he's Joyce's equal in firepower the tactic is sound. Joyce wins the first set in a tiebreaker. But three times in the tiebreaker Knowles yells at migratory spectators "Don't worry! It's only a tiebreaker in a professional match!" and is basically a wreck by the time the first set is over, and the second set is perfunctory, a formality that Joyce concludes as fast as possible and hurries back to the Players' Tent to pack carbohydrates and find out whether he has to play his first round in the main draw later this same day.

I have watched the Qualies — not even the main draw yet, mind you, but the competition between 64 fairly low-ranked world-class players for the eight qualifying slots in the Canadian Open field — with a mixture of awe and sad surprise. I have been brought up sharply. I do not play and never have played the same game as these low-ranked pros.

The craven game I spent so much of my youth perfecting would not work against these guys. For one thing, pros simply do not make unforced errors — or at any rate they make them so rarely that there's no way they're going to make the four unforced errors in seven points necessary for me to win a game. For another thing, they will take any shot that doesn't have simply ferocious depth and pace on it and — given even a fractional moment to line up a shot — hit a winner off it. For yet another thing, their own shots have such ferocious depth and pace that there's no way I'd be able to hit more than a couple of them back at any one time. I could not meaningfully *exist* on the same court with these obscure, hungry players. Nor could you. And it's not just a matter of talent or practice. There's something else.

Monday commences the main draw, and the grounds are packed. Most of the Qualies' players are in planes high above some ocean somewhere by now.

Going to a major ATP tournament is like a cross between going to a major-league ball game and going to the fair. You can buy a Grounds Pass and wander from match to match, sampling the fare. You can also buy specific expensive tickets for big-name matches in the Stadium and Grandstand. In the early rounds, these headline matches tend to feature the high seeds and household names — Agassi, Sampras, Chang — against main draw also-rans like Jacob Hlasek.[50]

Being a tennis spectator is different from being at a baseball game, though. Whether crowd-noise or -movement is any more distracting to

---

[50] Hlasek lost in the first round of the main draw Tuesday morning to obscure American Jonathan Stark, who then lost to Sampras in the second round on Wednesday in front of a capacity Stadium crowd.

someone getting ready to serve than it is to someone getting ready to shoot a freethrow, players and tournaments act like it is, and play itself is supposed to be conducted in as close to funereal silence as possible.[51] If you've got a seat for a Stadium match, you can leave and return only during the break that happens after every odd-numbered game, when the players get to sit under red umbrellas for a second. Ushers cordon off the exits during play, and a concession-laden mass of spectators always stretches from just behind these ropes all the way down the slanted ramps into the Stadium's bowels, waiting to get back in.

Stade Jarry has the same sort of crumbling splendor that characterizes a lot of Montreal. The Stadium/Grandstand structure used to house the Expos before Montreal built Olympic Stadium, and it's grimy and old and creaks alarmingly when crowds enter or exit. The "Players' Lounge," which at most tournaments is a temperature-controlled salon with plush chairs and video games and multiple massage rooms, is at Stade Jarry just a big tent with canvas partitions around the locker room, no video games, just one TV, and no AC. The parking lots are inadequate and tufted with crabgrass, and the easements between courts and facilities on the grounds are either dirt or some kind of blacktop that's decayed back to the point where it's just about dirt too. The whole thing's due to be torn down after the '95 Open's over, and a new Flushing Meadow–type tennis complex is going to be built by Tennis Canada[52] and a whole bunch of the corporations whose names are on the Stadium's brothelish bunting.

The tournament site's surrounding Parc du Jarry, on the other hand,

---

[51] This is in the Stadium and Grandstand, where the big names play, this ceremonial hush. Lesser players on the outlying courts have to live with spectators talking during points, people moving around so that whole rickety sets of bleachers rumble and clank, food service attendants crashing carts around on the paths just outside the windscreen or giggling and flirting in the food-prep tents just on the other side of several minor courts' fences.

[52] This is Canada's version of the U.S.T.A., and its logo — which obtrudes into your visual field as often as is possible here at the du Maurier Omnium — consists of the good old Canadian maple leaf with a tennis racquet for a stem. It's stuff like Tennis Canada's logo you want to point to when Canadians protest that they don't understand why Americans make fun of them.

is exquisite. From the top row of the Stadium's seats you can look out
in the sunshine and see rolling grass, a public pool, a pond replete with
stately fowl. In the distance to the north is the verdigrised dome of a
really big church; to the west is the EKG skyline of downtown Montreal.

But so you can wander between matches, stand around watching
the practice courts, join the lines for the restrooms, or elbow-fight with
little kids and autograph hunters outside the Players' Tent. Or you can
buy concessions. There's a booth outside one entrance to the Stadium
Court that sells only Evian water. There's Spanish peanuts and fudge
you can buy by the gram and eat or buy by the kilo and take home.[53]
The whole Stade Jarry grounds have a standard summer-touristic reek
of fried foods — French fries in cups, nachos, and in paper trays small
spiraled fried things I decline to examine closely. There are two booths
for Richard D's Bars, a kind of Quebecois cognate for Dove Bars (and
not quite as good, but pretty good). There are only two men's rooms
open to the public,[54] and the lines for both always resemble a run on a
midsize branch bank. There's the Rado® Smash Booth, where for $3.00
Canadian you can step inside a large cage with a much-handled racquet
and hit a serve into a frayed-looking net and have the speed of your
serve appear on a big liquid-crystal display above the cage. Most of the
people availing themselves of the Rado® Smash Booth are men, whose
girlfriends watch dutifully as the men step inside the cage with the same
testosteronic facial expression of men at fairs testing their marksman-
ship or sledge-swinging prowess — and the American men tend to be
very pleased and excited at the displayed speed of their serve until it
dawns on them that the readout's in kph instead of mph. There are hot
dogs and hamburgers and the ambient sizzle-sound of same over near

[53] (though best of luck getting fudge home in this heat . . .)

[54] "Le Média" has its own facilities, though they're up in the Press Box, about five
flights of rickety and crowded stairs up through the Stadium's interior and then exterior and then interior, with the last flight being that dense striated iron of like a fire
escape and very steep and frankly dangerous, so that when one has to "aller au pissoir"
it's always a hard decision between the massed horror of the public rest rooms and the
Sisyphean horror of the Press bathroom, and I learn by the second day to go very easy
on the Evian water and coffee as I'm wandering around.

the Grandstand entrances. Just east of the Grandstand and the second men's room, there's a whole sort of cafeteria in a big tent with patio tables arrayed on Astroturf that's laid over a low deck of extremely flimsy boards so that your table trembles and your Evian bottle falls over every time somebody walks by. Starting on Monday there are a lot of Canadian girls in really short tight shorts and a lot of muscle-shirted Canadian boyfriends who scowl at you if you react to the girlfriends in the way the girlfriends' tight shorts seem designed to make anyone with a healthy endocrine system react.

There are old people who sit on red Stade Jarry park benches all day without moving.

At just about every gate and important door on the Stade Jarry grounds there are attendants, young Quebeckers paid by the tournament — whether their function is security or what remains somewhat unclear — who sit all day with walkie-talkies and red and black du Maurier visors and the catatonically bored expressions of attendants everywhere.

There are four separate booths that sell good old U.S. soft drinks, you'll be glad to know, although the booths' promo-signs for "Soft Drinks" translate literally into "Gaseous Beverages," which might explain why most Canadian Open spectators opt for Evian instead of soft drinks.

Or you can stand in front of the Canadian Open Stringer's Tent and watch the Official ATP Tour Stringer work through a small mountain of racquets, using pliers and shears and what looks like a combination blacksmith's anvil and dentist's chair. Or you can join the battalion of kids outside the Players' Tent all trying to get their Official ATP Player Trading Cards[55] autographed by players entering or exiting, and you can witness a kind of near-riot when the passing player turns out to be Sampras or Courier or Agassi, and you can even get stiff-armed by a bodyguard in wraparound shades when Brooke Shields passes too close in her own wraparounds and floppy hat.

If the mood for more serious consumption strikes, you can walk due

---

[55] (a recent and rather ingenious marketing move by the ATP — I buy several just for the names)

east of the Stadium complex to the Promenade du Sportif, a kind of canvas strip mall selling every product even remotely associated with the Canadian Open: Prince, Wilson, Nike, Head, Boost® Vitamin/Energy Drink (free samples available), Swatch, Nature Valley Granola Bars,[56] Sony, and DecoTurf Inc.

And at this tournament you can (U.S. readers may want to sit down for this part) actually *buy* du Maurier–brand cigarettes — by the carton or broad flat Europack — from a special red and black booth right outside the main entrance to the Stadium Court.[57] People in Quebec smoke — heavily — and this booth does serious business. No part of Stade Jarry is nonsmoking, and at matches so many spectators are chain-smoking du Maurier cigarettes that at times a slight breeze will carry the crowd's exhaled cloud of smoke out over the court, transforming the players into nacreous silhouettes for a moment before the cloud ascends. And, in truth, accredited media don't even have to *buy* the du Mauriers; Press Box employees will give packs out free to journalists, though they don't announce this or make a big big deal of it.

It's the little things like public smoking that remind you that Canada's not home. Or e.g. Francophone ads, and these ads' lack of even a pretense of coy subtlety — someplace between the Radisson des Gouverneurs and Stade Jarry is a huge billboard for some kind of Quebecois ice cream. It's a huge photo of an ice cream cone poised at a phallic 45°, jutting, the dome of ice cream unabashedly glansular, and underneath is the pitch: "Donnez-moi ta bouche."[58] The brand's own trademark slogan, at the bottom, is that it's "La glace du lait plus lechée." One of the nice things

---

[56] It's not at all clear what N.V.G.B.'s have to do with the Omnium, and no free samples are available.

[57] Du Maurier cigarettes are like Australian Sterlings or French Gauloise — full-bodied, pungent, crackly when inhaled, sweet and yeasty when exhaled, and so strong that you can feel your scalp seem to leave your skull for a moment and ride the cloud of smoke. Du Maurier–intoxication may be one reason why the Canadian Open crowds seem so generally cheery and expansive and well-behaved.

[58] (="Give me your mouth" — not subtle at all)

Michael Joyce and his coach do is usually let me ride with them in their courtesy car[59] between the hotel and Jarry, to sort of lurk and soak up atmosphere, etc. We pass this billboard several times a day. Finally one time I point up at the glistening phallic ad and ask Joyce whether the ad strikes him as a little heavy, overt, uncoy. Joyce looks up at the billboard — maybe for the first time, because in the car he's usually staring commuterishly straight ahead, either gathering himself into a prematch focus or exiting gradually from same — and turns to me and says in all earnestness that he's tried this particular brand of Canadian ice cream and it's not all that good.

Plus, of course, once the main draw starts, you get to look up close and live at name tennis players you're used to seeing only as arrays of pixels. One of the highlights of Tuesday's second round of the main draw is getting to watch Agassi play MaliVai Washington. Washington, the most successful black American on the Tour since Ashe, is unseeded at the Canadian Open but has been ranked as high as #11 in the world, and is dangerous, and since I loathe Agassi with a passion it's an exciting match. Agassi looks scrawny and faggy and, with his shaved skull and beretish hat and black shoes and socks and patchy goatee, like somebody just released from reform school (a look you can tell he's carefully decided on with the help of various paid image-consultants, and now cultivates). Washington, who's in dark-green shorts and a red shirt with dark-green sleeves, was a couple of years ago voted by *People* one of the 50 Prettiest Human Beings or something, and on TV is indeed real pretty but in person is awesome. From twenty yards away he looks less like a human being than like a Michelangelo anatomy sketch: his upper

---

[59]   These are usually luxury cars provided by some local distributorship in return for promotional consideration. The Canadian Open's courtesy cars are BMWs, all so new they smell like glove compartments and so expensive and high-tech that their dashboards look like the control panels of nuclear reactors. The people driving the courtesy cars are usually local civilians who take a week off from work and drive a numbingly dull route back and forth between hotel and courts — their compensation consists of free tickets to certain Stadium matches and a chance to rub elbows with professional tennis players, or at least with their luggage.

body the V of serious weight lifting, his leg-muscles standing out even in repose, his biceps little cannonballs of fierce-looking veins. He's beautiful but doomed, because the slowness of the Stadium Court makes it impractical for anybody except a world-class net man to rush the net against Agassi, and Washington is not a net man but a power-baseliner. He stays back and trades groundstrokes with Agassi, and even though the first set goes to a tiebreaker you can tell it's a mismatch. Agassi has less mass and flat-out speed than Washington, but he has vision and timing that give his groundstrokes way more pace. He can stay back and hit nuclear groundstrokes and force Washington until Washington eventually makes a fatal error. There are two ways to make a fatal error against Agassi: the first is the standard way, hitting it out or into the net or something; the second is to hit anything shorter than a couple feet inside the baseline, because anything that Agassi can move up on he can hit for a winner. Agassi's facial expression is the slightly smug self-aware one of somebody who's used to being looked at and automatically assumes the minute he shows up anywhere that everybody's looking at him. He's incredible to see play in person, but his domination of Washington doesn't make me like him any better; it's more like it chills me, as if I'm watching the devil play.

Television tends to level everybody out and make them seem kind of blandly handsome, but at Montreal it turns out that a lot of the pros and stars are interesting- or even downright funny-looking. Jim Courier, former #1 but now waning and seeded tenth here,[60] looks like Howdy Doody in a hat on TV, but here he turns out to be a very big boy — the "Guide Média" lists him at 175 pounds but he's way more than that, with large smooth muscles and the gait and expression of a Mafia enforcer. Michael Chang, 23 and #5 in the world, sort of looks like two different people stitched crudely together: a normal upper body perched atop hugely muscular and totally hairless legs. He has a mushroom-shaped head, ink-black hair, and an expression of deep and

---

[60] He will lose badly to Michael Stich in the round of 16, the same Stich whom Michael Joyce beat at the Lipton Championships in Key Biscayne four months before; and in fact Joyce will himself beat Courier in straight sets next week at the Infiniti Open in Los Angeles, in front of Joyce's family and friends, for one of the biggest wins of his career so far.

intractable unhappiness, as unhappy a face as I've ever seen outside a Graduate Writing Program.[61] P. Sampras, in person, is mostly teeth and eyebrows, and he's got unbelievably hairy legs and forearms, hair in the sort of abundance that allows me confidently to bet that he has hair on his back and is thus at least not 100% blessed and graced by the universe. Goran Ivanisevic is large and tan and surprisingly good-looking — at least for a Croat; I always imagine Croats looking ravaged and katexic and like somebody out of a Munch lithograph — except for an incongruous and wholly absurd bowl haircut that makes him look like somebody in a Beatles tribute band. It is Ivanisevic who will beat Joyce in three sets in the main draw's second round. Czech former top-ten Petr Korda is another clastic-looking mismatch: at 6'3" and 160, he has the body of an upright greyhound and the face of — eerily, *uncannily* — a fresh-hatched chicken (plus soulless eyes that reflect no light and seem to "see" only in the way that fish's and birds' eyes "see").

And Wilander is here — Mats Wilander, Borg's heir, top-ten at age eighteen, #1 at 24, now 30 and unranked and trying a comeback after years off the Tour, here cast in the role of the wily old mariner, winning on smarts. Tuesday's best big-name match is between Wilander and Stefan Edberg,[62] 28 and Wilander's own heir[63] and now married to

---

[61] Chang's mother is here — one of the most infamous of the dreaded Tennis Parents of the men's and women's Tours, a woman who's reliably rumored to have done things like reach down her child's tennis shorts in public to check his underwear — and her attendance (she's seated hierophantically in the player-guest boxes courtside) may have something to do with the staggering woe of Chang's mien and play. Thomas Enqvist ends up beating him soundly in the quarterfinals on Wednesday night. (Enqvist, by the way, looks eerily like a young Richard Chamberlain, the Richard Chamberlain of *The Towering Inferno*, say, with this narrow, sort of rodentially patrician quality. The best thing about Enqvist is his girlfriend, who wears glasses and when she applauds a good point sort of hops up and down in her seat with refreshing uncoolness.)

[62] Who himself has the blond bland good looks of a professional golfer, and is reputed to be the single dullest man on the ATP Tour and possibly in the whole world, a man whose hobby is purported to be "staring at walls" and whose quietness is not the quietness of restraint but of blankness, the verbal equivalent of a dead channel.

[63] (Just as Enqvist now appears to be Edberg's heir . . . Swedish tennis tends to be like monarchic succession: they tend to have only one really great player at a time, and this player is always male, and he almost always ends up #1 in the world for a while. This

Annette Olson, Wilander's S.O. during his own glory days, which adds a delicious personal cast to the match, which Wilander wins 6–4 in the third. Wilander ends up getting all the way to the semifinals before Agassi beats him as badly as I have ever seen one professional beat another professional, the score being 6–0 6–2 and the match not nearly as close as the score would indicate.

Even more illuminating than watching pro tennis live is watching it with Sam Aparicio, Joyce's coach, who knows as much about tennis as anybody I've talked to and isn't obnoxious about it. Sam watches a lot of pro matches, scouting stuff for Michael. Watching tennis with him is like watching a movie with somebody who knows a lot about the technical aspects of film: he helps you see things you can't see alone. It turns out, for example, that there are whole geometric sublevels of strategy in a power-baseline game, all dictated by various P.B.ers' strengths and weaknesses. A P.B.er depends on being able to hit winners from the baseline. But, as Sam teaches me to see, Michael Chang can usually hit winners only at an acute angle, from either corner. An "inside-out" player like Jim Courier, on the other hand, can hit winners only at obtuse angles, from the center out. Hence canny and well-coached players tend to play Chang "down the middle" and Courier "out wide." One of the things that makes Agassi so good is that he's capable of hitting winners from anywhere on the court — he has no geometric restriction. Joyce, too, according to Sam, can hit a winner at any angle. He just doesn't do it quite as well as Agassi, or as often.

Michael Joyce in close-up person, like eating supper or riding in a courtesy car, looks slighter and younger than he does on-court. From close up he looks his age, which to me is basically a fetus. He's about 5'9" and 160; he's muscular but quietly so, without much definition. He likes to wear old T-shirts and a backwards cap. His hairline is receding in a subtle young-man way that makes his forehead look a little high. I forget whether he wore an earring. Michael Joyce's interests outside tennis consist mostly of big-budget movies and genre novels of the commercial paperback sort that one reads on planes. In other words, he really

is one reason marketers and endorsement-consultants are circling Enqvist like makos all through the summer.)

has no interests outside tennis. He has a tight and long-standing group of friends back home in LA, but one senses that most of his personal connections have been made via tennis. He's dated some. It's impossible to tell whether he's a virgin. It seems staggering and impossible, but my sense is he might be. Then again, I tended to idealize and distort him, I know, because of how I felt about what he could do on the court. His most revealing sexual comment is made in the context of explaining the odd type of confidence that keeps him from freezing up in a match in front of large crowds or choking on a point when there's lots of money at stake.[64] Joyce, who usually needs to pause about five beats to think before he answers a question, thinks the confidence is partly a matter of temperament and partly a function of hard work:

"If I'm in like a bar, and there's a really good-looking girl, I might be kind of nervous. But if there's like a thousand gorgeous girls in the stands when I'm playing, it's a different story. I'm not nervous then, when I play, because I know what I'm doing. I know what to do out there." Maybe it's good to let these be his last quoted words.

Whether or not he ends up in the top ten and a name anybody will know, Michael Joyce will remain a figure of enduring and paradoxical fascination for me. The restrictions on his life have been, in my opinion, grotesque; and in certain ways Joyce himself is a grotesque. But the radical compression of his attention and self has allowed him to become a transcendent practitioner of an art — something few of us get to be. It's allowed him to visit and test parts of his psyche that most of us do not even know for sure we have, to manifest in concrete form virtues like courage, persistence in the face of pain or exhaustion, performance under wilting scrutiny and pressure.

Michael Joyce is, in other words, a complete man (though in a grotesquely limited way). But he wants more. Not more completeness; he doesn't think in terms of virtues or transcendence. He wants to be the best, to have his name known, to hold professional trophies over his head as he patiently turns in all four directions for the media. He is an Ameri-

---

[64] Nerves and choking are a huge issue in a precision-and-timing sport like tennis, and a "bad head" washes more juniors out of the competitive life than any sort of deficit in talent or drive.

can and he wants to win. He wants this, and he will pay to have it — will pay just to pursue it, let it define him — and will pay with the regretless cheer of a man for whom issues of choice became irrelevant long ago. Already, for Joyce, at 22, it's too late for anything else: he's invested too much, is in too deep. I think he's both lucky and un-. He will say he is happy and mean it. Wish him well.

1995

1

Right now it's Saturday 18 March, and I'm sitting in the extremely full coffee shop of the Fort Lauderdale Airport, killing the four hours between when I had to be off the cruise ship and when my flight to Chicago leaves by trying to summon up a kind of hypnotic sensuous collage of all the stuff I've seen and heard and done as a result of the journalistic assignment just ended.

I have seen sucrose beaches and water a very bright blue. I have seen an all-red leisure suit with flared lapels. I have smelled what suntan lotion smells like spread over 21000 pounds of hot flesh. I have been addressed as "Mon" in three different nations. I have watched 500 upscale Americans dance the Electric Slide. I have seen sunsets that looked computer-enhanced and a tropical moon that looked more like a sort of obscenely large and dangling lemon than like the good old stony U.S. moon I'm used to.

I have (very briefly) joined a Conga Line.

I've got to say I feel like there's been a kind of Peter Principle in effect on this assignment. A certain swanky East-Coast magazine approved of the results of sending me to a plain old simple State Fair last year to do a directionless essayish thing. So now I get offered this tropical plum assignment w/ the exact same paucity of direction or angle. But this time there's this new feeling of pressure: total expenses for the State Fair were $27.00 excluding games of chance. This time *Harper's* has shelled out over $3000 U.S. before seeing pithy sensuous description one. They keep saying — on the phone, Ship-to-Shore, very patiently — not to fret about it. They are sort of disingenuous, I believe, these magazine people. They say all they want is a sort of really big experiential postcard — go, plow the Caribbean in style, come back, say what you've seen.

I have seen a lot of really big white ships. I have seen schools of little fish with fins that glow. I have seen a toupee on a thirteen-year-old boy. (The glowing fish liked to swarm between our hull and the cement of the pier whenever we docked.) I have seen the north coast of Jamaica. I have seen and smelled all 145 cats inside the Ernest Hemingway Residence in Key West FL. I now know the difference between straight Bingo and Prize-O, and what it is when a Bingo jackpot "snowballs." I have seen camcorders that practically required a dolly; I've seen fluorescent luggage and fluorescent sunglasses and fluorescent pince-nez and over twenty different makes of rubber thong. I have heard steel drums and eaten conch fritters and watched a woman in silver lamé projectile-vomit inside a glass elevator. I have pointed rhythmically at the ceiling to the 2:4 beat of the exact same disco music I hated pointing at the ceiling to in 1977.

I have learned that there are actually intensities of blue beyond *very, very bright* blue. I have eaten more and classier food than I've ever eaten, and eaten this food during a week when I've also learned the difference between "rolling" in heavy seas and "pitching" in heavy seas. I have heard a professional comedian tell folks, without irony, "But seriously." I have seen fuchsia pantsuits and menstrual-pink sportcoats and and maroon-and-purple warm-ups and white loafers worn without socks. I have seen professional blackjack dealers so lovely they make you want to run over to their table and spend every last nickel you've got playing blackjack. I have heard upscale adult U.S. citizens ask the Guest Relations Desk whether snorkeling necessitates getting wet, whether the skeetshooting will be held outside, whether the crew sleeps on board, and what time the Midnight Buffet is. I now know the precise mixological difference between a Slippery Nipple and a Fuzzy Navel. I know what a Coco Loco is. I have in one week been the object of over 1500 professional smiles. I have burned and peeled twice. I have shot skeet at sea. Is this enough? At the time it didn't seem like enough. I have felt the full clothy weight of a subtropical sky. I have jumped a dozen times at the shattering, flatulence-of-the-gods sound of a cruise ship's horn. I have absorbed the basics of mah-jongg, seen part of a two-day rubber of contract bridge, learned how to secure a life jacket over a tuxedo, and lost at chess to a nine-year-old girl.

(Actually it was more like I shot *at* skeet at sea.)

I have dickered over trinkets with malnourished children. I now know every conceivable rationale and excuse for somebody spending over $3000 to go on a Caribbean cruise. I have bitten my lip and declined Jamaican pot from an actual Jamaican.

I have seen, one time, from an upper deck's rail, way below and off the right rear hull, what I believe to have been a hammerhead shark's distinctive fin, addled by the starboard turbine's Niagaracal wake.

I have now heard — and am powerless to describe — reggae elevator music. I have learned what it is to become afraid of one's own toilet. I have acquired "sea legs" and would like now to lose them. I have tasted caviar and concurred with the little kid sitting next to me that it is: *blucky.*

I now understand the term "Duty Free."

I now know the maximum cruising speed of a cruise ship in knots.[1] I have had escargot, duck, Baked Alaska, salmon w/ fennel, a marzipan pelican, and an omelette made with what were alleged to be trace amounts of Etruscan truffle. I have heard people in deck chairs say in all earnestness that it's the humidity rather than the heat. I have been — thoroughly, professionally, and as promised beforehand — pampered. I have, in dark moods, viewed and logged every type of erythema, keratinosis, pre-melanomic lesion, liver spot, eczema, wart, papular cyst, potbelly, femoral cellulite, varicosity, collagen and silicone enhancement, bad tint, hair transplants that have not taken — i.e. I have seen nearly naked a lot of people I would prefer not to have seen nearly naked. I have felt as bleak as I've felt since puberty, and have filled almost three Mead notebooks trying to figure out whether it was Them or Just Me. I have acquired and nurtured a potentially lifelong grudge against the ship's Hotel Manager — whose name was Mr. Dermatis and whom

---

[1] (though I never did get clear on just what a knot is)

I now and henceforth christen Mr. Dermatitis[2] — an almost reverent respect for my waiter, and a searing crush on the cabin steward for my part of Deck 10's port hallway, Petra, she of the dimples and broad candid brow, who always wore a nurse's starched and rustling whites and smelled of the cedary Norwegian disinfectant she swabbed bathrooms down with, and who cleaned my cabin within a cm of its life at least ten times a day but could never be caught in the actual *act* of cleaning — a figure of magical and abiding charm, and well worth a postcard all her own.

2

More specifically: From 11 to 18 March 1995 I, voluntarily and for pay, underwent a 7-Night Caribbean (7NC) Cruise on board the m.v. *Zenith*,[3] a 47,255-ton ship owned by Celebrity Cruises Inc., one of the over twenty cruise lines that currently operate out of south Florida.[4]

---

[2] Somewhere he'd gotten the impression I was an investigative journalist and wouldn't let me see the galley, Bridge, staff decks, *anything*, or interview any of the crew or staff in an on-the-record way, and he wore sunglasses inside, and epaulets, and kept talking on the phone for long stretches of time in Greek when I was in his office after I'd skipped the karaoki semifinals in the Rendez-Vous Lounge to make a special appointment to see him; I wish him ill.

[3] No wag could possibly resist mentally rechristening the ship the m.v. *Nadir* the instant he saw the *Zenith*'s silly name in the Celebrity brochure, so indulge me on this, but the rechristening's nothing particular against the ship itself.

[4] There's also Windstar and Silversea, Tall Ship Adventures and Windjammer Barefoot Cruises, but these Caribbean Cruises are wildly upscale and smaller. The 20+ cruise lines I'm talking run the "Megaships," the floating wedding cakes with occupancies in four figures and engine-propellers the size of branch banks. Of the Megalines out of South FL there's Commodore, Costa, Majesty, Regal, Dolphin, Princess, Royal Caribbean, good old Celebrity. There's Renaissance, Royal Cruise Line, Holland, Holland America, Cunard, Cunard Crown, Cunard Royal Viking. There's Norwegian Cruise Line, there's Crystal, there's Regency Cruises. There's the WalMart of the cruise industry, Carnival, which the other lines refer to sometimes as "Carnivore." I don't

The vessel and facilities were, from what I now understand of the industry's standards, absolutely top-hole. The food was superb, the service impeccable, the shore excursions and shipboard activities organized for maximal stimulation down to the tiniest detail. The ship was so clean and so white it looked boiled. The Western Caribbean's blue varied between baby-blanket and fluorescent; likewise the sky. Temperatures were uterine. The very sun itself seemed preset for our comfort. The crew-to-passenger ratio was 1.2 to 2. It was a Luxury Cruise.

With a few minor niche-adaptive variations, the 7NC Luxury Cruise is essentially generic. All of the Megalines offer the same basic product. This product is not a service or a set of services. It's not even so much a good time (though it quickly becomes clear that one of the big jobs of the Cruise Director and his staff is to keep reassuring everybody that everybody's having a good time). It's more like a feeling. But it's also still a bona fide product — it's supposed to be *produced* in you, this feeling: a blend of relaxation and stimulation, stressless indulgence and frantic tourism, that special mix of servility and condescension that's marketed under configurations of the verb "to pamper." This verb positively studs the Megalines' various brochures: ". . . as you've never been pampered

---

recall which line *The Love Boat*'s *Pacific Princess* was supposed to be with (I guess they were probably more like a CA-to-Hawaii-circuit ship, though I seem to recall them going all over the place), but now Princess Cruises has bought the name and uses poor old Gavin MacLeod in full regalia in their TV ads.

The 7NC Megaship cruiser is a type, a genre of ship all its own, like the destroyer. All the Megalines have more than one ship. The industry descends from those old patrician trans-Atlantic deals where the opulence combined with actually getting someplace — e.g. the *Titanic, Normandie,* etc. The present Caribbean Cruise market's various niches — Singles, Old People, Theme, Special Interest, Corporate, Party, Family, Mass-Market, Luxury, Absurd Luxury, Grotesque Luxury — have now all pretty much been carved and staked out and are competed for viciously (I heard off-the-record stuff about Carnival v. Princess that'd singe your brows). Megaships tend to be designed in America, built in Germany, registered out of Liberia or Monrovia; and they are both captained and owned, for the most part, by Scandinavians and Greeks, which is kind of interesting, since these are the same peoples who've dominated sea travel pretty much forever. Celebrity Cruises is owned by the Chandris Group; the X on their three ships' smokestacks turns out not to be an X but a Greek chi, for Chandris, a Greek shipping family so ancient and powerful they apparently regarded Onassis as a punk.

before," ". . . to pamper yourself in our jacuzzis and saunas," "Let us pamper you," "Pamper yourself in the warm zephyrs of the Bahamas."

The fact that contemporary adult Americans also tend to associate the word "pamper" with a certain *other* consumer product is not an accident, I don't think, and the connotation is not lost on the mass-market Megalines and their advertisers. And there's good reason for them to iterate the word, and stress it.

3

This one incident made the Chicago news. Some weeks before I underwent my own Luxury Cruise, a sixteen-year-old male did a Brody off the upper deck of a Megaship — I think a Carnival or Crystal ship — a suicide. The news version was that it had been an unhappy adolescent love thing, a shipboard romance gone bad, etc. I think part of it was something else, something there's no way a real news story could cover.

There is something about a mass-market Luxury Cruise that's unbearably sad. Like most unbearably sad things, it seems incredibly elusive and complex in its causes and simple in its effect: on board the *Nadir* — especially at night, when all the ship's structured fun and reassurances and gaiety-noise ceased — I felt despair. The word's overused and banalified now, *despair,* but it's a serious word, and I'm using it seriously. For me it denotes a simple admixture — a weird yearning for death combined with a crushing sense of my own smallness and futility that presents as a fear of death. It's maybe close to what people call dread or angst. But it's not these things, quite. It's more like wanting to die in order to escape the unbearable feeling of becoming aware that I'm small and weak and selfish and going without any doubt at all to die. It's wanting to jump overboard.

I predict this'll get cut by the editor, but I need to cover some background. I, who had never before this cruise actually been on the ocean, have always associated the ocean with dread and death. As a little kid I used to memorize shark-fatality data. Not just attacks. Fatalities. The Albert Kogler fatality off Baker's Beach CA in 1959 (Great White). The U.S.S. *Indianapolis* smorgasbord off the Philippines in

1945 (many varieties, authorities think mostly Tigers and Blues)[5]; the most-fatalities-attributed-to-a-single-shark series of incidents around Matawan/Spring Lake NJ in 1916 (Great White again; this time they caught a *carcharias* in Raritan Bay NJ and found human parts *in gastro* (I know which parts, and whose)). In school I ended up writing three different papers on "The Castaway" section of *Moby-Dick,* the chapter where the cabin boy Pip falls overboard and is driven mad by the empty immensity of what he finds himself floating in. And when I teach school now I always teach Crane's horrific "The Open Boat," and I get bent out of shape when the kids find the story dull or jaunty-adventurish: I want them to feel the same marrow-level dread of the oceanic I've always felt, the intuition of the sea as primordial *nada,* bottomless, depths inhabited by cackling tooth-studded things rising toward you at the rate a feather falls. Anyway, hence the atavistic shark fetish, which I need to admit came back with a long-repressed vengeance on this Luxury Cruise,[6] and that I made such a fuss about the one (possible) dorsal fin I saw off starboard that my companions at supper's Table 64 finally had to tell me, with all possible tact, to shut up about the fin already.

[5] I'm doing this from memory. I don't need a book. I can still name every documented *Indianapolis* fatality, including some serial numbers and hometowns. (Hundreds of men lost, 80 classed as Shark, 7–10 August '45; the *Indianapolis* had just delivered Little Boy to the island of Tinian for delivery to Hiroshima, so ironists take note. Robert Shaw as Quint reprised the whole incident in 1975's *Jaws,* a film that, as you can imagine, was like fetish-porn to me at age thirteen.)

[6] And I'll admit that on the very first night of the 7NC I asked the staff of the *Nadir's* Five-Star Caravelle Restaurant whether I could maybe have a spare bucket of *au jus* drippings from supper so I could try chumming for sharks off the back rail of the top deck, and that this request struck everybody from the maître d' on down as disturbing and maybe even disturbed, and that it turned out to be a serious journalistic faux pas, because I'm almost positive the maître d' passed this disturbing tidbit on to Mr. Dermatitis and that it was a big reason why I was denied access to stuff like the ship's galley, thereby impoverishing the sensuous scope of this article. (Plus it also revealed how little I understood the *Nadir's* sheer size: twelve decks and 150 feet up, the *au jus* drippings would have dispersed into a vague red cologne by the time they hit the water, with concentrations of blood inadequate to attract or excite a serious shark, whose fin would have probably looked like a pushpin from that height, anyway.)

I don't think it's an accident that 7NC Luxury Cruises appeal mostly to older people. I don't mean decrepitly old, but I mean like age-50+ people, for whom their own mortality is something more than an abstraction. Most of the exposed bodies to be seen all over the daytime *Nadir* were in various stages of disintegration. And the ocean itself (which I found to be salty as *hell*, like sore-throat-soothing-gargle-grade salty, its spray so corrosive that one temple-hinge of my glasses is probably going to have to be replaced) turns out to be basically one enormous engine of decay. Seawater corrodes vessels with amazing speed — rusts them, exfoliates paint, strips varnish, dulls shine, coats ships' hulls with barnacles and kelp-clumps and a vague ubiquitous nautical snot that seems like death incarnate. We saw some real horrors in port, local boats that looked dipped in a mixture of acid and shit, scabbed with rust and goo, ravaged by what they float in.

Not so the Megalines' ships. It's not an accident they're all so white and clean, for they're clearly meant to represent the Calvinist triumph of capital and industry over the primal decay-action of the sea. The *Nadir* seemed to have a whole battalion of wiry little Third World guys who went around the ship in navy-blue jumpsuits scanning for decay to overcome. Writer Frank Conroy, who has an odd little essaymercial in the front of Celebrity Cruises' 7NC brochure, talks about how "It became a private challenge for me to try to find a piece of dull bright-work, a chipped rail, a stain in the deck, a slack cable or anything that wasn't perfectly shipshape. Eventually, toward the end of the trip, I found a capstan[7] with a half-dollar-sized patch of rust on the side facing the sea. My delight in this tiny flaw was interrupted by the arrival, even as I stood there, of a crewman with a roller and a bucket of white paint. I watched as he gave the entire capstan a fresh coat of paint and walked away with a nod."

Here's the thing. A vacation is a respite from unpleasantness, and since consciousness of death and decay are unpleasant, it may seem weird that Americans' ultimate fantasy vacation involves being plunked down in an enormous primordial engine of death and decay. But on a 7NC Luxury Cruise, we are skillfully enabled in the construction

---

[7] (apparently a type of nautical hoist, like a pulley on steroids)

of various fantasies of triumph over just this death and decay. One way to "triumph" is via the rigors of self-improvement; and the crew's amphetaminic upkeep of the *Nadir* is an unsubtle analogue to personal titivation: diet, exercise, megavitamin supplements, cosmetic surgery, Franklin Quest time-management seminars, etc.

There's another way out, too, w/r/t death. Not titivation but titillation. Not hard work but hard play. The 7NC's constant activities, parties, festivities, gaiety and song; the adrenaline, the excitement, the stimulation. It makes you feel vibrant, alive. It makes your existence seem noncontingent.[8] The hard-play option promises not a transcendence of death-dread so much as just drowning it out: "Sharing a laugh with your friends[9] in the lounge after dinner, you glance at your watch and mention that it's almost showtime. . . . When the curtain comes down after a standing ovation, the talk among your companions[10] turns to, 'What next?' Perhaps a visit to the casino or a little dancing in the disco? Maybe a quiet drink in the piano bar or a starlit stroll around the deck? After discussing all your options, everyone agrees: *'Let's do it all!'* "

Dante this isn't, but Celebrity Cruises' 7NC brochure is nevertheless an extremely powerful and ingenious piece of advertising. The brochure is magazine-size, heavy and glossy, beautifully laid out, its text offset by art-quality photos of upscale couples'[11] tanned faces locked in a kind of rictus of pleasure. All the Megalines put out brochures, and they're

---

[8] The *Nadir*'s got literally hundreds of cross-sectional maps of the ship on every deck, at every elevator and junction, each with a red dot and a YOU ARE HERE — and it doesn't take long to figure out that these are less for orientation than for some weird kind of reassurance.

[9] Always constant references to "friends" in the brochures' text; part of this promise of escape from death-dread is that no cruiser is ever alone.

[10] See?

[11] Always couples in this brochure, and even in group shots it's always groups of couples. I never did get hold of a brochure for an actual Singles Cruise, but the mind reels. There was a "Singles Get Together" (sic) on the *Nadir* that first Saturday night, held in Deck 8's Scorpio Disco, which after an hour of self-hypnosis and controlled breathing I steeled myself to go to, but even the Get Together was 75% established couples, and the few of us Singles under like 70 all looked grim and self-hypnotized, and the whole affair seemed like a true wrist-slitter, and I beat a retreat after half an

essentially interchangeable. The middle part of the brochures detail the different packages and routes. Basic 7NC's go to the Western Caribbean (Jamaica, Grand Cayman, Cozumel) or the Eastern Caribbean (Puerto Rico, Virgins), or something called the Deep Carribean (Martinique, Barbados, Mayreau). There are also 10- and 11-Night Ultimate Caribbean packages that hit pretty much every exotic coastline between Miami and the Panama Canal. The brochures' final sections' boilerplate always details costs,[12] passport stuff, Customs regulations, caveats.

But it's the first section of these brochures that really grabs you, the photos and italicized blurbs from *Fodor's Cruises* and *Berlitz,* the dreamy *mise en scènes* and breathless prose. Celebrity's brochure, in particular, is a real two-napkin drooler. It has little hypertextish offsets, boxed in gold, that say stuff like INDULGENCE BECOMES EASY and RELAXATION BECOMES SECOND NATURE and STRESS BECOMES A FAINT MEMORY. And these promises point to the third kind of death-and-dread-transcendence the *Nadir* offers, one that requires neither work nor play, the enticement that is a 7NC's real carrot and stick.

4

"Just standing at the ship's rail looking out to sea has a profoundly soothing effect. As you drift along like a cloud on water, the weight of everyday life is magically lifted away, and you seem to be floating on a sea of smiles. Not just among your fellow guests but on the faces of the ship's staff as well. As a steward cheerfully delivers your drinks, you mention

---

hour because *Jurassic Park* was scheduled to run on the TV that night, and I hadn't yet looked at the whole schedule and seen that *Jurassic Park* would play several dozen times over the coming week.

[12] From $2500 to about $4000 for mass-market Megaships like the *Nadir,* unless you want a Presidential Suite with a skylight, wet bar, automatic palm-fronds, etc., in which case double that.

all of the smiles among the crew. He explains that every Celebrity staff member takes pleasure in making your cruise a completely carefree experience and treating you as an honored guest.[13] Besides, he adds, there's no place they'd rather be. Looking back out to sea, you couldn't agree more."

Celebrity's 7NC brochure uses the 2nd-person pronoun throughout. This is extremely appropriate. Because in the brochure's scenarios the 7NC experience is being not described but *evoked.* The brochure's real seduction is not an invitation to fantasize but rather a construction of the fantasy itself. This is advertising, but with a queerly authoritarian twist. In regular adult-market ads, attractive people are shown having a near-illegally good time in some scenario surrounding a product, and you are meant to fantasize that you can project yourself into the ad's perfect world via purchase of that product. In regular advertising, where your adult agency and freedom of choice have to be flattered, the purchase is prerequisite to the fantasy; it's the fantasy that's being sold, not any

---

[13]   In response to some dogged journalistic querying, Celebrity's PR firm's Press Liaison (the charming and Debra Winger–voiced Ms. Wiessen) had this explanation for the cheery service: "The people on board — the staff — are really part of one big family — you probably noticed this when you were on the ship. They really love what they're doing and love serving people, and they pay attention to what everybody wants and needs."

This was not what I myself observed. What I myself observed was that the *Nadir* was one very tight ship, run by an elite cadre of very hard-ass Greek officers and supervisors, and that the preterite staff lived in mortal terror of these Greek bosses who watched them with enormous beadiness at all times, and that the crew worked almost Dickensianly hard, too hard to feel truly cheery about it. My sense was that Cheeriness was up there with Celerity and Servility on the clipboarded evaluation sheets the Greek bosses were constantly filling out on them: when they didn't know any guests were looking, a lot of the workers had the kind of pinched weariness about them that one associates with low-paid service employees in general, plus fear. My sense was that a crewman could get fired for a pretty small lapse, and that getting fired by these Greek officers might well involve a spotlessly shined shoe in the ass and then a really long swim.

What I observed was that the preterite workers did have a sort of affection for the passengers, but that it was a *comparative* affection — even the most absurdly demanding passenger seemed kind and understanding compared to the martinetism of the Greeks, and the crew seemed genuinely grateful for this, sort of the way we find even very basic human decency moving if we encounter it in NYC or Boston.

literal projection into the ad's world. There's no sense of any real kind of actual promise being made. This is what makes conventional adult advertisements fundamentally coy.

Contrast this coyness with the force of the 7NC brochure's ads: the near-imperative use of the second person, the specificity of detail that extends even to what you will say (*you will say* "I couldn't agree more" and "Let's do it all!"). In the cruise brochure's ads, you are excused from doing the work of constructing the fantasy. The ads do it for you. The ads, therefore, don't flatter your adult agency, or even ignore it — they supplant it.

And this authoritarian — near-parental — type of advertising makes a very special sort of promise, a diabolically seductive promise that's actually kind of honest, because it's a promise that the Luxury Cruise itself is all about honoring. The promise is not that you can experience great pleasure, but that you *will*. That they'll make certain of it. That they'll micromanage every iota of every pleasure-option so that not even the dreadful corrosive action of your adult consciousness and agency and dread can fuck up your fun. Your troublesome capacities for choice, error, regret, dissatisfaction, and despair will be removed from the equation. The ads promise that you will be able — finally, for once — truly to relax and have a good time, because you will *have no choice* but to have a good time.[14]

I am now 33 years old, and it feels like much time has passed and is passing faster and faster every day. Day to day I have to make all sorts of choices about what is good and important and fun, and then I have to live with the forfeiture of all the other options those choices foreclose. And I'm starting to see how as time gains momentum my choices will narrow and their foreclosures multiply exponentially until I arrive at some point on some branch of all life's sumptuous branching complexity at which I am finally locked in and stuck on one path and time speeds me through stages of stasis and atrophy and decay until I go down for the third time,

---

[14] "YOUR PLEASURE," several Megalines' slogans go, "IS OUR BUSINESS." What in a regular ad would be a double entendre is here a triple entendre, and the tertiary connotation — viz. "MIND YOUR OWN BLOODY BUSINESS AND LET US PROFESSIONALS WORRY ABOUT YOUR PLEASURE, FOR CHRIST'S SAKE" — is far from incidental.

all struggle for naught, drowned by time. It is dreadful. But since it's my own choices that'll lock me in, it seems unavoidable — if I want to be any kind of grownup, I have to make choices and regret foreclosures and try to live with them.

Not so on the lush and spotless m.v. *Nadir.* On a 7NC Luxury Cruise, I pay for the privilege of handing over to trained professionals responsibility not just for my experience but for my *interpretation* of that experience — i.e. my pleasure. My pleasure is for 7 nights and 6.5 days wisely and efficiently managed . . . just as promised in the cruise line's advertising — nay, just as somehow already *accomplished* in the ads, with their 2nd-person imperatives, which make them not promises but predictions. Aboard the *Nadir,* just as ringingly foretold in the brochure's climactic p. 23, I get to do (in gold): ". . . something you haven't done in a long, long time: *Absolutely Nothing.*"

How long has it been since you did Absolutely Nothing? I know exactly how long it's been for me. I know how long it's been since I had every need met choicelessly from someplace outside me, without my having to ask or even acknowledge that I needed. And that time I was floating, too, and the fluid was salty, and warm but not too-, and if I was conscious at all I'm sure I felt dreadless, and was having a really good time, and would have sent postcards to everyone wishing they were here.

5

A 7NC's pampering is a little uneven at first, but it starts at the airport, where you don't have to go to Baggage Claim because people from the Megaline get your suitcases for you and take them right to the ship.

A bunch of other Megalines besides Celebrity Cruises operate out of Fort Lauderdale,[15] and the flight down from O'Hare is full of festive-looking people dressed for cruising. It turns out the folks sitting next to me on the plane are booked on the *Nadir.* They're a retired couple

---

[15] Celebrity, Cunard, Princess, and Holland America all use it as a hub. Carnival and Dolphin use Miami; others use Port Canaveral, Puerto Rico, the Bahamas, all over.

from Chicago and this is their fourth Luxury Cruise in as many years. It is they who tell me about the news reports of the kid jumping overboard, and also about a legendarily nasty outbreak of salmonella or *E. coli* or something on a Megaship in the late '70s that gave rise to the C.D.C.'s Vessel Sanitation program of inspections, plus about a supposed outbreak of Legionnaire's disease vectored by the jacuzzi on a 7NC Megaship two years ago — it was possibly one of Celebrity's three cruise ships, the lady (kind of the spokesman for the couple) isn't sure; it turns out she sort of likes to toss off a horrific detail and then get all vague and blasé when a horrified listener tries to pump her for details. The husband wears a fishing cap with a long bill and a T-shirt that says BIG DADDY.

7NC Luxury Cruises always start and finish on Saturday. Right now it's Saturday 11 March, 1020h., and we are deplaning. Imagine the day after the Berlin Wall came down if everybody in East Germany was plump and comfortable-looking and dressed in Caribbean pastels, and you'll have a pretty good idea what the Fort Lauderdale Airport terminal looks like today. Over near the back wall, a number of brisk-looking older ladies in vaguely naval outfits hold up printed signs — HLND, CELEB, CUND CRN. What you're supposed to do (the Chicago lady from the plane is kind of talking me through it as BIG DADDY shoulders us a path through the fray) what you're supposed to do is find your particular Megaline's brisk lady and sort of all coalesce around her as she walks with printed sign held high to attract still more cruisers and leads the growing ectoplasm of *Nadir*ites all out to buses that ferry us to the Piers and what we quixotically believe will be immediate and hassle-free boarding.

Apparently Ft. Laud. Airport is always just your average sleepy midsize airport six days a week and then every Saturday resembles the fall of Saigon. Half the terminal's mob consists of luggage-bearing people now flying home from 7NCs. They are Syrianly tan, and a lot of them have eccentric and vaguely hairy-looking souvenirs of various sizes and functions, and they all have a glazed spacey look about them that the Chicago lady avers is the telltale look of post-7NC Inner Peace. We pre-7NCs, on the other hand, all look pasty and stressed and somehow combat-unready.

Outside, we of the *Nadir* are directed to deectoplasmize ourselves and all line up along some sort of tall curb to await the *Nadir*'s special chartered buses. We are exchanging awkward don't-know-whether-to-smile-and-wave-or-not glances with a Holland America herd that's lining up on a grassy median parallel to us, and both groups are looking a little narrow-eyed at a Princess-bound herd whose buses are already pulling up. The Ft. Laud. Airport's porters and cabbies and white-bandoliered traffic cops and bus drivers are all Cuban. The retired Chicago couple, clearly wily veterans about lines by their fourth Luxury Cruise, has butted into place way up. A second Celebrity crowd-control lady has a megaphone and repeats over and over not to worry about our luggage, that it will follow us later, which I am apparently alone in finding chilling in its unwitting echo of the Auschwitz-embarkation scene in *Schindler's List.*

Where I am in the line: I'm between a squat and chain-smoking black man in an NBC Sports cap and several corporately dressed people wearing badges identifying them as with something called the Engler Corporation.[16] Way up ahead, the retired Chicago couple has spread a sort of parasol. There's a bumpy false ceiling of mackerel clouds moving in from the southwest, but overhead it's just wispy cirrus, and it's seriously hot standing and waiting in the sun, even without luggage or luggage-angst, and through a lack of foresight I'm wearing my undertakerish black wool suitcoat and an inadequate hat. But it feels good to perspire. Chicago at dawn was 18° and its sun the sort of wan and impotent March sun you can look right at. It is good to feel serious sun and see trees all frothy with green. We wait rather a long time, and the *Nadir* line starts to recoalesce into clumps as people's conversations have time to progress past the waiting-in-line small-talk stage. Either there was a mixup getting enough buses for people in on A.M. flights, or (my theory) the same Celebrity Cruises brain trust responsible for the wildly seductive brochure has decided to make certain elements of pre-embarkation as difficult and unpleasant as

---

[16] I was never in countless tries able to determine just what the Engler Corporation did or made or was about, but they'd apparently sent a quorum of their execs on this 7NC junket together as a weird kind of working vacation or intracompany convention or something.

possible in order to sharpen the favorable contrast between real life and the 7NC experience.

Now we're riding to the Piers in a column of eight chartered Greyhounds. Our convoy's rate of speed and the odd deference other traffic shows gives the whole procession a kind of funereal quality. Ft. Laud. proper looks like one extremely large golf course, but the cruise lines' Piers are in something called Port Everglades, an industrial area, pretty clearly, zoned for Blight, with warehouses and transformer parks and stacked boxcars and vacant lots full of muscular and evil-looking Florida-type weeds. We pass a huge field of those hammer-shaped automatic oil derricks all bobbing fellatially, and on the horizon past them is a little fingernail clipping of shiny gray that I'm thinking must be the sea. Several different languages are in use on my bus. Whenever we go over bumps or train tracks, there's a tremendous mass clicking sound in here from all the cameras around everybody's neck. I haven't brought any sort of camera and feel a perverse pride about this.

The *Nadir*'s traditional berth is Pier 21. "Pier," though it had conjured for me images of wharfs and cleats and lapping water, turns out to denote something like what *airport* denotes, viz. a zone and not a thing. There is no real water in sight, no docks, no fishy smell or sodium tang to the air; but there are, as we enter the Pier zone, a lot of really big white ships that blot out most of the sky.

Now I'm writing this sitting in an orange plastic chair at the end of one of Pier 21's countless bolted rows of orange plastic chairs. We have debused and been herded via megaphone through 21's big glass doors, whereupon two more completely humorless naval ladies handed us each a little plastic card with a number on it. My card's number is 7. A few people sitting nearby ask me "what I am," and I figure out I'm to respond "a 7." The cards are by no means brand new, and mine has the vestigial whorls of a chocolate thumbprint in one corner.

From inside, Pier 21 seems kind of like a blimpless blimp hangar, high-ceilinged and very echoey. It has walls of unclean windows on three sides, at least 2500 orange chairs in rows of 25, a kind of desultory Snack Bar, and restrooms with very long lines. The acoustics are brutal and it's tremendously loud. Outside, rain starts coming down even though the sun's still shining. Some of the people in the rows of chairs appear to have been here for days: they have that glazed encamped look of people at airports in blizzards.

It's now 1132h., and boarding will not commence one second before 1400 sharp; a PA announcement politely but firmly declares Celebrity's seriousness about this.[17] The PA lady's voice is what you imagine a British supermodel would sound like. Everyone's clutching his numbered card like the cards are identity papers at Checkpoint Charley. There's an Ellis Island/pre-Auschwitz aspect to the massed and anxious waiting, but I'm uncomfortable trying to extend the analogy. A lot of the people waiting — Caribbeanish clothing notwithstanding — look Jewish to me, and I'm ashamed to catch myself thinking that I can determine Jewishness from people's appearance.[18] Maybe two-thirds of the total people in here are actually sitting in orange chairs. Pier 21's pre-boarding blimp hangar's not as bad as, say, Grand Central at 1715h. on Friday, but it bears little resemblance to any of the stressless pamper-venues detailed in the Celebrity brochure, which brochure I am not the only person in here thumbing through and looking at wistfully. A lot of people are also reading the *Fort Lauderdale Sentinel* and staring with subwayish blankness at other people. A kid whose T-shirt says SANDY DUNCAN'S EYE is carving something in the plastic of his chair. There are quite a few old people all travelling with really *desperately* old people who are pretty clearly the old people's parents. A couple different guys in different rows are field-stripping their camcorders with military-looking expertise. There's a fair share of WASP-looking passengers, as well. A lot of the WASPs are couples in their twenties and thirties, with a honeymoonish aspect to the way their heads rest on each other's shoulders. Men after a certain age simply should not wear shorts, I've decided; their legs are hairless in a way that's creepy; the skin seems

---

[17] The reason for the delay won't become apparent until next Saturday, when it takes until 1000h. to get everybody off the m.v. *Nadir* and vectored to appropriate transportation, and then from 1000 to 1400h. several battalions of jumpsuited Third World custodial guys will join the stewards in obliterating all evidence of us before the next 1374 passengers come on.

[18] For me, public places on the U.S. East Coast are full of these nasty little moments of racist observation and then internal P.C. backlash.

denuded and practically crying out for hair, particularly on the calves. It's just about the only body-area where you actually want *more* hair on older men. Is this fibular hairlessness a result of years of chafing in pants and socks? The significance of the numbered cards turns out to be that you're supposed to wait here in Pier 21's blimp hangar until your number is called, then you board in "Lots."[19] So your number doesn't stand for you, but rather for the subherd of cruisers you're part of. Some 7NC-veterans nearby tell me that 7 is not a great Lot-number and advise me to get comfortable. Somewhere past the big gray doors behind the restrooms' roiling lines is an umbilical passage leading to what I assume is the actual *Nadir*, which outside the south wall's windows presents as a tall wall of total white. In the approximate center of the hangar is a long table where creamy-complected women in nursish white from Steiner of London Inc. are doing free little makeup and complexion consultations with women waiting to board, priming the economic pump.[20] The Chicago lady and BIG DADDY are in the hangar's southeasternmost row of chairs playing Uno with another couple, who turn out to be friends they'd made on a Princess Alaska Cruise in '93.

Now I'm writing this sort of squatting with my bottom braced up against the hangar's west wall, which wall is white-painted cinderblocks, like a budget motel's wall, and also oddly clammy. By this time I'm down to slacks and T-shirt and tie, and the tie looks like it's been washed and hand-wrung. Perspiring has already lost its novelty. Part of what Celebrity Cruises is reminding us we're leaving behind is massed public waiting areas with no AC and indifferent ventilation. Now it's 1255h. Though the brochure says the *Nadir* sails at 1630h. EDT and that you

[19] This term belongs to an eight-cruise veteran, a 50ish guy with blond bangs and a big ginger beard and what looks weirdly like a T-square sticking out of his carry-on, who's also the first person who offers me an unsolicited narrative on why he had basically no emotional choice right now but to come on a 7NC Luxury Cruise.

[20] Steiner of London'll be on the *Nadir*, it turns out, selling herbal wraps and cellulite-intensive delipidizing massages and facials and assorted aesthetic pampering — they have a whole little wing in the top deck's Olympic Health Club, and it seems like they all but own the Beauty Salon on Deck 5.

can board anytime from 1400 to then, all 1374 *Nadir* passengers look already to be massed here, plus what must be a fair number of relatives and well-wishers, etc.[21]

A major advantage to writing some sort of article about an experience is that at grim junctures like this pre-embarkation blimp hangar you can distract yourself from what the experience feels like by focusing on what look like items of possible interest for the article. This is the occasion I first see the thirteen-year-old kid with the toupee. He's slumped pre-adolescently in his chair with his feet up on some kind of rattan hamper while what I'll bet is his mom talks at him nonstop; he is staring into whatever special distance people in areas of mass public stasis stare into. His toupee isn't one of those horrible black shiny incongruous Howard Cosell toupees, but it's not great either; it's an unlikely orange-brown, and its texture is like one of those local-TV-anchorman toupees where if you toussled the hair it would get broken instead of mussed. A lot of the people from the Engler Corporation are massed in some kind of round informal conference or meeting over near the Pier's glass doors, looking from the distance rather like a rugby scrum. I've decided the perfect description of the orange of the hangar's chairs is *waiting-room* orange. Several driven-looking corporate guys are talking into cellular phones while their wives look stoic. Close to a dozen confirmed sightings of J. Redfield's *The Celestine Prophecy*. The acoustics in here have the nightmarishly echoey quality of some of the Beatles' more conceptual stuff. At the Snack Bar, a plain old candy bar is $1.50, and soda-pop's even more. The line for the men's room extends NW almost to the Steiner of London table. Several Pier personnel with clipboards are running around w/o any discernible agenda. The crowd has a smattering of college-age kids, all with complex haircuts and already wearing poolside thongs. A little kid right near me is wearing the exact same kind of hat I am, which I might as well admit right now is a full-color Spiderman cap.[22]

[21] Going on a 7NC Luxury Cruise is like going to the hospital or college in this respect: it seems to be SOP for a mass of relatives and well-wishers to accompany you right up to the jumping-off point and then have to finally leave, w/ lots of requisite hugs and tears.

[22] Long story, not worth it.

I count over a dozen makes of camera just in the little block of orange chairs within camera-make-discernment range. That's not counting camcorders.

The dress code in here ranges from corporate-informal to tourist-tropical. I am the sweatiest and most disheveled person in view, I'm afraid.[23] There is nothing even remotely nautical about the smell of Pier 21. Two male Engler executives excluded from the corporate scrum are sitting together at the end of the nearest row, right leg over left knee and joggling their loafers in perfect unconscious sync. Every infant within earshot has a promising future in professional opera, it sounds like. Also, every infant being carried or held is being carried or held by its female parent. Over 50% of the purses and handbags are wicker/rattan. The women all somehow give the impression of being on magazine diets. The median age here is at least 45.

A Pier person runs by with an enormous roll of crepe. Some sort of fire alarm's been going for the last fifteen minutes, nerve-janglingly, ignored by everyone because the British bombshell at the PA and the Celebrity people with clipboards also appear to be ignoring it. Also now comes what sounds at first like a sort of tuba from hell, two five-second blasts that ripple shirt-fronts and contort everyone's faces. It turns out it's Holland America's S.S. *Westerdam*'s ship's horn outside, announcing All-Ashore-That's-Going because departure is imminent.

Every so often I remove the hat, towel off, and sort of orbit the blimp hangar, eavesdropping, making small-talk. Over half the passengers I chat up turn out to be from right around here in south Florida. Nonchalant eavesdropping provides the most fun and profit, though: an enormous number of small-talk-type conversations are going on all over the hangar. And a major percentage of this overheard chitchat consists of passengers explaining to other passengers why they signed up for this 7NC Cruise. It's like the universal subject of discussion in here, like chitchatting in the dayroom of a mental ward: "So, why are *you* here?" And the striking constant in all the answers is that not once

---

[23] Another odd demographic truth is that whatever sorts of people are neurologically disposed to go on 7NC Luxury Cruises are also neurologically disposed not to sweat — the one venue of exception on board the *Nadir* was the Mayfair Casino.

does somebody say they're going on this 7NC Luxury Cruise just to go on a 7NC Luxury Cruise. Nor does anybody refer to stuff about travel being broadening or a mad desire to parasail. Nobody even mentions being mesmerized by Celebrity's fantasy-slash-promise of pampering in uterine stasis — in fact the word "pamper," so ubiquitous in the Celebrity 7NC brochure, is not once in my hearing uttered. The word that gets used over and over in the explanatory small-talk is: *relax.* Everybody characterizes the upcoming week as either a long-put-off reward or as a last-ditch effort to salvage sanity and self from some inconceivable crockpot of pressure, or both.[24] A lot of the explanatory narratives are long and involved, and some are sort of lurid. Two different conversations involve people who've just finally buried a relative they'd been nursing at home for months as the relative lingered hideously. A floral wholesaler in an aqua MARLINS shirt talks about how he's managed to drag the battered remnants of his soul through the Xmas-to-Valentine rush only by dangling in front of himself the carrot of this week of total relaxation and renewal. A trio of Newark cops all just retired and had promised themselves a Luxury Cruise if they survived their 20. A couple from Fort Lauderdale sketch a scenario in which they've sort of been shamed by friends into 7NC Luxury Cruising, as if they were native New Yorkers and the *Nadir* the Statue of Liberty.

By the way, I have now empirically verified that I am the only ticketed adult here without some kind of camera equipment.

At some point, unnoticed, Holland's *Westerdam*'s snout has withdrawn from the west window: the window is clear, and a brutal sun is shining through a patchy steam of evaporated rain. The blimp hangar's emptier by half now, and quiet. BIG DADDY and spouse are long gone. They have called Lots 5 through 7 all in a sort of bunch, and

---

[24] I'm pretty sure I know what this syndrome is and how it's related to the brochure's seductive promise of total self-indulgence. What's in play here, I think, is the subtle universal shame that accompanies self-indulgence, the need to explain to just about anybody why the self-indulgence isn't in fact really self-indulgence. Like: I never go get a massage just to get a massage, I go because this old sports-related back injury's killing me and more or less *forcing* me to get a massage; or like: I never just "want" a cigarette, I always "*need*" a cigarette.

I and pretty much the whole massed Engler Corporation contingent are now moving in a kind of columnar herd toward Passport Checks and the Deck 3[25] gangway beyond. And now we are getting greeted (each of us) by not one but two Aryan-looking hostesses from the Hospitality staff, and now moving over plush plum carpet to the interior of what one presumes is the actual *Nadir,* washed now in high-oxygen AC that seems subtly balsam-scented, pausing for a second, if we wish, to have our pre-Cruise photo taken by the ship's photographer,[26] apparently for some kind of Before/After souvenir ensemble they'll try to sell us at week's end; and I start seeing the first of more WATCH YOUR STEP signs this coming week than anyone could count, because a Megaship's architecture's flooring is totally jerryrigged-looking and uneven and everywhere there are sudden little six-inch steplets up and down; and there's the delicious feel of sweat drying and the first nip of AC chill, and I suddenly can't even remember what the squall of a prickly-heated infant sounds like anymore, not in the plushly cushioned little corridors I'm walked through. One of the two Hospitality hostesses seems to have an orthopedic right shoe, and she walks with a very slight limp, and somehow this detail seems terribly moving.

And as Inga and Geli of Hospitality walk me on and in (and it's an endless walk — up, fore, aft, serpentine through bulkheads and steel-

[25] Like all Megaships, the *Nadir* designates each deck with some 7NC-related name, and on the Cruise it got confusing because they never referred to decks by numbers and you could never remember whether e.g. the Fantasy Deck was Deck 7 or 8. Deck 12 is called the Sun Deck, 11 is the Marina Deck, 10 I forget, 9's the Bahamas Deck, 8 Fantasy and 7 Galaxy (or vice versa), 6 I never did get straight. 5 is the Europa Deck and comprises kind of the *Nadir's* corporate nerve center and is one huge high-ceilinged bank-looking lobby with everything done in lemon and salmon with brass plating around the Guest Relations Desk and Purser's Desk and Hotel Manager's Desk, and plants, and massive pillars with water running down them with a sound that all but drives you to the nearest urinal. 4 is all cabins and is called I think the Florida Deck. Everything below 4 is all business and unnamed and off-limits w/ the exception of the smidgeon of 3 that has the gangway. I'm henceforth going to refer to the Decks by number, since that's what I had to know in order to take the elevator anywhere. Decks 7 and 8 are where the serious eating and casinoing and discos and entertainment are; 11 has the pools and café; 12 is on top and laid out for serious heliophilia.

[26] (a thoroughly silly and superfluous job if ever there was one, on this 7N photocopia)

railed corridors with mollified jazz out of little round speakers in a beige enamel ceiling I could reach an elbow up and touch), the whole three-hour pre-cruise gestalt of shame and explanation and Why Are You Here is transposed utterly, because at intervals on every wall are elaborate cross-sectioned maps and diagrams, each with a big and reassuringly jolly red dot with YOU ARE HERE, which assertion preempts all inquiry and signals that explanations and doubt and guilt are now left back there with all else we're leaving behind, handing over to pros.

And the elevator's made of glass and is noiseless, and the hostesses smile slightly and gaze at nothing as all together we ascend, and it's a very close race which of these two hostesses smells better in the enclosed chill.

And now we're passing little teak-lined shipboard shops with Gucci, Waterford and Wedgewood, Rolex and Raymond Weil, and there's a crackle in the jazz and an announcement in three languages about Welcome and *Willkommen* and how there'll be a Compulsory Lifeboat Drill an hour after sailing.

At 1515h. I am installed in *Nadir* Cabin 1009 and immediately eat almost a whole basket of free fruit and lie on a really nice bed and drum my fingers on my swollen tummy.

6

Departure at 1630h. turns out to be a not untasteful affair of crepe and horns. Each deck's got walkways outside, with railings made of some kind of really good wood. It's now overcast, and the ocean way below is dull-colored and frothy, etc. It smells less fishy or oceany than just salty. Our horn is even more planet-shattering than the *Westerdam*'s horn. Most of the people exchanging waves with us are cruisers along the rails of the decks of other 7NC Megaships, also just leaving, so it's a surreal little scene — it's hard not to imagine all of us cruising the whole Western Caribbean in a parallel pack, all waving at one another the entire time. Docking and leaving are the two times a Megacruiser's Captain is actually steering the ship; and m.v. *Nadir* Captain G. Panagiotakis has wheeled us around and pointed our snout at the open sea, and we, large and white and clean, are under sail.

7

The whole first two days and nights are bad weather, with high-pitched winds and heaving seas, spume[27] lashing the porthole's glass, etc. For 40+ hours it's more like a Luxury North Sea Cruise, and the Celebrity staff goes around looking regretful but not apologetic,[28] and in all fairness it's hard to find a way to blame Celebrity Cruises Inc. for the weather.[29]

On gale-force days like the first two, passengers are advised to enjoy the view from the railings on the lee side of the *Nadir*. The one other guy who ever joins me in trying out the non-lee side has his glasses blown off by the wind, and he does not appreciate my remarking to him that round-the-ear cable arms are better for high-wind view-enjoying. I keep waiting to see somebody from the crew wearing the traditional yellow slicker, but no luck. The railing I do most of my contemplative gazing from is on Deck 10, so the sea is way below, and the sounds of it slopping and heaving around are far-away and surflike, and visually it's a little like looking down into a flushing toilet. No fins in view.

In heavy seas, hypochondriacs are kept busy taking their gastric pulse every couple seconds and wondering whether what they're feeling is maybe the onset of seasickness and/or gauging the exact level of seasickness they're feeling. Seasickness-wise, though, it turns out that heavy seas are sort of like battle: there's no way to know ahead of time how you'll react. A test of the deep and involuntary stuff of a man. I myself turn out not to get seasick. An apparent immunity, deep and unchosen, and slightly miraculous, given that I have every other

---

[27] The single best new vocab word from this week: *spume* (second-best was *scheisser*, which one German retiree called another German retiree who kept beating him at darts).

[28] (this expression resembling a kind of facial shoulder-shrug, as at fate)

[29] (Though I can't help noting that the weather in the Celebrity 7NC brochure was substantially nicer.)

kind of motion sickness listed in the *PDR* and cannot take anything for it.[30] For the whole first rough-sea day I puzzle about the fact that every other passenger on the m.v. *Nadir* looks to have received identical little weird shaving cuts below their left ear — which in the case of female passengers seems especially strange — until I learn that the little round Band-Aidish things on everybody's neck are these special new nuclear-powered transdermal motion sickness *patches,* which apparently now nobody with any kind of clue about 7NC Luxury Cruising leaves home without.

Patches notwithstanding, a lot of the passengers get seasick anyway, these first two howling days. It turns out that a seasick person really does look green, though it's an odd, ghostly green, pasty and toadish, and more than a little corpselike when the seasick person is dressed in formal dinnerwear.

For the first two nights, who's feeling seasick and who's not and who's not now but was a little while ago or isn't feeling it yet but thinks it's maybe coming on, etc., is a big topic of conversation at good old Table 64 in the Five-Star Caravelle Restaurant.[31] Common suffering and fear of suffering turn out to be a terrific ice-breaker, and ice-breaking is important, because on a 7NC you eat at the same designated table with the same companions all seven nights.[32] Discussing nausea

---

[30] I have a deep and involuntary reaction to Dramamine whereby it sends me pitching forward to lie prone and twitching wherever I am when the drug kicks in, so I'm sailing the *Nadir* cold turkey.

[31] This is on Deck 7, the serious dining room, and it's never called just the "Caravelle Restaurant" (and *never* just "the Restaurant") — it's always "The Five-Star Caravelle Restaurant."

[32] There were seven other people with me at good old Table 64, all from south Florida — Miami, Tamarac, Fort Lauderdale itself. Four of the people knew each other in private landlocked life and had requested to be at the same table. The other three people were an old couple and their granddaughter, whose name was Mona.

I was the only first-time Luxury Cruiser at Table 64, and also the only person who referred to the evening meal as "supper," a childhood habit I could not seem to be teased out of.

With the conspicuous exception of Mona, I liked all my tablemates a lot, and I want

to get a description of supper out of the way in a fast footnote and avoid saying much about them for fear of hurting their feelings by noting any weirdnesses or features that might seem potentially mean. There were some pretty weird aspects to the Table 64 ensemble, though. For one thing, they all had thick and unmistakable NYC accents, and yet they swore up and down that they'd all been born and raised in south Florida (although it did turn out that all the T64 adults' own parents had been New Yorkers, which when you think about it is compelling evidence of the durability of a good thick NYC accent). Besides me there were five women and two men, and both men were completely silent except on the subjects of golf, business, transdermal motion sickness prophylaxis, and the legalities of getting stuff through Customs. The women carried Table 64's conversational ball. One of the reasons I liked all these women (except Mona) so much was because they laughed really hard at my jokes, even lame or very obscure jokes; although they all had this curious way of laughing where they sort of *screamed* before they laughed, I mean really and discernibly screamed, so that for one excruciating second you could never tell whether they were getting ready to laugh or whether they were seeing something hideous and screamworthy over your shoulder across the 5☆C.R., and this was disconcerting all week. Also, like many other 7NC Luxury Cruise passengers I observed, they all seemed to be uniformly stellar at anecdotes and stories and extended-set-up jokes, employing both hands and faces to maximum dramatic effect, knowing when to pause and when to go run-on, how to double-take and how to set up a straight man.

My favorite tablemate was Trudy, whose husband was back home in Tamarac managing some sudden crisis at the couple's cellular phone business and had given his ticket to Alice, their heavy and very well-dressed daughter, who was on spring break from Miami U, and who was for some reason extremely anxious to communicate to me that she had a Serious Boyfriend, the name of which boyfriend was Patrick. Alice's part of most of our interfaces consisted of remarks like: "You hate fennel? What a coincidence: my boyfriend Patrick absolutely *detests* fennel"; "You're from Illinois? What a coincidence: my boyfriend Patrick has an aunt whose first husband was from Indiana, which is right near Illinois"; "You have four limbs? What a coincidence: . . . ," and so on. Alice's continual assertion of her relationship-status may have been a defensive tactic against Trudy, who kept pulling professionally retouched 4×5 glossies of Alice out of her purse and showing them to me with Alice sitting right there, and who, every time Alice mentioned Patrick, suffered some sort of weird facial tic or grimace where one side's canine tooth showed and the other side's didn't. Trudy was 56, the same age as my own dear personal Mom, and looked — Trudy did, and I mean this in the nicest possible way — like Jackie Gleason in drag, and had a particularly loud pre-laugh scream that was a real arrhythmia-producer, and was the one who coerced me into Wednesday night's Conga Line, and got me strung out on Snowball Jackpot Bingo, and also was an incredible lay authority on 7NC Luxury Cruises, this being her sixth in a decade — she and her friend Esther (thin-faced, subtly ravaged-looking, the distaff part of the couple from Miami) had tales to tell about Carnival, Princess, Crystal, and Cunard too fraught with libel-potential to reproduce here, and one long review of what was apparently the worst cruise line in 7NC history — one "American

Family Cruises," which folded after just sixteen months — involving outrages too liter-ally incredible to be believed from any duo less knowledgeable and discerning than Trudy and Esther.

Plus it started to strike me that I had never before been party to such a minute and exacting analysis of the food and service of a meal I was just at that moment eat-ing. Nothing escaped the attention of T and E — the symmetry of the parsley sprigs atop the boiled baby carrots, the consistency of the bread, the flavor and mastication-friendliness of various cuts of meat, the celerity and flambé technique of the various pastry guys in tall white hats who appeared tableside when items had to be set on fire (a major percentage of the desserts in the 5☆C.R. had to be set on fire), and so on. The waiter and busboy kept circling the table, going "Finish? Finish?" while Esther and Trudy had exchanges like:

"Honey you don't look happy with the conch, what's the problem."

"I'm fine. It's fine. Everything's fine."

"Don't lie. Honey with that face who could lie. Frank am I right? This is a person with a face incapable of lying. Is it the potatoes or the conch? Is it the conch?"

"There's nothing wrong Esther darling I swear it."

"You're not happy with the conch."

"All right. I've got a problem with the conch."

"Did I tell you? Frank did I tell her?"

[Frank silently probes own ear with pinkie.]

"Was I right? I could tell just by looking you weren't happy."

"I'm fine with the potatoes. It's the conch."

"Did I tell you about seasonal fish on ships? What did I tell you?"

"The potatoes are good."

Mona is eighteen. Her grandparents have been taking her on a Luxury Cruise every spring since she was five. Mona always sleeps through both breakfast and lunch and spends all night at the Scorpio Disco and in the Mayfair Casino playing the slots. She's 6'2" if she's an inch. She's going to attend Penn State next fall because the agreement was that she'd receive a 4-Wheel-Drive vehicle if she went someplace where there might be snow. She was unabashed in recounting this college-selection criterion. She was an incredibly demanding passenger and diner, but her complaints about slight aesthetic and gustatory imperfections at table lacked Trudy and Esther's discernment and integ-rity and came off as simply churlish. Mona was also kind of strange-looking: a body like Brigitte Nielsen or some centerfold on steroids, and above it, framed in resplen-dent and frizzless blond hair, the tiny delicate pale unhappy face of a kind of corrupt doll. Her grandparents, who retired every night right after supper, always made a small ceremony after dessert of handing Mona $100 to "go have some fun" with. This $100 bill was always in one of those little ceremonial bank envelopes that has B. Franklin's face staring out of a porthole-like window in the front, and written on the envelope in red Magic Marker was always "We Love You, Honey." Mona never once said thank you for the money. She also rolled her eyes at just about everything her grandparents said, a habit that quickly drove me up the wall.

and vomiting while eating intricately prepared and heavy gourmet foods doesn't seem to bother anybody.

Even in heavy seas, 7NC Megaships don't yaw or throw you around or send bowls of soup sliding across tables. Only a certain subtle unreality to your footing lets you know you're not on land. At sea, a room's floor feels somehow 3-D, and your footing demands a slight attention good old planar static land never needs. You don't ever quite hear the ship's big engines, but when your feet are planted you can feel them, a kind of spinal throb — it's oddly soothing.

Walking is a little dreamy also. There are constant slight shifts in torque from the waves' action. When heavy waves come straight at a Megaship's snout, the ship goes up and down along its long axis — this is called *pitching*. It produces a disorienting deal where you feel like you're walking on a very slight downhill grade and then level and then on a very slight uphill grade. Some evolutionary retrograde reptile-brain part of the CNS is apparently reawakened, though, and manages all this so automatically that it requires a good deal of attention to notice anything more than that walking feels a little dreamy.

I find I'm not as worried about saying potentially mean stuff about Mona as I am about Trudy and Alice and Esther and Esther's mute smiling husband Frank.

Apparently Mona's special customary little gig on 7NC Luxury Cruises is to lie to the waiter and maître d' and say that Thursday is her birthday, so that at the Formal supper on Thursday she gets bunting and a heart-shaped helium balloon tied to her chair and her own cake and pretty much the whole restaurant staff comes out and forms a circle around her and sings to her. Her real birthday, she informs me on Monday, is 29 July, and when I observe that 29 July is also the birthday of Benito Mussolini, Mona's grandmother shoots me kind of a death-look, though Mona herself is excited at the coincidence, apparently confusing the names *Mussolini* and *Maserati*. Because it just so happens that Thursday 16 March really *is* the birthday of Trudy's daughter Alice, and because Mona declines to forfeit her fake birthday claim and instead counterclaims that her and Alice's sharing bunting and natal attentions at 3/16's Formal supper promises to be "radical," Alice has decided that she wishes Mona all kinds of ill, and by Tuesday 14 March Alice and I have established a kind of anti-Mona alliance, and we amuse each other across Table 64 by making subtly disguised little strangling and stabbing motions whenever Mona says anything, a set of disguised motions Alice told me she learned at various excruciating public suppers in Miami with her Serious Boyfriend Patrick, who apparently hates almost everyone he eats with.

Rolling, on the other hand, is when waves hit the ship from the side and make it go up and down along its crosswise axis.[33] When the m.v. *Nadir* rolls, what you feel is a very slight increase in the demands placed on the muscles of your left leg, then a strange absence of all demand, then demands on the right leg. The demands shift at the rate of a very long thing swinging, and again the action is usually so subtle that it's almost a meditative exercise to stay conscious of what's going on.

We never pitch badly, but every once in a while some really big *Poseidon Adventure*–grade single wave must come and hit the *Nadir*'s side, because every once in a while the asymmetric leg-demands won't stop or reverse and you keep having to put more and more weight on one leg until you're exquisitely close to tipping over and have to grab something.[34] It happens very quickly and never twice in a row. The cruise's first night features some really big waves from starboard, and in the casino after supper it's hard to tell who's had too much of the '71 Richebourg and who's just doing a roll-related stagger. Add in the fact that most of the women are wearing high heels, and you can imagine some of the vertiginous staggering/flailing/clutching that goes on. Almost everyone on the *Nadir* has come on in couples, and when they walk during heavy seas they tend to hang on each other like freshman steadies. You can tell they like it — the women have this trick of sort of folding themselves into the men and snuggling as they walk, and the men's postures improve and their faces firm up and you can tell they feel unusually solid and protective. A 7NC Luxury Cruise is full of these odd little unexpected romantic nuggets like trying to help each other walk when the ship rolls — you can sort of tell why older couples like to cruise.

[33] (Which, again, w/ a Megaship like this is subtle — even at its worst, the rolling never made chandeliers tinkle or anything fall off surfaces, though it did keep a slightly unplumb drawer in Cabin 1009's complex Wondercloset rattling madly in its track even after several insertions of Kleenex at strategic points.)

[34] This on-the-edge moment's exquisiteness is something like the couple seconds between knowing you're going to sneeze and actually sneezing, some kind of marvelous distended moment of transferring control to large automatic forces. (The sneeze-analogy thing might sound freaky, but it's true, and Trudy's said she'll back me up.)

Heavy seas are also great for sleep, it turns out. The first two mornings, there's hardly anybody at Early Seating Breakfast. Everybody sleeps in. People with insomnia of years' standing report uninterrupted sleep of nine hours, ten hours. Their eyes are wide and childlike with wonder as they report this. Everybody looks younger when they've had a lot of sleep. There's rampant daytime napping, too. By week's end, when we'd had all manner of weather, I finally saw what it was about heavy seas and marvelous rest: in heavy seas you feel rocked to sleep, with the windows' spume a gentle shushing, the engines' throb a mother's pulse.

8

Did I mention that famous writer and Iowa Writers Workshop Chairperson Frank Conroy has his own experiential essay about cruising right there in Celebrity's 7NC brochure? Well he does, and the thing starts out on the Pier 21 gangway that first Saturday with his family:[35]

> With that single, easy step, we entered a
> new world, a sort of alternate reality to
> the one on shore. Smiles, handshakes,
> and we were whisked away to our cabin
> by a friendly young woman from Guest
> Relations.

Then they're outside along the rail for the *Nadir*'s sailing:

[35] Conroy took the same Luxury Cruise as I, the Seven-Night Western Caribbean on the good old *Nadir*, in May '94. He and his family cruised for free. I know details like this because Conroy talked to me on the phone, and answered nosy questions, and was frank and forthcoming and in general just totally decent-seeming about the whole thing.

> . . . We became aware that the ship was
> pulling away. We had felt no warning, no
> trembling of the deck, throbbing of the
> engines or the like. It was as if the land were
> magically receding, like some ever-so-slow
> reverse zoom in the movies.

This is pretty much what Conroy's whole "My Celebrity Cruise, or *'All This and a Tan, Too'*" is like. Its full implications didn't hit me until I reread it supine on Deck 12 the first sunny day. Conroy's essay is graceful and lapidary and attractive and assuasive. I submit that it is also completely sinister and despair-producing and bad. Its badness does not consist so much in its constant and mesmeric references to fantasy and alternate realities and the palliative powers of pro pampering —

> I'd come on board after two months of
> intense and moderately stressful work, but
> now it seemed a distant memory.

> I realized it had been a week since I'd
> washed a dish, cooked a meal, gone to
> the market, done an errand or, in fact,
> anything at all requiring a minimum of
> thought and effort. My toughest decisions
> had been whether to catch the afternoon
> showing of *Mrs. Doubtfire* or play bingo.

— nor in the surfeit of happy adjectives, nor so much in the tone of breathless approval throughout —

> For all of us, our fantasies and expectations
> were to be exceeded, to say the least.

> When it comes to service, Celebrity
> Cruises seems ready and able to deal with
> anything.

> Bright sun, warm still air, the brilliant
> blue-green of the Caribbean under the vast
> lapis lazuli dome of the sky. . . .
>
> The training must be rigorous, indeed,
> because the truth is, the service was
> impeccable, and impeccable in every
> aspect from the cabin steward to the
> sommelier, from the on-deck waiter
> to the Guest Relations manager, from the
> ordinary seaman who goes out of his
> way to get your deck chair to the third
> mate who shows you the way to the
> library. It is hard to imagine a more
> professional, polished operation, and
> I doubt that many in the world can
> equal it.

Rather, part of the essay's real badness can be found in the way it reveals once again the Megaline's sale-to-sail agenda of micromanaging not only one's perceptions of a 7NC Luxury Cruise but even one's own interpretation and articulation of those perceptions. In other words, Celebrity's PR people go and get one of the U.S.A.'s most respected writers to pre-articulate and -endorse the 7NC experience, and to do it with a professional eloquence and authority that few lay perceivers and articulators could hope to equal.[36]

But the really major badness is that the project and placement of "My Celebrity Cruise . . ." are sneaky and duplicitous and far beyond whatever eroded pales still exist in terms of literary ethics. Conroy's "essay" appears as an insert, on skinnier pages and with different margins than the rest of the brochure, creating the impression that it has been excerpted from some large and objective thing Conroy wrote. But it hasn't been. The truth is that Celebrity Cruises paid Frank Conroy up-

---

[36] E.g. after reading Conroy's essay on board, whenever I'd look up at the sky it wouldn't be the sky I was seeing, it was the *vast lapis lazuli dome of the sky.*

front to write it,[37] even though nowhere in or around the essay is there anything acknowledging that it's a paid endorsement, not even one of the little "So-and-so has been compensated for his services" that flashes at your TV screen's lower right during celebrity-hosted infomercials. Instead, inset on this weird essaymercial's first page is an author-photoish shot of Conroy brooding in a black turtleneck, and below the photo is an author-bio with a list of Conroy's books that includes the 1967 classic *Stop-Time,* which is arguably the best literary memoir of the twentieth century and is one of the books that first made poor old yours truly want to try to be a writer.

In other words, Celebrity Cruises is presenting Conroy's review of his 7NC Cruise as an essay and not a commercial. This is extremely bad. Here is the argument for why it's bad. Whether it honors them well or not, an essay's fundamental obligations are supposed to be to the reader. The reader, on however unconscious a level, understands this, and thus tends to approach an essay with a relatively high level of openness and credulity. But a commercial is a very different animal. Advertisements have certain formal, legal obligations to truthfulness, but these are broad enough to allow for a great deal of rhetorical maneuvering in the fulfillment of an advertisement's primary obligation, which is to serve the financial interests of its sponsor. Whatever attempts an advertise-ment makes to interest and appeal to its readers are not, finally, for the reader's benefit. And the reader of an ad knows all this, too — that an

---

[37] Pier 21 having seasoned me as a recipient of explanatory/justificatory narratives, I was able to make some serious journalistic phone inquiries about how Professor Conroy's essaymercial came to be, yielding two separate narratives:

(1) From Celebrity Cruises's PR liaison Ms. Wiessen (after a two-day silence that I've come to understand as the PR-equivalent of covering the microphone with your hand and leaning over to confer w/ counsel): "Celebrity saw an article he wrote in *Travel and Leisure* magazine, and they were really impressed with how he could create these mental postcards, so they went to ask him to write about his Cruise experience for people who'd never been on a Cruise before, and they did pay him to write the article, and they really took a gamble, really, because he'd never been on a Cruise before, and they had to pay him whether he liked it or not, and whether they liked the article or not, but . . . [dry little chuckle] obviously they liked the article, and he did a good job, so that's the Mr. Conroy story, and those are his perspectives on his experience."

(2) From Frank Conroy (with the small sigh that precedes a certain kind of weary candor): "I prostituted myself."

ad's appeal is by its very nature *calculated* — and this is part of why our state of receptivity is different, more guarded, when we get ready to read an ad.[38]

In the case of Frank Conroy's "essay," Celebrity Cruises[39] is trying to position an ad in such a way that we come to it with the lowered guard and leading chin we properly reserve for coming to an essay, for something that is art (or that is at least trying to be art). An ad that pretends to be art is — at absolute best — like somebody who smiles warmly at you only because he wants something from you. This is dishonest, but what's sinister is the cumulative effect that such dishonesty has on us: since it offers a perfect facsimile or simulacrum of goodwill without goodwill's real spirit, it messes with our heads and eventually starts upping our defenses even in cases of genuine smiles and real art and true goodwill. It makes us feel confused and lonely and impotent and angry and scared. It causes despair.[40]

[38] This is the reason why even a really beautiful, ingenious, powerful ad (of which there are a lot) can never be any kind of real art: an ad has no status as gift, i.e. it's never really *for* the person it's directed at.

[39] (with the active complicity of Professor Conroy, I'm afraid)

[40] This is related to the phenomenon of the Professional Smile, a national pandemic in the service industry; and noplace in my experience have I been on the receiving end of as many Professional Smiles as I am on the *Nadir*: maître d's, Chief Stewards, Hotel Managers' minions, Cruise Director — their P.S.'s all come on like switches at my approach. But also back on land at banks, restaurants, airline ticket counters, on and on. You know this smile — the strenuous contraction of circumoral fascia w/ incomplete zygomatic involvement — the smile that doesn't quite reach the smiler's eyes and that signifies nothing more than a calculated attempt to advance the smiler's own interests by pretending to like the smilee. Why do employers and supervisors force professional service people to broadcast the Professional Smile? Am I the only consumer in whom high doses of such a smile produce despair? Am I the only person who's sure that the growing number of cases in which totally average-looking people suddenly open up with automatic weapons in shopping malls and insurance offices and medical complexes and McDonald'ses is somehow causally related to the fact that these venues are well-known dissemination-loci of the Professional Smile?

Who do they think is fooled by the Professional Smile?

And yet the Professional Smile's absence now *also* causes despair. Anybody who's ever bought a pack of gum in a Manhattan cigar store or asked for something to be stamped FRAGILE at a Chicago post office or tried to obtain a glass of water from a

At any rate, for this particular 7NC consumer, Conroy's ad-as-essay ends up having a truthfulness about it that I'm quite sure is unintentional. As my week on the *Nadir* wore on, I began to see this essaymercial as a perfect ironic reflection of the mass-market-Cruise experience itself. The essay is polished, powerful, impressive, clearly the best that money can buy. It presents itself as for my benefit. It manages my experiences and my interpretation of those experiences and takes care of them in advance for me. It seems to care about me. But it doesn't, not really, because first and foremost it wants something from me. So does the Cruise itself. The pretty setting and glittering ship and dashing staff and sedulous servants and solicitous fun-managers all want something from me, and it's not just the price of my ticket — they've already got that. Just what it is that they want is hard to pin down, but by early in the week I can feel it, and building: it circles the ship like a fin.

9

Celebrity's fiendish brochure does not lie or exaggerate, however, in the luxury department. I now confront the journalistic problem of not being sure how many examples I need to list in order to communicate the atmosphere of sybaritic and nearly insanity-producing pampering on board the m.v. *Nadir*.

How about for just one example Saturday 11 March, right after sailing but before the North Sea weather hits, when I want to go out to Deck 10's port rail for some introductory vista-gazing and thus decide I need some zinc oxide for my peel-prone nose. My zinc oxide's still in my big duffel bag, which at that point is piled with all Deck 10's other luggage

---

South Boston waitress knows well the soul-crushing effect of a service worker's scowl, i.e. the humiliation and resentment of being denied the Professional Smile. And the Professional Smile has by now skewed even my resentment at the dreaded Professional Scowl: I walk away from the Manhattan tobacconist resenting not the counterman's character or absence of goodwill but his lack of *professionalism* in denying me the Smile. What a fucking mess.

in the little area between the 10-Fore elevator and the 10-Fore staircase while little men in cadet-blue Celebrity jumpsuits, porters — entirely Lebanese, this squad seemed to be — are cross-checking the luggage tags with the *Nadir*'s passenger list Lot #s and organizing the luggage and taking it all up the Port and Starboard halls to people's cabins.

And but so I come out and spot my duffel among the luggage, and I start to grab and haul it out of the towering pile of leather and nylon, with the idea that I can just whisk the bag back to 1009 myself and root through it and find my good old ZnO;[41] and one of the porters sees me starting to grab the bag, and he dumps all four of the massive pieces of luggage he's staggering with and leaps to intercept me. At first I'm afraid he thinks I'm some kind of baggage thief and wants to see my claim-check or something. But it turns out that what he wants is my duffel: he wants to carry it to 1009 for me. And I, who am about half again this poor herniated little guy's size (as is the duffel bag itself), protest politely, trying to be considerate, saying Don't Fret, Not a Big Deal, Just Need My Good Old ZnO. I indicate to the porter that I can see they have some sort of incredibly organized ordinal luggage-dispersal system under way here and that I don't mean to disrupt it or make him carry a Lot #7 bag before a Lot #2 bag or anything, and no I'll just get the big old heavy weatherstained sucker out of here myself and give the little guy that much less work to do.

And then now a very strange argument indeed ensues, me v. the Lebanese porter, because it turns out I am putting this guy, who barely speaks English, in a terrible kind of sedulous-service double-bind, a paradox of pampering: viz. the The-Passenger's-Always-Right-versus-Never-Let-A-Passenger-Carry-His-Own-Bag paradox. Clueless at the time about what this poor little Lebanese man is going through, I wave off both his high-pitched protests and his agonized expression as mere servile courtesy, and I extract the duffel and lug it up the hall to 1009 and slather the old beak with ZnO and go outside to watch the coast of Florida recede cinematically à la F. Conroy.

Only later did I understand what I'd done. Only later did I learn that

---

[41] (Which by the way trust me, I used to lifeguard part-time, and fuck this SPF hooha: good old ZnO will keep your nose looking like a newborn's.)

that little Lebanese Deck 10 porter had his head just about chewed off
by the (also Lebanese) Deck 10 Head Porter, who'd had his own head
chewed off by the Austrian Chief Steward, who'd received confirmed
reports that a Deck 10 passenger had been seen carrying his own luggage
up the Port hallway of Deck 10 and now demanded rolling Lebanese
heads for this clear indication of porterly dereliction, and had reported
(the Austrian Chief Steward did) the incident (as is apparently SOP)
to an officer in the Guest Relations Dept., a Greek officer with Revo
shades and a walkie-talkie and officerial epaulets so complex I never did
figure out what his rank was; and this high-ranking Greek guy actually
came around to 1009 after Saturday's supper to apologize on behalf
of practically the entire Chandris shipping line and to assure me that
ragged-necked Lebanese heads were even at that moment rolling down
various corridors in piacular recompense for my having had to carry
my own bag. And even though this Greek officer's English was in lots of
ways better than mine, it took me no less than ten minutes to express
my own horror and to claim responsibility and to detail the double-
bind I'd put the porter in — brandishing at relevant moments the actual
tube of ZnO that had caused the whole snafu — ten or more minutes
before I could get enough of a promise from the Greek officer that
various chewed-off heads would be reattached and employee records
unbesmirched to feel comfortable enough to allow the officer to leave;[42]
and the whole incident was incredibly frazzling and angst-fraught and
filled almost a whole Mead notebook and is here recounted in only its
barest psychoskeletal outline.

It is everywhere on the *Nadir* you look: evidence of a steely
determination to indulge the passenger in ways that go far beyond
any halfway-sane passenger's own expectations.[43] Some wholly random

[42] In further retrospect, I think the only thing I really persuaded the Greek officer of
was that I was very weird, and possibly unstable, which impression I'm sure was shared
with Mr. Dermatitis and combined with that same first night's *au-jus*-as-shark-bait
request to destroy my credibility with Dermatitis before I even got in to see him.

[43] One of Celebrity Cruises' slogans asserts that they Look Forward To Exceeding
Your Expectations — they say it a lot, and they are sincere, though they are either
disingenuous about or innocent of this Excess's psychic consequences.

examples: My cabin bathroom has plenty of thick fluffy towels, but when I go up to lie in the sun[44] I don't have to take any of my cabin's towels, because the two upper decks' sun areas have big carts loaded with even thicker and fluffier towels. These carts are stationed at convenient intervals along endless rows of gymnastically adjustable deck chairs that are themselves phenomenally fine deck chairs, sturdy enough for even the portliest sunbather but also narcoleptically comfortable, with heavy-alloy skeletons over which is stretched some exotic material that combines canvas's quick-drying durability with cotton's absorbency and comfort — the material's precise composition is mysterious, but it's a welcome step up from public pools' deck chairs' surface of Kmartish plastic that sticks and produces farty suction-noises whenever you shift your sweaty weight on it — and the *Nadir*'s chairs' material is not striated or cross-hatched in some web but is a solid expanse stretched drum-tight over the frame, so that you don't get those weird pink chair-stripes on the side you're lying on. Oh, and each upper deck's carts are manned by a special squad of full-time Towel Guys, so that, when you're well-done on both sides and ready to quit and spring easily out of the deck chair, you don't have to pick up your towel and take it with you or even bus it into the cart's Used Towel slot, because a Towel Guy materializes the minute your fanny leaves the chair and removes your towel for you and deposits it in the slot. (Actually the Towel Guys are such overachievers about removing used towels that even if you just get up for a second to reapply ZnO or gaze contemplatively out over the railing, often when you turn back around your towel's gone, and your deck chair's refolded to the uniform 45° at-rest angle, and you have to readjust your chair all over again and go to the cart to get a fresh fluffy towel, of which there's admittedly not a short supply.)

Down in the Five-Star Caravelle Restaurant, the waiter[45] will not only bring you, e.g., lobster — as well as seconds and even thirds on

---

[44]   (to either Deck 11's pools or Deck 12's Temple of Ra)

[45]   Table 64's waiter is Tibor, a Hungarian and a truly exceptional person, about whom if there's any editorial justice you will learn a lot more someplace below.

lobster[46] — with methamphetaminic speed, but he'll also incline over you[47] with gleaming claw-cracker and surgical fork and dismantle the lobster for you, saving you the green goopy work that's the only remotely rigorous thing about lobster.

At the Windsurf Cafe, up on Deck 11 by the pools, where there's always an informal buffet lunch, there's never that bovine line that makes most cafeterias such a downer, and there are about 73 varieties of entrée alone, and incredibly good coffee; and if you're carrying a bunch of notebooks or even just have too many things on your tray, a waiter will materialize as you peel away from the buffet and will carry your tray — i.e. even though it's a cafeteria there're all these waiters standing around, all with Nehruesque jackets and white towels draped over left arms that are always held in the position of broken or withered arms, watching you, the waiters, not quite making eye-contact but scanning for any little way to be of service, plus plum-jacketed sommeliers walking around to see if you need a non-buffet libation . . . plus a whole other crew of maître d's and supervisors watching the waiters and sommeliers and tall-hatted buffet-servers to make sure they're not even thinking of letting you do something for yourself that they could be doing for you.[48]

Every public surface on the m.v. *Nadir* that isn't stainless steel or glass or varnished parquet or dense and good-smelling sauna-type wood is plush blue carpet that never naps and never has a chance to accumulate even one flecklet of lint because jumpsuited Third World guys are always at it with Siemens A.G. high-suction vacuums. The elevators are Euroglass and yellow steel and stainless steel and a kind of wood-

---

[46] Not until Tuesday's lobster night at the 5☆C.R. did I really emphatically understand the Roman phenomenon of the vomitorium.

[47] (not invasively or obtrusively or condescendingly)

[48] Again, you never have to bus your tray after eating at the Windsurf, because the waiters leap to take them, and again the zeal can be a hassle, because if you get up just to go get another peach or something and still have a cup of coffee and some yummy sandwich crusts you've been saving for last a lot of times you come back and the tray and the crusts are gone, and I personally start to attribute this oversedulous busing to the reign of Hellenic terror the waiters labor under.

grain material that looks too shiny to be real wood but makes a sound when you thump it that's an awful lot like real wood.[49] The elevators and stairways between decks[50] seem to be the particular objects of the anal retention of a whole special Elevator-and-Staircase custodial crew.[51,52]

And let's don't forget Room Service, which on a 7NC Luxury Cruise is called Cabin Service. Cabin Service is in addition to the eleven scheduled daily opportunities for public eating, and it's available 24/7, and it's free: all you have to do is hit x72 on the bedside phone, and

[49]   The many things on the *Nadir* that were wood-grain but not real wood were such marvelous and painstaking imitations of wood that a lot of times it seemed like it would have been simpler and less expensive simply to have used real wood.

[50]   Two broad staircases, Fore and Aft, both of which reverse their zag-angle at each landing, and the landings themselves have mirrored walls, which is wickedly great because via the mirrors you can check out female bottoms in cocktail dresses ascending one flight above you without appearing to be one of those icky types who check out female bottoms on staircases.

[51]   During the first two days of rough seas, when people vomited a lot (especially after supper and apparently *extra*-especially on the elevators and stairways), these puddles of vomit inspired a veritable feeding frenzy of Wet/Dry Vacs and spot-remover and all-trace-of-odor-eradicator chemicals applied by this Elite Special Forces–type crew.

[52]   By the way, the ethnic makeup of the *Nadir*'s crew is a melting-pot mélange on the order of like a Benetton commercial, and it's a constant challenge to trace the racio-geographical makeup of the employees' various hierarchies. All the big-time officers are Greek, but then it's a Greek-owned ship so what do you expect. Them aside, it at first seems like there's some basic Eurocentric caste system in force: waiters, bus-boys, beverage waitresses, sommeliers, casino dealers, entertainers, and stewards seem mostly to be Aryans, while the porters and custodians and swabbies tend to be your swarthier types — Arabs and Filipinos, Cubans, West Indian blacks. But it turns out to be more complex than that, because the Chief Stewards and Chief Sommeliers and maître d's who so beadily oversee the Aryan servants are *themselves* swarthy and non-Aryan — e.g. our maître d' at the 5☆C.R. is Portuguese, with the bull neck and heavy-lidded grin of a Teamsters official, and gives the impression of needing only some very subtle prearranged signal to have a $10000-an-hour prostitute or unimaginable substances delivered to your cabin; and our whole T64 totally loathes him for no single pinpointable reason, and we've all agreed in advance to fuck him royally on the tip at week's end.

ten or fifteen minutes later a guy who wouldn't even *dream* of hitting you up for a gratuity appears with this ... this *tray:* "Thinly Sliced Ham and Swiss Cheese on White Bread with Dijon Mustard," "The Combo: Cajun Chicken with Pasta Salad, and Spicy Salsa," on and on, a whole page of sandwiches and platters in the Services Directory — and the stuff deserves to be capitalized, believe me. As a kind of semi-agoraphobe who spends massive amounts of time in my cabin, I come to have a really complex dependency/shame relationship with Cabin Service. Since finally getting around to reading the Services Directory and finding out about it Monday night, I've ended up availing myself of Cabin Service every night — more like twice a night, to be honest — even though I find it extremely embarrassing to be calling up ×72 asking to have even *more* rich food brought to me when there've already been eleven gourmet eating-ops that day.[53] Usually what I do is spread out my notebooks and *Fielding's Guide to Worldwide Cruising 1995* and pens and various materials all over the bed, so when the Cabin Service guy appears at the door he'll see all this belletristic material and figure I'm working really hard on something belletristic right here in the cabin and have doubtless been too busy to have hit all the public meals and am thus legitimately entitled to the indulgence of Cabin Service.[54]

But it's my experience with the cabin cleaning that's maybe the ultimate example of stress from a pampering so extravagant that it messes with your head. Searing crush or no, the fact of the matter is I

[53] This is counting the Midnight Buffet, which tends to be a kind of lamely lavish Theme-slash-Costume-Partyish thing, w/ Theme-related foods — Oriental, Caribbean, Tex-Mex — and which I plan in this essay to mostly skip except to say that Tex-Mex Night out by the pools featured what must have been a seven-foot-high ice sculpture of Pancho Villa that spent the whole party dripping steadily onto the mammoth sombrero of Tibor, Table 64's beloved and extremely cool Hungarian waiter, whose contract forces him on Tex-Mex Night to wear a serape and a straw sombrero with a 17″ radius[53a] and to dispense Four Alarm chili from a steam table placed right underneath an ice sculpture, and whose pink and birdlike face on occasions like this expressed a combination of mortification and dignity that seem somehow to sum up the whole plight of postwar Eastern Europe.

[53a] (He let me measure it when the reptilian maître d' wasn't looking.)

[54] (I know, like I'm sure this guy even cares.)

rarely even see 1009's cabin steward, the diaphanous and epicanthically doe-eyed Petra. But I have good reason to believe she sees me. Because every time I leave 1009 for more than like half an hour, when I get back it's totally cleaned and dusted down again and the towels replaced and the bathroom agleam. Don't get me wrong: in a way it's great. I am kind of a slob, and I'm in Cabin 1009 a lot, and I also come and go a lot,[55] and when I'm in here in 1009 I sit in bed and write in bed while eating fruit and generally mess up the bed. But then whenever I dart out and then come back, the bed is freshly made up and hospital-cornered and there's another mint-centered chocolate on the pillow.[56]

I fully grant that mysterious invisible room-cleaning is in a way great, every true slob's fantasy, somebody materializing and deslobbing your room and then dematerializing — like having a mom without the guilt. But there is also, I think, a creeping guilt here, a deep accretive uneasiness, a discomfort that presents — at least in my own case — as a weird kind of pampering-paranoia.

Because after a couple days of this fabulous invisible room-cleaning, I start to wonder how exactly Petra knows when I'm in 1009 and when I'm not. It's now that it occurs to me how rarely I ever see her. For a while I try experiments like all of a sudden darting out into the 10-Port hallway to see if I can see Petra hunched somewhere keeping track of who is decabining, and I scour the whole hallway-and-ceiling area for evidence of some kind of camera or monitor tracking movements outside the cabin doors — zilch on both fronts. But then I realize that the mystery's even more complex and unsettling than I'd first thought, because my cabin gets cleaned always and only during intervals where I'm gone more than half an hour. When I go out, how can Petra or her supervisors possibly know how long I'm going to be gone? I try leaving 1009 a couple times and then dashing back after 10 or 15 minutes to see

---

[55] This was primarily because of the semi-agoraphobia — I'd have to sort of psych myself up to leave the cabin and go accumulate experiences, and then pretty quickly out there in the general population my will would break and I'd find some sort of excuse to scuttle back to 1009. This happened quite a few times a day.

[56] (This FN right here's being written almost a week after the Cruise ended, and I'm still living mainly on these hoarded mint-centered chocolates.)

whether I can catch Petra *in delicto,* but she's never there. I try making a truly unholy mess in 1009 and then leaving and hiding somewhere on a lower deck and then dashing back after exactly 29 minutes — and again when I come bursting through the door there's no Petra and no cleaning. Then I leave the cabin with exactly the same expression and appurtenances as before and this time stay hidden for 31 minutes and then haul ass back — and this time again no sighting of Petra, but now 1009 is sterilized and gleaming and there's a mint on the pillow's fresh new case. Know that I carefully scrutinize every inch of every surface I pass as I circle the deck during these little experiments — no cameras or motion sensors or anything in evidence anywhere that would explain how They know.[57] So now for a while I theorize that somehow a special crewman is assigned to each passenger and follows that passenger at all times, using extremely sophisticated techniques of personal surveillance and reporting the passenger's movements and activities and projected time of cabin-return back to Steward HQ or something, and so for about a day I try taking extreme evasive actions — whirling suddenly to check behind me, popping around corners, darting in and out of Gift Shops via different doors, etc. — never one sign of anybody engaged in surveillance. I never develop even a plausible theory about how They do it. By the time I quit trying, I'm feeling half-crazed, and my counter-surveillance measures are drawing frightened looks and even some temple-tapping from 10-Port's other guests.

I submit that there's something deeply mind-fucking about the Type-A-personality service and pampering on the *Nadir,* and that the manic invisible cabin-cleaning provides the clearest example of what's creepy about it. Because, deep down, it's not *really* like having a mom. *Pace* the guilt and nagging, etc., a mom cleans up after you largely because she loves you — you are the point, the object of the cleaning somehow.

---

[57] The answer to why I don't just ask Petra how she does it is that Petra's English is extremely limited and primitive, and in sad fact I'm afraid my whole deep feeling of attraction and connection to Petra the Slavanian steward has been erected on the flimsy foundation of the only two English clauses she seems to know, one or the other of which clauses she uses in response to every statement, question, joke, or protestation of undying devotion: "Is no problem" and "You are a funny thing."

On the *Nadir*, though, once the novelty and convenience have worn off, I begin to see that the phenomenal cleaning really has nothing to do with me. (It's been particularly traumatic for me to realize that Petra is cleaning Cabin 1009 so phenomenally well simply because she's under orders to do so, and thus (obviously) that she's not doing it for me or because she likes me or thinks I'm No Problem or A Funny Thing — in fact she'd clean my cabin just as phenomenally well even if I were a dork — and maybe conceivably behind the smile does consider me a dork, in which case what if in fact I really am a dork? — I mean, if pampering and radical kindness don't seem motivated by strong affection and thus don't somehow affirm one or help assure one that one is not, finally, a dork, of what final and significant value is all this indulgence and cleaning?)

The feeling's not all that dissimilar to the experience of being a guest in the home of somebody who does things like sneak in in the A.M. and make your guest bed up for you while you're in the shower and fold your dirty clothes or even launder them without being asked to, or who empties your ashtray after each cigarette you smoke, etc. For a while, with a host like this, it seems great, and you feel cared about and prized and affirmed and worthwhile, etc. But then after a while you begin to intuit that the host isn't acting out of regard or affection for you so much as simply going around obeying the imperatives of some personal neurosis having to do with domestic cleanliness and order . . . which means that, since the ultimate point and object of the cleaning isn't you but rather cleanliness and order, it's going to be a relief for her when you leave. Meaning her hygienic pampering of you is actually evidence that she doesn't want you around. The *Nadir* doesn't have the Scotchguarded carpet or plastic-wrapped furniture of a true anal-type host like this, but the psychic aura's the same, and so's the projected relief of getting out.

10

I don't know how a well a claustrophobe would do, but for the agoraphobe a 7NC Luxury Megacruiser presents a whole array of attractively enclosing options. The agoraphobe can choose not to leave the ship,[58] or can restrict herself only to certain decks, or can decline to leave the particular deck her cabin is on, or can eschew the view-conducive open-air railings on either side of that certain deck and keep exclusively to the deck's interior enclosed part. Or the agoraphobe can simply not leave her cabin at all.

I — who am not a true, can't-even-go-to-the-supermarket-type agoraphobe, but am what might be called a "borderline-" or "semi-agoraphobe" — come nevertheless to love very deeply Cabin 1009, Exterior Port.[59] It is made of a fawn-colored enamelish polymer and its walls are extremely thick and solid: I can drum annoyingly on the wall above my bed for up to five minutes before my aft neighbors pound (very faintly) back in annoyance. The cabin is thirteen size-11 Keds long by twelve Keds wide, with a little peninsular vestibule protruding out toward a cabin door that's got three separate locking technologies and trilingual lifeboat instructions bolted to its inside and a whole deck of DO NOT DISTURB cards hanging from the inside knob.[60] The vestibule is one-and-one-half times as wide as I. The cabin's bathroom is off one side of the vestibule, and off the other side is the Wondercloset, a complicated honeycomb of shelves and drawers and hangers and cubbyholes and Personal Fireproof Safe. The Wondercloset is so intricate in its utilization of every available cubic cm that all I can say is it must have been designed by a very organized person indeed.

All the way across the cabin, there's a deep enamel ledge running

[58] (At sea this is small agorapotatoes, but in port, once the doors open and the gangway extends, it represents a true choice and is thus agoraphobically valid.)

[59] "1009" indicates that it's on Deck 10, and "Port" refers to the side of the ship it's on, and "Exterior" means that I have a window. There are also, of course, "Interior" cabins off the inner sides of the decks' halls, but I hereby advise any prospective 7NC passenger with claustrophobic tendencies to make sure and specify "Exterior" when making cabin-reservations.

[60] The non-U.S. agoraphobe will be heartened to know that this deck includes "BITTE NICHT STÖREN," "PRIÈRE DE NE PAS DÉRANGER," "SI PREGA NON DISTURBARE," and (my personal favorite) "FAVOR DE NO MOLESTAR."

along the port wall under a window that I think is called my porthole.[61] As are the portholes in ships on TV, this porthole is indeed round, but it is not small, and in terms of its importance to the room's mood and *raison* it resembles a cathedral's rose window. It's made of that kind of very thick glass that Drive-Up bank tellers stand behind. In the corner of the porthole's glass is this:

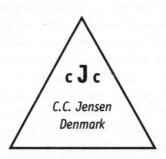

c **J** c

C.C. Jensen
Denmark

You can thump the glass with your fist w/o give or vibration. It's really good glass. Every morning at exactly 0834h. a Filipino guy in a blue jumpsuit stands on one of the lifeboats that hang in rows between Decks 9 and 10 and sprays my porthole with a hose, to get the salt off, which is fun to watch.

Cabin 1009's dimensions are just barely on the good side of the line between very very snug and cramped. Packed into its near-square are a big good bed and two bedside tables w/ lamps and an 18″ TV with five At-Sea Cable® options, two of which show continuous loops of the Simpson trial.[62] There's also a white enamel desk that doubles as a vanity, and a round glass table on which is a basket that's alternately

---

[61] If you're either a little kid or an anorectic you can probably sit on this ledge to do your dreamy contemplative sea-gazing, but a raised and buttock-hostile lip at the ledge's outer border makes this impractical for a full-size adult.

[62] There are also continual showings of about a dozen second-run movies, via what I get the sense is a VCR somewhere right here on board, because certain irregularities in tracking show up in certain films over and over. The movies run 24/7, and I end up watching several of them so many times that I can now do their dialogue verbatim. These movies include *It Could Happen to You* (the *It's a Wonderful Life*-w/-lottery twist

filled with fresh fruit and with husks and rinds of same. I don't know whether it's SOP or a subtle journalistic perq, but every time I leave the cabin for more than the requisite half-hour I come back to find a new basket of fruit, covered in snug blue-tinted Saran, on the glass table. It's good fresh fruit and it's always there. I've never eaten so much fruit in my life.

Cabin 1009's bathroom deserves extravagant praise. I've seen more than my share of bathrooms, and this is one bitchingly nice bathroom. It is five-and-a-half Keds to the edge of the shower's step up and sign to Watch Your Step. The room's done in white enamel and gleaming brushed and stainless steel. Its overhead lighting is luxury lighting, some kind of blue-intensive Eurofluorescence that's run through a diffusion filter so it's diagnostically acute without being brutal.[63] Right by the light switch is an Alisco Sirocco-brand hairdryer that's brazed right onto the wall and comes on automatically when you take it out of the mount; the Sirocco's *High* setting just about takes your head off. Next to the hairdryer there's both 115v and 230v sockets, plus a grounded 110v for razors.

The sink is huge and its bowl deep without seeming precipitous or ungentle of grade. Good C.C. Jensen plate mirror covers the whole wall over the sink. The steel soap dish is striated to let sog-water out and minimize that annoying underside-of-the-bar slime. The ingenious consideration of the anti-slime soap dish is particularly affecting.

Keep in mind that 1009 is a mid-price single cabin. The mind

---

thing), *Jurassic Park* (which does not stand up well: its essential plotlessness doesn't emerge until the third viewing, but after that the semi-agoraphobe treats it like a porno flic, twiddling his thumbs until the T. Rex and Velociraptor parts (which do stand up well)), *Wolf* (stupid), *The Little Rascals* (nauseous), *Andre* (kind of *Old Yeller* with a seal), *The Client* (with another incredibly good child actor — where do they *get* all these Olivier-grade children?), and *Renaissance Man* (w/ Danny DeVito, a movie that tugs at your sentiments like a dog at a pantcuff, except it's hard not to like any movie that has an academic as the hero).

[63] What it is is lighting for upscale and appearance-conscious adults who want a clear picture of whatever might be aesthetically problematic that day but also want to be reassured that the overall aesthetic situation is pretty darn good.

positively reels at what a luxury-penthouse-type cabin's bathroom must be like.[64]

And so but simply enter 1009's bathroom and hit the overhead lights and on comes an automatic exhaust fan whose force and aerodynamism give steam or your more offensive-type odors just no quarter at all.[65] The fan's suction is such that if you stand right underneath its louvered vent it makes your hair stand straight up on your head, which together with the concussive and abundantly rippling action of the Sirocco hairdryer makes for hours of fun in the lavishly lit mirror.

The shower itself overachieves in a big way. The Hot setting's water is exfoliatingly hot, but it takes only one preset manipulation of the shower-knob to get perfect 98.6° water. My own personal home should have such water pressure: the showerhead's force pins you helplessly to the stall's opposite wall, and at 98.6° the head's MASSAGE setting makes your eyes roll up and your sphincter just about give.[66] The showerhead and its flexible steel line are also detachable, so you can hold the head and direct its punishing stream just at e.g. your particularly dirty right knee or something.[67]

---

[64] Attempts to get to see a luxury cabin's loo were consistently misconstrued and rebuffed by upscale penthouse-type *Nadir*ites — there are disadvantages to Luxury Cruising as a civilian and not identifiable Press.

[65] 1009's bathroom always smells of a strange but not unnice Norwegian disinfectant whose scent resembles what it would smell like if someone who knew the exact organochemical composition of a lemon but had never in fact smelled a lemon tried to synthesize the scent of a lemon. Kind of the same relation to a real lemon as a Bayer's Children's Aspirin to a real orange.

The cabin itself, on the other hand, after it's been cleaned, has no odor. None. Not in the carpets, the bedding, the insides of the desk's drawers, the wood of the Wondercloset's doors: nothing. One of the very few totally odorless places I've ever been in. This, too, eventually starts giving me the creeps.

[66] Perhaps designed with this in mind, the shower's floor has a 10° grade from all sides to the center's drain, which drain is the size of a lunch plate and has audibly aggressive suction.

[67] This detachable and concussive showerhead can allegedly also be employed for non-hygienic and even prurient purposes, apparently. I overheard guys from a small U. of Texas spring-break contingent (the only college-age group on the whole *Nadir*)

Toiletry-wise, flanking the sink's mirror are broad shallow bolted steel minibaskets with all sorts of free stuff in them. There's Caswell-Massey Conditioning Shampoo in a convenient airplane-liquor-size bottle. There's Caswell-Massey Almond and Aloe Hand and Body Emulsion With Silk. There's a sturdy plastic shoehorn and a chamois mitt for either eyeglasses or light shoeshining — both these items are the navy-blue-on-searing-white that are Celebrity's colors.[68] There's not one but *two* fresh showercaps at all times. There's good old unpretentious unswishy Safeguard soap. There's washcloths w/o nubble or nap, and of course towels you want to propose to.

In the vestibule's Wondercloset are extra chamois blankets and hypoallergenic pillows and plastic CELEBRITY CRUISES–emblazoned bags of all different sizes and configurations for your laundry and optional dry cleaning, etc.[69]

But all this is still small potatoes compared to 1009's fascinating and potentially malevolent toilet. A harmonious concordance of elegant form and vigorous function, flanked by rolls of tissue so soft as to be without the usual perforates for tearing, my toilet has above it this sign: THIS TOILET IS CONNECTED TO A **VACUUM SEWAGE SYSTEM**. PLEASE DO NOT THROW INTO THE TOILET ANYTHING THAN ORDINARY TOILET WASTE AND TOILET PAPER[70]

---

regale each other about their ingenuity with the showerhead. One guy in particular was fixated on the idea that somehow the shower's technology could be rigged to administer fellatio if he could just get access to a "metric ratchet set" — your guess here is as good as mine.

[68] The *Nadir* itself is navy trim on a white field, and all the Megalines have their own trademark color schemes — lime-green on white, aqua on white, robin's-egg on white, barn-red on white (white apparently being a constant).

[69] You can apparently get "Butler Service" and automatic-send-out dry cleaning and shoeshining, all at prices that I'm told are not out of line, but the forms you have to fill out and hang on your door for all this are wildly complex, and I'm scared of setting in motion mechanisms of service that seem potentially overwhelming.

[70] The missing predicative preposition here is *sic* — ditto what looks to be an implied image of thrown excrement — but the mistakes seem somehow endearing, humanizing, and this toilet needed all the humanizing it could get.

Yes that's right a *vacuum toilet*. And, as with the exhaust fan above, not a lightweight or unambitious vacuum. The toilet's flush produces a brief but traumatizing sound, a kind of held high-B gargle, as of some gastric disturbance on a cosmic scale. Along with this sound comes a concussive suction so awesomely powerful that it's both scary and strangely comforting — your waste seems less removed than *hurled* from you, and hurled with a velocity that lets you feel as though the waste is going to end up someplace so far away from you that it will have become an abstraction . . . a kind of existential-level sewage treatment.[71,72]

[71] It's pretty hard not to see connections between the exhaust fan and the toilet's vacuums — an almost Final Solution–like eradication of animal wastes and odors (wastes and odors that are by all rights a natural consequence of Henry VIII–like meals and unlimited free Cabin Service and fruit baskets) — and the death-denial/-transcendence fantasies that the 7NC Luxury Megacruise is trying to enable.

[72] The *Nadir's* VACUUM SEWAGE SYSTEM begins after a while to hold such a fascination for me that I end up going hat in hand back to Hotel Manager Dermatitis to ask once again for access to the ship's nether parts, and once again I pull a boner with Dermatitis: I innocently mention my specific fascination with the ship's VACUUM SEWAGE SYSTEM — which boner is consequent to another and prior boner by which I'd failed to discover in my pre-boarding researches that there'd been, just a few months before this, a tremendous scandal in which the I think *QE2* Megaship had been discovered dumping waste over the side in mid-voyage, in violation of numerous national and maritime codes, and had been videotaped doing this by a couple of passengers who subsequently apparently sold the videotape to some network newsmagazine, and so the whole Megacruise industry was in a state of almost Nixonian paranoia about unscrupulous journalists trying to manufacture scandals about Megaships' handling of waste. Even behind his mirrored sunglasses I can tell that Mr. Dermatitis is severely upset about my interest in sewage, and he denies my request to eyeball the V.S.S. with a complex defensiveness that I couldn't even begin to chart out here. It is only later that night (Wednesday 3/15), at supper, at good old Table 64 in the 5☆C.R., that my cruise-savvy tablemates fill me in on the *QE2* waste-scandal, and they scream[72a] with mirth at the clay-footed naïveté with which I'd gone to Dermatitis with what was in fact an innocent if puerile fascination with hermetically-evacuated waste; and such is my own embarrassment and hatred of Mr. Dermatitis by this time that I begin to feel like if the Hotel Manager really *does* think I'm some kind of investigative journalist with a hard-on for shark dangers and sewage scandals then he might think it would be worth the risk to have me harmed in some way; and through a set of neurotic connections I won't even try to defend, I, for about a day and a half, begin to fear that the *Nadir's* Greek episcopate will somehow contrive to use the incredibly

11

Traveling at sea for the first time is a chance to realize that the ocean is not one ocean. The water changes. The Atlantic that seethes off the eastern U.S. is glaucous and lightless and looks mean. Around Jamaica, though, it's more like a milky aquamarine, and translucent. Off the Cayman Islands it's an electric blue, and off Cozumel it's almost purple. Same sort of deal with the beaches. You can tell right away that south Florida's sand is descended from rocks: it hurts your bare feet and has that sort of minerally glitter to it. But Ocho Rios's beach is more like dirty sugar, and Cozumel's is like clean sugar, and at places along the coast of Grand Cayman the sand's texture is more like flour, silicate, its white as dreamy and vaporous as clouds' white. The only real constant to the nautical topography of the m.v. *Nadir*'s Caribbean is something about its unreal and almost retouched-looking prettiness[73] — it's impossible to describe quite right, but the closest I can come is to say that it all looks: *expensive.*

12

Mornings in port are a special time for the semi-agoraphobe, because just about everybody else gets off the ship and goes ashore for Organized Shore Excursions or for unstructured peripatetic tourist stuff, and the m.v. *Nadir*'s upper decks have the eerily delicious deserted quality of your folks' house when you're home sick as a kid and everybody else is off at work and school, etc. Right now it's 0930h. on 15 March (Ides Wednesday) and we're docked off Cozumel, Mexico. I'm on Deck 12. A couple guys in software-company T-shirts jog fragrantly by every couple

---

potent and forceful 1009 toilet itself for the assassination — I don't know, that they'll like somehow lubricate the bowl and up the suction to where not just my waste but I myself will be sucked down through the seat's opening and hurled into some kind of abstract septic holding-tank.

[72a] (literally)

[73] It is not "beautiful"; it is "pretty." There's a difference.

minutes,[74] but other than that it's just me and the ZnO and hat and about a thousand empty and identically folded high-quality deck chairs. The 12-Aft Towel Guy has almost nobody to exercise his zeal on, and by 1000h. I'm on my fifth new towel.   -

Here the semi-agoraphobe can stand alone at the ship's highest port rail and gaze pensively out to sea. The sea off Cozumel is a kind of watery indigo through which you can see the powder-white of the bottom. In the middle distance, underwater coral formations are big cloud-shapes of deep purple. You can see why people say of calm seas that they're "glassy": at 1000h. the sun assumes a kind of Brewster's Angle w/r/t the surface and the harbor lights up as far as the eye can see: the water moves a million little ways at once, and each move makes a sparkle. Out past the coral, the water gets progressively darker in orderly baconish stripes — I think this phenomenon has to do with perspective. It's all extremely pretty and peaceful. Besides me and the T.G. and the orbiting joggers, there's only a supine older lady reading *Codependent No More* and a man standing way up at the fore part of the starboard rail videotaping the sea. This sad and cadaverous guy, who by the second day I'd christened Captain Video, has tall hard gray hair and Birkenstocks and very thin hairless calves, and he is one of the cruise's more prominent eccentrics.[75] Pretty much everybody on the *Nadir* qualifies as camera-crazy, but Captain Video camcords absolutely *everything*, including

---

[74] Seven times around Deck 12 is a mile, and I'm one of very few *Nadir*ites under about 70 who doesn't jog like a fiend up here now that the weather's nice. Early A.M. is the annular rush-hour of Deck 12 jogging. I've already seen a couple of juicy and Keystone-quality jogging collisions.

[75] Other eccentrics on this 7NC include: the thirteen-year-old kid with the toupee, who wears his big orange life jacket all week and sits on the wood floor of the upper decks reading Jose Philip Farmer paperbacks with three different boxes of Kleenex around him at all times; the bloated and dead-eyed guy who sits in the same chair at the same 21 table in the Mayfair Casino every day from 1200h. to 0300h., drinking Long Island Iced Tea and playing 21 at a narcotized underwater pace. There's The Guy Who Sleeps By The Pool, who does just what his name suggests, except he does it all the time, even in the rain, a hairy-stomached guy of maybe 50, a copy of *Megatrends* open on his chest, sleeping w/o sunglasses or sunblock, w/o moving, for hours and hours, in full and high-watt sun, and never in my sight burns or wakes up (I suspect that at night they move him down to his room on a gurney). There's also the two unbeliev-ably old and cloudy-eyed couples who sit in a quartet in upright chairs just inside the

meals, empty hallways, endless games of geriatric bridge — even leaping onto Deck 11's raised stage during Pool Party to get the crowd from the musicians' angle. You can tell that the magnetic record of Captain Video's Megacruise experience is going to be this Warholianly dull thing that is exactly as long as the Cruise itself. Captain Video's the only passenger besides me who I know for a fact is cruising without a relative or companion, and certain additional similarities between C.V. and me (the semi-agoraphobic reluctance to leave the ship in port, for one thing) tend to make me uncomfortable, and I try to avoid him as much as possible.

The semi-agoraphobe can also stand at Deck 12's starboard rail and look way down at the army of *Nadir* passengers being disgorged the Deck 3 gangway. They keep pouring out the door and down the narrow gangway. As each person's sandal hits the pier, a sociolinguistic transformation from *cruiser* to *tourist* is effected. At this very moment, 1300+ upscale tourists with currency to unload and experiences to experience and record compose a serpentine line stretching all the way down the Cozumel pier, which pier is poured cement and a good quarter-mile long and leads to the TOURISM CENTER,[76] a kind of mega-Quonset structure where Organized Shore Excursions[77] and cabs

---

clear plastic walls that enclose the area of Deck 11 that has the pools and Windward Cafe, facing out, i.e. out through the plastic sheeting, watching the ocean and ports like they're something on TV, and also never once visibly moving.

It seems relevant that most of the *Nadir*'s eccentrics are eccentric in *stasis:* what distinguishes them is their doing the same thing hour after hour and day after day without moving. (Captain Video is an active exception. People are surprisingly tolerant of Captain Video until the second-to-last night's Midnight Caribbean Blow-Out by the pools, when he keeps breaking into the Conga Line and trying to shift its course so that it can be recorded at better advantage; then there is a kind of bloodless but unpleasant uprising against Captain Video, and he lays low for the rest of the Cruise, possibly organizing and editing his tapes.)

[76] (its sign's in English, significantly)

[77] In Ocho Rios on Monday the big tourist-draw was apparently some sort of waterfall a whole group of *Nadir*ites could walk up inside with a guide and umbrellas to protect their cameras. In Grand Cayman yesterday the big thing was Duty-Free rum and something called Bernard Passmán Black Coral Art. Here in Cozumel it's supposedly silver jewelry hawked by hard-dickering peddlers, and more Duty-Free liquor, and a

or mopeds into San Miguel are available. The word around good old Table 64 last night was that in primitive and incredibly poor Cozumel the U.S. dollar is treated like a UFO: "They worship it when it lands."

Locals along the Cozumel pier are offering *Nadir*ites a chance to have their picture taken holding a very large iguana. Yesterday, on the Grand Cayman pier, locals had offered them the chance to have their picture taken with a guy wearing a peg-leg and hook, while off the *Nadir*'s port bow a fake pirate ship plowed back and forth across the bay all morning, firing blank broadsides and getting on everybody's nerves.

The *Nadir*'s crowds move in couples and quartets and groups and packs; the line undulates complexly. Everybody's shirt is some kind of pastel and is festooned with the cases of recording equipment, and 85% of the females have white visors and wicker purses. And everybody down below has on sunglasses with this year's fashionable accessory, a padded fluorescent cord that attaches to the glasses' arms so the glasses can hang around your neck and you can put them on and take them off a lot.[78]

Off to my right (southeast), now, another Megacruiser is moving in for docking someplace that must be pretty close to us, judging by its approach-vector. It moves like a force of nature and resists the idea that so much mass is being steered by anything like a hand on a tiller. I can't imagine what trying to maneuver one of these puppies into the pier is like. Parallel parking a semi into a spot the same size as the semi with a blindfold on and four tabs of LSD in you might come close. There's no empirical way to know: they won't even let me near the ship's Bridge, not after the *au-jus* snafu. Our docking this morning at sunrise involved an antlike frenzy of crewmen and shore personnel and an anchor[79] that spilled from the ship's navel and upward of a dozen ropes complexly

---

fabled bar in San Miguel called Carlos and Charlie's where they allegedly give you shots of something that's mostly lighter fluid.

[78] Apparently it's no longer in fashion to push the frames of the sunglasses up to where they ride just above the crown of your skull, which is what I used to see upscale sunglasses-wearers do a lot; the habit has now gone the way of tying your white Lacoste tennis sweater's arms across your chest and wearing it like a cape.

[79] The anchor is gigantic and must weigh a hundred tons, and — delightfully — it really is anchor-shaped, i.e. the same shape as anchors in tattoos.

knotted onto what look like giant railroad ties studding the pier. The crew insist on calling the ropes "lines" even though each one is at least the same diameter as a tourist's head.

I cannot convey to you the sheer and surreal scale of everything: the towering ship, the ropes, the ties, the anchor, the pier, the vast lapis lazuli dome of the sky. The Caribbean is, as ever, odorless. The floor of Deck 12 is tight-fitted planks of the same kind of corky and good-smelling wood you see in saunas.

Looking down from a great height at your countrymen waddling in expensive sandals into poverty-stricken ports is not one of the funner moments of a 7NC Luxury Cruise, however. There is something inescapably *bovine* about an American tourist in motion as part of a group. A certain greedy placidity about them. Us, rather. In port we automatically become *Peregrinator americanus, Die Lumpenamerikaner.* The Ugly Ones. For me, boviscopophobia[80] is an even stronger motive than semi-agoraphobia for staying on the ship when we're in port. It's in port that I feel most implicated, guilty by perceived association. I've barely been out of the U.S.A. before, and never as part of a high-income herd, and in port — even up here above it all on Deck 12, just watching — I'm newly and unpleasantly conscious of being an American, the same way I'm always suddenly conscious of being white every time I'm around a lot of nonwhite people. I cannot help imagining us as we appear to them, the impassive Jamaicans and Mexicans,[81] or especially to the non-Aryan preterite crew of the *Nadir.* All week I've

---

[80] (= the morbid fear of being seen as bovine)

[81] And in my head I go around and around about whether my fellow *Nadir*ites suffer the same steep self-disgust. From a height, watching them, I usually imagine that the other passengers are oblivious to the impassively contemptuous gaze of the local merchants, service people, photo-op-with-lizard vendors, etc. I usually imagine that my fellow tourists are too bovinely self-absorbed to even notice how we're looked at. At other times, though, it occurs to me that the other Americans on board quite possibly feel the same vague discomfort about their bovine-American role in port that I do, but that they refuse to let their boviscopophobia rule them: they've paid good money to have fun and be pampered and record some foreign experiences, and they'll be goddamned if they're going to let some self-indulgent twinge of neurotic projection about how their Americanness appears to malnourished locals detract from the 7NC Luxury Cruise they've worked and saved for and decided they deserve.

found myself doing everything I can to distance myself in the crew's eyes from the bovine herd I'm part of, to somehow unimplicate myself: I eschew cameras and sunglasses and pastel Caribbeanwear; I make a big deal of carrying my own cafeteria tray and am effusive in my thanks for the slightest service. Since so many of my shipmates shout, I make it a point of special pride to speak extra-quietly to crewmen whose English is poor.

At 1035h. there are just one or two small clouds in a sky so blue here it hurts. Every dawn so far in port has been overcast. Then the ascending sun gathers force and disperses the clouds somehow, and for an hour or so the sky looks shredded. Then by 0800h. an endless blue opens up like an eye and stays that way all A.M., one or two clouds always in the distance, as if for scale.

There are massed formicatory maneuvers among pier workers with ropes and walkie-talkies down there now as this other bright-white Megaship moves slowly in toward the pier from the right.

And then in the late A.M. the isolate clouds overhead start moving toward one another, and in the early P.M. they begin very slowly interlocking like jigsaw pieces, and by evening the puzzle will be solved and the sky will be the color of old dimes.[82]

But of course all this ostensibly unimplicating behavior on my part is itself motivated by a self-conscious and somewhat condescending concern about how I appear to others that is (this concern) 100% upscale American. Part of the overall despair of this Luxury Cruise is that no matter what I do I cannot escape my own essential and newly unpleasant Americanness. This despair reaches its peak in port, at the rail, looking down at what I can't help being one of. Whether up here or down there, I am an American tourist, and am thus *ex officio* large, fleshy, red, loud, coarse, condescending, self-absorbed, spoiled, appearance-conscious, ashamed, despairing, and greedy: the world's only known species of bovine carnivore.

---

[82] This dawn-and-dusk cloudiness was a pattern. In all, three of the week's days could be called substantially cloudy, and it rained a bunch of times, including all Friday in port in Key West. Again, I can see no way to blame the *Nadir* or Celebrity Cruises Inc. for this happpenstance.

Here, as in the other ports, Jet Skis buzz the *Nadir* all morning. There's about half a dozen this time. Jet Skis are the mosquitoes of Caribbean ports, annoying and irrelevant and apparently always there. Their noise is a cross between a gargle and a chain saw. I am tired of Jet Skis already and have never even been on a Jet Ski. I remember reading somewhere that Jet Skis are incredibly dangerous and accident-prone, and I take a certain unkind comfort in this as I watch blond guys with washboard stomachs and sunglasses on fluorescent cords buzz around making hieroglyphs of foam.

Instead of fake pirate ships, in Cozumel there are glass-bottom boats working the waters around the coral shadows. They move sluggishly because they're terribly overloaded with cruisers on an Organized Shore Excursion. What's neat about the sight is that everybody on the boats is looking straight down, a good 100+ people per boat — it looks prayerful somehow, and sets off the boat's driver, a local who stares dully ahead at the same nothing all drivers of all kinds of mass transport stare at.[83]

A red and orange parasail hangs dead still on the port horizon, a stick-figure dangling.

The 12-Aft Towel Guy, a spectral Czech with eyes so inset they're black from brow-shadow, stands very straight and expressionless by his cart, playing what looks like Rock-Paper-Scissors with himself. I've learned that the 12-Aft Towel Guy is immune to chatty journalistic probing — he gives me a look of what I can only call *withering neutrality* whenever I go get another towel. I am reapplying ZnO. Captain Video isn't filming now but is looking at the harbor through a square he's made of his hands. He's the type where you can tell without even looking closely that he's talking to himself. This other Megacruise ship is now docking right next to us, a procedure which apparently demands a lot of coded blasts on its world-ending horn. But maybe the single best A.M. visual in the harbor is another big organized 7NC-tourist thing: A group of *Nadir*ites is learning to snorkel in the lagoonish waters just

---

[83] A further self-esteem-lowerer is how bored all the locals look when they're dealing with U.S. tourists. We bore them. Boring somebody seems way worse than offending or disgusting him.

offshore; off the port bow I can see a good 150 solid citizens floating on their stomachs, motionless, the classic Dead Man's Float, looking like the massed and floating victims of some hideous mishap — from this height a macabre and riveting sight. I have given up looking for dorsal fins in port. It turns out that sharks, apparently being short on aesthetic sense, are never seen in pretty Caribbean ports, though a couple Jamaicans had lurid if dubious stories of barracudas that could take off a limb in one surgical drive-by. Nor in Caribbean ports is there ever any evident kelp, glasswort, algaeic scuz, or any of the sapropel the regular ocean's supposed to have. Probably sharks like murkier and scuzzier waters; potential victims could see them coming too easily down here.

Speaking of carnivores, Carnival Cruises Inc.'s good ships *Ecstasy* and *Tropicale* are both anchored all the way across the harbor. In port, Carnival Megaships tend to stay sort of at a distance from other cruise ships, and my sense is that the other ships think this is just as well. The Carnival ships have masses of 20ish-looking people hanging off the rails and seem at this distance to throb slightly, like a hi-fi's woofer. The rumors about Carnival 7NC's are legion, one such rumor being that their Cruises are kind of like floating meat-market bars and that their ships bob with a conspicuous carnal *squeakatasqueakata* at night. There's none of this kind of concupiscent behavior aboard the *Nadir*, I'm happy to say. By now I've become a kind of 7NC snob, and when Carnival or Princess are mentioned in my presence I feel my face assume Trudy and Esther's expression of classy distaste.

But so there they are, the *Ecstasy* and *Tropicale;* and now right up alongside the *Nadir* on the other side of the pier is finally docked and secured the m.v. *Dreamward,* with the peach-on-white color scheme that I think means it's owned by Norwegian Cruise Line. Its Deck 3 gangway protrudes and almost touches our Deck 3 gangway — sort of obscenely — and the *Dreamward*'s passengers, identical in all important respects to the *Nadir*'s passengers, are now streaming down the gangway and massing and moving down the pier in a kind of canyon of shadow formed by the tall walls of our two ships' hulls. The hulls hem them in and force a near-defile that stretches endlessly. A lot of the *Dreamward*'s passengers turn and crane to marvel at the size of what's just disgorged them. Captain Video, now inclined way over the starboard rail so that only the toes of his sandals are still touching deck, is filming them as they look up at us, and more than a few of the *Dreamward*ites way below lift their own camcorders and point them up our way in a kind of almost defensive or retaliatory gesture, and for just a moment they and C.V. compose a tableau that looks almost classically postmodern.

Because the *Dreamward* is lined up right next to us, almost porthole to porthole, with its Deck 12's port rail right up flush[84] against our Deck 12's starboard rail, the *Dreamward*'s semi-agoraphobic shore-shunners and I can stand at the rails and sort of check each other out in the sideways way of two muscle cars lined up at a stoplight. We can sort of see how we stack up against each other. I can see the *Dreamward*'s rail-leaners looking the *Nadir* up and down. Their faces are shiny with high-SPF sunblock. The *Dreamward* is blindingly white, white to a degree that seems somehow aggressive and makes the *Nadir*'s own white look more like buff or cream. The *Dreamward*'s snout is a little more tapered and aerodynamic-looking than our snout, and its trim is a kind of fluorescent peach, and the beach umbrellas around its Deck 11 pools[85] are also peach — our beach umbrellas are light orange, which has always seemed odd given the white-and-navy motif of the *Nadir*, and now seems to me ad hoc and shabby. The *Dreamward* has more pools on Deck 11 than we do, plus what looks like a whole other additional pool behind glass on Deck 6; and their pools' blue is that distinctive chlorine-blue — the *Nadir*'s two small pools are both seawater and kind of icky, even though the pools in the Celebrity brochure had sneakily had that electric-blue look of good old chlorine.

On all its decks, all the way down, the *Dreamward*'s cabins have little white balconies for private open-air sea-gazing. Its Deck 12 has a full-court basketball setup with color-coordinated nets and backboards as white as communion wafers. I notice that each of the myriad towel carts on the *Dreamward*'s Deck 12 is manned by its very own Towel Guy, and that their Towel Guys are ruddily Nordic and nonspectral and have nothing resembling withering neutrality or boredom about their mien.

[84] (which on scale of these ships means something around 100 m)

[85] On all 7NC Megaships, Deck 12 forms a kind of mezzanineish ellipse over Deck 11, which is always about half open-air (11 is) and always has pools surrounded by plastic/Plexiglass walls.

The point is that, standing here next to Captain Video, looking, I start to feel a covetous and almost prurient envy of the *Dreamward*. I imagine its interior to be cleaner than ours, larger, more lavishly appointed. I imagine the *Dreamward*'s food being even more varied and punctiliously prepared, the ship's Gift Shop less expensive and its casino less depressing and its stage entertainment less cheesy and its pillow mints bigger. The little private balconies outside the *Dreamward*'s cabins, in particular, seem just way superior to a porthole of bank-teller glass, and suddenly private balconies seem absolutely crucial to the whole 7NC Megaexperience I'm expected to try to convey.

I spend several minutes fantasizing about what the bathrooms might be like on the good old *Dreamward*. I imagine its crew quarters being open for anybody at all to come down and moss out and shoot the shit, and the *Dreamward*'s crew being open and genuinely friendly, with M.A.s in English and whole leatherbound and neatly printed diaries full of nautical lore and wry engaging 7NC observations. I imagine the *Dreamward*'s Hotel Manager to be an avuncular Norwegian with a rag sweater and a soothing odor of Borkum Rif about him, a guy w/o sunglasses or hauteur who throws open the pressurized doors to the *Dreamward*'s Bridge and galley and Vacuum Sewage System and personally takes me through, offering pithy and quotable answers to questions before I've even asked them. I experience a sudden rush of grievance against *Harper's* magazine for booking me on the m.v. *Nadir* instead of the *Dreamward*. I calculate by eye the breadth of the gap I'd have to jump or rappel to switch to the *Dreamward*, and I mentally sketch out the paragraphs that would detail such a bold and William T. Vollmannish bit of journalistic derring-do as literally jumping from one 7NC Megaship to another.

This saturnine line of thinking proceeds as the clouds overhead start to coalesce and the sky takes on its regular clothy P.M. weight. I am suffering here from a delusion, and I know it's a delusion, this envy of another ship, and still it's painful. It's also representative of a psychological syndrome that I notice has gotten steadily worse as the Cruise wears on, a mental list of dissatisfactions and grievances that started picayune but has quickly become nearly despair-grade. I know that the syndrome's cause is not simply the contempt bred of a week's familiarity with the poor old *Nadir*, and that the source of all the dissatisfactions isn't the *Nadir* at all but rather plain old humanly conscious me, or, more precisely, that ur-American part of me that craves and responds to pampering and passive pleasure: the Dissatisfied Infant part of me, the part that always and indiscriminately WANTS. Hence this syndrome by which, for example, just four days ago I experienced such embarrassment over the perceived self-indulgence of ordering even more gratis food from Cabin Service that I littered the bed with fake evidence of hard work and missed meals, whereas by last night I find myself looking at my watch in real annoyance after fifteen minutes and wondering where the fuck *is* that Cabin Service guy with the tray already. And by now I notice how the tray's sandwiches are kind of small, and how the wedge of dill pickle[86] always soaks into the starboard crust of the bread, and how the damn Port hallway is too narrow to really let me put the used Cabin Service tray outside 1009's door at night when I'm done eating, so that the tray sits in the cabin all night and in the A.M. adulterates the olfactory sterility of 1009 with a smell of rancid horseradish, and how this seems, by the Luxury Cruise's fifth day, deeply dissatisfying.

Death and Conroy notwithstanding, we're maybe now in a position to appreciate the lie at the dark heart of Celebrity's brochure. For this — the promise to sate the part of me that always and only WANTS — is the central fantasy the brochure is selling. The thing to notice is that the real fantasy here isn't that this promise will be kept, but that such a promise is keepable at all. This is a big one, this lie.[87] And of course I want to believe it — fuck the Buddha — I want to believe that maybe this Ultimate Fantasy Vacation will be *enough* pampering, that this time the luxury and pleasure will be so completely and faultlessly administered that my Infantile part will be sated.[88]

---

[86] (I hate dill pickles, and C.S. churlishly refuses to substitute gherkins or butter chips)

[87] It may well be *the* Big One, come to think of it.

[88] The fantasy they're selling is the whole reason why all the subjects in all the brochures' photos have facial expressions that are at once orgasmic and oddly slack: these expressions are the facial equivalent of going *"Aaaahhhhh,"* and the sound is not just that of somebody's Infantile part exulting in finally getting the total pampering it's always wanted but also that of the relief all the other parts of that person feel when the Infantile part finally *shuts up.*

But the Infantile part of me is insatiable — in fact its whole essence or *dasein* or whatever lies in its a priori insatiability. In response to any environment of extraordinary gratification and pampering, the Insatiable Infant part of me will simply adjust its desires upward until it once again levels out at its homeostasis of terrible dissatisfaction. And sure enough, on the *Nadir* itself, after a few days of delight and then adjustment, the Pamper-swaddled part of me that WANTS is now back, and with a vengeance. By Ides Wednesday I'm acutely conscious of the fact that the AC vent in my cabin hisses (*loudly*), and that though I can turn off the reggae Muzak coming out of the speaker in the cabin I cannot turn off the even louder ceiling-speaker out in the 10-Port hall. By now I notice that when Table 64's towering busboy uses his crumb-scoop to clear crumbs off the tablecloth between courses he never seems to get quite *all* the crumbs. By now the nighttime rattle of my Wondercloset's one off-plumb drawer sounds like a jackhammer. Mavourneen of the high seas or no, when Petra makes my bed not all the hospital corners are at *exactly* the same angle. My desk/vanity has a small but uncannily labial-looking hairline crack in the bevel of its top's right side, which crack I've come to hate because I can't help looking right at it when I open my eyes in bed in the morning. Most of the nightly Celebrity Showtime live entertainment in the Celebrity Show Lounge is so bad it's embarrassing, and there's a repellent hotel-art-type seascape on the aft wall of 1009 that's bolted to the wall and can't be removed or turned around, and Caswell-Massey Conditioning Shampoo turns out to be harder to rinse all the way out than most other shampoos, and the ice sculptures at the Midnight Buffet sometimes look hurriedly carved, and the vegetable that comes with my entrée is continually overcooked, and it's impossible to get really *numbingly* cold water out of 1009's bathroom tap.

I'm standing here on Deck 12 looking at a *Dreamward* that I bet has cold water that'd turn your knuckles blue, and, like Frank Conroy, part of me realizes that I haven't washed a dish or tapped my foot in line behind somebody with multiple coupons at a supermarket checkout in a week; and yet instead of feeling refreshed and renewed I'm anticipating just how totally stressful and demanding and unpleasurable regular landlocked adult life is going to be now that even just the premature removal of a towel by a sepulchral crewman seems like an assault on my basic rights, and plus now the sluggishness of the Aft elevator is an outrage, and the absence of 22.5-lb dumbbells in the Olympic Health Club's dumbbell rack is a personal affront. And now as I'm getting ready to go down to lunch I'm mentally drafting a really mordant footnote on my single biggest peeve about the *Nadir: soda-pop is not free,* not even at dinner: you have to order a Mr. Pibb from the 5☆C.R.'s maddeningly E.S.L.-hampered cocktail waitress just like it was a fucking Slippery Nipple, and then you have to sign for it right there at the table, and they *charge* you — and they don't even *have* Mr. Pibb; they foist Dr Pepper on you with a maddeningly unapologetic shrug when any *fool* knows Dr Pepper is *no substitute* for Mr. Pibb, and it's an absolute goddamned travesty, or at any rate extremely dissatisfying indeed.[89]

---

[89] This right here is not the mordant footnote projected *supra,* but the soda-pop issue bears directly on what was for me one of the true mysteries of this Cruise, viz. how Celebrity makes a profit on Luxury 7NCs. If you accept *Fielding's Worldwide Cruises 1995*'s per diem on the *Nadir* of about $275.00 a head, then you consider that the m.v. *Nadir* itself cost Celebrity Cruises $250 million to build in 1992, and that it's got 600 employees of whom at least the upper echelons have got to be making serious money (the whole Greek contingent had the unmistakable set of mouth that goes with salaries in six figures), plus simply hellacious fuel costs — plus port taxes and insurance and safety equipment and space-age navigational and communications gear and a computerized tiller and state-of-the-art maritime sewage — and then start factoring in the luxury stuff, the top-shelf decor and brass ceiling-tile, chandeliers, a good three dozen people aboard as nothing more than twice-a-week stage entertainers, plus then the professional Head Chef and the lobster and Etruscan truffles and the cornucopic fresh fruit and the imported pillow mints . . . then, even playing it very conservative, you cannot get the math to add up. There doesn't look to be any way Celebrity can be coming out ahead financially. And yet the sheer number of different Megalines offering 7NCs constitutes reliable evidence that Luxury Cruises must be very profitable indeed. Again, Celebrity's PR lady Ms. Wiessen was — notwithstanding a phone-voice that was a total pleasure to listen to — not particularly helpful with this mystery:

> The answer to their affordability, how they offer such a great product, is really based on their management. They really are in touch with all the details of what's important to the public, and they pay a lot of attention to those details.

Libation revenues provide part of the real answer, it turns out. It's a little bit like the microeconomics of movie theaters. When you hear how much of the gate they have to kick back to films' distributors, you can't figure out how theaters stay in business.

13

Every night, the 10-Port cabin steward, Petra, when she turns down your bed, leaves on your pillow — along with the day's last mint and Celebrity's printed card wishing you sweet dreams in six languages — the next day's *Nadir Daily*, a phatic little four-page ersatz newspaper printed on white vellum in a navy-blue font. The *ND* has historical nuggets on upcoming ports, pitches for Organized Shore

---

But of course you can't go just by ticket revenues, because where movie theaters really make their money is at the concession stand.

The *Nadir* sells a shitload of drinks. Full-time beverage waitresses in khaki shorts and Celebrity visors are unobtrusively everywhere — poolside, on Deck 12, at meals, entertainments, Bingo. Soda-pop is $2.00 for a very skinny glass (you don't pay cash right there; you sign for it and then they sock you with a printed Statement of Charges on the final night), and exotic cocktails like Wallbangers and Fuzzy Navels go as high as $5.50. The *Nadir* doesn't do tacky stuff like oversalt the soup or put bowls of pretzels all over the place, but a 7NC Luxury Cruise's crafted atmosphere of indulgence and endless partying — "Go on, You Deserve It" — more than conduces to freeflowing wine. (Let's not forget the cost of a fine wine w/supper, the ever-present sommeliers). Of the different passengers I asked, more than half estimated their party's total beverage tab at over $500. And if you know even a little about the beverage markups in any restaurant/bar operation, you know a lot of that $500's going to end up as net profit. Other keys to profitability: a lot of the ship's service staff's income isn't figured into the price of the Cruise ticket: you have to tip them at week's end or they're screwed (another peeve is that the Celebrity brochure neglects to mention this). And it turns out that a lot of the paid entertainment on the *Nadir* is "vended out" — agencies contract with Celebrity Cruises to supply teams like the Matrix Dancers for all the stage shows, the Electric Slide lessons, etc.

Another contracted vendor is Deck 8's Mayfair Casino, whose corporate proprietor pays a flat weekly rate plus an unspecified percentage to the *Nadir* for the privilege of sending their gorgeous dealers and four-deck shoes against passengers who've learned the rules of 21 and Caribbean Stud Poker from an "Educational Video" that plays continuously on one of the At-Sea TV's channels. I didn't spend all that much time in the Mayfair Casino — the eyes of 74-year-old Cleveland grandmothers pumping quarters into the slots of twittering machines are not much fun to spend time looking at — but I was in there long enough to see that if the *Nadir* gets even a 10% vig on the Mayfair's weekly net, then Celebrity is making a killing.

Excursions and specials in the Gift Shop, and stern stuff in boxes with malaprop-headlines like QUARANTINES ON TRANSIT OF FOOD and MISUSE OF DRUG ACTS 1972.[90]

Right now it's Thursday 16 March, 0710h., and I'm alone at the 5☆C.R.'s Early Seating Breakfast, Table 64's waiter and towering busboy hovering nearby.[91] We've rounded the final turn and are on our return trajectory toward Key West, and today is one of the week's two "At-Sea" days when shipboard activities are at their densest and most organized; and this is the day I've picked to use the *Nadir Daily* as a Baedeker as I leave Cabin 1009 for a period well in excess of half an hour and plunge headfirst into the recreational fray and keep a precise and detailed log of some really representative experiences as together now we go In Quest of Managed Fun. So everything that follows from here on out is from this day's p.&d. experiential log:

---

[90] Snippet of latter item: "All persons entering each island [?] are warned that it is a CRIMINAL OFFENSE to import or have possession of narcotics and other Controlled Drugs, including marijuana. Penalties for drug offenders are severe." Half of the Port Lecture before we hit Jamaica consisted of advice about stuff like two-timing street dealers who'll sell you a quarter-oz. of crummy pot and then trot down to a constable and collect a bounty for fingering you. Conditions in the local jails are described just enough to engage the grimmer parts of the imagination.

Celebrity Cruises' own onboard drug policy remains obscure. Although there are always a half-dozen humorless Security guys standing burlily around the *Nadir*'s gangway in port, you never get searched when you reboard. I never saw or smelled evidence of drug use on the *Nadir* — as with concupiscence, it just doesn't seem like that kind of crowd. But there must be colorful incidents in the *Nadir*'s past, because the Cruise staff became almost operatic in their cautions to us as we headed back to Fort Lauderdale on Friday, though every warning was preceded by an acknowledgment that the exhortation to flush/toss anything Controlled *surely* couldn't apply to anyone on this particular cruise. Apparently Fort Lauderdale's Customs guys regard homebound 7NC passengers sort of the way small-town cops regard out-of-state speeders in Saab Turbos. An old veteran of many 7NCLCs told one of the U. Texas kids ahead of me in the Customs line the last day "Kiddo, if one of those dogs stops at your bag, you better hope he lifts his leg."

[91] It's a total mystery when these waiters sleep. They serve at the Midnight Buffet every night, and then help clean up after, and then they appear in the 5☆C.R. in clean tuxes all over again at 0630h. the next day, always so fresh and alert they look slapped.

0645h.: A triple ding from the speakers in cabin and halls and then a cool female voice says Good Morning, the date, the weather, etc. She says it in a gentle accented English, repeats it in an Alsatian-sounding French, then again in German. She can make even German sound lush and postcoital. Hers is not the same PA voice as at Pier 21, but it's got the exact same quality of sounding the way expensive perfume smells.

0650–0705h.: Shower, play with Alisco Sirocco hairdryer & exhaust fan & hair in bathroom mirror, read from *Daily Meditations for the Semiphobically Challenged*, go over *Nadir Daily* with yellow HiLiter pen.

0708–0730h.: E.S. Breakfast at Table 64 in 5☆C.R. Last night everybody announced intentions to sleep through breakfast and grab some scones or something at the Windsurf Cafe later. So I'm alone at Table 64, which is large and round and right up next to a starboard window.

Table 64's waiter's name is, as mentioned before, Tibor. Mentally I refer to him as "The Tibster," but never out loud. Tibor has dismantled my artichokes and my lobsters and taught me that extra-well-done is not the only way meat can be palatable. We have sort of bonded, I feel. He is 35 and about 5'4" and plump, and his movements have the birdlike economy characteristic of small plump graceful men. Menu-wise, Tibor advises and recommends, but without the hauteur that's always made me hate the gastropedantic waiters in classy restaurants. Tibor is omnipresent without being unctuous or oppressive; he is kind and warm and fun. I sort of love him. His hometown is Budapest and he has a postgraduate degree in Restaurant Management from an unpronounceable Hungarian college. His wife back home is expecting their first child. He is the Head Waiter for Tables 64–67 at all three meals. He can carry three trays w/o precarity and never looks harried or on-the-edge the way most multitable waiters look. He seems like he cares. His face is at once round and pointy, and rosy. His tux never wrinkles. His hands are soft and pink, and his thumb-joint's skin is unwrinkled, like the thumb-joint of a small child.

Tibor's cuteness has been compared by the women at Table 64 to that of a button. But I have learned not to let his cuteness fool me. Tibor is a pro. His commitment to personally instantiating the *Nadir*'s fanatical commitment to excellence is the one thing about which he shows no sense of humor. If you fuck with him in this area he will feel pain and will make no effort to conceal it. See for example the second night, Sunday, at supper: Tibor was circling the table and asking each of us how our entrée was, and we all regarded this as just one of those perfunctory waiter-questions and all perfunctorily smiled and cleared our mouths and said Fine, Fine — and Tibor finally stopped and looked down at us all with a pained expression and changed his timbre slightly so it was clear he was addressing the whole table: "Please. I ask each: is excellent? Please. If excellent, you say, and I am happy. If not excellent, please: do not say excellent. Let me fix. Please." There was no hauteur or pedantry as he addressed us. He just meant what he said. His expression was babe-naked, and we heard him, and nothing was perfunctory again.

Good old Wojtek, the towering bespectacled Pole, age 22 and at least 6'8", Table 64's busboy — in charge of water, bread supply, crumb-removal, and using a big tower of a mill to put pepper on pretty much anything you don't lean forward and cover with your upper body — good old Wojtek works exclusively with Tibor, and they have an involved minuet of service that's choreographed down to the last pivot, and they speak quietly to each other in a Slavicized German pidgin you can tell they've evolved through countless quiet professional exchanges; and you can tell Wojtek reveres Tibor as much as the rest of us do.

This morning The Tibster wears a red bow tie and smells faintly of sandalwood. Early Seating Breakfast is the best time to be around him, because he's not very busy and can be initiated into chitchat without looking pained at neglecting his duties. He doesn't know I'm on the *Nadir* as a pseudojournalist. I'm not sure why I haven't told him — somehow I think it might make things hard for him. During E.S.B. chitchat I never ask him anything about Celebrity Cruises or the *Nadir*,[92] not out of deference to Mr. Dermatitis's pissy injunctions but because I feel like I'd just about die if Tibor got into trouble on my account.

---

[92]   (except for precise descriptions of whatever dorsal fins he's seen)

Tibor's ambition is someday to return to Budapest[93] for good and with his *Nadir*-savings open a sort of newspaper-and-beret-type sidewalk cafe that specializes in something called Cherry Soup. With this in mind, two days from now in Ft. Lauderdale I'm going to tip The Tibster way, way more than the suggested $3.00 U.S./diem,[94] balancing out total expenses by radically undertipping both the liplessly sinister maître d' and our sommelier, an unctuously creepy Ceylonese guy the whole table has christened The Velvet Vulture.

0815h.: Catholic Mass is celebrated with Father DeSandre, Location: Rainbow Room, Deck 8.[95]

There's no chapel per se on the *Nadir*. The Father sets up a kind of folding credence table in the Rainbow Room, the most aftward of the Fantasy Deck lounges, done in salmon and sere yellow with dados of polished bronze. Genuflecting at sea turns out to be a tricky business. There are about a dozen people here. The Father's backlit by a big port window, and his homily is mercifully free of nautical puns or references to life being a voyage. The communal beverage is a choice of either wine or Welch's-brand unsweetened grape juice. Even the *Nadir*'s daily mass's communion wafers are unusually yummy, biscuitier than your normal host and with a sweet tinge to the pulp it becomes in your teeth.[96] Cynical observations about how appropriate it is that a 7NC Luxury Cruise's daily worship is held in an overdecorated bar seem too easy to take up space on. Just how a diocesan priest gets a 7NC Megacruiser as a parish — whether Celebrity maybe has clerics on retainer, sort of like the army, and they get assigned to different ships in rotation, and whether the R.C. Church gets paid just like the other vendors who provide

[93] (he pronounces the "-pest" part of this "-persht")

[94] The last night's *ND* breaks the news about tipping and gives tactful "suggestions" on going rates.

[95] All boldface stuff is verbatim and *sic* from today's *Nadir Daily*.

[96] If Pepperidge Farm made communion wafers, these would be them.

service and entertainment personnel, etc. — will I'm afraid be forever unclear: Father DeSandre explains he has no time after the recessional for professional queries, because of

0900h.: **Wedding Vow Renewal with Father DeSandre.** Same venue, same porta-altar setup. No married couples show up to renew their wedding vows, though. There's me and Captain Video and maybe a dozen other *Nadir*ites sitting around in salmon chairs, and a beverage waitress makes a couple circuits with her visor and pad, and Father DeS. stands patiently in his cassock and white cope till 0920, but no older-type couples appear or step forward to renew. A few of the people in the R.R. sit in proximities and attitudes that show they're couples, but they sort of apologetically tell the Father they're not even married; the surprisingly cool and laid back Father DeS.'s invitation to make use of the setup and twin candles and priest w/ sacramentary *Book of Rites* opened to just the right page produces some shy laughter from the couples, but no takers. I don't know what to make of the W.V.R.'s no-shows in terms of death/despair/pampering/insatiability issues.

0930h.: **The Library is open for check-out of games, cards, and books, Location: Library,[97] Deck 7.**
    The *Nadir*'s Library is a little glassed-in salon set obliquely off Deck 7's Rendez-Vous Lounge. The Library's all good wood and leather and three-way lamping, an extremely pleasant place, but it's open only at weird and inconvenient times. Only one wall is even shelved, and most of the books are the sorts of books you see on the coffeetables of older people who live in condominiums near unchallenging golf courses: folio-sized, color-plated, with titles like *Great Villas of Italy* and *Famous Tea Sets of the Modern World,* etc. But it's a great place to just hang around and moss out, the Library. Plus this is where the chess sets are. This week also features an unbelievably large and involved jigsaw puzzle that sits about half-done on an oak table in

[97] Duh.

the corner, which all sorts of different old people come in and work on in shifts. There's also a seemingly endless game of contract bridge always going on in the Card Room right next door, and the bridge players' motionless silhouettes are always there through the frosted glass between Library and C.R. when I'm mossing out and playing with the chess sets.

The *Nadir*'s Library's got cheapo Parker Brothers chess sets with hollow plastic pieces, which any good chess player has got to like.[98] I'm not nearly as good at chess as I am at Ping-Pong, but I'm pretty good. Most of the time on the *Nadir* I play chess with myself (not as dull as it may sound), for I have determined that — no offense — the sorts of people who go on 7NC Megacruises tend not to be very good chess players.

Today, however, is the day I am mated in 23 moves by a nine-year-old girl. Let's not spend a lot of time on this. The girl's name is Deirdre. She's one of very few little kids on board not tucked out of sight in Deck 4's Daycare Grotto.[99] Deirdre's mom never leaves her in the Grotto but also never leaves her side, and has the lipless and flinty-eyed look of a parent whose kid is preternaturally good at something.

I probably should have seen this and certain other signs of impending humiliation as the kid first comes over as I'm sitting there trying a scenario where both sides of the board deploy a Queen's Indian and tugs on my sleeve and asks if I'd maybe like to play. She really does tug on my sleeve, and calls me Mister, and her eyes are roughly the size of sandwich plates. In retrospect it occurs to me that this girl was a little *tall* for nine, and worn-looking, slump-shouldered, the way usually only much older girls get — a kind of poor psychic posture. However good she may be at chess, this is not a happy little girl. I don't suppose that's germane.

---

[98] Heavy expensive art-carved sets are for dorks.

[99] This is something else Mr. Dermatitis declined to let me see, but by all reports the daycare on these Megaships is phenomenal, w/squads of nurturing and hyperkinetic young daycare ladies keeping the kids manically stimulated for up to ten-hour stretches via an endless number of incredibly well-structured activities, so tuckering the kids out that they collapse mutely into bed at 2000h. and leave their parents free to plunge into the ship's nightlife and Do It All.

Deirdre pulls up a chair and says she usually likes to be black and informs me that in lots of cultures black isn't thanatotic or morbid but is the spiritual equivalent of what white is in the U.S. and that in these other cultures it's *white* that's morbid. I tell her I already know all that. We start. I push some pawns and Deirdre develops a knight. Deirdre's mom watches the whole game from a standing position behind the kid's seat,[100] motionless except for her eyes. I know within seconds that I despise this mom. She's like some kind of stage-mother of chess. Deirdre seems like an OK type, though — I've played precocious kids before, and at least Deirdre doesn't hoot or smirk. If anything, she seems a little sad that I don't turn out to be more of a stretch for her.

My first inkling of trouble is on the fourth move, when I fianchetto and Deirdre knows what I'm doing is fianchettoing and uses the term correctly, again calling me Mister. The second ominous clue is the way her little hand keeps flailing out to the side of the board after she moves, a sign that she's used to a speed clock. She swoops in with her developed QK and forks my queen on the twelfth move and after that it's only a matter of time. It doesn't really matter. I didn't even *start* playing chess until my late twenties. On move 17 three desperately old and related-looking people at the jigsaw puzzle table kind of totter over and watch as I hang my rook and the serious carnage starts. It doesn't really matter. Neither Deirdre nor the hideous mom smiles when it's over; I smile enough for everybody. None of us says anything about maybe playing again tomorrow.

0945–1000h.: Back briefly for psychic recharging in good old 1009E.P., I eat four pieces of some type of fruit that's like a tiny oversweetened tangerine and watch, for the fifth time this week, the Velociraptors-stalk-precocious-children-in-gleaming-institutional-kitchen part of *Jurassic Park*, noting an unprecedented sympathy for the Velociraptors this time around.

---

[100] The only chairs in the Library are leather wing chairs with low seats, so only Deirdre's eyes and nose clear the board's table as she sits across from me, adding a Kilroyishly surreal quality to the humiliation.

1000–1100h.: Three simultaneous venues of Managed Fun, all aft on Deck 9: **Darts Tournament, take aim and hit the bull's-eye!; Shuffleboard Shuffle, join your fellow guests for a morning game; Ping Pong Tournament, meet the Cruise Staff at the tables, Prizes to the Winners!**

Organized shuffleboard has always filled me with dread. Everything about it suggests infirm senescence and death: it's like it's a game played on the skin of a void and the rasp of the sliding puck is the sound of that skin getting abraded away bit by bit. I also have a morbid but wholly justified fear of darts, stemming from a childhood trauma too involved and hair-raising to discuss here, and as an adult I avoid darts like cholera.

What I'm here for is the Ping-Pong. I am an exceptionally good Ping-Pong player. The *ND*'s use of "Tournament" is euphemistic, though, because there are never any draw sheets or trophies in sight, and no other *Nadir*ites are ever playing. The constant high winds on 9-Aft may account for Ping-Pong's light turnout. Today three tables are set up (well off to the side of the Darts Tournament, which given the level of darts-play over there seems judicious), and the m.v. *Nadir*'s very own Ping-Pong Pro (or "3P," as he calls himself) stands cockily by the center table, amusing himself by bouncing a ball off the paddle between his legs and behind his back. He turns when I crack my knuckles. I've come to Ping-Pong three different times already this week, and nobody's ever here except the good old 3P, whose real first name is Winston. He and I are now at the point where we greet each other with the curt nods of old and mutually respected foes.

Below the center table is an enormous box of fresh Ping-Pong balls, and apparently several more of these boxes are in the storage locker behind the Golf-Drive Net, which again seems judicious given the number of balls in each game that get smashed or blown out to sea.[101] They also have a big peg-studded board on the bulkhead's wall with over a dozen different paddles, both the plain-wooden-grip-and-head-

---

[101] I imagine it would be pretty interesting to trail a Megaship through a 7NC Cruise and just catalogue the trail of stuff that bobs in its wake.

with-thin-skin-of-cheap-pebbly-rubber kind and the fancy-wrapped-grip-and-head-with-thick-mushy-skin-of-unpebbled-rubber kind, all in Celebrity's snazzy white/navy motif.[102]

I am, as I believe I may already have stated, an extraordinarily fine Ping-Pong player,[103] and it turns out that I am an even finer Ping-Pong player outdoors in tricky tropical winds; and, although Winston is certainly a good enough player to qualify as a 3P on a ship where interest in Ping-Pong is shall we say less than keen, my record against him thus far is eight wins and only one loss, with that one loss being not only a very close loss but also consequent to a number of freakish gusts and a net that Winston himself admitted later may not have been regulation I.T.T.F. height and tension. Winston is under the curious (and false) impression that we've got some kind of tacit wager going on whereby if the 3P ever beats me three games out of five he gets my full-color Spiderman hat, which hat he covets and which hat I wouldn't dream ever of playing serious Ping-Pong without.

Winston only moonlights as a 3P. His primary duty on the *Nadir* is serving as Official Cruise Deejay in Deck 8's Scorpio Disco, where every night he stands behind an incredible array of equipment wearing hornrim sunglasses and working both the CD player and the strobes frantically till well after 0200h., which may account for a sluggish and slightly dazed quality to his A.M. Ping-Pong. He is 26 years old and, like much of the *Nadir*'s Cruise and Guest Relations staff, is good-looking in the vaguely unreal way soap opera actors and models in Sears catalogues are good-looking. He has big brown Help-Me eyes and a black fade that's styled into the exact shape of a nineteenth-century blacksmith's anvil, and he plays Ping-Pong with his thick-skinned paddle's head down in the chopsticky way of people who've received professional instruction.

---

[102] Only the fear of an impromptu Fort Lauderdale Customs search and discovery keeps me from stealing one of these paddles. I confess that I did end up stealing the chamois eyeglass-cleaners from 1009's bathroom, though maybe you're meant to take those home anyway — I couldn't tell whether they fell into the Kleenex category or the towel category.

[103] I've sure never lost to any prepubescent females in fucking *Ping-Pong,* I can tell you.

Outside and aft, the *Nadir*'s engines' throb is loud and always sounds weirdly lopsided. 3P Winston and I have both reached that level of almost Zen-like Ping-Pong mastery where the game kind of plays us — the lunges and pirouettes and smashes and recoveries are automatic outer instantiations of a kind of intuitive harmony between hand and eye and primal Urge To Kill — in a way that leaves our forebrains unoccupied and capable of idle chitchat as we play:

"Wicked hat. I want that hat. Boss hat."

"Can't have it."

"Wicked motherfucking hat. Spiderman be dope."[104]

"Sentimental value. Long story behind this hat."

Insipidness notwithstanding, I've probably exchanged more total words with 3P Winston on this 7NC Luxury Cruise than I have with anybody else.[105] As with good old Tibor, I don't probe Winston in any serious journalistic way, although in this case it's not so much because I fear getting the 3P in trouble as because (nothing against good old Winston personally) he's not exactly the brightest bulb in the ship's intellectual chandelier, if you get my drift. E.g. Winston's favorite witticism when deejaying in the Scorpio Disco is to muff or spoonerize some simple expression and then laugh and slap himself in the head and go "Easy for me to say!" According to Mona and Alice, he's also unpopular with the younger crowd at the Scorpio Disco because he always wants to play Top-40ish homogenized rap instead of real vintage disco.[106]

It's also not necessary to ask Winston much of anything at all, because

---

[104] Winston also sometimes seemed to suffer from the verbal delusion that he was an urban black male; I have no idea what the story is on this or what conclusions to draw from it.

[105] This is not counting my interfaces with Petra, which though lengthy and verbose tended of course to be one-sided except for "You are a funny thing, you."

[106] The single most confounding thing about the young and hip cruisers on the *Nadir* is that they seem truly to love the exact same cheesy disco music that we who were young and hip in the late '70s loathed and made fun of, boycotting Prom when Donna Summer's "MacArthur Park" was chosen Official Prom Theme, etc.

he's an incredible chatterbox when he's losing. He's been a student at the U. of South Florida for a rather mysterious seven years, and has taken this year off to "get fucking *paid* for a change for a while" on the *Nadir*. He claims to have seen all manner of sharks in these waters, but his descriptions don't inspire much real confidence or dread. We're in the middle of our second game and on our fifth ball. Winston says he's had the chance to do some serious ocean-gazing and soul-searching during his off hours these last few months and has decided to return to U.S.F. in Fall '95 and start college more or less all over, this time majoring not in Business Administration but in something he claims is called "Multimediated Production."

"They have a department in that?"

"It's this interdisciplinarian thing. It's going to be fucking *phat*, Homes. You know. CD-ROM and shit. Smart chips. Digital film and shit."

I'm up 18–12. "Sport of the future."

Winston agrees. "It's where it's all going to be at. The Highway. Interactive TV and shit. Virtual Reality. *Interactive* Virtual Reality."

"I can see it now," I say. The game's almost over. "The Cruise of the Future. The *Home Cruise*. The Caribbean Luxury Cruise you don't have to leave home for. Strap on the old goggles and electrodes and off you go."

"Word up."

"No passports. No seasickness. No wind or sunburn or insipid Cruise staff.[107] Total Virtual Motionless Stay-At-Home Simulated Pampering."

"Word."

---

[107] Interfacing with Winston could be kind of depressing in that the urge to make cruel sport of him was always irresistible, and he never acted offended or even indicated he knew he was being made sport of, and you went away afterward feeling like you'd just stolen coins from a blind man's cup or something.

1105h.: **Navigation Lecture — Join Captain Nico and learn about the ship's Engine Room, the Bridge, and the basic "nuts 'n bolts" of the ship's operation!**

The m.v. *Nadir* can carry 460,000 gallons of nautical-grade diesel fuel. It burns between 40 and 70 tons of this fuel a day, depending on how hard it's travelling. The ship has two turbine engines on each side, one big "Papa" and one (comparatively) little "Son."[108] Each engine has a propeller that's 17 feet in diameter and is adjustable through a lateral rotation of 23.5° for maximum torque. It takes the *Nadir* 0.9 nautical miles to come to a complete stop from its standard speed of 18 knots. The ship can go slightly faster in certain kinds of rough seas than it can go in calm seas — this is for technical reasons that won't fit on the napkin I'm taking notes on. The ship has a rudder, and the rudder has two complex alloy "flaps" that somehow interconfigure to allow a 90° turn. Captain Nico's[109] English is not going to win any elocution ribbons, but he is a veritable blowhole of hard data. He's about my age and height but is just ridiculously good-looking,[110] like an extremely fit and tan Paul Auster. The venue here is Deck 11's Fleet Bar,[111] all blue and white and trimmed

---

[108] Choosing from among 2^4 options, they can run on all four, or one Papa and one Son, or two Sons, etc. My sense is that running on Sons instead of Papas is kind of like switching from warp drive to impulse power.

[109] The *Nadir* has a Captain, a Staff Captain, and four Chief Officers. Captain Nico is actually one of these Chief Officers; I do not know why he's called Captain Nico.

[110] Something else I've learned on this Luxury Cruise is that no man can ever look any better than he looks in the white full-dress uniform of a naval officer. Women of all ages and estrogen-levels swooned, sighed, wobbled, lash-batted, growled, and hubba'd when one of these navally resplendent Greek officers went by, a phenomenon that I don't imagine helped the Greeks' humility one bit.

[111] The Fleet Bar was also the site of **Elegant Tea Time** later that same day, where elderly female passengers wore long white stripper-gloves and pinkies protruded from cups, and where among my breaches of **Elegant Tea Time** etiquette apparently were: (a) imagining people would be amused by the tuxedo-design T-shirt I wore because I hadn't taken seriously the Celebrity brochure's instruction to bring a real tux on the Cruise; (b) imagining the elderly ladies at my table would be charmed by the off-color

in stainless steel, and so abundantly fenestrated that the sunlight makes Captain Nico's illustrative slides look ghostly and vague. Captain Nico wears Ray-Bans but w/o a fluorescent cord. Thursday 16 March is also the day my paranoia about Mr. Dermatitis's contriving somehow to jettison me from the *Nadir* via Cabin 1009's vacuum toilet is at its emotional zenith, and I've decided in advance to keep a real low journalistic profile at this event. I ask a total of just one little innocuous question, right at the start, and Captain Nico responds with a witticism —

"How do we start engines? Not with the key of ignition, I can tell you!"

— that gets a large and rather unkind laugh from the crowd.

It turns out that the long-mysterious "m.v." in "m.v. *Nadir*" stands for "motorized vessel." The m.v. *Nadir* cost $250,310,000 U.S. to build. It was christened in Papenburg FRG in 10/92 with a bottle of ouzo instead of champagne. The *Nadir*'s three onboard generators produce 9.9 megawatts of power. The ship's Bridge turns out to be what lies behind the very intriguing triple-locked bulkhead near the aft towel cart on Deck 11. The Bridge is "where the equipments are — radars, indication of weathers and all these things."

Rorschach jokes I made about the rather obscene shapes the linen napkins at each place were origami-folded into; (c) imagining these same ladies might be interested to learn what sorts of things have to be done to a goose over its lifetime in order to produce pâté-grade liver; (d) putting a 3-ounce mass of what looked like glossy black buckshot on a big white cracker and then putting the whole cracker in my mouth; (e) assuming one second thereafter a facial expression I'm told was, under even the most charitable interpretation, inelegant; (f) trying to respond with a full mouth when an elderly lady across the table with a pince-nez and buff-colored gloves and lipstick on her right incisor told me this was Beluga caviar, resulting in (f(1)) the expulsion of several crumbs and what appeared to be a large black bubble and (f(2)) the distorted production of a word that I was told sounded to the entire table like a genital expletive; (g) trying to spit the whole indescribable nauseous glob into a flimsy *paper* napkin instead of one of the plentiful and sturdier *linen* napkins, with results I'd prefer not to describe in any more detail than as *unfortunate;* and (h) concurring, when the little kid (in a bow tie and [no kidding] *tuxedo-shorts*) seated next to me pronounced Beluga caviar "blucky," with a spontaneous and unconsidered expression that was, indeed and unmistakably, a genital expletive.

Let us draw the curtain of charity over the rest of that particular bit of Managed Fun. This will, at any rate, explain the 1600h.–1700h. lacuna in today's p.&d. log.

Two years of sedulous postgraduate study is required of officer-wannabes just to get a handle on the navigational math involved; "also there is much learning for the computers."

Of the 40 or so *Nadir*ites at this lecture, the total number of women is: 0. Captain Video is here, of course, Celebrating the Moment from a camcorded crouch on the Fleet Bar's steel bartop; he's wearing a nylon warm-up suit of fluorescent maroon and purple that makes him look like a huge macaw, and his knees crackle whenever he shifts position and rehunches. By this time Captain Video's really getting on my nerves.

A deeply sunburned man next to me is taking notes with a Mont Blanc pen in a leatherbound notebook with ENGLER embossed on it.[112] Just one moment of foresight on the way from Ping-Pong to Fleet Bar would have prevented my sitting here trying to take notes on paper napkins with a big felt-tip HiLiter. The *Nadir*'s officers have their quarters, mess, and a private bar on Deck 3, it turns out. "In the Bridge also we have different compass to see where we are going." The ship's four patro-filial turbines cannot ever be turned off except in drydock. What they do to deactivate an engine is simply disengage its propeller. It turns out that parallel parking a semi on LSD doesn't even come close to what Captain G. Panagiotakis experiences when he docks the m.v. *Nadir*. The Engler man next to me is drinking a $5.50 Slippery Nipple, which comes with not one but two umbrellas in it. The rest of the *Nadir*'s crew's quarters are on Deck 2, which also houses the ship's laundry and "the areas of processing of garbage and wastes." Like all Megacruisers, the *Nadir* needs no tugboat in port; this is because it's got "the sternal thrusters and bow thrusters."[113]

The lecture's audience consists of bald solid thick-wristed men over 50 who all look like the kind of guy who rises to CEO a company

---

[112] All week the Englerites have been a fascinating subcultural study in their own right — moving only in herds and having their own special Organized Shore Excursions and constantly reserving big party-rooms with velveteen ropes and burly guys standing by them with their arms crossed checking credentials — but there hasn't been room in this essay to go into any serious Englerology.

[113] (not — mercifully — "bowal thrusters")

out of that company's engineering dept. instead of some fancy MBA program.[114] A number of them are clearly Navy veterans or yachtsmen or something. They all compose a very knowledgeable audience and ask involved questions about the bore and stroke of the engines, the management of multiradial torque, the precise distinctions between a C-Class Captain and a B-Class Captain. My attempts at technical notes are bleeding out into the paper napkins until the yellow letters are all ballooned and goofy like subway graffiti. The male 7NC cruisers all want to know stuff about the hydrodynamics of midship stabilizers. They're all the kind of men who look like they're smoking cigars even when they're not smoking cigars. Everybody's complexion is hectic from sun and salt spray and a surfeit of Slippery Nipples. 21.4 knots is a 7NC Megaship's maximum possible cruising speed. There's no way I'm going to raise my hand in this kind of crowd and ask what a knot is.

Several unreproduceable questions concern the ship's system of satellite navigation. Captain Nico explains that the *Nadir* subscribes to something called GPS: "This Global Positioning System is using the satellites above to know the position at all times, which gives this data to the computer." It emerges that when we're not negotiating ports and piers, a kind of computerized Autocaptain pilots the ship.[115] There's no actual "tiller" or "con" anymore, is the sense I get; there's certainly no protrusive-spoked wooden captain's wheel like these that line the walls

---

[114] In other words, the self-made brass-balled no-bullshit type of older U.S. male whom you least want the dad to turn out to be when you go over to a girl's house to take her to a movie or something with dishonorable intentions rattling around in the back of your mind — an ur-authority figure.

[115] This helps explain why Captain G. Panagiotakis usually seems so phenomenally unbusy, why his real job seems to be to stand in various parts of the *Nadir* and try to look vaguely presidential, which he would (look presidential) except for the business of wearing sunglasses inside,[115a] which makes him look more like a Third World strongman.

> [115a] All the ship's officers wore sunglasses inside, it turned out, and al-
> ways stood off to the side of everything with their hands behind their
> backs, usually in groups of three, conferring hieratically in technical
> Greek.

of the jaunty Fleet Bar, each captain's wheel centered with thole pins that hold up a small and verdant fern.

1150h.: There's never a chance to feel actual physical hunger on a Luxury Cruise, but when you've gotten accustomed to feeding seven or eight times a day, a certain foamy emptiness in the gut always lets you know when it's time to feed again.

Among the *Nadir*ites, only the radically old and formalphiliacal hit Luncheon at the 5☆C.R., where you can't wear swim trunks or a floppy hat. The really happening place for lunch is the buffet at the Windsurf Cafe off the pools and plasticene grotto on Deck 11. Just inside both sets of the Windsurf's automatic doors, in two big bins whose sides are decorated to look like coconut skin, are cornucopiae of fresh fruit[116] presided over by ice sculptures of a madonna and a whale. The crowds' flow is skillfully directed along several different vectors so that delays are minimal, and the experience of waiting to feed in the Windsurf Cafe is not as bovine as lots of other 7NC experiences.

Eating in the Windsurf Cafe, where things are out in the open and not brought in from behind a mysterious swinging door, makes it even clearer that everything ingestible on the *Nadir* is designed to be absolutely top-of-the-line: the tea isn't Lipton but *Sir Thomas Lipton* in a classy individual vacuum packet of buff-colored foil; the lunch meat is the really good fat- and gristle-free kind that gentiles usually have to crash kosher delis to get; the mustard is something even fancier-tasting than Grey Poupon that I keep forgetting to write down the brand of. And the Windsurf Cafe's coffee — which burbles merrily from spigots in big brushed-steel dispensers — the coffee is, quite simply, the kind of coffee you marry somebody for being able to make. I normally have a firm and neurologically imperative one-cup limit on coffee, but the Windsurf's coffee is so good,[117] and the job of deciphering the big

---

[116] As God is my witness no more fruit ever again in my whole life.

[117] And it's just coffee qua coffee — it's not Blue Mountain Hazlenut Half-Caf or Sudanese Vanilla With Special Chicory Enzymes or any of that bushwa. The *Nadir*'s is a level-headed approach to coffee that I hereby salute.

yellow Rorschachian blobs of my Navigation Lecture notes so taxing, that on this day I exceed my limit, by rather a lot, which may help explain why the next few hours of this log get kind of kaleidoscopic and unfocused.

1240h.: I seem to be out on 9-Aft hitting golf balls off an Astroturf square into a dense-mesh nylon net that balloons impressively out toward the sea when a golf ball hits it. Thanatotic shuffleboard continues over to starboard; no sign of 3P or any Ping-Pong players or any paddles left behind; ominous little holes in deck, bulkhead, railing, and even the Astroturf square testify to my wisdom in having steered way clear of the A.M. Darts Tourney.

1314h.: I am now seated back in Deck 8's Rainbow Room watching "Ernst," the *Nadir*'s mysterious and ubiquitous Art Auctioneer,[118] mediate spirited bidding for a signed Leroy Neiman print. Let me iterate this. Bidding is spirited and fast approaching four figures for a signed Leroy Neiman print — not a signed Leroy Neiman, a signed Leroy Neiman *print*.

1330h.: Poolside Shenanigans! Join Cruise Director Scott Peterson and Staff for some crazy antics and the Men's Best Legs Contest judged by all the ladies at poolside!
    Starting to feel the first unpleasant symptoms of caffeine toxicity, hair tucked at staff suggestion into a complimentary Celebrity Cruises swimcap, I take full and active part in the prenominate Shenanigans, which consist mostly of a tourney-style contest where gals in the Gal division and then guys in the Guy division have to slide out on a

---

[118] One of very few human beings I've ever seen who is both blond and murine-looking, Ernst today is wearing white loafers, green slacks, and a flared sportcoat whose pink I swear can be described only as menstrual.

plastic telephone pole slathered with Vaseline[119] and face off against another gal/guy and try to knock each other off the pole and into the pool's nauseous brine by hitting each other with pillowcases filled with balloons. I make it through two rounds and then am knocked off by a hulking and hairy-shouldered Milwaukee newlywed who actually *hits me with his fist* — which as people start to lose their balance and compensate by leaning far forward[120] can happen — knocking my swimcap almost clear off my head and toppling me over hard to starboard into a pool that's not only got a really high Na-content but is also now covered with a shiny and full-spectrum scum of Vaseline, and I emerge so icky and befouled and cross-eyed from the guy's right hook that I blow what should have been a very legitimate shot at the title in the Men's Best Legs Contest, in which I end up placing third but am told later I would have won the whole thing except for the scowl, swollen and strabismic left eye, and askew swimcap that formed a contextual backdrop too downright goofy to let the full force of my gams' shapeliness come through to the judges.

1410h.: I seem now to be at the daily Arts & Crafts seminar in some sort of back room of the Windsurf Cafe, and aside from noting that I seem to be the only male here under 70 and that the project under construction on the table before me involves Popsicle sticks and crepe and a type of glue too runny and instant-adhesive to get my trembling overcaffeinated hands anywhere near, I have absolutely no fucking idea what's going on. 1415h.: In the public loo off the elevators on Deck 11-Fore, which has four urinals and three commodes, all Vacuum-Suction, which if activated one after the other in rapid succession produce a cumulative sound that is exactly like the climactic D^b-$G^\#$ melisma

---

[119] (the pole)

[120] This is what I did, leaned too far forward and into the guy's fist that was clutching the hem of his pillowcase, which is why I didn't cry Foul, even though the vision in my right eye still drifts in and out of focus even back here on land a week later.

at the end of the 1983 Vienna Boys Choir's seminal recording of the medievally lugubrious *Tenebrae Factae Sunt.* 1420h.: And now I'm in Deck 12's Olympic Health Club, in the back area, the part that's owned by Steiner of London,[121] where the same creamy-faced French women who'd worked 3/11's crowd at Pier 21 now all hang out, and I'm asking to be allowed to watch one of the "Phytomer/Ionithermie Combination Treatment De-Toxifying Inch Loss Treatments"[122] that some of the heftier ladies on board have been raving about, and I am being told that it's not really a spectator-type thing, that there's nakedness involved, and that if I want to see a P./I.C.T.D.-T.I.L.T. it's going to have to be as the subject of one; and between the quoted price of the treatment and the sensuous recall of the smell of my own singed nostril-hair in Chem. 205 in 1983, I opt to forfeit this bit of managed pampering. If you back off from something really big, the creamy ladies then try to sell you on a facial, which they say "a great large number" of male *Nadir*ites have pampered themselves with this week, but I also decline the facial, figuring that at this point in the week the procedure for me would consist mostly in exfoliating half-peeled skin. 1425h.: Now I'm in the small public loo of the Olympic Health Club, a one-holer notable only

---

[121] (also in the *ND* known as Steiner Salons and Spas at Sea)

[122] So you can see why nobody with a nervous system would want to miss watching one of these, some hard data from the Steiner brochure:

> **IONITHERMIE — HOW DOES IT WORK?** Firstly you will be measured in selected areas. The skin is marked and the readings are recorded on your program. Different creams, gels and ampoules are applied. These contain extracts effective in breaking down and emulsifying fat. Electrodes using faradism and galvanism are placed in position and a warm blue clay covers the full area. We are now ready to start your treatment. The galvanism accelerates the products into your skin, and the faradism exercises your muscles.[122a] The cellulite or 'lumpy fat,' which is so common amongst women, is emulsified by the treatment, making it easier to drain the toxins from the body and disperse them, giving your skin a smoother appearance.

> > [122a] And, as somebody who once brushed up against a college chemistry lab's live induction coil and had subsequently to be pried off the thing with a wooden mop handle, I can personally vouch for the convulsive-exercise benefit of faradic current.

because O. Newton-John's "Let's Get Physical" plays on an apparently unending loop out of the overhead speaker. I'll go ahead and admit that I have, this week, come in a couple times between UV bombardments and pumped a little iron here in the *Nadir*'s Olympic Health Club. Except in the O.H.C. it's more like pumping ultrarefined titanium alloy: all the weights are polished stainless steel, and the place is one of these clubs with mirrors on all four walls that force you into displays of public self-scrutiny that are as excruciating as they are irresistible, and there are huge and insectile-looking pieces of machinery that mimic the aerobic demands of staircases and rowboats and racing bikes and improperly waxed cross-country skies, etc., complete with heart-monitor electrodes and radio headphones; and on these machines there are people in spandex whom you really want to take aside and advise in the most tactful and loving way not to wear spandex.

1430h.: We're back down in the good old Rainbow Room for **Behind the Scenes — Meet your Cruise Director Scott Peterson and find out what it's really like to work on a Cruise Ship!**

Scott Peterson is a deeply tan 39-year-old male with tall rigid hair, a constant high-watt smile, an escargot mustache, and a gleaming Rolex — basically the sort of guy who looks entirely at home in sockless white loafers and a mint-green knit shirt from Lacoste. He is also one of my least favorite Celebrity Cruises employees, though with Scott Peterson it's a case of mildly enjoyable annoyance rather than the terrified loathing I feel for Mr. Dermatitis.

The very best way to describe Scott Peterson's demeanor is that it looks like he's constantly posing for a photograph nobody is taking.[123] He mounts the Rainbow Room's low brass dais and reverses his chair and sits like a cabaret singer and begins to hold forth. There are maybe 50 people attending, and I have to admit that some of them seem

---

[123] He's also a bit like those small-town politicians and police chiefs who go to shameless lengths to get mentioned in the local newspaper. Scott Peterson's name appears in each day's *Nadir Daily* over a dozen times: **"Backgammon Tournament with your Cruise Director Scott Peterson"; " 'The World Goes Round' with Jane McDonald,**

to like Scott Peterson a lot, and really do enjoy his talk, a talk that, not surprisingly, turns out to be more about what it's like to be Scott Peterson than what it's like to work on the good old *Nadir*. Topics covered include where and under what circumstances Scott Peterson grew up, how Scott Peterson got interested in cruise ships, how Scott Peterson and his college roommate got their first jobs together on a cruise ship, some hilarious booboos in Scott Peterson's first months on the job, every celebrity Scott Peterson has personally met and shaken the hand of, how much Scott Peterson loves the people he gets to meet working on a cruise ship, how much Scott Peterson loves just working on a cruise ship in general, how Scott Peterson met the future Mrs. Scott Peterson working on a cruise ship, and how Mrs. Scott Peterson now works on a different cruise ship and how challenging it is to sustain an intimate relation as warm and in all respects wonderful as that of Mr. and Mrs. Scott Peterson when you (i.e., Mr. and Mrs. Scott Peterson) work on different cruise ships and lay eyes on each other only about every sixth week, except how but now Scott Peterson's tickled to be able to announce that Mrs. Scott Peterson happens to be on a well-earned vacation and is as a rare treat here this week cruising on the m.v. *Nadir* with him, Scott Peterson, and is as a matter of fact right here with us in the audience today, and wouldn't Mrs. S.P. like to stand up and take a bow.

I swear I am not exaggerating: this occasion is a real two-handed head-clutcher, awesome in its ickiness. But now, just as I need to leave in order not to be late for 1500h.'s much-anticipated skeetshooting, Scott Peterson starts to relate an anecdote that engages my various on-board dreads and fascinations enough for me to stay and try to write down. Scott Peterson tells us how his wife, Mrs. Scott Peterson, was in the shower in the Mr. and Mrs. Scott Peterson Suite on Deck 3 of the *Nadir* the other night when — one hand goes up in the gesture of someone searching for just the right delicate term — when nature

---

Michael Mullane, and the Matrix Dancers, and your host, Cruise Director Scott Peterson"; "Ft. Lauderdale Disembarkation Talk — Your Cruise Director Scott Peterson explains everything you need to know about your transfer from the ship in Ft. Lauderdale"; etc., ad naus.

called. So Mrs. Scott Peterson apparently gets out of the shower still wet and sits down on Scott Peterson's stateroom's bathroom's commode. Scott Peterson, in a narrative aside, says how perhaps we've all noticed that the commodes on the m.v. *Nadir* are linked to a state-of-the-art Vacuum Sewage System that happens to generate not a weak or incidental flush-suction. Other *Nadir*ites besides just me must fear their toilet, because this gets a big jagged tension-related laugh. Mrs. Scott Peterson[124] is sinking lower and lower in her salmon-colored chair. Scott Peterson says but so Mrs. Scott Peterson sits down on the commode, still naked and wet from the shower, and attends to nature's summons, and when she's done she reaches over and hits the commode's Flush mechanism, and Scott Peterson says that, in Mrs. Scott Peterson's wet slick condition, the incredible suction of the *Nadir*'s state-of-the-art V.S.S. starts actually *pulling her down through the seat's central hole,*[125] and apparently Mrs. Scott Peterson is just a bit too broad abeam to get sucked down all the way and hurled into some abstract excremental void but rather *sticks,* wedged, halfway down in the seat's hole, and can't get out, and is of course stark naked, and starts screeching for help (by now the live Mrs. Scott Peterson seems very interested in something going on down underneath her table, and mostly only her left shoulder — leather-brown and stippled with freckles — is visible from where I'm sitting); and Scott Peterson tells us that he, Scott Peterson, hears her and comes rushing into the bathroom from the stateroom where he'd been practicing his Professional Smile

[124] Mrs. S.P. is an ectomorphic and sort of leather-complected British lady in a big-brimmed sombrero, which sombrero I observe her now taking off and stowing under her brass table as she loses altitude in the chair.

[125] At this point in the anecdote I'm absolutely rigid with interest and empathic terror, which will help explain why it's such a huge letdown when this whole anecdote turns out to be nothing but a cheesy Catskills-type joke, one that Scott Peterson has clearly been telling once a week for eons (although maybe not with poor Mrs. Scott Peterson actually sitting right there in the audience, and I find myself hopefully imagining all sorts of nuptial vengeance being wreaked on Scott Peterson for embarrassing Mrs. Scott Peterson like that), the dweeb.

in the bedside table's enormous vanity mirror,[126] comes rushing in
and sees what's happened to Mrs. Scott Peterson and tries to pull her
out — her feet kicking pathetically and buttocks and popliteals purpling
from the seat's adhesive pressure — but he can't pull her out, she's been
wedged in too tight by the horrific V.S.S. suction, and so thanks to
some quick thinking Scott Peterson gets on the phone and calls one
of the *Nadir*'s Staff Plumbers, and the Staff Plumber says Yes Sir Mr.
Scott Peterson Sir I'm on my way, and Scott Peterson runs back into the
bathroom and reports to Mrs. Scott Peterson that professional help is on
the way, at which point it only then occurs to Mrs. Scott Peterson that
she's starkers, and that not only are her ectomorphic breasts exposed to
full Eurofluorescent view but a portion of her own personal pudendum
is clearly visible above the rim of the occlusive seat that holds her fast,[127]
and she screeches Britishly at Scott Peterson to for the bloody love of
Christ do something to cover her legally betrothed nethers against the
swart blue-collar gaze of the impending Staff Plumber, and so Scott
Peterson goes and gets Mrs. Scott Peterson's favorite sun hat, a huge
sombrero, in fact the very same huge sombrero Scott Peterson's beloved
wife is wearing right . . . umm, just a couple seconds ago was wearing
right here in this very Rainbow Room; and but so via the quick and
resourceful thinking of Scott Peterson the sombrero is brought from
the stateroom into the bathroom and placed over Mrs. Scott Peterson's
inbent concave naked thorax, to cover her private parts. And the *Nadir*'s
Staff Plumber knocks and comes in all overlarge and machine-oil-
redolent, w/ tool-belt ajingle, and badly out of breath, and sure enough
swart, and he comes into the bathroom and appraises the situation and
takes certain complex measurements and performs some calculations
and finally tells Mr. Scott Peterson that he thinks he (the Staff Plumber)
can get indeed get Mrs. Scott Peterson out of the toilet seat, but that

---

126   [authorial postulate]

127   [Again an authorial postulate, but it's the only way to make sense of the remedy
she's about to resort to (at this point I still don't know this is all just a corny joke — I'm
rigid and bug-eyed with empathic horror for both the intra- and extranarrative Mrs.
S.P.).]

extracting that there Mexican fellow in there with Mrs. S.P. is going to be a whole nother story.

—

1305h.: I've darted just for a second into Deck 7's Celebrity Show Lounge to catch some of the rehearsals for tomorrow night's climactic Passenger Talent Show. Two crew-cut and badly burned U. Texas guys are doing a minimally choreographed dance number to a recording of "Shake Your Groove Thing." Asst. Cruise Director "Dave the Bingo Boy" is coordinating activities from a canvas director's chair at stage left. A septuagenarian from Halifax VA tells four ethnic jokes and sings "One Day at a Time (Sweet Jesus)." A retired Century 21 Realtor from Idaho does a long drum solo to "Caravan." The climactic Passenger Talent Show is apparently a 7NC tradition, as was Tuesday night's Special Costume Party.[128] Some of the *Nadir*ites are deeply into this stuff and have brought their own costumes, music, props. A lithe Canadian couple does a tango complete w/ pointy black shoes and an interdental rose. Then the finale of the P.T.S. is apparently going to be four consecutive stand-up comedy routines delivered by very old men. These men totter on one after the other. One has one of those three-footed canes, another a necktie that looks uncannily like a Denver omelette, another an excruciating stutter. What follow are four successive interchangeable routines where the manner and humor are like exhumed time capsules of the 1950s: jokes about how impossible it is to understand women, about how very much men want to play golf and how their wives try to keep them from playing golf, etc. The routines have the same kind of flamboyant unhipness that makes my own grandparents objects of my pity, awe, and embarrassment all at once. One of the senescent quartet refers to his appearance tomorrow night as a "gig." The one with the tridential cane stops suddenly in the middle of a long joke about skipping

---

[128] It was this kind of stuff that combined with the micromanagement of activities to make the *Nadir* weirdly reminiscent of the summer camp I attended for three straight Julys in early childhood, another venue where the food was great and everyone was sunburned and I spent as much time as possible in my cabin avoiding micromanaged activities.

his wife's funeral to play golf and, pointing the cane's tips at Dave the Bingo Boy, demands an immediate and accurate estimate of what the attendance will be for tomorrow night's Passenger Talent Show. Dave the Bingo Boy sort of shrugs and looks at his emery board and says that it's hard to say, that it like varies week to week, whereupon the old guy kind of brandishes his cane and says well it better be substantial because he god*damn* well hates playing to an empty house.

1320h.: The *ND* neglects to mention that the skeetshooting is a *competitive* Organized Activity. The charge is $1.00 a shot, but you have to purchase your shots in sets of 10, and there's a large and vaguely gun-shaped plaque for the best X/10 score. I arrive at 8-Aft late; a male *Nadir*ite is already shooting skeet, and several other men have formed a line and are waiting to shoot skeet. The *Nadir*'s wake is a big fizzy V way below the aft rail. Two sullen Greek NCOs run the show, and between their English and their earmuffs and the background noise of shotguns — plus the fact that I've never touched any kind of gun before and have only the vaguest idea of which end even to point — negotiations over my late entry and the forwarding of the skeetshooting bill to *Harper's* are lengthy and involved.

I am seventh and last in line. The other contestants in line refer to the skeet as "traps" or "pigeons," but what they really look like is tiny discuses painted the Day-Glo orange of high-cost huntingwear. The orange, I posit, is for ease of visual tracking, and the color must really help, because the trim bearded guy in aviator glasses currently shooting is perpetrating absolute skeetocide in the air over the ship.

I assume you already know the basic skeetshooting conventions from movies and TV: the lackey at the weird little catapultish device, the bracing and pointing and order to *Pull,* the combination thud and *kertwang* of the catapult, the brisk crack of the weapon, and the midair disintegration of the luckless skeet. Everybody in line with me is male, though there are a number of females in the crowd that's watching the competition from the 9-Aft balcony above and behind us.

From the line, watching, three things are striking: (a) what on TV is a brisk crack is here a whooming roar that apparently is what a shotgun really sounds like; (b) skeetshooting looks comparatively easy, because now the stocky older guy who's replaced the trim bearded guy at the rail is also blowing these fluorescent skeet away one after the other, so that a steady rain of lumpy orange crud is falling into the *Nadir*'s wake; (c) a flying skeet,[129] when shot, undergoes a frighteningly familiar-looking midflight peripeteia — erupting material, changing vector, and plummeting seaward in a distinctive corkscrewy way that all eerily recalls footage of the 1986 *Challenger* disaster.

Striking thing (b) turns out to be an illusion, one not unlike the illusion I'd had about the comparative easiness of golf from watching golf on TV before I'd actually ever tried to play golf. The shooters who precede me do all seem to fire with a kind of casual scorn, and they all get 8/10 or above. But it turns out that, of these six guys, three have military-combat backgrounds, another two are insufferable East-Coast retro-Yuppie brothers who spend weeks every year hunting various fast-flying species with their "Pa*pa*" in southern Canada, and the last has not only his own earmuffs, plus his own shotgun in a special crushed-velvet-lined case, but also his own skeetshooting range in his backyard[130] in North Carolina. When it's finally my turn, the earmuffs they give me have somebody else's ear-oil on them and don't fit my head. The gun itself is shockingly heavy and stinks of what I'm told is cordite, small pubic spirals of which are still exiting the barrel from the Korea-vet who preceded me and is tied for first with 10/10. The two Yuppie brothers are the only entrants even near my age; both got scores of 9/10 and are now appraising me coolly from identical prep-school-slouch positions against the starboard rail. The Greek non-coms seem extremely bored. I am handed the heavy gun and told to "be bracing a hip" against the aft rail and then to place the stock of the weapon against no *not* the shoulder of my hold-the-gun arm but the shoulder of my pull-the-trigger arm — my initial error in this latter regard results in a severely distorted aim that makes the Greek by the catapult do a rather neat drop-and-roll.

---

[129] (these skeet made, I posit, from some kind of extra-brittle clay for maximum frag)

[130] !

OK, let's not spend a lot of time drawing this whole incident out. Let me simply say that, yes, my own skeetshooting score was noticeably lower than the other entrants' scores, then simply make a few disinterested observations for the benefit of any novice contemplating shooting skeet from the rolling stern of a 7NC Megaship, and then we'll move on: (1) A certain level of displayed ineptitude with a firearm will cause everyone in the vicinity who knows anything about firearms to converge on you all at the same time with cautions and advice and handy tips passed down from Papa. (2) A lot of the advice in (1) boils down to exhortations to "lead" the launched skeet, but nobody explains whether this means that the gun's barrel should move across the sky with the skeet or should instead lie in a sort of static ambush along some point in the skeet's projected path. (3) TV skeetshooting is not totally unrealistic in that you really are supposed to say "*Pull*" and the weird little catapultish thing really does produce a kertwanging thud. (4) Whatever a "hair trigger" is, a shotgun does not have one. (5) If you've never fired a gun before, the urge to close your eyes at the precise moment of concussion is, for all practical purposes, irresistible. (6) The well-known "kick" of a fired shotgun is no misnomer: it does indeed feel like being kicked, and hurts, and sends you back several steps with your arms pinwheeling wildly for balance, which, when you're holding a gun, results in mass screaming and ducking and then on the next shot a conspicuous thinning of the crowd in the 9-Aft gallery above.

Finally, (7), know that an unshot skeet's movement against the vast lapis lazuli dome of the open ocean's sky is sun-like — i.e. orange and parabolic and right-to-left — and that its disappearance into the sea is edge-first and splashless and sad.

1600h. – 1700h.: Lacuna.

1700h. – 1815h.: Shower, personal grooming, third viewing of the heart-tweaking last act of *Andre,* attempted shower-steam-rehabilitation of wool slacks and funereal sportcoat for tonight's 5☆C.R. supper, which in the *ND* is designated sartorially "Formal."[131]

1815h.: The cast and general atmospherics of the 5☆C.R.'s T64 have already been covered. Tonight's supper is exceptional only in its tension. The hideous Mona has, recall, opted to represent today as her birthday to Tibor and the maître d', resulting tonight in bunting and a tall cake and a chair-balloon, plus in Wojtek leading a squad of Slavic busboys in a ceremonial happy-birthday mazurka around Table 64, and in an overall smug glow of satisfaction from Mona (who when The Tibster sets her cake down before her claps her hands once before her face like a small depraved child) and in an expression of blank tolerance from Mona's grandparents that's impossible to read or figure.

Additionally, Trudy's daughter Alice — whose birthday, recall, really *is* today — has in silent protest against Mona's fraud said nothing all

---

[131] Look, I'm not going to spend a lot of your time or my emotional energy on this, but if you are male and you ever do decide to undertake a 7NC Luxury Cruise, be smart and take a piece of advice I did not take: *bring Formalwear*. And I do not mean just a coat and tie. A coat and tie are appropriate for the two 7NC suppers designated "Informal" (which term apparently comprises some purgatorial category between "Casual" and "Formal"), but for Formal supper you're supposed to wear either a tuxedo or something called a "dinner jacket" that as far as I can see is basically the same as a tuxedo. I, dickhead that I am, decided in advance that the idea of Formalwear on a tropical vacation was absurd, and I steadfastly refused to buy or rent a tux and go through the hassle of trying to figure out how even to pack it. I was both right and wrong: yes, the Formalwear thing is absurd, but since every *Nadir*ite except me went ahead and dressed up in absurd Formalwear on Formal nights, *I* — having, of course, ironically enough spurned a tux precisely because of absurdity-considerations — was the one who ends up looking absurd at Formal 5☆C.R. suppers — painfully absurd in the tuxedo-motif T-shirt I wore on the first Formal night, and then even more painfully absurd on Thursday in the funereal sportcoat and slacks I'd gotten all sweaty and rumpled on the plane and at Pier 21. No one at Table 64 said anything about the absurd informality of my Formal-supper dress, but it was the sort of deeply tense absence of comment which attends only the grossest and most absurd breaches of social convention, and which after the Elegant Tea Time debacle pushed me right to the very edge of ship-jumping. Please, let my dickheadedness and humiliation have served some purpose: take my advice and *bring Formalwear*, no matter how absurd it seems, if you go.

week to Tibor about it — i.e. her own birthday — and sits tonight across from Mona wearing just the sort of face you would expect from one privileged child watching another privileged child receive natal treats and attentions that are by all rights her own.

The result of all this is that stony-faced Alice and I[132] have tonight established a deep and high-voltage bond across the table, united in our total disapproval and hatred of Mona, and are engaging in a veritable ballet of coded little stab-, strangle-, and slap-Mona pantomimes for each other's amusement, Alice and I are, which I've got to say is for me a fun and therapeutic anger-outlet after the day's tribulations.

But the supper's tensest development is that Alice's mother and my own new friend Trudy — whose purslane-and-endive salad, rice pilaf, and Tender Medallions of Braised Veal are simply too perfect tonight to engage any of her critical attention, and who I should mention has, all week, made little secret of the fact that she's not exactly crazy about Alice's Serious Boyfriend Patrick, or about his and Alice's Serious Relationship[133] — that Trudy notices and misconstrues my and Alice's coded gestures and stifled giggles as signs of some kind of burgeoning romantic connection between us, and Trudy begins yet once again extracting and spreading out her purse's 4×5s of Alice, and relating little tales of Alice's childhood designed to make Alice appear adorable, and talking Patrick down, and in general I have to say acting like a procuress . . . and this would be bad enough, tension-wise (especially when Esther gets into the act), but now poor Alice — who, even though deeply preoccupied with birthday-deprivation and Mona-hatred, is by no means dim or unperceptive — quickly sees what Trudy's doing, and, apparently terrified that I might possibly share her mother's mispercep-

---

[132] (an I who, recall, am reeling from the triple whammy of first ballistic humiliation and then Elegant Tea Time disgrace and now being the only person anywhere in sight in a sweat-crusted wool sportcoat instead of a glossy tux, and am having to order and chug three Dr Peppers in a row to void my mouth of the intransigent aftertaste of Beluga caviar)

[133] (which S.R. apparently includes living together on Alice's $$ and "co-owning" Alice's 1992 Saab)

tion of my connection with her as anything more than an anti-Mona alliance, begins directing my way a kind of Ophelia-type mad monologue of unconnected Patrick-references and Patrick-anecdotes, all of which causes Trudy to start making her weird dentally asymmetric grimace at the same time she begins cutting at her Tender Medallions of Braised Veal so hard that the sound of her knife against the 5☆C.R.'s bone china gives everybody at the table tooth-shivers; and the mounting tension causes fresh sweatstains to appear in the underarms of my funereal sportcoat and spread nearly to the perimeter of the faded salty remains of Pier 21's original sweatstains; and when Tibor makes his customary post-entrée circuit of the table and asks How Is All Of Everything, I am for the first time since the educational second night unable to say anything other than: Fine.

2045h.

CELEBRITY SHOWTIME

Celebrity Cruises Proudly Presents

HYPNOTIST

NIGEL ELLERY

Hosted by your Cruise Director Scott Peterson

PLEASE NOTE: *Video and audio taping of all shows is strictly prohibited.*
Children, please remain seated with your parents during shows.
No children in the front row.

CELEBRITY SHOW LOUNGE

Other Celebrity Showtime headline entertainments this week have included a Vietnamese comedian who juggles chain saws, a husband-and-wife team that specializes in Broadway love medleys, and, most notably, a singing impressionist named Paul Tanner, who made simply an enormous impression on Table 64's Trudy and Esther, and whose impressions of Engelbert Humperdinck, Tom Jones, and particularly Perry Como were apparently so stirring that a second Popular Demand

Encore Performance by Paul Tanner has been hastily scheduled to follow tomorrow night's climactic Passenger Talent Show.[134]

Stage-hypnotist Nigel Ellery is British[135] and looks uncannily like 1950s B-movie villain Kevin McCarthy. Introducing him, Cruise Director Scott Peterson informs us that Nigel Ellery "has had the honor of hypnotizing both Queen Elizabeth II and the Dalai Lama."[136] Nigel Ellery's act combines hypnotic highjinks with a lot of rather standard Borscht Belt patter and audience abuse. And it ends up being such a ridiculously apposite symbolic microcosm of the week's whole 7NC Luxury Cruise experience that it's almost like a setup, some weird form of journalistic pampering.

First off, we learn that not everyone is susceptible to serious hypnosis — Nigel Ellery puts the C.S.L.'s whole 300+ crowd through some simple in-your-seat tests[137] to determine who in the C.S.L.'s crowd is "suggestibly gifted" enough to participate in the "fun" to come.

---

[134] At least guaranteeing the old *Nadir*ite comedian w/ cane a full house, I guess.

[135] His accent indicates origins in London's East End.

[136] (Not, one would presume, at the same time.)

[137] One is: Lace your fingers together and put them in front of your face and then unlace just your index fingers and have them sort of face each other and imagine an irresistible magnetic force drawing them together and see whether the two fingers do indeed as if by magic move slowly and inexorably together until they're pressed together whorl to whorl. From a really scary and unpleasant experience in seventh grade,[137a] I already know I'm excessively suggestible, and I skip all the little tests, since no force on earth could ever get me up on a hypnotist's stage in front of over 300 entertainment-hungry strangers.

> [137a] (viz. when at a school assembly a local psychologist put us all under a supposedly light state of hypnosis for some "Creative Visualization," and ten minutes later everybody in the auditorium came out of the hypnosis except unfortunately yours truly, and I ended up spending four irreversibly entranced and pupil-dilated hours in the school nurse's office, with the increasingly panicked shrink trying more and more drastic devices for bringing me out of it, and my parents very nearly litigated over the whole episode, and I calmly and matter-of-factly decided to steer well clear of all hypnosis thereafter)

Second, when the six most suitable subjects — all still locked in complex contortions from the in-your-seat tests — are assembled onstage, Nigel Ellery spends a long time reassuring them and us that absolutely nothing will happen that they do not wish to have happen and voluntarily submit to. He then persuades a young lady from Akron that a loud male Hispanic voice is issuing from the left cup of her brassiere. Another lady is induced to smell a horrific odor coming off the man in the chair next to her, a man who himself believes that the seat of his chair periodically heats to 100°C. The other three subjects respectively flamenco, believe they are not just nude but woefully ill-endowed, and are made to shout "Mommy, I want a wee-wee!" whenever Nigel Ellery utters a certain word. The audience laughs very hard at all the right times. And there is something genuinely funny (not to mention symbolically microcosmic) about watching these well-dressed adult cruisers behave strangely for no reason they understand. It is as if the hypnosis enables them to construct fantasies so vivid that the subjects do not even know they are fantasies. As if their heads were no longer their own. Which is of course funny.

Maybe the single most strikingly comprehensive 7NC symbol, though, is Nigel Ellery himself. The hypnotist's boredom and hostility are not only undisguised, they are incorporated kind of ingeniously into the entertainment itself: Ellery's boredom gives him the same air of weary expertise that makes us trust doctors and policemen, and his hostility — via the same kind of phenomenon that makes Don Rickles a big star in Las Vegas, I guess — is what gets the biggest roars of laughter from the lounge's crowd. The guy's stage persona is extremely hostile and mean. He does unkind imitations of people's U.S. accents. He ridicules questions from both the subjects and the audience. He makes his eyes burn Rasputinishly and tells people they're going to wet the bed at exactly 3:00 A.M. or drop trou at the office in exactly two weeks. The spectators — mostly middle-aged, it looks like — rock back and forth with mirth and slap their knee and dab at their eyes with hankies. Each moment of naked ill will from Ellery is followed by an enormous circumoral constriction and a palms-out assurance that he's just kidding and that he loves us and that we are a simply marvelous bunch of human beings who are clearly having a very good time indeed.

For me, at the end of a full day of Managed Fun, Nigel Ellery's act is not particularly astounding or side-splitting or entertaining — but neither is it depressing or offensive or despair-fraught. What it is is weird. It's the same sort of weird feeling that having an elusive word on the tip of your tongue evokes. There's something crucially key about Luxury Cruises in evidence here: being entertained by someone who clearly dislikes you, and feeling that you deserve the dislike at the same time that you resent it. All six subjects are now lined up doing syncopated Rockette kicks, and the show is approaching its climax, Nigel Ellery at the microphone getting us ready for something that will apparently involve furiously flapping arms and the astounding mesmeric illusion of flight. Because my own dangerous susceptibility makes it important that I not follow Ellery's hypnotic suggestions too closely or get too deeply involved, I find myself, in my comfortable navy-blue seat, going farther and farther away inside my head, sort of Creatively Visualizing a kind of epiphanic Frank Conroy–type moment of my own, pulling mentally back, seeing the hypnotist and subjects and audience and Celebrity Show Lounge and deck and then whole motorized vessel itself with the eyes of someone not aboard, visualizing the m.v. *Nadir* at night, right at this moment, steaming north at 21.4 knots, with a strong warm west wind pulling the moon backwards through a skein of clouds, hearing muffled laughter and music and Papas' throb and the hiss of receding wake and seeing, from the perspective of this nighttime sea, the good old *Nadir* complexly aglow, angelically white, lit up from within, festive, imperial, palatial . . . yes, this: like a palace: it would look like a kind of floating palace, majestic and terrible, to any poor soul out here on the ocean at night, alone in a dinghy, or not even in a dinghy but simply and terribly floating, a man overboard, treading water, out of sight of all land. This deep and creative visual trance — N. Ellery's true and accidental gift to me — lasted all through the next day and night, which period I spent entirely in Cabin 1009, in bed, mostly looking out the spotless porthole, with trays and various rinds all around me, feeling maybe a little bit glassy-eyed but mostly good — good to be on the *Nadir* and good soon to be off, good that I had survived (in a way) being pampered to death (in a way) — and so I stayed in bed. And even though the tranced stasis caused me to miss the final night's climactic P.T.S. and the Farewell Midnight Buffet and then Saturday's docking and a chance to have my After photo taken with Captain G. Panagiotakis, subsequent reentry into the adult demands of landlocked real-world life wasn't nearly as bad as a week of Absolutely Nothing had led me to fear.

1995

The following people helped make various of the foregoing better than they (various of the foregoing) would have been otherwise and are hereby thanked:

Mary Ann Babbe, Will Blythe, Mark ("Action Boy") Costello, Will Dana, Richard Ellis, Jonathan ("This Isn't Nearly as Bad as One Might Have Expected") Franzen, K. L. Harris, Colin ("Let's Explore Once Again Why This Doesn't Quite Work") Harrison, Jack Hitt, Jay ("I'm Suffering Right Along With You") Jennings, Steve Jones, Glenn ("The Mollifier") Kenny, Nora Krug, Michael Martone, Mike Mattil, Bill McBride, Michael Milburn, Steve Moore, Bonnie Nadell, Linda Perla, Michael Pietsch, Erin Poag, Ellen Rosenbush, Greg Sharko, Lee ("What, Aren't All Page Proofs Set in Tocharian B?") Smith, David Travers, Paul Tough, Kristin ("The Blunt Machete") von Ogtrop, Amy ("Just How Much Reader-Annoyance Are You Shooting For Here Exactly?") Wallace, Deborah Wuliger.

INFINITE JEST

David Foster Wallace

Somewhere in the not-so-distant future the residents of Ennet House, a Boston halfway house for recovering addicts, and students at the nearby Enfield Tennis Academy are ensnared in the search for the master copy of Infinite Jest, a movie said to be so dangerously entertaining its viewers become entranced and expire in a state of catatonic bliss . . .

'An exploding star of a novel . . . reading the book is itself a sort of addiction . . . Wallace writes with authority, deep feeling and caustic wit'
The Spectator

'Scenes of gruesome hilarity and some of genuine tragedy . . . The most relevant portrayal of American culture to appear in recent years, *Infinite Jest* is fascinating, ridiculous and excruciating, and a stimulating injection into contemporary American culture'
Independent on Sunday

'One of the best books about addiction and recovery to appear in recent memory . . . positively sings with lyrical insight and wry humour'
Sunday Times

ABACUS
978-0-349-12108-6

BRIEF INTERVIEWS WITH HIDEOUS MEN

David Foster Wallace

'Very, very funny, and also deadly serious . . . a book of
formidable creative intelligence'
Observer

'Wallace's talent is such that you can't help wondering: how
good can he get?'
Time Out

In this startling and singular short story collection, David
Foster Wallace nudges at the boundaries of fiction with
inimitable wit and seductive intelligence. Venturing inside
minds and landscapes that are at once recognisable and utterly
strange, these stories reaffirm Wallace's reputation as one of
his generation's pre-eminent talents, expanding our ideas of
the pleasures fiction can afford.

'Contains longish stretches of genius'
Geoff Nicholson, *Independent*

'His skills as a literary innovator are immense . . . this is an
entertaining and dazzlingly innovative work . . . a dizzying
gallop across the wild frontier of contemporary fiction'
Daily Telegraph

'As clever and intriguing as Wallace's past work . . . these
strong, sad voices ring powerfully clear'
The Times

ABACUS
978-0-349-11188-9

GIRL WITH CURIOUS HAIR

David Foster Wallace

David Foster Wallace is one of the most prodigiously talented young writers in America today and *Girl With Curious Hair* is repelete with his remarkable and unsettling re-imaginations of reality. From an eerily 'real', almost holographic evocation of Lyndon B. Johnson, to over-televised game-show hosts and late-night comedians, to the title story, where terminal punk nihilism meets Young Republicanism, Wallace renders the incredible comprehensible, the bizarre normal, the absurd hilarious, the familiar strange.

'A collection of stories as varied in length and theme as they are imaginative, and downright bizarre as any collection by one author has a right to be. Truly funny surreal humour'
San Francisco Chronicle

'Wallace is one of the big talents of his generation, a writer of virtuosic talents who can seemingly do anything'
New York Times

ABACUS
978-0-349-11102-5

To buy any of our books and to find out
more about Abacus and Little, Brown, our authors
and titles, as well as events and book clubs,
visit our website

www.littlebrown.co.uk

and follow us on Twitter

@AbacusBooks
@LittleBrownUK

To order any Abacus titles p & p free in the UK,
please contact our mail order supplier on:

+ 44 (0)1832 737525

Customers not based in the UK should contact
the same number for appropriate postage
and packing costs.